COPTIC CHRISTIANS AND MUSLIMS IN EGYPT

Two Communities, One Nation

COPTIC CHRISTIANS AND MUSLIMS IN EGYPT

Fikry F. Andrawes
Alison Orr-Andrawes

The American University in Cairo Press
Cairo New York

First published in 2019 by
The American University in Cairo Press
113 Sharia Kasr el Aini, Cairo, Egypt
200 Park Ave., Suite 1700, New York, NY 10166
www.aucpress.com

Dar el Kutub No. 22050/17
ISBN 978 977 416 870 3

Dar el Kutub Cataloging-in-Publication Data

Andrawes, Fikry F., Alison Orr-Andrawes
Coptic Christians and Muslims in Egypt: Two Communities, One Nation / Fikry F. Andrawes and Alison Orr-Andrawes.— Cairo: The American University in Cairo Press, 2019.
p. cm.
ISBN 978 977 416 870 3
1. Islam—Relations—Egypt—Christianity
2. Islam and Christianity
3. Orr-Andrawes, Alison (jt. auth.)
281.720962

1 2 3 4 5 23 22 21 20 19

Designed by Adam el-Sehemy
Printed in the United States of America

CONTENTS

Preface xi

Notes on Transliteration, Translation, and Dates xiii

Acknowledgments xv

Introduction 1

1 Christianity in Egypt 9

Early Christianity in Egypt 9

The Catechetical School of Alexandria 11

Monastic Egypt 15

Diocletian and the Persecution of Christians 18

Athanasius and the Separation of the Coptic Church 22

2 The Coming of Islam 33

Egypt before the Arab Invasion 33

The Arabs Arrive in Egypt 36

Was Egypt Acquired by a Treaty or by Force? 41

How the Arabs Saw Egypt for the First Time 41

The Library of Alexandria 42

Conditions Imposed on Non-Muslims 43

Early Administration under 'Amr ibn al-'As 44

3 Early Arab Dynasties: The Umayyads and the Abbasids 49

The Umayyad Dynasty (AD 661–750) 52

The Abbasid Dynasty (AD 750–1517) 57

4 The Era of the Independent Muslim Dynasties 63
The Tulunid Dynasty (AD 884–96) 63
The Ikhshidi Dynasty (AD 935–69) 66
The Fatimid Dynasty (AD 909–1171) 67
The Ayyubid Dynasty (AD 1171–1250) 78

5 The Mamluk Era (AD 1250–1517) 83

6 The Islamization of Egypt 93
Threats to Islam from Mongols and Europeans 94
Changing Demography in the South of Egypt 96
Rich Coptic Administrators and Tax Collectors 98
Marriage and Conversion 98
The Shift from Coptic to Arabic Language 99

7 Egypt under the Ottomans (1517–1798) 103
Turkish Rule 103
Coptic–Muslim Relations 105
The Decline of the Ottoman Dynasty 109

8 The French Adventure in Egypt (1798–1801) 111
Under Napoleonic Rule 113
Mu'allim Ya'qub: Visionary or Traitor? 117
The End of the French Adventure in Egypt and Its Effects 119

9 Muhammad 'Ali Dynasty (1805–1952) 123
The Founder of Modern Egypt 124
The Dynasty after the Death of Muhammad 'Ali 127
The Coptic Church and Colonialism 132

10 The Urabi Revolt (1879–82) 135

11 Egypt under the British (1881–1954) 141
The British, the Muslims, and the Copts 142

12 From Revolt to Revolution (1919–52) 151
The Wafd Party (1923–52) 156
Political Islam 160
The Copts and Political Islam 164
Coptic–Muslim Relations among Intellectuals 166
The Problem of Building Churches in Twentieth-Century Egypt 169

13 The 1952 Revolt and the Nasser Era (1954–70) 173
The Coptic Church in Transition 178

14 The Sadat Era (1970–81) 183
Financing and Political Islam 184
The Rise of Political Islam under Sadat 186
Sadat's Difficult Years 189

15 The Mubarak Era (1981–2011) 201
The Return of Pope Shenouda 205
A Changing Political, Social, and Economic Climate 207

16 The January 25 Revolution and Its Aftermath 217

Epilogue 229
Appendix 1 Six Outstanding Individuals of the Egyptian Enlightenment Period 231
Taha Hussein (1889–1973) 231
Salama Musa (1887–1958) 234
Muhammad Talaat Harb (1867–1941) 239
Rose al-Yusuf (1888–1958) 242
Makram Ebeid (1889–1961) 243
Jurji Zaydan (1861–1914) 247
Appendix 2 Summary of Parliamentary Elections 251
Notes 253
Bibliography 279
Index 289

To Sonallah Ibrahim

PREFACE

The original Arabic edition of this book first appeared in 2010, a few months before the Egyptian revolution of 25 January 2011, when Copts and Muslims came together to demonstrate national unity and to bring an end to the Mubarak regime. Unfortunately, as new political freedoms became possible for the first time in more than half a century, the resulting upheaval once again led to increased tension and occasional violence between the two communities, precipitated in part by the emergence of a strain of radical political Islam.

Tension between Christians and Muslims is not a new phenomenon in Egyptian history. The Arabic edition of this book described the historical roots of this conflict and provided a background for understanding what is happening in Egypt today. This English edition, designed for a wider audience, includes additional new material and makes available in English some source material that previously could only be found in Arabic or Coptic. It examines Christian–Muslim relations in the context of what was happening in Egypt during each successive historical period.

NOTES ON TRANSLITERATION, TRANSLATION, AND DATES

This book includes a number of Arabic words and names written using the English alphabet. Readers who know Arabic should have no difficulty in deciphering them. Some Arabic words, such as 'caliph' and 'shaykh,' and familiar names such as Naguib Mahfouz, have English spellings which are established by general use. But there are many Arabic words and names that can be transliterated in multiple ways. We have tried to use forms that will be most easily recognized by readers, rather than striving for phonetic consistency. Transliterated words have been italicized and presented in their colloquial Egyptian forms.

Unless otherwise stated, the translation of passages from Arabic to English is our own. While we referenced sources that can be found in English translation by others whenever possible, on some occasions we reference both. For example, a reference is provided for the English translation of *Al-Jabarti's History of Egypt* (edited by Jane Hathaway), as well as for the original Arabic version. Readers of both languages will be able to spot some variations or inconsistent translation between the two.

With respect to dating, we use the Islamic calendar (Hijri) along with the Western calendar until the third century Hijri, after which we use Western dates only.

ACKNOWLEDGMENTS

The authors would like to express their deep gratitude to the following people who all helped make this book possible.

Gawdat Gabra was a source of encouragement and much important information. He was most generous with his time for lengthy discussions.

Sabri al-Baga provided us with the voting results of the parliamentary election after 1952.

Jude Berman and John Swan did the first editing of the manuscript and made helpful suggestions along the way.

Many thanks to the publishing staff of AUC Press for their cooperation, support, and understanding. We would especially like to express our thanks to Ms. Nadia Naqib, Mr. Tarek Ghanem, and Ms. Lucy Hanna.

INTRODUCTION

Relations between the Coptic and Muslim communities in Egypt have become increasingly strained in recent decades. This is not a new phenomenon; periods of sectarian tension have alternated with peaceful coexistence ever since Islam's arrival in the seventh century. In order to understand the present, it is helpful to know the past. But where is the general reader to turn? Popular media coverage—in both the West and the Middle East—often focuses on recent events and looks at surface issues, without penetrating to the historical roots of the problem. Westerners with no connection to the Middle East may know little about either the Coptic or the Muslim communities. Copts, as a minority group, are generally more familiar with the dominant Islamic culture than vice versa; Egyptians are taught selective aspects of Islamic history as part of the regular school curriculum, but they are taught little or nothing about the Coptic culture that prevailed before the Arabs arrived. The average Egyptian would be astonished to learn that Egypt had ever been a Coptic Christian country. To complicate matters, each sectarian community often views its own history in a highly selective way. This book is an attempt to provide some historical background. It, too, is inevitably selective and has its own points of view. Despite the authors' efforts to be evenhanded, some readers will strongly disagree with some of the views presented here. No doubt everyone can find something to be offended by. References are provided for those who wish to explore in greater depth.

This work surveys the flow of historical events that have influenced the relationship between Egyptian Muslims and Copts over some fourteen centuries. It makes no claims to be comprehensive, scholarly, or original. Rather, it draws on work done by others, both ancient and modern, presented in a way we hope will be informative and occasionally even entertaining. Its main objective is to offer the general reader a rough chronological framework within which Coptic–Muslim relations can be understood in the context of what was happening in Egypt at the time.

Much has been written on the history of Islam; somewhat less is available on the history of the Coptic (Egyptian Orthodox) Church. There are three important scholarly books dealing with Copts written in the modern era: *Christians versus Muslims in Modern Egypt* by S.S. Hassan;[1] *The Copts of Egypt: The Challenges of Modernization and Identity* by Vivian Ibrahim;[2] and *The Coptic Question in the Mubarak Era* by Sebastian Elsässer.[3] But few writers have focused specifically on the relationship between the two communities as it has fluctuated in response to changes in the broader political climate. A single outstanding book on this subject, by Jacques Tagher, was published in Arabic in 1951. It covers the period from AD 640 to 1922. The only English translation was by Ragai N. Makar in 1998.[4] The story behind Tagher's book is worth mentioning as an example of the difficulties of publishing scholarly work in Egypt on the subject of Christian–Muslim relations.

When Tagher's book appeared in 1951, it was strongly opposed by the Islamists of the time, especially the Muslim Brotherhood and al-Azhar. Muhammad al-Hudaybi, the head of the Muslim Brotherhood, did not want to oppose the book directly because any attention it received might boost its distribution. So, as a countermeasure, he asked the well-known Azharite shaykh Muhammad al-Ghazali to author a book presenting the Islamic point of view on the subject of tolerance and intolerance between Christianity and Islam.[5] Al-Ghazali's book selectively showed that Islamic views and policies dealing with minorities were more tolerant than those of Christianity. It disputed some of what Tagher described with regard to discrimination against Copts. Despite the fact that it did not rise to the level of Tagher's scholarly work, it was popular among Islamists and caused Tagher's book to remain controversial. The first printing of Tagher's book quickly disappeared from the shelves; it was not printed again until sixty years later (2010), when it was reissued by one of the government publishing houses. At that time, the government felt threatened by the rise in political Islam, and was motivated to reprint Tagher's book which exposed facts Islamists found unflattering.

The teaching of history in Egypt, especially when related to religious matters, is often selective, biased, and used for political purposes. Muhammad 'Afifi, a modern Muslim historian, has expressed the view that Egyptians need to have a more comprehensive and objective view of their history so they are not held hostage by biased views from the past.[6] The Arabic edition of this book, published in 2010 and now in its fifth printing, was an attempt to address this need.[7]

The present English edition has been revised to address a wider English-speaking readership, and updated to cover recent events in Egypt. As in the Arabic edition, the earlier chapters draw heavily on a number of references by ancient historians, both Muslims and Copts. This was done for two reasons. First, some of these are eyewitness accounts that convey the sentiment of the time and events they describe. Second, using Arabic sources may give the text greater credibility in the eyes of those readers who tend to mistrust modern Western writers. Since much of this early history is available only in Arabic or Coptic, we provide English translations of paragraphs from some of the older Coptic and Arabic references, many of which have never been translated into English.

We begin by looking at how Christianity and Islam each came to Egypt, and then follow the historical developments in Coptic–Muslim relations until the present time. The first chapter covers the period from the first to the seventh century AD, tracing the development of the Coptic Church from the time Christianity arrived in Egypt until the coming of Islam. It describes the Roman persecution of Christians; the famous Christian theology school of Alexandria; Origen, the father of the allegorical interpretation of the Bible; the beginnings of monasticism in Egypt and its spread to the rest of the Christian world; the end of Roman persecution; the emergence of a national church in Egypt; the theological differences over the nature of Jesus, which led to the separation of the Coptic Church from the Western church in the fifth century; and a second wave of Coptic persecution by the Byzantines, bringing us to the time of the Arabs' arrival in the seventh century.

The second chapter covers the state of Egypt when the Arabs arrived; the success of the Arab invasion; the nature of the occupation and what has been said about it by Copts and Muslims; and how Egyptians were treated by early Muslim rulers. Special attention is given to tax collection, a field that was dominated by Copts until the nineteenth century. This fact at times had a devastating effect on Coptic–Muslim relations.

Chapter three deals with the Umayyad and the Abbasid dynasties. These two dynasties were quite similar. Their representatives ruled Egypt for short periods, two to three years on average, and their major objective was to collect excessive taxes, while neglecting the needs of the country. This was a time of precipitous decline in the economy, persecution of Copts, and several popular revolts. The transformation of Egypt from a Coptic-speaking Christian country to an Arabic-speaking Islamic one began during this period.

Chapter four covers the independent Muslim rulers of Egypt. They comprise the Tulunid, Ikhshidi, Fatimid, and Ayyubid dynasties. During this period, general conditions in Egypt improved significantly. During the Fatimid dynasty, Copts experienced some of the best and also some of the worst treatment at the hands of Muslim rulers. At times, they were treated almost as equal to Muslims, but under the third Fatimid caliph, al-Hakim, they experienced terrible persecution and the destruction of almost every church in the country. This period saw a significant reduction in the Coptic population.

Chapter five deals with the period of the Mamluks, white slave warriors who seized control of Egypt and ruled for 274 years. The chapter explores the role played by Muslim religious leaders in legitimizing the Mamluk dynasty. This period witnessed conflicts between warring factions of the Mamluk ruling class, which weakened the country and opened the door once again for conflict between Copts and Muslims. Relations reached a low point, during which many churches from Alexandria to Aswan were destroyed in a single day. The Copts retaliated by burning mosques and Muslim homes. We also discuss the presence of European Crusaders in Egypt and Palestine, their effect on Coptic–Muslim relations, and the eventual defeat of the Crusaders at the hands of the Mamluks.

Chapter six deals with the Islamization of Egypt—its language, religion, and culture. The thirteenth and fourteenth centuries witnessed a devastating deterioration in Coptic–Muslim relations. During this period, Islam was under attack by Mongols from the east, European Crusaders in Syria and Palestine, and Catholics in Spain. In Egypt, Copts became a scapegoat for the anger Muslims felt due to their suffering at the hands of Christians in general.

Chapter seven covers Egypt under the Ottoman Empire, a period that lasted from the middle of the sixteenth until the end of the eighteenth century. During this period, the real power was still in the hands of the Mamluks, who owed formal allegiance to the Ottomans. Religious practice among both Christians and Muslims declined, as did their economic status.

Chapter eight covers the Napoleonic expedition in Egypt, which lasted for only three years but ushered in the beginnings of modern Egypt. Napoleon's occupation set the foundation for a political and legal system that was influenced by the French Revolution. We discuss the episode surrounding Mu'allim Ya'qub, an influential Copt who allied himself with the French occupiers. He became a general and led Coptic troops against the Muslims, who were supported by the Mamluks. When the

French finally returned to Europe, he accompanied them in the hope of finding Europeans who would help rid Egypt of Ottoman and Mamluk rule and bring modernity to Egypt. Ya'qub remains a controversial figure to this day. He is seen as a patriot or a traitor, perspectives that tend to reflect the viewer's religious affiliation.

Chapter nine describes the rise of the Muhammad 'Ali dynasty, which lasted from 1805 until 1952. The high and low points of Muhammad 'Ali's reign are described, including his military adventures to expand his empire, and his eventual downfall at the hands of Western European powers. The Muhammad 'Ali dynasty was a time of great change. There were two popular revolts, foreign experts and modern ideas flooded into Egypt, and the government provided scholarships for Egyptians to study abroad as part of a drive toward modernity. Restraints on Copts were loosened, the *jizya* (poll tax on non-Muslims) was abolished, Copts were drafted into the army for the first time, and some Copts began to enter mainstream political life. One consequence of greater contact with Europe was the attempt of Western missionaries to win converts among both Copts and Muslims in Egypt. This effort met with little success among Muslims, but made inroads among Copts, leading the government to support the Coptic Church in its efforts to stop the intrusion of Western influence. The Egyptian governments of this period were strong, and the historical records make no mention of significant problems between Copts and Muslims. The Suez Canal was built during this period.

Chapter ten deals with the Urabi revolt. This revolt began as an attempt by native Egyptian officers to gain greater influence within an army led primarily by Turkish and Circassian officers. It gradually expanded into a movement, supported by both Christian and Muslim Egyptians, expressing their opposition to Turkish domination and European interference. This attempt to bring greater independence and democratization ultimately failed. Urabi was exiled and the British colonized Egypt for nearly seventy years.

Chapter eleven covers the British imperial ambitions in Egypt. These increased after the opening of the Suez Canal, eventually leading to the military invasion and occupation of Egypt. This chapter discusses British attempts to cause a rift between Copts and Muslims aimed at facilitating British control. The role of the Copts during the British occupation is discussed, as well as the rise and decline of tension between Copts and Muslims. Some Coptic aristocrats attempted to modernize the Coptic Church, but faced resistance from the church.

Chapter twelve covers the first half of the twentieth century with emphasis on the period between the 1919 revolution and the 1952 revolution. These three decades witnessed the beginning and end of the democratic nationalistic movement in Egypt. It was a time of great ferment that saw the rise of political parties, the adoption of a national constitution, and the representation of Copts within the political system. In a push for greater self-determination, most Egyptians, Copts and Muslims alike, resisted both the British and the monarchy. In this context, we discuss the role of Muslim religious leaders and their influence in politics. Conservative Islamic forces, such as al-Azhar University, supported the monarchy against secularism. We also discuss the emergence of the Muslim Brotherhood, the beginning of the modern revival of the Coptic Church, the appearance of prominent Coptic politicians, and the effect of growing Islamic influence in the educational system.

Chapter thirteen begins with the 1952 officers' revolt and covers the Nasser period, an era rich in successes and failures as Nasser attempted to implement a new social agenda, expand education, and encourage industrialization. This period witnessed a war against the British, French, and Israelis in 1956, and another war with Israel in 1967. Under Nasser, independent democratic institutions were weakened, Coptic and Muslim elites were marginalized or disappeared, and a new military class dominated the administration. Although the Coptic role in politics was much reduced from what it had been in the first half of the century, the Copts experienced little direct discrimination, except in the upper levels of government. During this time, educated Copts rose to the highest ranks of church leadership and started a popular revival of Coptic traditions. The church started to assume a greater role in representing Copts in the political arena. The 1950s and 1960s saw persecution of leftists, intellectuals, and the Muslim Brotherhood.

Chapter fourteen covers Egypt under President Sadat, who courted the Muslim Brotherhood and other jihadists to help neutralize the influence of the leftists and Nasserites. Ironically, this policy strengthened political Islam and eventually resulted in Sadat's assassination. During this period, conflict between the president and the Coptic patriarch reached a level of hostility not seen in centuries. This period also witnessed the Arab-Israeli war of 1973 which ended with the Camp David Accords between Egypt and Israel. Corruption within Egypt started to increase significantly and dissent was stifled. The period ended with widespread jailing of anyone who objected to Sadat's policy, followed by Sadat's assassination by Muslim radicals.

Chapter fifteen covers the Mubarak era, which lasted for thirty years. This period witnessed increasing corruption, weakening of civil institutions, and strengthening of the government security apparatus, bureaucracy, and the army. Political Islam increased in power and popularity, and violence against Copts reached a high point. Under Mubarak, a declared state of emergency allowed the government to suspend due process in order to control any opposition. This period ended with the popular revolt of 25 January 2011, which resulted in Mubarak stepping down from power.

Chapter sixteen brings us up to the time of this writing. The chapter begins with the Revolution of 25 January 2011, which removed Mubarak from power and installed the Supreme Council of the Armed Forces (SCAF) as temporary head of the government. A brief period of hope and enthusiasm gave way to political unrest as various factions, including the Muslim Brotherhood, competed to fill the power vacuum. In the absence of law enforcement and security, attacks on Copts and churches increased. The year 2012–13 saw the election of President Muhammad Morsi; installation of a government dominated by the Muslim Brotherhood; moves by Morsi to subvert democratic safeguards; and widespread demonstrations by the people, calling for his removal. The army forcibly removed Morsi, setting off a wave of violence and counter-demonstrations by his supporters, which were ruthlessly suppressed. Former general 'Abd al-Fattah al-Sisi was elected president, and sectarian tensions have declined somewhat as of this writing. What the future holds remains to be seen.

1
CHRISTIANITY IN EGYPT

Early Christianity in Egypt

Strong trade relations between Jerusalem and Alexandria and the presence of a large Jewish community in both cities played a significant role in introducing Christianity to Egypt in the first century. At that time, the message of Christianity was still directed toward the Jewish people. Egyptian church tradition holds that St. Mark the Evangelist brought Christianity to Egypt in about AD 60. He is considered the first patriarch of the Coptic Church.

Unfortunately, little documentation from that time has survived, with the result that most of the information that has been handed down about the earliest years of the church in Egypt is sketchy and anecdotal. For example, *The History of the Patriarchs (Tarikh al-batarika)*, written near the end of the tenth century by Sawirus Ibn al-Muqaffa' (or Severus of Ashmunayn; died in AD 987), gives only a few lines about each of the first eleven patriarchs, even though some of them headed the church for more than twenty years. His entry for Anianus, who succeeded St. Mark as patriarch after the latter was martyred in Alexandria in AD 68, says simply

> When St. Mark the Evangelist died, he was followed by Anianus. The number of the brothers in Christ increased. He ordained priests and servants of the church. He served for twenty-two years and passed away on the twentieth of Hathor in the second year of Domathios, King of Rome.[1]

We know very little more about Demetrius I—who became the twelfth patriarch in AD 189—than we do about his eleven predecessors. However, he is remembered for two things: the story of his selection and his condemnation of Origen, one of the great thinkers of Christianity. The story of his selection is worth mentioning as a typical example of the miraculous accounts found in early Coptic Church history. Severus of Ashmunayn tells the following:

> The patriarch preceding Demetrius, Yulianus [Julian, 180–89], was visited by an angel who told him, "The one who visits you with a grapevine will be the next patriarch." The next morning, an illiterate farmer by the name of Demetrius came to visit the patriarch. He had gone to his field to prune his vineyard and found a cluster of grapes growing out of season, so he brought the grapes to the patriarch as a present. The patriarch announced to the people, "This is your next patriarch, as the angel foretold last night." When Demetrius resisted, he was bound in chains and anointed. In this way, he became the twelfth patriarch and was blessed by God.[2]

However, because Demetrius was married, there was opposition to his selection. So the story continues:

> Acting on the advice of the angel, one day, after the church service, Demetrius asked for some burning charcoal to be brought and placed on his and his wife's tunics. He then walked next to his wife through the church without either tunic burning [a sign that the couple had not had sexual relations]. Since Demetrius was married at a young age, the angel used to come every night and sleep between him and his wife and cover each one of them with one of his wings until the morning, when the angel left.[3]

Coptic Church history has many stories like this. Thought to be useful in strengthening the faith of simple people, they were passed on by oral tradition for many years before being written down. Some Copts believe them even today.

The historian Ra'fat 'Abd al-Hamid describes Demetrius as a talented administrator of church affairs,[4] but not a scholar on the same level as those who studied or taught at the Catechetical School of Alexandria. It was Demetrius who appointed Origen as head of the school at the unusually young age of about twenty, and then later condemned him, as will be discussed in the next section.

The Catechetical School of Alexandria

The Catechetical School of Alexandria was the first institution of theological learning in Christian antiquity. Believed to have been founded in the middle of the second century, the school was a beacon of light that helped to guide Christianity in its early years. Some of the school's graduates became priests, bishops, or patriarchs, both within Egypt and abroad. We have greater knowledge about early Christianity beginning in the late second century, largely as a result of the writings of the Catechetical School of Alexandria. The school's intellectual caliber drew students from all over the Christian world, and allowed the Coptic Church to be regarded as the preeminent authority on theological matters. This period ended when the Coptic Church, along with several other Eastern churches, separated from the Roman/Byzantine church and those allied with it in AD 451.

At the time the school was founded, Alexandria was the largest and most influential center of learning in the ancient world. Although we lack information about how the school was founded, it is clear that its creation was influenced by classical scholars of the Museum of Alexandria and its famous Royal Library. Compelled to defend the new religion, Christianity had to interact with and learn from the philosophers of the time, and the Royal Library of Alexandria was a renowned source of classical learning. In addition to theology, the Catechetical School began to offer courses in philosophy, mathematics, and languages.

The first head of the school was Athenagoras, who is believed to have been a teacher at the Museum. His successor was Pantaenus. The Coptic Church credits Pantaenus with having introduced the Coptic alphabet, using Greek letters and adding seven more letters from the old demotic language. Some believe that translation of the Bible into Coptic started about that time (that is, in the late second century).[5] However, according to *The Coptic Encyclopedia*, the translation took place in the middle of the fifth century. Pantaenus left the school when, at the request of the patriarch, he went on a mission to India, then Ethiopia, Arabia, and Yemen.

Among the later heads of the school are two prominent leaders who left their mark: Clement and Origen. Clement of Alexandria (Titus Flavius Clemens) was a Greek, born about AD 150. He became head of the school in AD 190 and was one of the first to interpret the Bible allegorically. Clement held that all learning, whatever its source, is sacred; that ignorance is worse than sin; and that faith and knowledge are complementary. He opposed religious myth and applied principles from Greek philosophy to the study of Christianity, comparing Christians who feared philosophy to children who are afraid of the dark. Clement, whose primary goal was to improve education within the church, was a scholar who retained his love for secular literature. He wrote three books. The first, *Protrepticus*, was an appeal for education, addressed to the Greeks. The second, *Paedagogus*, dealt with manners and morals and was written for the wealthy class. The third, *Stramata*, was a collection of miscellaneous studies. During Clement's tenure, the school placed special emphasis on general education and manners. In AD 202 Clement fled to Palestine to escape Roman persecution.[6]

The second outstanding leader of the Catechetical School was Origen, who was appointed by Patriarch Demetrius I to succeed Clement as head of the school in AD 198. Although today he is little known in his native country, this ancient Egyptian scholar is widely recognized as one of the greatest early Christian philosophers. During his tenure as head of the school, Origen expanded the curriculum to include the study of astronomy, natural sciences, and music. He also established the foundation for theology studies, including allegorical interpretation of texts, following the practice used in Greek philosophy. Even though he was the head of the school, he attended Ammonius's classes at the Museum of Alexandria on the new Platonism. Origen was a broad-minded scholar, especially in light of the fact that Ammonius was a former Christian who had renounced the faith. Origen traveled widely, journeying to Rome, Greece, Arabia, and Palestine to lecture in major cities.[7]

Origen believed that understanding a text depended on the individual. This is essentially what 'Ali ibn Abi Talib, the fourth Muslim caliph (AD 656–61), meant when he said the Qur'an does not talk, but people make the Qu'ran speak. Similarly, Origen believed that a text has two meanings: one literal, the other allegorical. The allegorical reading of the text is for those who have reached a high spiritual level, while the literal understanding is sufficient for the common man. This is similar to words of the Prophet of Islam: "Behind the verses of the Qur'an, knowledge doesn't reveal itself for those who stop at the literal meaning of the words.

Origen was the author of about six hundred books and commentaries. His most important work was the *Hexapla*, a parallel comparison of six versions of the Old Testament text: one written in old Hebrew, another in Hebrew written in Greek letters, the Septuagint (Hebrew translated into Greek, traditionally by seventy rabbis in Alexandria), and three other Greek editions. This monumental effort took twenty-eight years to complete and comprises fifty volumes. To aid his work, wealthy patrons supplied him with secretaries and scribes, who functioned like a small publishing house.

Origen's other works include numerous writings on the Gospels and treatises that sought to integrate Platonic thought with Christian theology, including lengthy rebuttals to anti-Christian philosophers.[8]

In AD 231, Patriarch Demetrius, who had appointed and supported Origen, excommunicated him. Origen left Egypt for Palestine, in AD 233, and founded a school in Caesarea, where he continued his research and writings until his death in AD 254. Why was he excommunicated? Eusebius of Caesarea, a church historian in the third and fourth centuries, thought Demetrius turned against Origen because he was jealous of the younger man's fame,[9] but there is more to it than that. Origen and his work were condemned again and again in the centuries following his death.

The most serious condemnation of Origen's work came more than a century later, when he was declared a heretic by the churches of Egypt, Constantinople, and Rome. Origen's condemnation by Patriarch Theophilus of Alexandria (AD 385–412) was part of an effort by Theophilus to control the monks of Nitria (south of Alexandria) during a controversy over whether God could be conceived of as having a human image, as the uneducated monks claimed, or whether God was a spiritual principle, as suggested by Origen. Theophilus initially agreed with Origen's views, but when great numbers of monks converged on Alexandria to protest, even threatening the patriarch's life, Theophilus changed his position and condemned Origen at a church council held in AD 403.[10] A second condemnation came in AD 542, at a council in Constantinople, and was followed by another condemnation by Emperor Justinian in AD 543. So Origen eventually was condemned by all the major churches, as well as by the state. Why did the church repeatedly condemn him between the third and sixth centuries? Most historians think it was because Origen relied on the allegorical explanation of the text, based on aspects of Greek philosophy.

This was the beginning of a dark age, during which the church and the state were unified, and their combined power was used to control what people could write or read. Some at the time believed that differences of opinion about religion represented a threat to the unity of the empire. Following Emperor Justinian's condemnation, it was forbidden to read or possess any of Origen's works. Much of what he wrote was destroyed, but some of his works survived in Latin translation. Other works are known only indirectly through the writings of others.

Ever since the beginning of the European Enlightenment, Origen has attracted the attention of Western scholars and churchmen. In recent times, Egyptian church historian Iris Habib al-Masri[11] tried to persuade the late patriarch Pope Cyril VI (1959–71) to rescind the excommunications that the Egyptian church had imposed on Origen in 231 and again in 403. The patriarch reportedly told her, "My daughter, as I have received the church, so will I leave it." He would not change what his predecessors had done. Memory of Origen and his work has almost completely vanished in Egypt. Only recently have Coptic scholars begun to rediscover Origen's work through the writings of Western scholars. Origen is one of the most important figures in early Egyptian church history. Yet Egyptian church historians still seem reluctant to acknowledge his importance. Although international conferences on Origen's work have been held since 1973, few Egyptian scholars participate in them, and we still await the day when publishers in Egypt credit Origen's works as part of Egyptian history.

Heracles succeeded Origen as head of the Catechetical School and subsequently became patriarch of the Coptic Church (AD 231–47). Heracles tried unsuccessfully to persuade Origen to return to Alexandria. According to the twentieth-century historian Iris Habib al-Masri, Heracles rescinded Demetrius's excommunication of Origen. However, the later excommunication by Theophilus is still in force from the Coptic Church's point of view. It is said that Heracles was the first patriarch to be called "papa" or "pope," after he increased the number of local bishops to twenty.[12] Beginning in the ninth century, the Western church adopted this term to refer exclusively to the bishop of Rome. However, the Coptic Church still uses it to refer to their patriarch.

Didymus the Blind (AD 313–98) was one of the last important heads of the school. He invented a system of engraved writing, which may have been the first attempt in human history to help the blind read. In doing so, he preceded Braille by fifteen centuries.[13] Didymus also authored a book in which he demonstrated the errors committed by those who accused Origen of heresy. A defender of Origen's thinking, Didymus maintained that those who accused Origen of heresy were incapable of understanding Origen's teachings because they lacked his level of intellect and spirituality. Although some historians dismiss Didymus as a marginal figure, in 1941, during the Second World War, a chance discovery near the site of the ancient Quseir Monastery on the Egyptian plateau of Tura (on the outskirts of Cairo) brought the work of Didymus back to light and revealed him to be one of the great thinkers of the fourth century.[14] The discovery consisted of eight manuscripts by Origen and Didymus, including almost two thousand pages from five commentaries by the latter. Both men had been condemned by the Fifth Ecumenical Council in Constantinople in AD 553. At that time, the allegorical interpretation of scripture was being suppressed, so it is likely these manuscripts were hidden to preserve them from destruction. Didymus was considered by Evagrius Ponticus of the fourth century to be a great gnostic teacher. His writings include *On the Trinity* (three books), *On the Holy Spirit*, and *Discourse Against Arius and Sabellius*.[15]

After the fourth century, the small Christian community that had flourished in the competitive and diverse atmosphere of Alexandria vanished. Powerful bishops came to dominate Christian life and thought, with a stifling effect on what had once been one of the most vibrant centers of Christianity. There is general agreement that whatever was left of the Catechetical School and its library moved to St. Macarius Monastery in the desert northwest of Cairo. Founded in AD 360, the monastery attracted some four thousand monks from all around the Mediterranean. It became the unofficial seat of the patriarchs after the Egyptian, Ethiopian, and Armenian churches separated from the rest of the Christendom in AD 451, which might explain why this single monastery produced twenty-nine out of 117 patriarchs.[16] Although St. Macarius Monastery was able to preserve many texts and manuscripts, the open-minded discourse that had marked the thinking of cosmopolitan scholars such as Clement, Origen, and Didymus gradually became a thing of the past.

Monastic Egypt

We will now take a step back to look at early developments in the Christian church in the wider Egyptian community, outside the rarefied atmosphere of the Catechetical School of Alexandria. One of the most important of these was the development of monasticism. In the second and third centuries, Egyptians suffered political, religious, and economic persecution under the Romans. Egyptians were treated as second- or third-class citizens, considered of lower status than the Jews of Alexandria.[17] Many Christians believed Jesus' return was imminent, and it was in this climate that monasticism arose. Individuals moved away from the settled areas along the Nile Valley and went out into the desert in large numbers to pray and meditate.[18] In the span of one century, monastic life developed as an institution, and monks achieved wide fame for spirituality and miracles. At that time, visits to Egyptian monks and monasteries became important pilgrimage destinations. Returning pilgrims, in turn, spread knowledge of monasticism to other parts of the Christian world. As a result, Egyptian models of monastic life were widely copied.

The first known monk was St. Anthony (circa AD 250–354). Anthony, who reportedly lived to be more than a hundred years old, came to be known as the father of Christian monasticism in the East and the West. According to Egyptian tradition, Anthony was born into a wealthy family in Lower Egypt. Following the death of his parents, he gave away all his possessions and took up solitary life in an old cemetery. Later he moved to the desert west of the Gulf of Suez. There he lived in a cave near the top of a mountain, close to a spring. Renouncing all earthly comforts, he spent his days and nights in prayer and meditation. Though he lived in a remote area, far from civilization, word of his austere life and spiritual development spread throughout Egypt and beyond. Others followed his example. There was no formal organization at first. Individuals simply went to the desert, found a cave or built a small hut, and tried to imitate his way of life. Many of these early hermits settled in the vicinity of St. Anthony's cave near the Red Sea. This was the first gathering of monks in Christian history, and the site is considered the oldest documented Christian site in Egypt. It has been occupied by monks continuously from then until now, with the exception of the period between AD 1419 and 1441, when it was abandoned for unknown reasons.[19]

Only seven letters written by Anthony have survived. For some time, it was thought that he was an uneducated man, but recent analysis of these letters proves that he was aware of Greek philosophy as well as of some of Origen's writings.[20] St. Anthony's life was described by some of his contemporaries, the most important of whom was Athanasius I, who will be described in more detail later.[21] The form of monasticism that St. Anthony inspired was loosely structured. Monks might gather for services, but their primary activity was to pursue spiritual development in solitary cells. This is the predominant form of monasticism that survives in Egypt today.

Meanwhile, in the south of Egypt near Luxor, a different form of monasticism was developing. A monk named Pachomius (AD 292–346) is credited with organizing groups of monks into the first highly structured residential communities. He founded eleven monasteries for monks and two for nuns. About fifty thousand monks are estimated to have inhabited these monasteries.[22] They had scheduled times for work, prayer, meals, and sleep. Monks were housed three to a room. They wore special dress and were assigned specific tasks. Some specialized in writing and copying manuscripts, others specialized in bookkeeping, agriculture, and so on. There was an administrative staff and an annual meeting to assign administrative duties. The rules established by Pachomius were translated into other languages, with some modifications. Pachomian monasteries flourished for only about a century, before declining in Egypt.[23] However, the concept was taken up throughout the early Christian world. These early monasteries set the pattern from which Roman Catholic monasticism gradually developed. For more information about Pachomius, his life, and monastic rules, one can consult Philip Rousseau's Pachomius: *The Making of Community in Fourth-Century Egypt*.[24]

In 1945, farmers digging for fertilizer in Upper Egypt discovered thirteen ancient papyrus codices, which have come to be known as the Nag Hammadi Library. This collection contains forty-five separate works, thirty-six of which had been previously unknown in any form. Among these are a number of gnostic gospels. It is believed that these manuscripts originally came from one of the Pachomian monasteries and were buried after Patriarch Athanasius I banned them in AD 367. Most of the Nag Hammadi texts are now in the Coptic Museum in Cairo. They have all been translated from Coptic into various modern languages,[25] but only a few sections have been translated into Arabic.[26]

The fourth and the fifth centuries witnessed explosive growth in the monastic movement in Egypt. In the desert west of the Delta, the monastic communities at Nitria, Kellia, and Wadi al-Natrun housed monks numbering in the tens of thousands. Not all the monks in these communities were Egyptians; monastic life in Egypt was a magnet for Christians from all over the area.

Around the end of the fourth century, St. Shenoute (whose name means 'son of God' in the pharaonic language, and who died about AD 449) founded a monastic order based on the Pachomian Rule. He built a monastery in the region of Akhmim (about five hundred kilometers south of Cairo) that housed 2,200 monks, and another monastery nearby accommodating 1,800 nuns. The monastery's church was built of stone blocks taken from ancient Egyptian temples. The plaster finish has eroded over time, exposing the ancient pharaonic carving in the stone beneath. Shenoute taught the illiterate monks how to read and write. He emerged as a leader who spoke on behalf of the poor against the wealthy Greeks and Romans. He was an inspiring preacher and writer. The library of his monastery has preserved some of his commentaries, which are still used in the liturgy today. Shenoute improved the Saidi (south Egypt) dialect of the Coptic language and filtered out some of the Greek words. His legacy includes several beautiful works of Coptic literature.[27]

The early monastic movement in Egypt was relatively independent until the patriarch Athanasius I (AD 326–73) brought it under the control of the church. Monks and monasteries represented power to the church, and at times, to the patriarchs. Certain Egyptian monks, noted for their spirituality, became widely known and were visited by leaders and dignitaries seeking blessings or cures for various illnesses. There is evidence that between the fifth and the ninth centuries, Christianity in Ireland and England was influenced by Coptic monks, some of whom may have traveled there.[28] Monks from those lands also journeyed great distances to study at Coptic monasteries around the Mediterranean.

Coptic monasteries, especially St. Macarius Monastery in Wadi al-Natrun, preserved many old manuscripts and books containing a wealth of information about Coptic culture and heritage.[29] Despite some losses during turbulent periods of Muslim rule, these collections remained relatively intact over the centuries, until the beginning of the sixteenth century, when Europeans set out to gather wealth, artifacts, books, and manuscripts from the East. The popes of Rome, for example, sent representatives to acquire whatever they could from the treasures of the Coptic monasteries. Poverty and poor conditions in the monasteries made their task easier. Some manuscripts were bought outright, while others were obtained by guile. The net result was a large flow of books and manuscripts out of Egypt. Some disappeared forever, lost to the Nile during transportation.[30] If it were not for some Ethiopian translations, for example, we would have lost the writings of John of Nikiou, who chronicled the period of the Arab invasion of Egypt.[31]

The numbers of monks steadily declined after the Arabs arrived in Egypt in the seventh century. By the middle of the twentieth century, the total number of monks remaining in Egypt did not exceed one hundred. In the past sixty years, however, a vigorous revival movement has increased that number several-fold. Today, four monasteries survive in Wadi al-Natrun, and a few other monasteries are scattered around the country.

Diocletian and the Persecution of Christians

Christianity began spreading across the Mediterranean in the first century, but it did not spread as quickly as some have thought. The number of Christians did not increase significantly until the beginning of the fourth century, when Christianity became one of the official religions of Constantine's empire in AD 381.

The Roman Empire included members of many religions. Initially, there was no significant discrimination against Christianity, which was still considered a sect of Judaism. As the number of Christians increased, however, they became more visible. One factor that aided the spread of Christianity was that it became the religion of the poor and oppressed, who were attracted by the promise of a better life, if not in this world, then in the next. Gradually, members of the upper and middle classes, as well as leaders of other religions, began to realize that Christianity called for the exclusive worship of one God and for improving the conditions of the poor. This posed a threat to the religious, economic, and social status quo. Christians began to face persecution from the government as well as from other religions. As a result, they started to hold clandestine meetings and to pray in secret. This added to their troubles because they then were accused of being a secret society with political ambitions. Government persecution increased against Christians all over the empire, especially against the heads of the churches. Many church historians have written about this period, including the Egyptian historian Severus of Ashmunayn, in *The History of the Patriarchs*, and Eusebius, in *History of the Church*.[32]

By the end of the third century, chaos prevailed in some parts of the empire. The central government was weak, and some local rulers declared their independence. In this climate, Diocletian (AD 284–305) came to power, unified the empire, and reorganized the administration, the army, and the financial system. He separated the army from civil administration and divided the empire into two and then four semi-independent states, each ruled by a Caesar or an Augustus. In doing so, Diocletian set the administrative pattern for the Byzantine Empire in the East.

Emperor Diocletian tried to restore the glory of the empire by reviving the old Roman religions, particularly the cults of Apollo and Jupiter. Apparently this did not cause much conflict with the Christians, who by this time constituted a growing proportion of the population in Egypt. However, in the last three years of his reign, and for reasons that are unclear, the persecution against Christians became extremely severe. Eusebius of Caesarea, the church historian, says, "In the ninth year of Diocletian's rule, royal orders were issued everywhere to destroy churches, to burn holy books, to expel Christians from influential positions, and to prevent servants from working in the royal palaces if they insisted on staying in the Christian faith."[33]

Egypt was treated particularly harshly. It was the bread basket of the Roman army, and thus a vital resource. In addition to Christianity's religious non-conformity, it was perceived as a political threat. Internal revolts occurred in the cities of Coptos and Busiris, but the most important revolt was in Alexandria, where the ruler, Achilleus, declared independence.[34] Diocletian eventually succeeded in subduing the city by force. The Egyptian church historian John of Nikiou describes it as follows:

> When Diocletian the Egyptian (sic) ruled Egypt, he oppressed the believers. He couldn't control Alexandria or Egypt. He prepared a large army under his leadership with his three ruling partners. After Egypt surrendered to him, he destroyed Alexandria and built a palace in the eastern part of the city. He stayed there for a long time, because he wasn't able to enter the city until some people pointed out to him a hidden entrance. His huge army was able to enter the city after a fierce battle. Diocletian set the city on fire and burned everything. He made offerings to his evil gods and persecuted Christians. He was like a wild beast, hating every good thing. He opposed God because all Roman authority was at his disposal. He killed priests and monks, men, women, and children. He had no mercy; blood was everywhere. They were like cannibals and they were everywhere.[35]

It was a dangerous time for Christians. As a result, some church leaders fled—among them, Peter I, who was patriarch from AD 300–11. This had important implications which we will return to later. Under pressure, some Christians pretended to give up their religion and were forced to make offerings to the Roman gods. Others refused and were martyred. Later, the Coptic Church honored them by resetting the years of the Coptic calendar to begin with the date Diocletian become emperor (August 29, AD 284). As a result, year 1 of the Coptic calendar ended on August 28, AD 285.[36] The names of the Coptic calendar months remained the same as in the ancient Egyptian calendar—they are still used by Egyptian farmers today. It is impossible to know the number killed during this period of persecution, but estimates range from 144,000 to 800,000.[37]

Diocletian saw the unrest in Alexandria as a revolt against the empire. The fact that Christianity was a well-organized religion under a centrally controlled hierarchy of patriarch, bishops, priests, deacons, and monks was perceived as a threat to Roman rule. It was also troubling that Christians often met in secret and that their organization was not under the emperor's control. Rome's subjugation of Alexandria did not succeed in making Christians give up their religion. However, it brought Egypt firmly back under the authority of the empire.

Initially, Diocletian did not persecute Christians, nor was he interested in Christianity. His rule began in AD 284, and persecution against Christians did not occur until eighteen years later.[38] What accounts for this change in policy? Some historians think the motivating force behind the persecution was Galerius, one of Diocletian's four rulers and also his son-in-law and successor. Galerius hated Christians and wanted to get rid of them. Around this time, a revolt took place in Syria, during which the imperial palace was twice set on fire. Galerius[39] persuaded Diocletian that Christians were involved in a conspiracy to overthrow him. As a result, Diocletian issued three imperial orders in AD 303 to destroy churches, burn holy books, and jail and torture the heads of the churches. In AD 304, he issued another decree, ordering all people to offer sacrifices to the Roman gods.[40] After this, persecution against Christians became widespread, though its severity differed according to local circumstances.

In AD 305, Diocletian abdicated his position as emperor. He may have been the first Roman emperor ever to do so. This did not bring an end to the persecution, however. Persecution against Christians continued until AD 312, when Constantine came to power after a series of adroit political and military maneuvers. Constantine had a more tolerant policy. He had served in Diocletian's court when his own father, Constantius, was the caesar of the West, and had seen that persecuting Christians only increased their numbers. Perhaps that was the reason he allowed freedom of religion.[41]

Constantine succeeded in becoming the sole ruler of the empire after waging a number of wars. One of the most important of these was fought in AD 312 against Maxentius in Rome. According to legend, before the battle, Constantine saw a vision of a cross in the sky with the motto *In hoc signo vince*, "By this sign, you will conquer." Constantine ordered the Christian monogram, with the superimposed letters *chi* and *rho*, emblazoned on his soldiers' standards. After winning the battle, it is said that Constantine converted to Christianity and ordered the making of a gold cross decorated with precious stones.[42] Eusebius relates the story of the cross in the sky in his book on Constantine's life.[43] This account, however, has been criticized by both early and recent historians. Eusebius wrote about the supposed event twenty-five years after it occurred. There was no mention of it before that date.

When Constantine came to power, he brought the church under the authority of the empire and called himself *pontifex maximus* (chief priest), as had been a Roman tradition. He flooded the church leaders with gifts, so that they became his powerful allies.[44] This ushered in a period of political and theological conflicts, during which emperors could intervene and dictate their opinions. State intervention in church affairs turned out to be a mixed blessing for the church. On the one hand, the church (at least those in the church who agreed with the state) benefited from state support; on the other hand, the church lost a measure of control over its internal affairs.

Did Constantine convert to Christianity out of conviction or mere political expediency? At that time, the number of Christians was increasing among the masses as well as in the army. Some historians have questioned the authenticity of Constantine's conversion, while others have accepted it, to the point of calling him the "thirteenth disciple" of Jesus. It is reported that Constantine himself continued to make public obeisance to Sol, the Roman god of the sun, and that he was not baptized until he was on his deathbed, in AD 337.[45]

In AD 324, Constantine was named supreme Augustus by the Roman senate, and the empire was united under his control. Christianity became one of the empire's religions, but it did not become the official religion until AD 381. The number of Christians during this period was not large, but they were united and well organized. Constantine used Christianity for his political gain and tried to tame the church to serve the empire and to serve himself personally. He united church and state, diverting state funds into church coffers and bringing bishops into the service of the state. As a result, under Constantine, the government became more autocratic than ever.[46] Although he considered himself a bishop who possessed the truth and who ruled in the name of God, Constantine did not know much about theological matters. His letters to Alexandria regarding what became known as the Arian heresy (which dealt with the nature of Christ) are evidence of this. These letters show that he did not consider this a matter worth debating, even though it had become an ongoing theological issue, whose ramifications persist to the present day.

Politics influenced the church, and the Egyptian church played an important role in Roman politics until the year AD 451, when it, along with the Armenian, Syrian, and Ethiopian churches, decided to separate from the official Roman church in a declaration of independence.

Athanasius and the Separation of the Coptic Church

As a result of the freedom of religion permitted by Constantine, a multiplicity of religious interpretations flourished. Most of the major theological controversies in the early centuries of Christianity were centered on the nature of Jesus Christ. We will not discuss these different opinions, except for those that had an effect on Egypt. Many church councils were convened.

Some worked locally to resolve specific problems or answer internal questions; others had implications for the entire early Christian world. The first council of the latter kind was held in Nicea in AD 325. Christianity by then was one of the official religions of the empire. This council took place one year after the empire had been unified under Constantine, and is an example of an early attempt by the state to bring the church under its control.

The Nicene Council was convened to deal with the Arian heresy.[47] Arius (AD 270–336) was a priest of Libyan descent who preached, in Alexandria, that Jesus was created—meaning that Jesus was not of the same substance as God, but was a creation of God. Arianism, in its essence, tried to base Christianity on logical principles that could be easily understood. The opposing view, adopted by the bishop of Alexandria, claimed that Jesus combined both godly and human natures; he was God, in the sense that a person in a high spiritual state can be one with God. This represented a difference between spiritual and intellectual understanding. The theological point at issue was both subtle and abstract. The Catechetical School of Alexandria had believed in this spiritual understanding of Jesus. It is also possible this viewpoint had roots in ancient Egyptian religion, wherein Isis, Osiris, and Horus formed a trinity of God—one in all, and all in one.

Almost a century before the Arian heresy, Origen commented on different kinds of Christianity by saying, "A variety of schools of thought is often desirable."[48] But as we have seen, the church itself was often less tolerant. Under pressure from the Alexandrian clergy, Arius and his followers were excommunicated. They left Alexandria and went to Constantinople, where they had supporters. Emperor Constantine tried to resolve this theological dispute by sending letters to both parties, downplaying their differences. This failed to bring about a reconciliation, so Constantine convened an ecumenical church council, the first of its kind. Held in May AD 325 in Nicea, near the emperor's residence in Nicomedia, it was attended by many clergy, mostly from the East. The resulting decision, stated in the Nicene Creed, took the side of Alexandria's bishop, and the Egyptian church holds this position to this day.

The problem of the nature of Jesus has continued to haunt the church. Since Nicea, four other ecumenical councils have dealt with the same problem in one form or another.[49] The Egyptian (Coptic) church was influential in shaping these councils, all of which confirmed the conclusion reached at the Nicene Council. We will discuss the fifth council in a moment, because this was the council where the Egyptian church separated from the rest. The split was due in part to the controversy over the nature of

Jesus, although politics also played a role. This conflict eventually led to the separation of the Coptic Church, as will be discussed later in the chapter.

Athanasius attended the Nicene Council as secretary and deacon to Egyptian Pope Alexander I (AD 312–26). He also acted as Alexander's envoy to heads of various churches outside Egypt, thereby gaining exposure and experience. Eventually Athanasius succeeded Alexander as patriarch and bishop of Alexandria. He went on to lead the church for almost half a century (AD 326–73). Athanasius was one of the most important individuals in the history of the church at large, but particularly that of the Coptic Church. Edward Gibbon described him as a person of superior character and abilities. He helped significantly in shaping the independent character of the Coptic Church and to conserve the Nicene Creed, but he paid a high personal price for it.[50]

When Athanasius was selected as the twentieth patriarch, there was division in the Coptic Church. Three factions opposed his selection. The first group saw Athanasius's age as a problem. At the time, he was probably between twenty-nine and thirty years old, and church law required patriarchs to be at least thirty. The second objection came from the Arian camp. Athanasius was strongly opposed to Arianism, so naturally the Arians opposed his selection. A third objection to Athanasius's selection came from the Melitians.[51] Melitius was a bishop of Lycopolis (modern Asyut, in Upper Egypt). During the great persecutions of Diocletian, when the patriarch Peter was in hiding, Melitius took it upon himself to appoint replacements for those bishops and priests who had fled or been martyred. When Peter returned briefly to his post, before his own martyrdom in AD 311, he excommunicated Melitius and his appointees because their appointments had violated normal procedures. This issue was raised at the Nicene Council, where it was decided that priests ordained by Melitius could retain their status, as could the bishops he appointed if their see would otherwise be vacant. Melitius also retained his title and post. But the problem was not really resolved. Thirty-five bishops and hundreds of priests and monks continued to follow Melitius. So the problem persisted, and the split continued until the fifth century.[52]

Athanasius took a hard line against Melitius, Arius, and their followers. In this climate, selecting Athanasius was not easy.[53] There are some contradictions in the accounts of how this was done. Father Matthew the Poor, a modern Coptic historian, says that Athanasius was selected by ninety-four bishops and opposed by thirty-five bishops from the Arian and Melitian camps.[54] This opinion represents the official position of the Coptic Church.

But Timothy D. Barnes[55] states that the total number of bishops was only forty-five, and that before a decision was agreed upon, seven bishops from Athanasius's supporters selected and ordained him the next patriarch, while the Melitians selected a rival bishop.[56] Some political maneuvering undoubtedly led to the selection of Athanasius at such a young age.

However it came about, Athanasius become the patriarch and eventually was able to win the support of most Egyptians and to unify the Egyptian church to a large degree. As time passed, he became widely admired. He remained the head of the church for many years. His enemies tried to have him removed or exiled, but with limited success. They managed to exile him and replace him a number of times, but he always succeeded in returning to his post.[57] Even when he was exiled or replaced, Egyptians considered him their patriarch. At times, he stood alone against the imperial establishment in Constantinople, a stance that increased his popularity among Egyptians. Athanasius has been credited by modern historians with unifying the Coptic Church of Egypt. According to Edward Gibbon, Athanasius displayed "a superiority of character and abilities which would have qualified him, far better than the degenerate sons of Constantine, for the government of a great monarchy."[58]

But the followers of Arius and Melitius, some of whom were close to the emperor and his court, continued to make trouble. They fabricated one accusation after another against Athanasius while he was far from Constantinople and unable to defend his views before the emperor. This was reflected in the number of times Athanasius was removed or exiled.[59] In addition, a degree of personal jealousy came into play because Athanasius was independent, had a strong personality, and was widely admired in Egypt.

Animosity from Constantinople toward the bishops of Alexandria became a pattern that continued even after the separation of the Coptic Church in AD 451. A later example of this comes to us from Iohannis Ephesini (John of Ephesus) in the sixth century, during the rule of Emperor Tiberius II.[60]

When the patriarch Yuhanna (John) was complaining to the emperor Tiberius every day about those who believe in the one nature of Jesus—the Orthodox—the emperor asked him if he could swear that they were heretics. Even though the patriarch was misleading the emperor, when he had to swear he could not lie. He answered, "They aren't heretics and their faith is correct, but they are far from us and from the official church and they don't want to share the ritual with us." The emperor said, "If you testify that they are good Christians, why do you always slander them? Do you want me to persecute them like Diocletian? It is enough that we have wars with the barbarians; we don't need to get in trouble with our followers as well."

This might be part of what happened behind the scenes that caused trouble for the Copts and their church.

Athanasius's enemies slandered him, but he stood firm in his beliefs. His steadfastness is summarized in an apocryphal story, related by Father Matthew the Poor. When Athanasius was told by a contemporary, "The world is against you, Athanasius," he replied, "And Athanasius is against the world." As a result of his intransigence, he spent time in exile, both within and without Egypt, but always managed to hold onto his position. During his twenty-eight years as patriarch, he was exiled or disappeared within Egypt five times, for a total of seventeen to eighteen years, hiding in various monasteries.[61] Despite these troubles, Athanasius published forty-five books and commentaries and achieved much for the church.[62]

Objective assessment of the man is difficult even today, especially within Egypt. Most of the sources available in Arabic contain only the official church position, which is highly laudatory. For example, the Coptic Church honors Athanasius by giving him the title of 'apostle' to equate him with Jesus's apostles. In the eyes of many Copts, he is a legendary figure. Other opinions are hard to find in Coptic or Arabic, though they can be found in scholarly and mostly non-Arabic books, some of which are cited here.[63]

In 381, Emperor Theodoretus (AD 378–95) outlawed paganism and declared Christianity to be the only official religion of the empire. The unity of the church became an important tool to bolster the unity of the state. In pursuit of this goal, Theodoretus issued a decree imposing the Nicene version of the Christian faith on everyone. He considered anyone who failed to accept the Nicene Creed to be a heretic. The church was encouraged to comply because it depended on support from the state. Church leaders played an important social and political role, one that was inextricably interwoven with their religious role.[64] From the end of the fourth century until the middle of the fifth century, the empire was officially Christian, but this does not mean that all its people were. In Egypt, pockets of the ancient Egyptian religion remained even as late as the Arab invasion in the seventh century.

Between the end of the fourth and the middle of the fifth century, three patriarchs emerged who had a profound influence on the Coptic Church. They were Theophilus, his nephew Cyril, and Dioscorus. These Alexandrian patriarchs had a strong influence both inside and outside Egypt, which led to some envy and jealousy from heads of other churches, especially those associated with the emperors in Rome and Constantinople. Ultimately, theological disputes and the struggle for supremacy among various versions of Christianity led to the separation of the Egyptian church, as we will see.

Theophilus (AD 385–412) was a complex and controversial figure. He gained power and influence from the state, from the increasing number of Christians, and from the decline of other religions. While patriarch, he was an active collaborator in Emperor Theodosius's program to stamp out paganism and to Christianize the population. For example, the emperor gave Theophilus the keys to all pagan temples in Egypt, from Alexandria to Aswan, and authorized him to use whatever wealth he found there to build churches.[65] Under Theophilus's leadership, Christians dismantled pagan buildings and built churches and monasteries, often on the same site and using the disassembled building material. The Egyptian patriarch also took the lead in instigating mobs to storm the Serapion, a Greek temple that housed the Library of Alexandria, one of the world's largest collections of books and manuscripts (about forty thousand).[66] In one of history's greatest acts of vandalism, the Serapion and its irreplaceable library were demolished and burned, and a church and monastery were built on its site.[67] The Library of Alexandria will be discussed in more detail in the next chapter.

Theophilus's fixation on building churches rather than helping the poor did not sit well with the simple ascetic monks who followed Origen's teachings. This added to the patriarch's growing problems because the monks played an important role in helping him stamp out paganism.[68] Theophilus initially followed the teachings of Origen, favoring a more allegorical, less literal, interpretation of scripture. When he expressed doubts about the doctrine of anthropomorphism (which held that Adam was created in the image of God) in one of his letters, many non-Origenist monks accused the patriarch himself of heresy. Some monks went to Alexandria and rallied against him. Reportedly, some even plotted to have him killed. As a result, Theophilus underwent a sudden change of heart; he told the monks that God had human characteristics, saying, "I see you as the face of God." When the monks pressed him, he denounced the theology of Origen, which he had until then embraced.[69] This in turn caused a problem with the Origenist monks, who already were displeased that he was spending extravagant sums on ostentatious church buildings.

After Theophilus withdrew his support for Origen's theology and espoused the views of the more literal-minded monks, he cracked down on all opposition, which came primarily from the intelligentsia of the church. He excommunicated and ordered the expulsion of the Origenist monks from all monasteries. He sent military troops to Nitria, where about five thousand monks lived, to expel all dissenting monks by force and to quell the resistance. Some of the expelled monks asked for clemency, but Theophilus turned them down, so they went to Constantinople to seek help from the patriarch John Chrysostom. Theophilus refused to accept the mediation of Chrysostom and excommunicated him as well at the Synod of Oak in AD 403.[70] Chrysostom was a popular spiritual leader, but as a result of Theophilus's action, he was forced to leave his post and died in exile. Under Theophilus's successor, the Coptic Church withdrew the excommunication against Chrysostom, whose name now is often mentioned in Coptic services and who is considered one of the saints.

When Theophilus died, his nephew Cyril (AD 412–44) succeeded him as patriarch three days later. Cyril was another controversial figure. The Coptic Church calls him Cyril the Great or the Pillar of Religion. He was influential in the church councils he attended, and wrote several important theological commentaries.[71] Cyril followed in his uncle's footsteps. During his tenure, there was civil unrest and sporadic violence against pagans and Jews, which the historian Steven J. Davis believes may have been instigated by Cyril. In one particularly brutal episode,[72] Hypatia, the famous Alexandrian Platonic philosopher and the first notable woman mathematician, was dragged from her carriage to the Caesarion church and killed. Her body was then mutilated and burned. This incident, among others, brought disgrace upon Cyril and his church.[73] The Jews of Alexandria were harassed and expelled from some of their quarters. Their synagogues were converted into churches.

Another problem that surfaced between Constantinople and Alexandria during Cyril's time was, yet again, over the nature of Jesus. Nestorius, the bishop of Constantinople, taught that Mary was the mother of Jesus, not the mother of God. This was seen as conflicting with the Nicene Creed, which stated that God and Jesus were the same. The old argument had never really been laid to rest, so Emperor Theodosius II ordered another council to deal with this problem. It was held in Ephesus in AD 431, with Cyril presiding. Nestorius was condemned and excommunicated by unanimous decision, but the votes were cast without the presence of the Antiochene party. The Antiochenes then held their own council and excommunicated Cyril. It was a war of excommunications. When the emperor learned about this, he decided to nullify all the decisions. No compromise could be reached and it took three years for Alexandria and

Antioch to reconcile. Nestorius left public life, went back to his monastery, relinquished his episcopate, and was exiled for five years.[74]

In 2008, the Sufi scholar Youssef Ziedan wrote a historical novel about this period.[75] The book was very well received by Muslims but rejected by some Christian clergy, who considered it anti-Christian because they did not appreciate the differences between historical novels, scholarly history, and church history. The controversy over this novel attracted much media attention and is an example of how ancient sectarian disputes can contribute to modern sectarian tensions.

As the Coptic Church grew, the ancient Egyptian religion—which had persisted since the time of the pharaohs—suffered from Christian persecution. It did not disappear from Egypt until the sixth or even the seventh century. Most of the old temples were destroyed or mutilated, and their stone blocks were used to construct churches and monasteries. Saint Shenoute's White Monastery near Sohag in Upper Egypt is a good example. The ancient Egyptian carvings are quite obvious on some of the blocks. Sometimes old temples, such as the one at Philae, were left standing and were converted into churches. This pattern of modifying the sites of an older religion to serve a newer one was repeated centuries later, when churches were converted into mosques.

By the fourth and fifth centuries, the Coptic Church in Egypt had become a powerful influence on other churches, especially those in Constantinople and Rome, where the emperors resided. This had serious consequences. Although Alexandria had highly respected theologians and Egyptian monasteries fostered many spiritual monks who came from all over the Christian world, the political power lay in Constantinople and in Rome. As a result, the imperial courts, especially the one in Constantinople, continued their campaign to reduce the influence of Alexandria. Things came to a head after Cyril died and Dioscorus (AD 444–54) replaced him as patriarch of the Coptic Church. Jacques Tagher quotes Dioscorus as saying, "Egypt belongs to me more than the emperor, and I request sovereignty over it."[76] Regardless of his motives, a theological and political storm was gathering. Events quickly got out of control, with serious consequences.

This storm began with the revival of the old controversy over the nature of Jesus. A monk named Eutychius, who was the head of a monastery near Constantinople, preached that Jesus had one nature. The bishops of Constantinople and Rome objected. Alexandria supported Eutychius, based on the Coptic understanding of the one nature of God, which had been formulated at the Nicene Council of AD 325. To address this issue, another church council was held at Ephesus in 499, presided over by Dioscorus of Alexandria. At this council, the bishop of Constantinople was deposed, a decision supported by the emperor Theodosius. But when the emperor died one year later, the climate in Constantinople changed and the clouds over Alexandria began to darken.[77]

When the emperor died in AD 450, his widow, Pulcheria, married the officer Marcian, who became the next emperor. Pulcheria was worried about the growing power of Alexandria and was not pleased that Alexandria had arranged to have the bishop of Constantinople deposed. Pulcheria also sympathized with Leo, the bishop of Rome. Leo had been excommunicated by Dioscorus after the Council of Ephesus because he had forgiven some of the bishops who had been excommunicated at the previous ecumenical council. Leo's action meant that a local council in Rome could countermand the decision of an ecumenical council. Now the power in Constantinople shifted heavily against Alexandria, and there was a movement to depose Dioscorus.

The last ecumenical council the Egyptians attended was held in AD 451 at Chalcedon, a town near present-day Istanbul. The council was attended by 520 bishops or their representatives. It was planned so that most of the attendees opposed the bishop of Alexandria, Dioscorus. The Alexandrian position was that Jesus has a divine and human nature that are united as one within him. The other position, which prevailed at the council of Chalcedon, was that Jesus has two distinct natures, both existing in the person of Jesus. However, the Eastern churches found the council's decision unacceptable and refused to be bound by it. Dioscorus was put on trial and deposed.[78] The Coptic, Armenian, and Syrian churches joined the position of the Egyptian church. The American scholar Cyrus Gordon reflected the feeling of the Egyptians regarding that council by saying, "When the Egyptians went to Chalcedon, they were proud of their Pharaonic heritage and rightly so; they were proud of their Alexandrian fathers and rightly so; they frankly told the whole world what they believed and when the world refused to listen, they walked out, and rightly so."[79]

After AD 451, the Egyptians stuck to their version of the nature of Jesus. Several attempts were made to reunify the churches, but these did not succeed. The Egyptian church has kept its independence since then, sometimes paying a high price. When Byzantine rulers imposed Chalcedonian patriarchs on Egypt, the Egyptians selected their own anti-Chalcedonian (monophysite) leaders. On one occasion, the appointed Chalcedonian patriarch, Proterius, was killed by the Egyptians[80] and, though not a Christian act, it was considered by some to be a nationalistic act. This struggle continued until the Arabs arrived in the seventh century, starting another historical era that brought with it a new set of challenges.

It has taken fifteen centuries for the Coptic and Catholic churches to reconcile. In 1988, the two churches finally agreed on a document stating, "Jesus is perfect in his divinity and perfect in his humanity. He made his humanity one with his divinity without mixture, nor mingling, nor confusion. His divinity was not separated from his humanity even for a moment or twinkling of an eye." The document was signed in St. Bishoi Monastery in Egypt.[81]

Christianity came to Egypt through the back door, as a religion for the slaves, the servants, and the poor. It preached equality between the Egyptians and their masters—the Romans and the Byzantine Greeks. As a result, some Egyptians were able to stand up to those who enslaved and persecuted them. Church leaders, especially in the fourth and fifth centuries, brought authentically Egyptian leadership that had been absent since pharaonic times.

For centuries, before the Arabs came to Egypt, Coptic Christianity sustained the national identity of the indigenous Egyptian population in the face of outside political domination by the Roman and Byzantine Empires. Coptic religion and language united the people and shaped their unique culture. One might even say the secession of the Coptic Church was an expression of national identity; religious independence was gained in lieu of political independence. When churches in other parts of the Christian world bowed to imperial dictates and received help and support in return, Egyptians resisted. Emperors and patriarchs came and went, but the Coptic Church maintained its autonomy, as it has until the present day.

2
THE COMING OF ISLAM

Egypt before the Arab Invasion

By the time the Arabs arrived in Egypt in the seventh century, the Roman Empire had been in a slow decline for about three centuries. In the West, Germanic tribes had invaded much of the territory once held by Rome. In the East, Emperor Constantine's successors continued to rule a decaying empire from the imperial seat in Constantinople (Byzantium). The last strong emperor in the East was Justinian (AD 527–65), who attempted to revive the old Roman Empire and managed to regain some of its lost territories in the West. During his reign, the empire extended from the Caucasus and Arabia to the Pillars of Hercules. In Constantinople, the Cathedral of St. Sophia, now a mosque, still stands as a testament to the greatness of Byzantine architecture in that period. To guard the borders, Justinian established a series of garrisons, including outposts at St. Catherine's Monastery in Sinai and at St. Anthony's Monastery near the Red Sea. Like his predecessors, Justinian tried to bring the stubborn Copts in line with the rest of the churches in his empire, but in vain.

Justinian was followed by a succession of weak emperors, the worst of whom was the vicious and corrupt Phocas (AD 602–10). Phocas was crowned by the patriarch Cyriacus in the church of St. John at Constantinople. As the empire deteriorated under poor leadership, Heraclius (AD 610–41), the prefect of Africa, took control of the capital, killed Phocas, and became the next emperor.[1]

It was precisely at this time that Muhammad, the Prophet of Islam, started spreading his message. As Islam began to take root in Arabia, the weakened Byzantine Empire came under assault by the Persians, who were expanding their empire. In AD 614, the Persians invaded Syria and Palestine, and wrested these provinces from the Byzantines. In Jerusalem, the Persians destroyed some of the great churches, killed upwards of ninety thousand people, and imprisoned another thirty-five thousand.[2]

Many Christian clergy escaped to Alexandria, where they were welcomed. Friendly ties between the two communities were reinforced when, years later, the Coptic Church helped to rebuild Jerusalem.[3]

In AD 616, having seized Syria and Palestine, the Persians invaded Egypt and Libya. The Persians showed a savage ferocity which passes all of reason and necessity. They met little resistance, except in Alexandria, which was well fortified and encircled by water. In the environs of Alexandria, there were no fewer than six hundred monasteries. Severus of Ashmunayn, the Coptic church historian of the late tenth century, stated that the Persians killed most of the monks, destroyed libraries, and made off with many treasures.[4] The Egyptian historian al-Maqrizi of the fifteenth century described the Persian invasion as follows in his work titled *Kitab al-mawa'iz wa-l-i'tibar bi-dhikr al-khitat wa-l-athar*.

> The Persian army entered Syria and Palestine, killed all the Christians, and then came to Egypt and killed a great number of them. They were helped by the Jews in fighting the Christians and destroying the churches. The Jews took their revenge on the Christians for what they had suffered at their hands. The Persians ruined two churches in Jerusalem, burned Christian holy places, took the Holy Rood, and captured the Jerusalem patriarch and other clergy. [5]

In Egypt, after their initial brutal invasion, the Persian rulers pursued a more lenient policy of conciliation and sought to maintain the status quo in social policy and economic affairs.[6] After taking the eastern provinces, the Persian emperor Chosroes turned his attention to Constantinople, the Byzantine capital and seat of the emperor Heraclius. Chosroes came from Iraq to assault the city, but was unsuccessful. The siege dragged on for fourteen years. While the Persians blockaded Constantinople, Turkish tribes were attacking along the Byzantine frontiers. Emperor Heraclius was desperate. Trapped in his capital along with his impotent army, he looked for a way out. He tried to make a peace agreement with the Persians, but Chosroes demanded that Heraclius surrender and replace Christianity with the worship of the Persian sun deity.[7] Heraclius refused, and was left with no real choice but to fight. The patriarch in Constantinople, Sergius, placed his church treasure at the disposal of the emperor, who used it to rebuild his army, eventually giving him military success.[8] After breaking the blockade, Heraclius defeated the Persians and drove them out of Asia Minor, liberating all the countries the Persians had occupied. The war lasted for six years, and the Byzantine victory was one of the most dramatic triumphs in history.[9]

Those who had backed the losing side paid a high price. As al-Maqrizi says:

> In Palestine, the Jews presented Heraclius with valuable gifts and asked him to protect their lives, which he agreed to do. But when the church leaders informed Heraclius about the Jewish support of the Persians and what the Jews had done to the Christians and their churches, Heraclius believed them and turned against the Jews. It was catastrophic for the Jews, most of whom were killed; the only survivors were those who fled.[10]

In Egypt, the Persians were driven out and the Byzantines returned. During this transition, Egypt was in chaos. The historian Alfred Butler translates the report of the seventh-century historian John of Nikiou as follows: "The clash of arms was often heard in Alexandria itself, while not only was Upper Egypt haunted by bands of brigands and harried by raids of Beduins or Nubians, but even the Delta was the scene of riots and feuds little short of civil war."[11]

Heraclius, remembering how the church had supported him against the Persians in his time of need, remained a firm supporter of the Chalcedonian church. He reestablished Chalcedonian bishops in the dissenting provinces and supported them with financial aid and economic advantages. He went even further by trying to impose his own doctrine, which was called monothelitism (from Greek, meaning 'one will'). According to this doctrine, Christ had two natures but only one will, or *energeia*.[12] The emperor chose Cyrus (AD 631–42) from the Caucasus to impose this creed on the Egyptians. To give him sufficient power to attain this aim, Heraclius appointed him simultaneously Byzantine patriarch of Alexandria, civil viceroy, and military commander of the imperial forces in Egypt.

Cyrus used brutality and humiliation in an attempt to force unity on the church, but his efforts failed. In AD 631, the Coptic patriarch Benjamin I left Alexandria in anticipation of persecution. He took refuge in monasteries for about ten years, and remained in hiding until the Arabs invaded in AD 640. Unable to find Benjamin I, Cyrus captured Benjamin's brother, Mina, and tortured him in an effort to make him reveal his brother's hiding place and force the patriarch to accept the new creed imposed by Heraclius.

When all this failed, Cyrus had Mina put in a sack weighed down with stones and drowned in the Nile.

While Cyrus governed in Egypt, the Copts suffered one of the worst periods of persecution in their history. The arrival of the Arabs in Egypt gave the Copts hope that their lot would improve. Indeed, this initially was the case. The new Arab ruler, 'Amr ibn al 'As, did not interfere in Coptic religious affairs, even though spreading the faith was one of the pillars of Islam. The problems came later as more and more Copts converted to Islam. Eventually, the Copts become a small minority. Butler speculates about how the Copts anticipated the arrival of Islam in Egypt.

> What did the Egyptians feel with regard to that great movement which had sprung from Arabia and was already shaking the cities of Syria? To their honor, be it said, there is not the slightest reason to think that they looked upon it with sympathy: yet when they heard that even the Muslims granted a measure of toleration to the Christians, the thought may have risen in their hearts that subjection to the Muslims would make life less unbearable, that the yoke of Mohammed would be lighter than the yoke of the most Christian Emperor Heraclius. That they abhorred the religion of Islam is proved by every page of their history: but during those ten years of hopeless misery, the sword of Cyrus had cut through well-nigh the last thread which bound their allegiance to the Roman Empire; and they regarded the advent of the Muslims as a plague sent by divine vengeance upon their persecutors.[13]

The Arabs Arrive in Egypt

By the time the Prophet Muhammad died in AD 632, Arabia had become a predominantly Muslim country and the Arabs had begun spreading into Syria and Palestine. By AD 640 (AH 19), they had completed their conquest of these provinces. Ibn al-'As, the Muslim general who was one of the leaders in the campaign to conquer Syria, persuaded 'Umar ibn al-Khattab, the second caliph, to extend the campaign to Egypt. In this climate, with the Byzantine Empire struggling and Syria already captured, Egypt was poised to fall to the Arabs like a ripe fruit.

The operation on the Egyptian front began in December AD 639 (AH 18) with only thirty-five hundred to four thousand fighters, according to ninth-century sources. The Arabs must have had great self-confidence after defeating the Byzantines in Syria and Palestine, or they would not have embarked on this campaign with such a small number of warriors. Nevertheless, the Arabs crossed Sinai and reached Cairo, meeting almost no resistance until they were stopped in front of the fortress of Babylon in Old Cairo. Here they were unable to progress farther, so they laid siege to the fortress. The leader of the campaign in Egypt, Ibn al-'As, realized he would not be able to occupy Egypt without reinforcements, which he asked for and received.[14] While awaiting their arrival, a group of Arab fighters explored the nearby towns, reaching as far as the Fayum oasis (fifty miles from Cairo), where they supplied themselves with provisions by seizing the goods of the defenseless people.

In the following excerpt, John of Nikiou gives us a contemporaneous account of the first armed confrontation between the Byzantine defensive forces and the Arabs.

> The city of Fayum was held by the governor Domentianus while Theodosius the Prefect of the province was with Anastasius, Prefect of Alexandria, in the Delta not far from Nikiou. The defense of the province was entrusted to John, the general of the militia, or to local levies commanded by John of Maros. The point of entrance to Fayum was strongly guarded, and an observation post was established by the Romans [i.e., Byzantines] at Hajar al Lahun [near Fayum]. A force of cavalry archers was also sent against the Arabs to arrest their march. The Saracen army seems to have found it impossible to break through the Byzantine cordon and edged off to the desert hills, capturing a large quantity of cattle on their way. They advanced in this way to a town called Bahnasa which they took by storm, and slaughtered all before them—men, women, and children. 'Amr ibn al 'As now faced about suddenly as he heard that John with a small force of fifty men had been following and spying on his movements and was at some distance from his support. John realized his danger and endeavored by a rapid retreat to regain his camp at Aboutat, no great distance on the bank of the Nile. His troops marched by night, taking cover by day in palm groves and thickets. But their hiding place was betrayed to 'Amr by a Bedouin chief. They were surrounded, and slain to the last man.[15]

In June AD 640 (AH 19), the Arab reinforcements requested by Ibn al-'As arrived to aid the siege of the fortress of Babylon. According to the historians Ibn 'Abd al-Hakam and Butler, they numbered about twelve to fifteen thousand.[16] Even with the attacking force thus strengthened, the defenders were able to hold out for nearly seven more months before negotiating a settlement. During this time, in February/March 641, Emperor Heraclius died, leaving the Byzantines without strong leadership. Heraclius was succeeded by his son Constantine, who was ill and survived for only a hundred days. According to John of Nikiou, the Byzantines surrendered and evacuated the fortress of Babylon on Monday, April 6, AD 641 (AH 20), during the Easter holy days. Ibn al-'As allowed them to leave, taking with them a few belongings and their gold, but abandoning their military equipment and their ships.[17]

After Constantine's death, his illegitimate half-brother, Heraclius the Small, became the new child emperor. Under these circumstances, with no real leader in Constantinople or in Egypt, and after the loss of Syria and Palestine, the remaining Byzantine troops in Egypt were demoralized and ready to go home. Military and civilian leaders started to abandon their posts, going first to Alexandria, then to Constantinople. The Egyptians were not sorry to see them go. Butler quotes John of Nikiou's description of the Byzantines:

> "Those enemies of Christ who have defiled the Church by an unclean faith, and who have wrought apostasies and deeds of violence such as neither pagan nor barbarian hath wrought: they have despised Christ and His servants, and we have not found such evildoers even among the worshippers of false idols."[18]

It may seem hard to believe that a band of twelve thousand Arabs or more with relatively primitive weapons could defeat twenty thousand professional Byzantine soldiers, but the Arabs were strongly motivated. First, they were impelled by a desire to spread their new and still pure religion based on justice and the oneness of God. Second, their lives in Arabia were rough, and they were looking for a share of the wealth they saw in the territories of older imperial civilizations. They had significant financial inducements. During the early Islamic campaigns, it was the custom of the Prophet Muhammad to divide the captured goods among his warriors, based on their participation in his campaign. He set aside about 20 percent for the good of the community and divided the remainder among the warriors so each man was given one share, a horse received two shares, and a man on a horse received three shares.[19] This principle was useful in forming a highly motivated volunteer army, in contrast with the complacent Byzantine army, which quickly collapsed in Syria, Palestine, and then Egypt.

The Arab army continued to advance north toward Alexandria. Their progress was aided by the fact that, as Byzantine authority was collapsing, the native Egyptian inhabitants of the Delta were divided: some wanted to fight the Arabs, while others were willing to join them.[20] The new administration in Constantinople, headed by the boy emperor, decided to pull its troops out of Egypt and send Cyrus (the same Cyrus who had governed Egypt disastrously for ten years under Emperor Heraclius) to negotiate terms of surrender with the Arabs. Cyrus successfully negotiated an evacuation treaty with Ibn al-'As in the second half of AD 641. During the negotiations, the Byzantines were impressed by several features of their enemy: the Arabs preferred death to living with the humiliation of defeat; they did not have distinctions of rank (their commander was considered one of them); and they all prayed at fixed times.[21]

The most comprehensive reporting and commentary on the treaty was published by Butler, based on accounts by John of Nikiou in the seventh century AD and al-Tabari at the end of the ninth century AD (third century AH), as well as by other researchers, both Muslim and Christian. The terms of the treaty are translated by Butler as follows:

> In the name of the God, the Merciful, the Compassionate.
>
> 1. This is what 'Amr ibn al-'As granted the people of Misr [Egypt]—to wit, security for their persons and their religion and their property, their churches and their crosses, their land and their water. In none of these things shall there be any encroachment nor any abatement of their rights.
> 2. The Nubians shall not settle among them.
> 3. The people of Misr are bound to pay the poll-tax, if they agree upon this treaty of peace and the inundation of their river has reached full level—fifty millions.
> 4. They are responsible for any acts of their brigands.
> 5. If any of them refuse [the terms of the treaty], the total of the poll-tax shall be reduced for them in proportion; and we are free of obligation to protect those who refuse.
> 6. If their river does not rise to its usual level, then the sum [of taxation] shall be reduced for them in proportion.
> 7. Whosoever of the Romans or the Nubians enters into their treaty, for him are the same rights as for them (i.e., the people of Misr) and the same obligations.
> 8. Whosoever refuses [these terms] and chooses to depart, he shall be safe until he reaches his own place of security or quits our domination.

9. The tribute imposed is to be paid by three equal installments, one third at each payment.
10. For what is written in this treaty stands the pledge and warranty of God, the warranty of His Prophet, the warranty of the Caliph, the Commander of the Faithful, and the warranty of the Faithful.
11. For the Nubians who come under this treaty, it is prescribed that they shall furnish so many head (of cattle) and so many horses; and in return they shall not be plundered nor hindered in their trade, coming or going.[22]

For further details about the treaty, one should consult the commentary in Butler's appendix, as well as John of Nikiou and al-Tabari. John of Nikiou mentions that Ibn al-'As did not respect the treaty "because he was of barbarian origins," and notes that he increased the taxes three times.[23] In fact, according to al-Maqrizi, when a Copt asked Ibn al-'As, "'Tell us how much poll tax we have to pay,' Ibn al-'As replied, while pointing to a corner in a church, 'If you give me from the floor to the ceiling, I will not tell you. You are like a safe to us. If we need more, we will get it from you; if our demands decrease, we will ask you for less.'"[24] As we will see in the next chapter, under this policy, the actual revenue decreased significantly due to poor management.

After the treaty was signed, the Egyptians were given three choices: (1) convert to Islam and be accepted as brothers; (2) pay two dinars as poll tax *(jizya)* and receive state protection, but accept an inferior status; or (3) continue to fight until God decides the outcome.[25] A few converted to Islam at this time to avoid paying the *jizya*, while others became Muslims out of conviction. Those who converted to Islam were still a small minority, but were an asset to the Arabs. They mediated between the population and the new rulers, and became the eyes and ears of the latter.

The conquest of Egypt was the easiest and swiftest of the Arab invasions. It took less than three years, while the conquest of Syria and Palestine took about eight years, the conquest of Iraq took about eighteen years, and the conquest of East Africa about fifty.

After the treaty, Ibn al-'As gained power and began to control Egypt with great political acumen. In addition to the *jizya*, taxes were collected on land *(kharaj)*. Clergy were exempted from paying the *jizya*. Church property was protected, and none of it was confiscated.[26] Ibn al-'As also issued a decree to grant safety to Benjamin I, the Coptic patriarch, who had been in hiding from Byzantine persecution under Cyril for thirteen years. The decree stated, "In whatever place the patriarch of the Egyptian Christians is living, to that place we grant protection and security and tranquility, to administer the affairs of his church and to govern his nation."[27] The Muslims had no interest in the theological fine points of the Chalcedonian debate and were content to let Cyril lead his church as he saw fit. Thus, the Copts were initially much better off under their new rulers than they had been under the terror of the Byzantines. In this new atmosphere of religious freedom under Ibn al-'As, the Coptic Church flourished and soon realized its aim to be considered the Church of Egypt.[28]

Was Egypt Acquired by a Treaty or by Force?

According to some later interpretations of Islamic *fiqh* (Muslim law), whether or not the Copts have the right to build and maintain churches depends on whether Egypt was acquired by treaty or by force. If Egypt was acquired by a treaty, the Copts would have the right to build and keep their churches. But if Egypt was taken by force, they would not. The issue of building churches was not a major problem in the early days of Islam, when Muslims numbered only a few thousand and Copts numbered a few million. For example, the treaty we have just discussed (between the Byzantines and the Arabs) said nothing about a restriction in this regard. It was not until more than a century later, as the demographic pattern shifted, that building new churches—and even restoring existing ones—became at times difficult or even impossible. The Islamic *fiqh* dealing with this matter was mentioned for the first time nearly two centuries after the Islamic invasion of Egypt. Ibn 'Abd al-Hakam, a ninth-century Egyptian Muslim historian, discussed the question of treaty versus force extensively.[29]

During his lifetime, the Prophet distributed the booty among his warriors according to the formula already described. Some Arabs assumed this formula would be extended to the new land they had captured. After conquering Alexandria, some of Ibn al-'As's leaders wanted to divide Egypt among themselves, but Ibn al-'As disagreed. He asked the caliph Ibn al-Khattab to decide this matter. The caliph's decision was not to divide Egypt, but to keep it as an asset for all Muslims, not just for the benefit of a few.[30] Because Egypt was not divided, some Arab writers argue that the country was not treated as the spoils of war, and therefore should be considered territory acquired by treaty. But the question has never been permanently settled.

How the Arabs Saw Egypt for the First Time

One can imagine how the Arabs, who came from desert territories where water and grazing were scarce and who lived in tents or simple buildings, must have reacted to their new surroundings. In Egypt, they found abundant green vegetation, large buildings, wide streets, plenty of food, and a broad river continuously flowing with sweet water (which some said flowed from paradise). No wonder they were fascinated. Above all, they admired the Egyptian people and even liked them. 'Abdullah ibn 'Umar wrote, "The Egyptians are the best among the people we conquered. They are generous. They are also relatives of the Arabs, especially of the Quraysh tribe [elite families from around Mecca, birthplace of the Prophet]. If you want to see Paradise on earth, look at Egypt with its green plants and colorful fruits. Alexandria is a great wonder."[31]

Other Arab writers of the time were also enchanted with Egypt. They were particularly impressed with the size and splendor of Alexandria. After securing his hold on Egypt, Ibn al-'As wrote a letter to the caliph Ibn al-Khattab in Arabia. In it he said, "I have taken a city of which I can but say that it contains four thousand palaces, four thousand baths, four hundred theaters, twelve thousand sellers of green vegetables, and forty thousand tributary Jews paying the *jizya*."[32]

Butler offers quotations by other writers: "Alexandria is a city containing marble in pavements, buildings, and columns." "The city was all white and bright by night as well as by day." "It was painful to go out by night for the moonlight reflecting from the white marble made the city so bright that a tailor could see to thread his needle without a lamp."[33]

The Muslim historian al-Mas'udi (AD 896–957) gives another example of how the early Arabs used fanciful descriptions to convey their delight: "The lighthouse was built on a foundation of glass in the form of a crab, on a tongue of land extending into the sea. It has three hundred rooms, so that it is hard to find your way in it without a guide. The elevation of the lighthouse is about the height of three hundred men. The mirror [lens] in the lighthouse could see Constantinople."[34]

The churches of Egypt must have been wonders, as well. The great church of St. Mark, located near the harbor of Alexandria and containing the marble tomb of the saint, is one example. But even more renowned than St. Mark's was the church called the Caesarion, which stood in the same quarter. According to Butler, "This church had almost usurped the place of the Cathedral. Its vast fabric, with the two ancient Egyptian obelisks standing in its fore-court, towered above the city walls, and was the most conspicuous object in the near foreground of the view."[35]

The Library of Alexandria

Some have accused the Arabs of destroying the famous Royal Library of Alexandria. However, it is unclear whether it even existed at the time of the

Arab conquest. In the previous chapter, we alluded to the damage done to the old pagan temples by Patriarch Theophilus (AD 385–412) and his successor, Cyril (AD 412–44). It is quite likely that the library, which contained the world's largest collection of manuscripts at that time, was destroyed during this period, because it, too, was a symbol of paganism. Butler, who devotes a chapter in his book to this subject, concluded that the Arabs played no part in the destruction of the library, which he and others believe vanished long before the Arab conquest.[36]

When facts are few, rumors are likely to flourish. The following story of the Library of Alexandria is attributed to Abu-l Faraj, of the fourteenth century, a priest who had been deprived of his office due to a charge of heresy. According to Abu-l Faraj, when Ibn al-'As, the ruler of Egypt, learned of the library he asked the caliph 'Umar ibn al-Khattab in Arabia what he should do with all these books. The caliph replied, "If the books you mentioned agree with the Book of God, they aren't required; if the books disagree with the Book of God, they aren't desired." So Ibn al-'As burned the books to heat the water in the public baths. It took about six months (or seventy days, according to another account) to consume the books as fuel.[37]

This story was repeated by the Muslim historian al-Maqrizi. Coming from such a respected source, it gained popularity among some Copts and Muslims. However, the story was not mentioned by any writers, Muslim or Copt, before the thirteenth century. Furthermore, no travelers from the late fifth century to the seventh century made any mention of the library. If there were any truth to this story, John of Nikiou certainly would have mentioned it. It is probable that the library had already been damaged or destroyed during the anti-pagan turmoil that swept the city during the tenure of Patriarch Theophilus (AD 385–412), when he incited a mob to storm and destroy the Serapion (the Greek temple that housed the library).[38] In any case, even if a collection of scrolls survived the violence, it is unlikely they would have survived the humid and salty atmosphere of Alexandria during the subsequent two centuries until the arrival of the Arabs.

Conditions Imposed on Non-Muslims

Under Islamic law, Christians and Jews were called *ahl al-dhimma*, which means 'protected people.' As non-Muslims, they were required to pay the *jizya*. In return, they did not have to serve in the army, and all their belongings, including lands, were protected. During the first two centuries of Islamic rule, these protections were observed. But as the number of Muslims increased and the number of Copts decreased, other laws and codes were drawn up that were designed to elevate the status of Muslims above that of non-Muslims, and to humiliate the latter. These new regulations included dress codes, building and restoration codes for churches, and regulations for religious festivals. Some of these codes went so far as to limit the kinds of horses Copts were allowed to ride. Other laws made it a criminal offense to call the Prophet a liar or to speak of the Prophet contemptuously. No Christian man could marry a Muslim woman, but a Muslim man could marry a Christian woman and their children would be Muslims. It was forbidden for a non-Muslim to try to induce a Muslim to renounce Islam.[39]

To give some legitimacy to these rules and conditions, they were attributed to the second caliph, Ibn al-Khattab. There are reasons to question this attribution, however, and it is believed that some of these discriminatory conditions were added at a later period. Some of these restrictions were enforced during periods of weak government, while others became part of the culture. In addition, there are varying interpretations of the Qu'ran, both ancient and modern. We know a great deal about Caliph 'Umar, including the fact that he was a scrupulously ethical ruler and would have been unlikely to support such discriminatory code.[40]

Early Administration under 'Amr ibn al-'As

How did the Arabs, who came from a simple tribal society, administer the lands they had so quickly acquired—countries with ancient civilizations and complex administrative systems? In Egypt, administrators who had worked under the Byzantines were allowed to keep their positions if they agreed to pay the *jizya* and to work under the new Muslim rulers. After the Byzantines left, most of the administrators and tax collectors were Copts, a situation that continued until nearly the end of the nineteenth century, when Egypt was colonized by the British.

According to the Muslim historian Ibn 'Abd al-Hakam, Caliph Ibn al-Khattab recommended that Ibn al-'As seek the advice of the Coptic patriarch Benjamin I regarding the best way to administer Egypt. The patriarch told the governor that taxes should be collected only once, after the end of the harvest season; that dikes and sluice gates should be kept in repair; that canals should be dug out yearly; and that no unjust ruler should be appointed. Unfortunately, these recommendations were seldom followed, especially after the tenure of 'Amr ibn al-'As. As a result, the revenue of Egypt declined from 20 million dinars during the Byzantine period to 12 million dinars during Ibn al-'As's rule. This was the beginning of a downward trend. By the end of the Abbasid dynasty (AD 868/AH 254), revenues had declined to only about 800,000 dinars, as will be discussed in the next chapter.

Ibn al-'As was by far the most knowledgeable and sympathetic ruler the Egyptians had during the first two centuries of Arab rule. He was a good military leader and a just governor, but he did not produce the revenue the caliph expected. The second, third, and fourth caliphs did not trust Ibn al-'As's financial reports, and suspected that the governor was skimming off some of Egypt's revenues. This is evident in the correspondence between Caliph 'Umar and his governor, Ibn al-'As.[42] The following excerpt is an example. In a letter to the governor, the caliph wrote, "I didn't send you to Egypt to sate your lusts and those of your people, but because I hoped you would, by good administration, increase our revenue. Therefore, upon receipt of this letter, send me the taxes, for I have here people in great need." In another account, the caliph accuses the governor of neglect and fraud, and demands he turn over to the treasury one half of his personal possessions. In one incident, Ibn al-'As's response is to ask for a delay until the time of harvest, as suggested by Benjamin I, the Coptic patriarch. Ibn al-'As argues that he could not raise more taxes without doing injustice to the people, and that it would be better to be merciful to them than to burden and oppress them. Butler believes that the taxation under the treaty by the Arabs was less burdensome than taxation had been under the Romans.[43]

Despite Ibn al-'As's personal sense of justice, the administrative system suffered from a lack of oversight. Under the second caliph, Ibn al-Khattab, so much wealth was being collected so fast that it outran the administration's ability to control it. The governors and tax collectors took advantage of the system by diverting an undue share for themselves. The caliph realized that his governors and army leaders had started to acquire great personal wealth, but he did not know how to deal with it. Some individuals became extremely wealthy. Ibn al-Khattab is recorded as saying, "If I could, I would take a great deal of these wealthy people's assets and return it to the poor."[38] But this was not possible; divisions of wealth and class had already become deeply entrenched. A small minority of Muslims, primarily from the Quraysh tribe of Mecca, were the new aristocrats, with extreme wealth. Below them were the military classes—those who defended the borders. At the bottom of the social scale were the majority of the people, poor farmers who worked the earth.[44]

When the third caliph, Osman, came to power, he removed Ibn al-'As and appointed a new governor. The new governor promptly increased revenues by about two million dinars. When Osman mentioned this to Ibn al-'As, the latter acknowledged the changes, but pointed out that they would ultimately harm Egypt. Indeed, revenues decreased from that time on. It is generally accepted that the Arabs were more merciful in their taxation during the early Islamic period than the Byzantines had been. The Byzantine tax system was complex, unfair, and inefficient. The only beneficiaries of that system were the very rich at the top of society. The late prominent writer and analyst Ahmad Baha' al-Din has repeatedly urged that Islamic history be corrected to reflect facts, not remain based on stories and traditions.[40]

By the time of the third caliph, Osman, things had gotten worse. The Muslim historian Ibn Sa'd Besinda (ninth century AD, second century AH) cites a number of examples of the extreme wealth of a few individuals in the conquered lands.[41] One example is al-Zubayr ibn al-'Awam, one of Ibn al-'As's generals, who died leaving a fortune of 51 million dinars, in addition to properties in Egypt, Iraq, and Saudi Arabia. Another example is Ibn al-'As himself, who acquired considerable wealth from ruling Egypt and was removed by the third caliph, Osman, for that reason. But 'Amr ibn al-'As returned to rule Egypt again under the fifth caliph, and acquired even more wealth, as we shall see shortly.[45]

The fourth caliph, 'Ali ibn Abi Talib, was a cousin of the Prophet and also the Prophet's son-in-law. He came to power after a tumultuous period that ended with the assassination of Caliph Osman. The fourth caliph's tenure was plagued by war and by the assassinations that ended his life and the lives of his two sons. It was a transitional period marked by a struggle between (1) supporters of Ibn Abi Talib, who wished to return Islam to its purity and to institute a system whereby each new caliph would be selected by the people, and (2) those who wanted succession of the caliphate to proceed according to the old dynastic system that had preceded Islam. The latter prevailed. The struggles of this period set the stage for the foundation of the Shi'a sect. Ibn Abi Talib himself appears to have been a man of high principles. As caliph, he advised his governor in Egypt to show mercy to the people and be kind to them. He admonished him to remember that there are only two kinds of people: those who are your brothers in religion and those who are your brothers in humanity. When Ibn Abi Talib was killed, his only worldly possessions were a Qu'ran, his sword, and about ten dinars.

As mentioned, Ibn al-'As was removed from ruling Egypt during the tenure of the third caliph, Osman, but he resented this and hoped to rule

Egypt again. When the fourth caliph, Ibn Abi Talib, came to power, he was not about to appoint Ibn al-ʻAs to rule Egypt or any other territory because he questioned Ibn al-ʻAs's integrity. Ibn al-ʻAs knew this, so he conspired with the ruler of Syria, Muʻawiya ibn Abi Sufyan, to remove Ibn Abi Talib and replace him with Ibn Abi Sufyan. This conspiracy succeeded, and Ibn Abi Sufyan became the fifth caliph, a position he held for the next twenty years. As a reward, Ibn al-ʻAs was reinstated as ruler of Egypt for five more years. By then, the purity of Islam was a thing of the past.

At the end of his life, when Ibn al-ʻAs saw death approaching, he brought together all the personal wealth he had collected in Egypt and told his son, "When I die, return all this money to its real owners." This treasure filled seventy hides of oxen. When Caliph Ibn Abi Sufyan, then residing in Syria, heard of this, he seized the money for himself, saying, "We need this money to defend ourselves and Islam against our enemies."[46.]

Ibn Abi Sufyan became the founder of the Umayyad dynasty, which was named after his tribe and ruled the vast Islamic world for just about a century (AD 633–749, AH 43–132). Its leaders often governed in an oppressive and autocratic manner, using religion as a cover to justify their own actions, including misconduct and unethical behavior, as we will discuss in the next chapter. Nevertheless, the Umayyads established one of the world's great empires, setting the foundation that enabled Islam to spread across much of the world, from Spain to China.

Many books, including those cited above by Taha Hussein *(al-Fitna al-kubra, Othman)*, Ibn Saʻd Besinda *(al-Tabaqat al-kubra)*, and Muhammad ibn Ahmad ibn Iyas *(Badi' al-zuhur fi waqaiʻ)* show that corruption within the Islamic empire began shortly after the Prophet died and continued with only a few exceptions after that early period. That is why Ahmad Baha' al-Din, one of the greatest intellectuals of our time, mentioned the need to rewrite the Islamic history of this period.[47]

3

EARLY ARAB DYNASTIES: THE UMAYYADS AND THE ABBASIDS

After the Arabs subdued Egypt, their goals, like those of the Byzantines and Romans before them, included collecting wealth, spreading their religion, securing their borders, and weakening or absorbing local powers. This was the beginning of the period of Arab colonization. Some contemporary Muslim Egyptians may be offended by hearing Arabs described as a colonizing power. They may argue that Egypt was acquired by treaty and not by force, as if the Arabs came to Egypt at the request of the Egyptians, or for the mutual benefit of both parties. But this was not the case. An example of the one-sided nature of the relationship was expressed by the second caliph, Ibn al-Khattab, who demanded more wheat from Egypt, saying to his governor, "Let God destroy Egypt for the benefit and prosperity of Medina"[1] (the Arab capital at the time).

The Arabs replaced the Byzantines as the new aristocracy, a ruling class backed by military force. In spite of the fact that Islam preached equality before God, a social class difference existed between Arabs and non-Arabs, even in cases in which the latter had converted to Islam. In Egypt, social inequality between Arabs and non-Arabs persisted for centuries, only diminishing gradually over time as the two groups intermarried and integrated. One way to reduce the class gap in the early days was for a local family to claim an association with an Arab tribe. According to the modern Egyptian historian 'Abd al-'Aziz Jamal al-Din, it was common for Egyptian families to buy a genealogy in order to prove Arab ancestry.[2] This practice persisted even into modern times. For example, King Fu'ad of Egypt (1917–22), an Albanian, managed to obtain a document supposedly proving his descent from the Prophet. He needed this recognition to sustain his hope of inheriting the caliphate after it was abolished in Turkey by Kamal Atatürk in 1923. Even today, some Egyptians like to claim descent from the early Arab arrivals, in order to associate themselves with early Islam and thereby enhance their status.

In fact, the actual number of Arabs who immigrated to Egypt from Arabia was insignificant compared with the much larger population of Egyptians, whose territory the Arabs controlled. Initially, there were marked differences in language, religion, and culture between the two groups. The former were Arabic-speaking Muslims from a nomadic, desert culture, while Egyptians were Coptic-speaking, predominantly Christian, members of an agrarian society. Despite the disparity in numbers, the religion and language of the newcomers gradually came to dominate Egyptian life and culture. This process began under the Umayyad and Abbasid dynasties and continued for many centuries. The Arabs gave the Egyptians Islam, at times imposing it by force. The Egyptians, in turn, played an important role in influencing Islamic art, architecture, and literature. Over time, some Egyptians became prominent Islamic scholars *(ulamas)*, and Egypt became the center of authority on Islamic matters thanks to al-Azhar, the prominent theological center founded in the late tenth century.

Muslim caliphs (Arabs and non-Arabs) and their representatives ruled Egypt for almost thirteen centuries. This continuity of rule included the many dynasties that claimed Islamic legitimacy by ruling through a puppet caliph. The governors appointed by the caliphs to rule Egypt often knew very little of the country. They remained in their posts for only a few years, which did not allow them time to understand the real problems of Egypt or how to improve and modernize the country. From the time the Arabs arrived until the end of the Abbasid dynasty in Egypt (AD 640–868/AH 19–254), the average time a governor stayed in Egypt was two and a half years. Sometimes the caliph sent two representatives to rule Egypt: one to collect taxes (called the taxation amir), and the other to administer the country and the army (called the prayer amir). The aim of this policy was to assure that neither of these governors would be able to seize total power. During the twenty-one years that the caliph al-Rashid of the Abbasid dynasty ruled (AD 787–808/AH 171–93), he appointed twenty-four governors in Egypt.[3] This policy had a devastating effect on the country, as we shall see.

Since the time of the second caliph, Ibn al-Khattab, caliphs had been aware that revenues from Egypt were declining, but either they did not understand the reasons for this, or they did not know how to remedy it. The historian Ibn 'Abd al-Hakam of the ninth century AD (third century AH) tells us that when the governor Ibn al-Khattab asked an Egyptian why the revenue was declining, the Egyptian replied, "Before the Arabs came, nothing was taken from the collected taxes until the infrastructure was repaired and maintained. But your governor doesn't care about the infrastructure and the needs of the country. He collects the taxes as if he intends to collect [them] for only one year."[4]

The governors of Egypt were aware that they would not be allowed to run the country independently and that their tenure would be short, so they tried to extract as much as they could for their own benefit. The caliphs, for their part, were unwilling to compromise their standard of living or stop their expansion into new territories, which required a growing army and increased financial resources. The rulers resorted to increasing taxation aggressively, which eventually led to unrest and many revolts, beginning in AD 723 (AH 105).[5] Increasing taxation was hard on all Egyptians, but had a particular effect on the Copts as well on Coptic–Muslim relations, as we will see.

During its long history, Egypt's well-being paralleled that of its central government. When the government was strong, Egypt was prosperous; when the government was weak, the opposite was true. This is not a new observation. Napoleon Bonaparte, who ruled Egypt for less than two years at the end of the eighteenth century, observed in his autobiography, "No country needs a strong central government as much as Egypt does." While in exile he wrote,

> If power in the hands of Egypt's rulers is well used, the channels and barrages will be well maintained and the water will run smoothly to cover most of the land during the flood season, resulting in good crops. But if the government is poor, the channels will fill with silt and the barrages will clog up, so the flood will cover only a part of the land and the crops will deteriorate and the entire country will suffer.[6]

For more than two centuries, under the first four caliphs and their successors of the Umayyad and Abbasid dynasties, Egypt did not have a strong central government. The Arab ruling class would not allow it. 'Amr ibn al-'As, the first Arab ruler of Egypt, was the lone exception. His tenure followed the Byzantine period, and he listened to the advice of those who knew Egypt well. It is possible that Ibn al-'As's concern for Egypt's welfare was motivated by his hope that he would one day become its independent ruler.[7]

As mentioned previously, the Byzantines used to collect about 20 million dinars annually; by the end of the Abbasid dynasty, this may have declined to as little as 800,000 dinars.[8] Al-Maqrizi comments on this period by saying, "The revenue of Egypt deteriorated as a result of wars and after the spreading of corruption in most of the land, so the Umayyad and the Abbasid dynasties collected under three million dinars."[9]

The Umayyad Dynasty (AD 661–750)

Mu'awiya ibn Abi Sufyan, the fifth caliph, was the first ruler of the Umayyad dynasty. He died in AD 679 (AH 60) after ensuring his son Yazid would become the next caliph.

Before we embark on the details of Coptic–Muslims relations in this period, it may be helpful to discuss the nature of the tax system, tax collectors, and administrators. Most of the tax collectors were Copts, and this fact undoubtedly had an effect on Coptic–Muslim relations. A small number of Copts dominated this very profitable profession until the British colonized Egypt in the late nineteenth century. Most tax collectors were not well liked by the people, regardless of their religion, because they tended to be well off financially while the majority of the people were poor. This antipathy was magnified when the tax collectors were seen to belong to a minority group.

Tax collectors were well connected with the ruling class no matter who the rulers were. They frequently gave large gifts to the houses of the ruling class and to Muslim leaders, especially on Islamic occasions, such as religious festivals.[10] These gifts were often seen as bribes or as a means for tax collectors to ingratiate themselves with the rulers for their own benefit. To mollify the Coptic community, tax collectors sometimes used their influence to obtain building permits which were otherwise difficult for Copts to secure. Historically, the wealth of this class of Copts caused problems for the rest of the Coptic community, especially during periods when the government was weak, as we will discuss in chapter six.

There were two basic types of taxes. The first was the *jizya*, a poll tax imposed on non-Muslims (but sometimes on Muslims, as we will discuss). The second included taxes on the land and its yield. Taxes were also levied on merchants, buildings, and industries, but the total sum of these was insignificant because most Egyptians were farmers. The *jizya* was collected from adult men who were capable of working; old men, women, and children were excluded. Some of the early Arab historians failed to make a distinction between different kinds of taxes and instead lumped them under one category. The *jizya* was not an Arab invention; the word itself is Persian. When the Crusaders colonized the Holy Land, they imposed the *jizya* on Muslims.[11]

In Egypt, the *jizya* was not an insignificant amount. It usually came to about 35 percent of the total tax burden, but sometimes amounted to as much as 50 percent.[12] The usual amount of *jizya* was two dinars per person. According to Severus of Ashmunayn, in the ninth century AD, one dinar purchased twenty-five ardebs of wheat,[13] or the equivalent of 140 bushels. According to al-Maqrizi, in the fifteenth century, the dinar purchased twelve ardebs, or about sixty-seven bushels of wheat.[14] So the *jizya* amounted to the equivalent of 134 to 280 bushels of wheat per person, which would have been a considerable burden on a small farmer or hired laborer.

The churches and clergy were exempted from paying taxes under the Byzantines and during the early Islamic period. Some Copts who either would not or could not afford to pay the *jizya* took to the desert and became monks, resulting in an increase in the number of monks.[15] As tax revenue declined and the financial needs of the empire increased, the governor of Egypt, ʻAbd al-ʻAziz ibn Marwan (AD 684/AH 65), imposed the *jizya* on clergy for the first time. His justification was that if the poor had to pay the *jizya*, the rich church should not be exempt. He took a census of all members of the clergy and imposed a tax on all bishops and church property. In addition to boosting tax revenues, collecting taxes from clergy decreased the number of monks and weakened the monasteries, which were an important and influential institution within the church. The nineteenth-century Coptic historian Yaʻqub Nakhla Rufila[16] mentioned above suggests that by levying stiff taxes, the administration increased its revenues and simultaneously weakened a powerful potential adversary.

For similar reasons, the governor of Egypt sometimes intervened to delay selection of the patriarch. Patriarchs were considered state officials and were appointed by a decree from the caliph. This tradition was a continuation of Byzantine policy. Weakening local leaders was an objective for some rulers, who feared church leaders could organize an opposition movement. However, this danger never materialized. Nevertheless, it was common for a patriarchal seat to remain vacant for long periods of time.[17]

The *jizya* was especially important during the early Islamic centuries, when the majority of Egyptians were Copts. According to Islamic law, a Copt who converted to Islam should not have to pay the *jizya*. But during the Umayyad dynasty, this was not the case. At first, Copts were not encouraged to convert to Islam, and those who did still paid the *jizya*, so there was no real financial incentive to convert. When ʻUmar ibn ʻAbd al-ʻAziz, the eleventh caliph, who came to power in AD 714/AH 96, learned that non-Arab Muslims were paying *jizya*, he instructed his governors to stop this practice. However, this injunction lasted only for a short time. Ibn 'Abd al-'Aziz also decided to remove the *jizya* imposed on the clergy. Still, he was harsh on the Copts in other ways. He put pressure on Copts and Jews to convert to Islam, and issued a decree that they be expelled from official government posts unless they became Muslims. After ruling for two years and three months, Ibn 'Abd al-'Aziz was killed, most likely as a result of poisoning by a family member.[18] After his death, his successor, Yazid bin 'Abd al-Malik, reinstated the *jizya* on monks and even increased it.[19] Revenues continued to decline, while taxation increased. Al-Maqrizi describes this period as follows:

> The patriarch's seat was vacant for three years, until finally the Copts selected Alexandros II [in the year AD 700/AH 81]. He ruled the church for twenty-five years. During his tenure he suffered many hardships; he was removed twice, and forced to pay a ransom of six thousand dinars before being allowed to resume his position. Ibn Marwan, the governor, took a census of all the monks and collected one dinar *jizya* from each. This was the first *jizya* collected from the monks. When 'Abd al-Malik bin Marwan, the new ruler, was appointed to govern Egypt, he became even harder on the Copts. During the tenure of Kora Ibn Sheriek (AD 708–15/AH 90–96), the Copts suffered greater hardships than ever before. The tax collector, al-Habhab, increased all taxes. This led to the first revolt against the Arab rulers. The Muslims put down the revolt using military force, killing a large number of Copts. In the year AD 725/AH 107, al-Habhab was followed by Usama ibn Zayd al-Tanuhi, who was even harder on Copts. He confiscated their wealth and ordered monks to put an iron bracelet around their wrist identifying the monk by name and monastery. Any monk found without this bracelet had his hand cut off. All Copts were forced to carry an identification card; any Copt without this card had to pay a ten-dinar penalty. When al-Tanuhi had the monasteries inspected, monks found without a bracelet had their heads chopped off or were beaten to death. The churches were destroyed, crosses were broken, and all statues were broken and destroyed.[20]

Al-Maqrizi continues:

> When the next caliph, Hisham ibn 'Abd al-Malik, came to power, he ordered his rulers to allow Copts to live under the humane

> conditions stated in the original treaty [the treaty between Ibn al-'As and the Byzantines, mentioned in the previous chapter]. When Hanzala ibn Safwan became the ruler of Egypt for the second time [he ruled for the first time in AH 102–104, his second tenure was AH 119–24] he become even harder on Copts and increased taxes and took a census of all people and animals. He forced all Copts to be tattooed with a picture of a lion and whoever was found without this tattoo had his hand cut off.[21]

Al-Maqrizi does not explain the meaning of the lion tattoo, but it may have been chosen for its association with St. Mark, considered the founder of the Coptic Church. In church icons, he was always depicted next to a lion.

The Coptic historian Severus of Ashmunayn speaks of conditions similar to those al-Maqrizi describes, saying, "How great was the sadness and misery that plagued Egypt. Kora Ibn Sheriek [governor of Egypt] brought down great disasters on Copts and Muslims alike and put them in prison."[22] Severus also mentions that the rulers in this period took the beautiful marble columns from the churches for their own use, leaving the churches in ruins.[23] Jailing the Coptic patriarch and asking for ransom to release him was intended to humiliate Copts and destroy their spirit. This action was repeated by some later rulers, as will be mentioned in the next chapters. Ibn Iyas, another Muslim historian in the sixteenth century, described Kora Ibn Sheriek as an ignorant, immoral, and corrupt person who would drink liquor on the roof of the mosque.[24]

As a result of government policies that overburdened the Egyptians with taxes and neglected the infrastructure on which irrigation depended, some farmers were forced to abandon their land when it became insufficiently productive. This, in turn, further reduced state revenues. The emir in charge of tax collection, 'Abdullah al-Habhab (AD 727/AH 109), asked the caliph in Damascus, Ibn 'Abd al-Malik, to allow the immigration of some Arabs from Arabia to cultivate the deserted land, particularly that in the eastern part of the Delta around Belbeis. The caliph agreed and ordered about 3,500 members of the Quas tribe to settle in the eastern part of the Delta. This was the first time an Arab tribe immigrated to Egypt for permanent settlement. Their taxes were reduced to 50 percent of what Egyptians paid, even Egyptians who had converted to Islam. In addition, the state supported them with horses and camels.[25] Not long after the imported Arabs settled in this area, some of them resorted to violence, stealing, and stirring up trouble against their neighbors.[26]

Taxes continued to be a burden on Egyptians, the majority of whom were still Copts. Al-Maqrizi describes the period of the patriarch Khail I (AD 744–67/AH 127–50) as follows:

> During his tenure, the south revolted and fought the Arabs, but they were defeated and many of them were killed. Another revolt started in Samanud, in the Nile's Delta, led by Behnis, who fought but was defeated and many Copts were killed. Yet another revolt started in Rosetta. It, too, was put down after Marwan ibn Muhammad the caliph (from AD 744–48/AH 125–32) came to the aid of the governor. The governor, 'Abd al-Malik ibn Musa, arrested the patriarch, Khail I, and demanded a ransom. The patriarch and some bishops were allowed to travel around Egypt to collect the ransom, but they found the people in great hardship. All these revolts were brutally suppressed. Marwan's troops arrested some nuns. When he tried to have sex with one of them, she misled him by claiming to have a secret oil, which, if rubbed on the body, would prevent a sword from going through it. She offered to demonstrate the oil on herself. Marwan then tested his sword against her and killed her, thus fulfilling her wish to die rather than be violated.[27]

The Coptic historian Severus adds more information about the revolts of this period. Toward the end of the Umayyad dynasty, another revolt broke out in the lowlands of the northern part of the Nile Delta, in the district of Bashmur. It was called the Bashmuric Revolt, after the people who lived there. When they refused to pay any taxes, the governor, Ibn Marwan, tried to compel them by force, but was unsuccessful. Eventually, the caliph himself, Marwan ibn Muhammad, the last caliph of the Umayyad dynasty, came to Egypt, after escaping with his troops from the increasing pressure of the Abbasids in Iraq and Iran. In Egypt, he promised to forgive the people of Bashmur if they would surrender. But they would not. The caliph then went to Alexandria, where he caused considerable damage and took whatever he could lay his hands on. Patriarch Khail I was arrested for a second time, and ransom was demanded. However, the people had no money left to give, so he was tied to a large ball of iron and forced to follow the caliph as his prisoner. He remained in this position until Marwan was killed by Abbasid troops near present-day Cairo, after burning the Old City in a desperate attempt to stop the Abbasid army.[28]

The harsh Umayyad policy was directed not only toward the Copts; it was directed against any people who revolted in any of their territories, even in the heart of the Islamic world. In AD 683 (AH 64), when the Umayyads faced opposition from the people of Mecca and Medina, the Umayyads did not hesitate to use military force against them. The fighting was so fierce that the cover of the Ka'ba *(al-Masjid al-Haram)* was burned during the conflict. After the defeat of Mecca and Medina, the Umayyad troops were allowed to loot and pillage the two cities for three days in what was called the Battle of al-Harra.[29]

For more than seventy years, the Melchite (Chalcedonian) Christians in Egypt did not have a Melchite patriarch. During this period, the Copts controlled all the churches of Egypt and marginalized the Melchites. The Byzantine emperor sent a gift to the caliph Ibn 'Abd al-Malik (AD 723–41/ AH 105–24) and asked him to return control of the Melchite churches to the Melchites. Ibn 'Abd al-Malik returned one church to the Melchites, and it became the seat of the newly appointed Melchite patriarch.[30]

The Umayyads ruled for about one hundred years. They built a vast empire, which extended from the Chinese border to Spain. Toward the end of the dynasty, corruption increased and the Umayyad Empire started to weaken as the result of poor management and the brutal treatment of its subjects. Revolts occurred in many territories. In addition, the tribes surrounding the empire began to attack the borders. In AD 736 (AH 118), the Byzantines returned to Egypt briefly and occupied Alexandria and parts of the Egyptian Delta, causing considerable damage. Meanwhile, a rival faction based in Persia, the Abbasids, was quietly growing in strength and waiting for its opportunity to strike.

The Abbasid Dynasty (AD 750–1517)

The Abbasid dynasty was named after the Prophet's younger uncle, Abbas. It started as a secret movement in reaction to the Umayyads' policy of Arab superiority. Non-Arab Muslims, such as the Persians and the Turks, resented having to pay the *jizya*. The Persians, in particular, were instrumental in supporting a reform movement that promised to enforce justice, uphold the equality of all Muslims, and implement a policy whereby caliphs must be chosen from among the descendants of the Prophet *(ahl al-bayt)*. With the help of Abu Muslim al-Kharasani, a charismatic Persian political and military leader, this movement garnered support, which allowed the Abbasids to rise to power. Al-Kharasani is considered the real force behind the founding of this dynasty. Unfortunately, the original principles of equality and justice did not carry over into practice.

In AD 750, the Abbasids defeated the last Umayyad caliph, Marwan II, at the Battle of Zab River, in what is now present-day Iraq. The first Abbasid caliph was Abu-l 'Abbas al-Saffah (*al-Saffah* means mass murderer, and his actions show he was well named). One of his first orders was to dig up Umayyad graves and whip the bodies. He also rounded up all the living members of the Umayyad ruling class and ordered them to be put to death. As they lay dead or dying, he had a carpet placed over their bodies. Then he ordered a meal to be served to him as he sat on the carpet. After he and his friends had finished eating, he said he had never eaten a better meal.[31]

After the Abbasids had consolidated their power, the second Abbasid caliph, Abu Ja'far al-Mansur, killed al-Kharasani in AD 754 (AH 137).[32] The Turks and Persians, who often held influential positions within the empire, played an active role in the power struggles within the dynasty. For example, the first minister of the Abbasid dynasty, Abu Salma Hifs ibn Sulayman, was a Persian,[33] and some of the later caliphs fell under the influence of their Turkish or Persian mothers. As a result of internal conflicts among the Abbasids, independent dynasties began to appear in many parts of the empire, including the Fatimids and the Mamluks in Egypt. The caliphs were marginalized, and the real power shifted to the Turks and the Persians.[34]

The Abbasid Empire was the largest empire in the world at that time. Al-Mansur founded Baghdad as its capital in AD 762. The fifth caliph, Harun al-Rashid, is remembered as one of the greatest patrons of science and art. His son, al-Ma'mun, founded Bayt al-Hikma (the House of Wisdom), which housed many manuscripts and books representing the best of the Old World literature. Bayt al-Hikma was open to both Muslims and non-Muslims. Its scholars were active in translating important works of the ancient civilizations, and many mathematical and scientific discoveries of that time came from Bayt al-Hikma. During al-Ma'mun's tenure, Hindi numerals first became known in the Islamic world, paving the way for the adoption in later centuries of Arabic numerals as standard throughout the Western world.

An important development in Islamic religion was the introduction of Mu'tazili theology during the Abbasid dynasty. This movement incorporated aspects of Greek philosophy, and in particular, the belief that religion should be based on reason. This school held that God could be understood through rational inquiry. Unfortunately for Islam and Muslims, this school did not last very long. After al-Ma'mun's reign, Mu'tazili theology was suppressed and its followers were persecuted by the caliph al-Mutawakkil (AD 847–61/AH 235–42). However, Mu'tazili theology had opened the door for a more flexible interpretation of the Qur'an. Modern times have witnessed an attempt to bring rationality to the practice of Islam, based on the principles of Mu'tazili interpretation.

In the beginning, the Egyptians welcomed the Abbasids, hoping they would implement their stated principles of justice and equality. At first, things looked encouraging. The Abbasids promised to protect church property and quickly released Patriarch Khalil I, who had been held captive by the last Umayyad caliph. They also forgave the rebellious people of Bashmur for all the back taxes they had refused to pay to the previous dynasty. But the promised reforms evaporated quickly. Once established, the Abbasids followed the Umayyads' policy of collecting as much in taxes as they could, with little regard for the people's or the country's needs. They also resorted to brutality as a means to extract payment, despite the interpretation *(fiqh)* of some Islamic scholars stating that torture should not be used against those who could not pay taxes or *jizya*. In many respects, the Abbasids were harsher on the Copts than their predecessors had been; their rule witnessed the beginning of the end of Coptic culture.

During this dynasty, over a period of about seventy-five years (AD 767–833/AD 149–217) thirteen uprisings were caused by increased taxation.[35] One of the most significant revolts occurred in AD 797 (AH 181), when the governor, al-Eith ibn al-Fadl, ordered a survey of all cultivated land. To inflate the amount of tax to be collected on the land, his surveyors used a measure that was shorter than the standard one. The people—Copts and Muslims alike—refused to pay the taxes, and the governor had to put down the revolt by force, killing many.[36]

Meanwhile, the central authority in Baghdad was in turmoil over which of two brothers would succeed to the caliphate after the death of their father, al-Rashid. The designated heir was al-Amin, al-Rashid's son by an Arab mother, but his claim was contested by his brother al-Ma'mun, whose mother was Persian. The conflict ignited a civil war. The war ended when, with the help of the Persians, al-Amin was killed, al-Ma'mun was installed as caliph, and the Persians took over Baghdad. Al-Maqrizi describes some of the events of this period, which extended from AD 800 to 830 (AH 184–215), saying,

> During the tenure of Patriarch Marcos II there was a struggle for power between the two sons of the caliph al-Rashid, al-Amin and al-Ma'mun. The Copts were robbed in Alexandria and many of their properties were burned down. The monasteries of Wadi

> al-Natrun were also robbed and burned; few monks remained there. During this time, the Melchite [Chalcedonian Christian] patriarch went to Baghdad to treat one of the caliph's favorite women, since he was skilled in medicine. The woman recovered. In gratitude, the caliph ordered the Copts to return to the Melchites all the churches they had taken from them. After Patriarch Marcos II's death came Patriarch Jacob. During his tenure, the monasteries were re-inhabited and churches were restored, including the Coptic church in Jerusalem. But in the year AD 831/AH 216, the Copts revolted and were subdued by force. The caliph, al-Ma'mun, ordered the men killed and the women and children sold as slaves. After these events, Copts were so thoroughly defeated that they stopped fighting overtly and turned to indirect means of opposition.[37]

Al-Kindi tells essentially the same story, adding that the whole of Egypt had rebelled so violently that the caliph, al-Ma'mun, was forced to come to Egypt to deal with the situation in person. After quelling the revolt, the caliph blamed the governor, ordered him removed, and forced him to strip and walk before the people in his white underwear as a sign of humiliation.[38]

Ya'qub Nakhla Rufila states that when al-Ma'mun first came to Egypt, he met with Patriarch Yusab I (AD 830–49/AH 215–35) in an attempt to defuse the situation.[39] The caliph asked the patriarch, Yusab, to tell the Copts to surrender and he would personally see to it that they would receive fair treatment. All the Copts obeyed the patriarch's wishes, except for those of Bashmur, who revolted several times, just as they had previously revolted against the Umayyads. Although the swampy terrain in which they fought favored their campaign, the uprising was eventually put down. Bashmuri houses and churches were destroyed, and their women and children were taken as slaves. Al-Ma'mun stayed in Egypt for two months after the end of the revolt to reorganize the government and improve conditions. As part of this effort, he forgave the Egyptians' unpaid taxes.

Jamal al-Din adds that one reason the defeated Bashmuri people were taken as slaves was to help reclaim the swamps in southern Iraq, along the Persian Gulf. The land in that area was similar to the Bashmuris' native terrain. Jamal al-Din also says the Bashmuris may have participated in the Zanj rebellion that occurred in Iraq in the middle of the ninth century AD. This uprising involved slaves and former slaves, and consisted of two waves, each lasting about fifteen years.[40]

During the Abbasid dynasty, the Copts began to convert to Islam in large numbers because converts were not required to pay the *jizya*. Another factor that may have persuaded some Copts—and Christians in general—to accept Islam was the Mu'tazili movement. This movement produced a large volume of literature that refuted Christian doctrines, and thus may have served both evangelical and catechetical purposes.[41]

During his rule as caliph, al-Mutawakkil passed an edict that called for the destruction of renovated churches and the dismissal of non-Muslims from civil service posts. Mark Swanson, in *The Coptic Papacy in Islamic Egypt 641–1517*, quotes John the Writer, a Coptic Nestorian Christian (AD 850–53/AH 236–39) as saying,

> [Al-Mutawakkil] brought down upon the churches in every place innumerable afflictions which were that he ordered all the churches to be demolished, and that none of the Orthodox Christians, Melchites, Nestorians, or Jews should wear white garments, but that they should wear dyed garments so that they might be distinguished among the Muslims. He ordered that frightful pictures should be made on wooden boards and that they should be nailed over the doors of the Christians. He forced most of them to embrace al-Islam, and ordered that Christians should not serve in the employment of the Sultan at all, but only Muslims and those who had gone over to al-Islam.[42]

Severus of Ashmunayn, the author of *The History of the Patriarchs*, gives a similar account with different details.

> The governor of Egypt, Enbesa Ibn Issak al-Dabbi [AD 852–56/AH 238–42], brought much misery on the Egyptians. He prohibited Copts from ringing church bells, broke all crosses, and forbade the making of wine in an effort to hinder Communion. He also forbade allowing Copts to occupy any official position unless they converted to Islam. He ordered all the churches destroyed and forced a dress code to distinguish Copts from Muslims. He committed many evil deeds against Copts.[43]

Ibn al-Mudabbir, one of the last rulers in charge of collecting taxes in Egypt during this dynasty (AD 861–68/AH 247–54), used innovative but harsh methods—such as taxing fisheries, trees, animal grazing, and salt mining—to create more revenue. More revolts occurred, but these were brutally suppressed. As a result of the heavy taxation, the country became so impoverished that tax revenues only amounted to 10 to 20 percent of what the Byzantines and early Arabs had been able to collect.

During the Abbasid period, the violence against Egyptians was not always due to their religion, but rather to the poor policies and greed of the central government. Christians and Muslims both suffered. However, increased taxation, brutal suppression of revolts, and the additional burden of the *jizya* led to the first major wave of Coptic conversions to Islam. More serious waves are described in the following three chapters. The poor policies of the Abbasid dynasty weakened the empire, the caliphs became marginalized, and the real power started to move elsewhere, as we will examine next.

4

THE ERA OF THE INDEPENDENT MUSLIM DYNASTIES

The Tulunid Dynasty (AD 884–96)

As the late Abbasid caliphs in Baghdad became weaker, they began to lose control over their far-flung territories. Though the office of caliph was widely respected throughout the Muslim world as a symbol of Islam—during Friday prayers, the name of the caliph was called out as the head of the Muslim world, for example—this recognition gradually became a mere formality. Loss of political control was hastened by the practice of offering territorial governorships in exchange for money. Some of these governors then sold their posts to others, cashing in on their appointments without ever having to renounce their comfortable lives in Baghdad. This was not a system that encouraged good governance. During this time, taxes in Egypt were collected independently of the annual flood and without regard for the economic condition of the country, causing hardship to many.[1] Although the patronage system was usually detrimental to Egypt's well-being, in one instance it turned out to be advantageous. It had become a tradition that the governor of Egypt should be a Turk. One of those appointed was Azgor the Turk, who sent his stepson, Ahmad ibn Tulun, to rule Egypt in his place. This was a fortunate choice for Egypt. After clever political maneuvers, Ibn Tulun was able to assert his independence and soon restored the country's economy. This was the beginning of a new era for Egypt.

Ibn Tulun came to Egypt in AD 868 (AH 257) at the age of thirty-three, and ruled for sixteen years. This was the longest any individual had governed Egypt since the Arab invasion two and a half centuries earlier. Ibn Tulun removed excessive taxation to relieve the economic burden of the Egyptians. He restored the barrages and the canals to assure adequate water supply to the land, and improved the deteriorated infrastructure by building hospitals and public baths. He established a new city, called al Qata'i', now a part of metropolitan Cairo. In this city, he built a palace and a new, magnificent, and unique mosque, which is still one of Cairo's important ancient Islamic sites. He also built a strong army and extended his influence to Syria and Palestine.[2]

Ibn Tulun died at the age of forty-nine after achieving significant improvements in Egypt. During his tenure, the collected revenue increased from 800,000 to four million dinars as a result of improved infrastructure. At the time of his death, Ibn Tulun's personal assets amounted to about ten million dinars.[3]

Some Muslim rulers, while moderate in their treatment of Copts as a whole, were hard on the Coptic patriarchs. Ibn Tulun was one such ruler. This could be attributed to a number of things. Whether accurate or not, the widespread belief that the church was wealthy made it a tempting target from which the government could extort money. Internal personal conflicts and scandals within the church gave the ruler a pretext to intervene in church affairs. Jacques Tagher gives the following example.[4] When Ibn Tulun needed more money to finance his campaign in Syria, he used a church scandal as a pretext to order the patriarch to deliver all his assets to the state, arguing that monks (the patriarch was originally a monk) selected a life of poverty and should not have any wealth. This was correct. The patriarch, as head of the church, was responsible for church affairs, including collecting money from the rich to support the poor. But he did not have any personal wealth of his own, and church assets were not his to give, so Ibn Tulun had him imprisoned in a small jail cell for about a year. Some affluent members of Ibn Tulun's court were able to release the patriarch after he promised to collect twenty thousand dinars in two installments. The patriarch traveled the country to collect donations from Copts, but for all his efforts, he was able to collect only ten thousand dinars after the church was forced to sell some of its properties. When the patriarch was unable to pay the full amount, he was put in jail again, and there he remained until after Ibn Tulun had died and been replaced by his son Khumarawayh. The latter freed the patriarch and excused him from having to pay the rest of the sum. This story has been described by both Muslim and Coptic historians. This incident shows that the church was not as wealthy as it appeared. It also raises the question of why Ibn Tulun, who was moderate in his treatment of Copts as a whole, would single out the patriarch for such harsh treatment. The patriarch, as the head of the church, had no real political power outside the church. But Ibn Tulun might have feared the possibility that the patriarch could use his moral authority to lead a movement against the government. This had never happened before, and there is no evidence to support this fear at the time of Ibn Tulun, even though Copts still made up a large percentage of the population. However, humiliating the patriarch and jailing him might have been seen as weakening the Copts' morale, thereby reducing the chance they would cause trouble to the government.

On the whole, Ibn Tulun was considerate of the Copts. There is a telling story concerning the famous Ibn Tulun mosque. According to al-Maqrizi and others,[5] when Ibn Tulun wished to build a magnificent mosque, he was told he would need about three hundred columns for the construction. He could have taken these from old churches, but his conscience did not let him. So the mosque, built by a Coptic engineer named Sa'd ibn Katib al-Faggani,[6] was constructed with no columns, except for a single one for the *mihrab* (a semicircular niche in the wall of a mosque that indicates the direction of Mecca).

Not all rulers were so accommodating. The Coptic historian Severus of Ashmunayn mentions a number of stories about other rulers who destroyed old churches to use their beautiful marble columns and floors for their own buildings. Some of these stones were transported all the way to Baghdad.[7] The ruins of the ancient site of St. Mina's complex, west of Alexandria, is a visible example of how some beautiful churches were vandalized by removing columns and stones for use elsewhere. One can see that this site had once been a magnificent complex, prior to being plundered for building material.

Another story with a different message, well known in the Arab world, concerns 'Umar ibn al-Khattab, the second caliph. The caliph was visiting the patriarch of Jerusalem, and when prayer time came, he refused to pray inside the church so it could not be appropriated later on as a place of prayer for Muslims. He prayed only on the threshold of the church, and issued a decree forbidding Muslims from praying there, except for one person at a time. By this act, he preserved the church.[8] This story is often cited as an example of Islamic tolerance—as indeed it is—although this tolerant attitude did not always prevail. Ibn Tulun died in AD 883–84 and was succeeded by his son Khumarawayh, who was good to the Copts. Khumarawayh was killed in AD 895 in one of his military campaigns in Damascus, and was succeeded by two weaker members of the family.

The Tulunid dynasty lasted for forty-six years, until AD 905, when the Abbasid military leader Muhammad ibn Sulayman came to Egypt and claimed the country back for the Abbasid Empire, bringing an end to Egyptian autonomy. He burned the city of Ibn Tulun, al-Qata'i', and his army sacked and pillaged the city. Women were raped, and resisters were crucified on the trunks of palm trees.[9]

After being in Egypt for a year, Muhammad ibn Sulayman left Egypt for Damascus. On the way, he was met by the caliph's representative, who ordered him to hand over all the treasures and money he had taken from Egypt. This was estimated to be about two million dinars.[9] Once again, Egypt returned to the condition it had been in before Ibn Tulun came to Egypt. For the next thirty years, it remained under the thumb of Baghdad, until the Ikhshidis came to power and repeated Ibn Tulun's attempt to rule Egypt independently and improve its lot.

The Ikhshidi Dynasty (AD 935–69)

Muhammad ibn Tughj al-Ikshid, also a Turk, was sent to Egypt to rule on behalf of the Abbasid caliph in AD 935 (AH 324). Like Ibn Tulun, he took advantage of the weak caliph in Baghdad to strive for political independence. His family ruled Egypt for forty-three years, a period marked by tolerance and harmony. The rulers respected Coptic traditions and even shared some of the Copts' festivities. The Arab historian al-Mas'udi gives an eyewitness account that will stand as an example. He describes how Egypt celebrated the holy day commemorating Jesus's baptism.

> I was present in the year 303 [AD 915] during the night celebrating Jesus's baptism. Muhammad ibn Tughj al-Ikshid, in his palace known by the name "the Chosen," on an island surrounded by the Nile, ordered one thousand torches to be lit, in addition to the torches and candles lit by the Copts. This holy day was attended by thousands of Copts and Muslims, both in boats and on the banks of the Nile. All shops were opened. All the people were happy, many of them diving in the Nile, which they claimed would cure all diseases.[10]

Except for specifically Islamic positions, all jobs within the Ikhshidi administration were open to Copts. This was not an entirely unmixed blessing and may have hastened the decline of the Coptic language. Most Copts up to this time had kept their own language—the language of ancient Egypt. As Copts began to work in government positions, they had to learn Arabic, which had been declared the only official language of the administration by Ibn 'Abd al-Malik, the viceroy of Egypt (AD 705), about sixty years after the Arab conquest.

During the Ikhshidi dynasty, the relationship between Copts and Muslims within Egypt was strained by events taking place outside its borders.

In AD 906 (AH 295), the Byzantines entered Syria and Palestine, where they destroyed some mosques. When news of this Christian aggression reached Egypt, angry Muslim mobs retaliated by ruining one of the old churches. Some Muslim poets further excited the mobs by composing inflammatory poetry and attributing it to a Christian poet.[11] This pattern occurred repeatedly. Whenever the Byzantines achieved victory, there was a backlash against Copts in Egypt. It is important to note that this was the response of people in the street, not official policy, which was quite the reverse. The government did not encourage anti-Coptic outbursts, and in some cases, actively used force to quell them. In AD 925, the caliph in Baghdad issued a decree to the entire Abbasid Empire, urging calm and attempting to reduce anti-Christian sentiments. Authorities decreased the *jizya* demanded from the bishops, monks, and the poor as a gesture of support for the Christian community.[12]

After Muhammad ibn Tughj al-Ikshid died, four of his sons succeeded him, but they were weak. The real power was wielded by Kafur, a Nubian or Ethiopian slave, who was raised to become one of Muhammad ibn Tughj al-Ikhshidi's leaders, his confidant, and the tutor of his sons. Kafur became the last ruler of the dynasty, which had been in power for thirty-five years. By that time, the Ikhshidi dynasty had become so weak that they could not fend off the Byzantines, who were aggressively expanding on their eastern border. This set the stage for the Fatimid dynasty, which came to rule Egypt for about two centuries.

The Fatimid Dynasty (AD 909–1171)

The Fatimid dynasty, like the Umayyad and Abbasid dynasties discussed in chapter three, originated in Mecca, the cultural center of Arabia and birthplace of the Prophet Muhammad. Unlike the Umayyads and Abbasids, who were Sunni Muslims, the Fatimids were of the Shi'a branch of Islam. During their reign, Shi'ism became the official religion of the government and courts. To understand its origins and significance, we need to return briefly to the early days of Islam.

When the Prophet Muhammad died in AD 632, there was no universally recognized method for choosing his successor, or caliph (which means 'successor' in Arabic). Different factions backed rival claimants, contributing to the eventual schism between Sunni and Shi'a branches of Islam. The Sunni recognize the legitimacy of the first four caliphs, while the Shiites recognize only that of the fourth, 'Ali bin Abi Talib, Muhammad's cousin and son-in-law, whom Shiites believe should have succeeded Muhammad in the first place. After Abi Talib was assassinated in 661, power fell successively to the rulers of the Umayyad and then the Abbasid dynasties, which the Shiites did not (and still do not) recognize as legitimate.

As the Abbasid dynasty (named after the Prophet's uncle) began to consolidate its power in Baghdad, it was actively opposed by a branch of Shi'ism, the Isma'ilis, who claimed to represent the legitimate leaders of Islam through descent from Fatma, the Prophet Muhammad's daughter and wife of Abi Talib, the fourth caliph. The Isma'ilis preached revolt against the Sunni establishment, represented by the Abbasids, and actively spread their teachings abroad by establishing groups of followers in Yemen and across North Africa. The Abbasids persecuted this faction, forcing many to flee from Abbasid-controlled lands. Unable to overthrow and replace the Abbasids, the Isma'ilis built up their strength in North Africa. In AD 909 (AH 297), they declared their own leader to be the true caliph, set up a capital in Tunisia, and founded the dynasty known as the Fatimid, after Fatma.

Once established, the Fatimids set their sights on Egypt. They mounted unsuccessful invasions in AD 913 (AH 301) and again in AD 919 (AH 307), almost reaching the administrative capital at al-Fustat, before being turned back.[13] Finally, in AD 972 (AH 362), when the deteriorating Ikhshidi dynasty became so weak it could no longer defend its borders, the Fatimids were able to enter Egypt with almost no resistance. Their area of control eventually expanded to include Syria and Palestine, Arabia, Sudan, and Sicily, in addition to North Africa, their first holding. They built a new capital, Cairo, near the old capital of al-Fustat. The old section of Cairo and the well-known al-Azhar Mosque (the 'Great Mosque') were built by the Fatimid leader Jawhar al-Siqilli.[14]

The Fatimids brought with them the Shi'a sect of Islam and established a Shi'a caliph in Egypt, al-Mu'izz li-Din Illah (AD 932–75). They tried to make Shi'ism the official form of Islam by ordering judges to comply with its rules, and by requiring that high Islamic posts be held by Shi'as. They also tried to spread Shi'ism among the Sunni majority in Egypt, but without much success.

Three factors distinguish the Fatimid period in Egypt: (1) for the first time, the country was ruled by a dynasty that was based in Egypt and totally independent of Baghdad; (2) the Shi'a sect was introduced to Egypt and became Egypt's official state religion for the first and last time; and (3) under the Fatimids, the Copts experienced their best and their worst periods. During one period, Copts and Muslims enjoyed almost complete equality; in another, a terrible persecution of both Copts and Jews resulted in the destruction of about three thousand churches and monasteries in

Egypt and Palestine, including the Church of the Holy Sepulcher. The destruction of the Holy Sepulcher was one of the motivating factors behind several of the European Crusades during the Middle Ages.

When the Fatimids first arrived in Egypt, they exerted their authority over the Copts by ignoring them and forbidding their public religious festivals, such as the celebration of Christ's baptism. In contrast with the tolerance of Ikhshidi ruler Muhammad Ibn Tughj, the Fatimid caliph al-Mu'izz li-Din Illah issued a decree to hang anyone who celebrated Christ's baptism. However, once the Fatimids became settled in Egypt, al-Mu'izz showed great tolerance, employing Copts and Jews in the upper ranks of his administration. Copts held many administrative posts and dominated the area of tax collection, in particular. At that time, the percentage of the population who were Copts had declined to about one-third of the total population.

Al-Mu'izz was very interested in acquiring and spreading knowledge. He established a good library in al-Azhar Mosque that became, and still is, a leading institute of Islamic learning. After establishing his authority, he became very tolerant of other religions, and organized seminars in al-Azhar Mosque to discuss religious matters, including Christianity and Judaism.[15] His minister, Ya'qub ibn Killis, a Jew who had converted to Islam, was very influential in these intellectual debates. During the thirty-three year reign of al-Mu'izz and his son al-'Aziz (AD 973–96), ibn Killis became an authority on Islamic matters, especially the Shi'a sect.[16] He lectured and preached in al-Azhar Mosque and was also active in spreading Shi'a thought.

After al-Mu'izz died, al-'Aziz succeeded him (AD 975–96/AH 367–86). During his reign, Egypt was prosperous in agriculture, industry, and commerce. Taxation was not a serious problem because of the much-improved economy. Al-'Aziz was known for his religious tolerance. He called for total equality between Copts and Muslims, though Copts were still required to pay the *jizya*. Al-'Aziz ordered the restoration of old churches and the building of new ones. When some Muslim leaders and clergy objected, al-'Aziz provided the needed protection.[17]

Al-'Aziz married a Christian from the Melchite Church. She was the mother of the next caliph, al-Hakim, and his sister, Sitt al-Mulk (meaning 'the lady of the kingdom'). It seems that Sitt al-Mulk and her mother were sympathetic to Christians and influenced al-'Aziz in that regard. He intervened in the Melchites' church affairs by appointing his two brothers-in-law as patriarchs—one in Alexandria and the other in Antioch.[18]

In AD 996, al-'Aziz decided to fight the Byzantines, who were attacking the borders in the north of Syria. While the fleet was preparing to sail, it caught fire, and most of it was destroyed. The mob accused Roman merchants, who were bringing trade to Egypt, of starting the fire. One hundred sixty of them were killed. Encouraged by some Moroccans, the mob burned two churches. Al-'Aziz severely punished those who had participated in the mob and ordered the restoration of the churches.[19]

As a result of the visibility of some Jews and Copts in high posts, both groups later suffered considerable persecution. Whether they converted to Islam or not, Jews and Copts were still envied and resented. This can be seen in poems of that period. Hassan Ibn Bishr from Damascus wrote:

> Conversion to Christianity is the right thing to do.
> This era has proved it.
> Admit the trinity of God and ignore the rest.
> Ya'qub [ibn Killis] "the minister" is the father, al-'Aziz is the son,
> and praise the Holy Ghost.[20]

The poet al-Hassan ibn Khakan reflected Muslims' frustration with the Jews in a poem in which he says

> The Jews of this era achieved all their desires.
> Egyptian people, I advise you to convert to Judaism.
> The whole galaxy has already converted to Judaism.[21]

Lack of sensitivity by some minority members of the government also contributed to frustration on the part of some members of the majority. 'Issa ibn Nastoris, a Copt, was fired from his post as vizier because he relied too heavily on Copts. Caliph al-'Aziz could not replace him and therefore asked him back, but did so on the condition that Nastoris hire some Muslims in the administration.[22]

The exclusion of Muslims from highly profitable jobs, such as administration and tax collection, was largely the result of an educational system which passed down knowledge of trades and professions within the family or within a small group. This situation did not change until Egypt introduced a public education system in the nineteenth century. Until that time, Copts held a virtual monopoly on tax collection and top-tier administrative jobs, as well as jobs that required mathematical knowledge, such as land surveying.

Some Muslim leaders had reservations about dealing with non-Muslims, based on Qur'anic verses, such as verse number 51 of Surat al-Ma'ida:

> O you who believe, take not the Jews and the Christians for allies. They are friends of each other. And whoever amongst you takes them for friends he is indeed one of them. Surely Allah guides not the unjust people.

Also verses 6, 7, and 8 of al-Tawba:

> And if any one of the nonbelievers seeks your protection, then grant him protection so that he may hear the words of Allah. Then deliver him to his place of safety. That is because they are a people who do not know. How [can there be a treaty] while, if they gain dominance over you, they do not observe concerning you any pact of kinship or covenant of protection? They satisfy you with their mouths, but their hearts refuse [compliance], and most of them are defiantly disobedient.

These verses are often selectively quoted by those who wish to restrict non-Muslims from holding positions of leadership. Even today, some Muslims, especially among political Islamists and jihadists, preach the exclusion of non-Muslims from leadership positions. But many other verses are kind to People of the Book *(ahl al-kitab)*, as Christian and Jews are called. Islamic history has many examples of non-Muslims who held high administrative positions. One wonders whether the appointment of Copts and Jews to high-profile jobs was due to their religious affiliation or in spite of it. Copts, in particular, were generally considered competent and loyal; they never developed a political base that could be considered threatening. The resentment against the Copts subjected them and the Jews to a collective punishment that came like a tsunami a few years later, when Egypt was ruled by al-Hakim, as we will describe shortly.

Al-'Aziz died in AD 996 (AH 386), and the next nine caliphs were children when they ascended the throne. The first was al-Hakim bi-Amr Illah, who was eleven when he became the third Fatimid caliph in Egypt. At the beginning of his reign, while al-Hakim was a minor, Burjuwan al-Siqilli ruled the country as regent, with the assistance of Fahd ibn Ibrahim, a Copt. The young caliph was completely marginalized—or at least that was his perception. In AD 1000, at the age of fifteen, al-Hakim decided to remove Burjuwan. He conspired and succeeded in having him killed. From then on, al-Hakim began to run the country singlehandedly, at his young age. He appears to have governed erratically, making bizarre decisions based on his mood at the time. Possibly al-Hakim had some kind of mental disorder. It is also possible that some of the horrible things written about his character and actions were exaggerated or fictionalized.

In the history of Coptic–Muslim relations, there were three periods in which the Copts suffered extreme brutality. The first was during the Abbasid dynasty, during the reign of al-Ma'mun (see chapter three). The second was during al-Hakim's reign. The third was during the reign of the Mamluk Muhammad Ibn Qalawun in AD 1320 (which will be described in chapters 5 and 6). Al-Hakim ruled for about a quarter of a century. His reign was a long episode of suffering and brutality for all Egyptians, but it was particularly so for the Copts.

Before we get into the details of what happened to the Copts and Jews during al-Hakim's reign, let us consider his personality, as revealed by some of his administrative orders. These included forbidding people from planting *Corchorus olitorius* (also called Jew's mallow) or eating a green vegetable soup made from it called *mulukhiya*, a popular dish in Egypt even today. He also forbade people to eat zucchini—because he claimed the first caliph (Abu Bakr) had liked it—and forbade them to eat fish that did not have scales. One day, while al-Hakim was in Cairo, he reportedly saw some people eating the green soup he had outlawed. He ordered that they be whipped, paraded around Cairo under guard, and finally decapitated at one of the city gates where many people could see them.

All the taxes collected in the city of Cairo were earmarked for al-Hakim's personal use, and inspecting the city markets was one of his pleasures and duties. He would ride his white mule, followed by a tall, strong black slave named Mas'ud. These stories reflect what many people believed and wrote about.

If al-Hakim found any merchant cheating or hiding grain, he would ask Mas'ud to anally rape him in front of his shop while the crowd watched. The name Mas'ud became a symbol for punishment, and is still used that way today. For example, a popular saying is, "If you don't behave well, Mas'ud will get you."

Al-Hakim ordered people to close their shops during the day and open them at night. He forbade women from going to public baths. One day, as he was walking in town, he heard women's voices coming from one of the baths. He ordered the exits to be permanently walled up while they were inside, leaving the women to die a slow death, and he personally watched while the order was carried out. He also had schools built, teachers appointed to work in them, and then had the schools destroyed.

These are a few examples of what al-Hakim purportedly did that illustrate some aspects of his behavior, as mentioned by the sixteenth-century historian Ibn Iyas.[23] However, it is hard to tell whether these accurately described an erratic or sadistic individual, or whether the accounts themselves were exaggerated or fabricated.

Nevertheless, it is clear that what happened to the Copts and Jews during this period was brutal. Some converted to Islam to survive the trauma, and others left Egypt and went to Nubia, Ethiopia, or the Byzantine Empire.[24] The Roman Empire ceased to exist, but the Byzantine Empire survived until 1453. Here is what al-Maqrizi wrote in a chapter of *al-Khitat al-maqriziya* dedicated to the Copts.

> The tenure of the patriarch Zakharias (AD 996–1035), overlapped with that of al-Hakim for nine years. [According to Aziz S. Atiya, the entire tenure of Zakharias was during al-Hakim's reign.[25]] During this time, Zakharias was arrested for three months. He was thrown to the lions, along with a Nubian named Susta. However, the Copts claim that they were not harmed. During Zakharias's tenure, many miseries descended on the Copts, including things that had never happened to them before. Persecution began against Copts who were in control of administrative and financial affairs. Some Copts were important ministers; they became very rich and arrogant, and some abused their power, causing trouble for Muslims, which made al-Hakim angry. When angry, al-Hakim could not control himself. He arrested the Coptic minister 'Issa ibn Nastoris and had his head chopped off. He then arrested Fahd ibn Ibrahim, Burjuwan's secretary, and chopped his head off, as well. Al-Hakim persecuted all Christians, and imposed the dress code mentioned before on both Copts and Jews. He stopped their customary holy day festivities, including Palm Sunday and Holy Cross Day. He issued decrees confiscating all church belongings and endowments. He also ordered the burning of many crosses. Copts were not allowed to own slaves. Many churches, inside and outside of Cairo, were destroyed. He allowed mobs to vandalize churches and to take whatever they could [get] their hands on. The extent of mob looting was greater than can be described. The public took advantage of the mayhem and claimed churches as their private property. Al-Hakim approved all of this. The famous Quseir Monastery on the outskirts of Cairo was looted and

> destroyed. He forbade the Copts from celebrating Christ's baptism with festivities on the Nile, as they were accustomed to doing. The Copts were forced to hang a wooden cross weighing five pounds around their necks. [The heavy weight left a blue bruise mark on their necks; thus, Copts were nicknamed "blue bones." The term persists even today, though most Egyptians do not know its origin.] Copts were not allowed to ride horses; they could only ride mules or donkeys, using a modest bridle that was not decorated with silver or gold. Neither Copts nor Jews were allowed to rent a donkey from a Muslim. Al-Hakim ordered the destruction of all churches. Churches became fair game for the mobs, and all were looted. Mosques were built in place of the destroyed churches. Muslims began to pray in St. Shenouda's famous church in Cairo. Anyone who wanted to claim a church was given permission to do so. Valuable church belongings of gold and silver were sold in Cairo's markets. He ordered his lieutenants to allow Muslims to destroy churches. These destructions continued for three years. A reliable estimate of the number of churches destroyed in Egypt, Syria, and Palestine by the end of AD 1014 is about three thousand. These included the Church of the Holy Sepulcher in Jerusalem and some of the old churches that dated back to the Roman period. Copts were forced to wear crosses in the public baths, while Jews were forced to wear heavy bells around their necks. Finally, he ordered the expulsion of all the Copts and Jews from Egypt. The Copts and Jews gathered before his palace, weeping and crying, and begging for his forgiveness, until he relented. During this difficult time, many converted to Islam.[26]

The Coptic historian Severus of Ashmunayn gave a version similar to that of al-Maqrizi, except in greater detail. Severus mentions that the patriarch Zakharias was jailed and tortured. When he was released, he and the rest of the bishops retired to the monastery of Saint Macarius in Wadi al-Natrun. Matta al-Miskin (Matthew the Poor), a contemporary church historian, mentioned that the monasteries at Wadi al-Natrun escaped destruction because they were located so far into the desert.[27]

The sanctioned persecution and killing of Copts and Muslims, including leaders, judges, and court personnel continued.[28] The Copts never fully regained the status they had formerly enjoyed; their spirit was broken and their numbers were reduced. The discrimination against Copts during al-Hakim's reign was the opposite of the tolerance that had characterized the Fatimids' policy. In spite of the persecution, four Copts were allowed to hold ministerial positions during al-Hakim's tenure, probably because their administrative knowledge was indispensable.

It is not clear why al-Hakim caused so much destruction. 'Abd al-'Aziz Jamal al-Din, a contemporary Muslim historian, noted that the harsh treatment of non-Muslims was not a new Islamic policy; what was new was the magnitude of it. Since the early days after the second caliph, 'Umar, many restrictions had been imposed on Copts and Jews, even on those who had converted to Islam. However, during al-Hakim's reign, the severity of persecution reached a new high. Many Copts felt forced either to leave Egypt or to convert to Islam. They did so not out of conviction but as a matter of survival. As a result, the Copts underwent a second major wave of conversions to Islam.[29] Al-Hakim's personality contained contradictory and controversial elements. In addition to his reputation for harsh and erratic behavior, he had an intellectual side. He was interested in astronomy, and built an observatory for that purpose. As previously mentioned, he also built an important school, called Dar al-Hikma ('House of Wisdom'), in 1005. He provided the school with a great library that, according to some accounts, contained 1,200 copies of Tabari's history, beautifully bound. Dar al-Hikma was open to the public.[30]

Al-Hakim's end is a bit of a mystery. He disappeared in AD 1021. According to some accounts, near the end of his reign, al-Hakim became a Sufi. Some Coptic historians claimed that he converted to Christianity toward the end of his life and became a monk in the Wadi al-Natrun Monastery. However, this has been disputed by Muslim historians. In AD 1017, a new religious movement grew up in Cairo around the belief that al-Hakim was divine. This new esoteric religion grew out of Isma'ili Shi'a teachings. The group took its name (Druze) from one of the leaders, Muhammad al-Duruzi. When al-Hakim vanished in 1021 under mysterious circumstances, the Druze were forced to leave Egypt. They migrated to Lebanon, Palestine, and Syria, where they still exist today. The Druze believe that al-Hakim did not die, but that he simply disappeared and will reappear one day to establish a new golden age.[31]

How did the persecution of the Copts during al-Hakim's reign affect Coptic–Muslim relations? There is no doubt that most if not all Egyptians felt relieved by his mysterious disappearance. The effect on Muslims was short-lived; memory of his deeds has faded or become the subject of jokes and entertaining stories. But for Copts it was a different story. The destruction of their churches and monasteries, and the widespread robbing and murder of Copts, has left a residue of fear and insecurity which persists to some degree in their collective memory.

After al-Hakim's disappearance, his son al-Zahir became the next caliph (reigned AD 1021–36). Since he was just a young boy when he came to the throne, his aunt Sitt al-Mulk, a strong woman, acted as regent. Copts and Jews who had converted to Islam under pressure were permitted to go back to their original religion if they chose, even though this was contrary to certain Islamic laws. The Copts were also allowed to celebrate their holy days, although Muslims were not allowed to share in the festivities, as they had done before.[32] Some of the churches which had been destroyed or converted to mosques were returned to the Copts and were allowed to be restored.

The next caliph, al-Mustansir, was only seven years old when he succeeded al-Zahir in 1036. He continued on the throne for sixty years, but wielded little power. By this time, the Fatimid dynasty had begun to weaken, though the empire it ruled was still vast. It included Syria, Palestine, North Africa, Arabia, and Yemen. The army that enforced Fatimid rule in Egypt at that time was made up of Sudanese and Turkish soldiers. These two factions struggled with each other for power. The Turks prevailed, took control of the caliph in his palace, and seized both his wealth and his power. The Sudanese soldiers escaped to the south, where they robbed the churches and monasteries and killed a number of monks.[33]

As if political upheaval were not enough, each year between AD 1052 and 1077, the Nile flooded very poorly or not at all. Without irrigation, crops failed and Egyptians suffered one of the worst famines in their recorded history. Wheat was hard to find even at astronomical prices. About one-third of the population died from starvation. To survive, some people were forced to eat dogs and cats, and even human flesh.[34] It was a chaotic period. Finding himself unable to maintain order, the caliph sought help from Badr al-Jamali, head of the army in Syria. Al-Jamali was an Armenian Christian who had converted to Islam. In response to the caliph's appeal, al-Jamali brought his Syrian army to Egypt in 1073. There he took control and readily ended the chaos in Egypt. Once he had restored order, he relied on the Copts to help him run the country. Thus, some Copts were able to regain important posts they had previously held.[35]

Al-Jamali was followed by his son al-Afdal. They ruled Egypt successively for a total of fifty years. The last Armenian ruler was Bahram (reigned AD 1135–37), who, like his predecessors, was pro-Christian. Although these

Armenian rulers themselves had become Muslims, they maintained a working relationship with the Copts as well as with the Armenian Christian community, which had a long history in Egypt. As the Fatimid caliphate lost power, Armenian influence in Egypt increased, especially within the administration and the military. The Armenian rulers allowed the building of new churches and monasteries. They depended heavily on Copts they considered reliable, especially those who did not have a political base or any military power that might be threatening.

During this time, Crusaders from Palestine reached Egypt. Some Muslims, resentful of the positions held by Copts and Armenians, made no distinction between the invading Catholic Crusaders and the Egyptian-born Orthodox Armenians and Copts; they identified all of them as enemies of Islam. Radwan ibn Walkashi, a local ruler from the central Delta region, called for jihad against the Armenians and the Copts. He gathered an army of Muslims and headed toward Cairo where more fighters joined them, with Qu'rans held high. Ibn Walkashi defeated the army of the Armenian Muslim ruler, Bahram, and seized control of the country. Many Armenians were forced to escape to the south of Egypt. Some settled in Qus, a town 645 kilometers south of Cairo, while others, including Bahram, were allowed to stay nearby in the area of the White Monastery, near Akhmim, north of Luxor.[36]

Ibn Walkashi was now the first Sunni Muslim vizier. He replaced the Christians in the upper administration with Muslims and ordered dress codes for Christians and Jews that were similar to those imposed by al-Hakim. He also increased their *jizya*. During this time, churches were plundered and many Christians were killed, while others converted to Islam as a result of financial and social pressure.[37] The influence of Ibn Walkashi did not last long; the caliph plotted against him and succeeded in having him killed.

By this time, the Fatimid dynasty was on its last legs. Its final decades were marked by violent infighting. One of the last caliphs, 'Abd al-Majid al-Hafiz (reigned AD 1130–49), killed his own son al-Hassan, who was conspiring against him. The Copts had generally been able to obtain just treatment from the Fatimid administration; but in 1134, during al-Hassan's revolt against his father, al-Hassan arrested the patriarch Gabriel and imprisoned him until he paid one thousand dinars in ransom.[38]

The final chapter of Fatimid rule began when the caliph al-Fayiz (reigned AD 1154–60) threw out the ruler of the south, Abu Shuja' Shawir. Shawir responded by gathering some soldiers and leading them to Cairo, where he killed the caliph and put the caliph's nine-year-old son, al-'Adid li-Din Illah (reigned AD 1160–71), in his place. By then, the power of the caliphs had become so weak that a poet at the time compared them to parrots in a cage, repeating only what they were told.[39]

Shawir became engaged in a power struggle with Dirgham, a minister of the flailing Fatimid dynasty. When this struggle did not produce a winner, both men sought outside help. Shawir escaped to Damascus and sought the help of its king, Nur al-Din Mahmud. He offered Mahmud one-third of Egypt's revenue in return for his help. Dirgham, on the other hand, asked the help of Amalric, the Crusader king of Jerusalem (also called Almaric, reigned AD 1164–74). Both kings were glad to help, each hoping to gain control of Egypt. The king of Jerusalem and his Crusader army headed to Egypt, arriving in Cairo before the Syrians. There, they tried to elicit help from the Copts, but without success. The historian Qadri Qal'aji summarized the Coptic response as follows: "We are all Egyptians; the Muslims are our brothers; their country is ours. Religion does not separate us. We respect their religion, and they respect ours. Even our Christianity, which you think you share with us, is different from yours."[40] Coptic antipathy toward the Crusaders is understandable; during the Crusader campaigns in Palestine, Copts were not permitted to go to Jerusalem on pilgrimage and were considered heretics.[41]

The Syrian army sent to Egypt by Mahmud was headed by Assad al-Din Shirku and his nephew Salah al-Din. The latter played an important role in the fate of the region. After many skirmishes, the Syrian army gained the upper hand. The Egyptians welcomed the Syrian army's victory over the European Crusaders. A new government was established, which later controlled the entire region. Egypt was stabilized, and life for the Copts improved as well.

The Ayyubid Dynasty (AD 1171–1250)

When the last Fatimid caliph, al-'Adil, died in 1171, Salah al-Din, who was a Sunni Muslim Kurd, became the de facto ruler of Egypt, bringing a peaceful end to the Fatimid era after 262 years. Egypt returned to following the Abbasid dynasty formally, but the caliph in Baghdad was just as weak as the late Fatimid caliphs in Cairo had been. They held power in name only. The major difference for Egyptians was that now the Muslims called out the name of the caliph in Baghdad during Friday services, instead of the name of the former Fatimid caliph in Cairo.

Salah al-Din refused to take up residence in any of the magnificent Fatimid palaces, preferring to stay in government houses. Later he built the

Citadel, which has a strategic location overlooking the city and has become one of Old Cairo's important historical sites.

Salah al-Din was well aware of the Syrian king's and the Crusaders' expansionist intentions toward Egypt. But he was able to escape both threats by a combination of good planning and good luck. The Crusader Amalric I, king of Jerusalem (AD 1136–74), supported by the Fatimids, launched an unsuccessful invasion of Egypt and was badly defeated. He died shortly after that and was succeeded by his son, who also died soon afterward, due to illness. The Syrian king Mahmud also attempted to invade Egypt and organized a campaign for that purpose, but he died before his army had left for Egypt. He was succeeded by his son, who was eleven years old. After the death of Mahmud, Syria was torn apart by a power struggle. Salah al-Din saw his opportunity, mounted a counter-campaign, invaded Syria, and unified it under his supervision in 1174. He gained considerable power and subsequently expanded his domain from Tunisia in the west, to Arabia and Yemen in the east, and to Syria and northern Iraq in the north. Salah al-Din was left with no serious challengers. The caliph in Baghdad recognized Salah al-Din as the sultan of all the territories under his domain.

In the beginning of his career in Egypt, Salah al-Din did not trust the remaining supporters of the Fatimids, including Christians and Jews. He imposed discriminatory rules and a dress code on all Christians and Jews early in his reign. As a result of these rules, mobs destroyed some churches, and a number of Christian scribes were forced to convert to Islam. However, after Salah al-Din had consolidated his political and military power, he removed the discriminatory provisions and developed a working relationship with the Copts. Eventually, he trusted them to the point that they were employed in the upper levels of his administration and in military positions as noncombatants.[42] Jamal al-Din mentions that Salah al-Din trusted neither the Melchite Christians nor the Armenians, who were sympathetic to the Fatimids, but he did trust the Copts. Not surprisingly, Coptic historians have looked favorably on Salah al-Din's tenure, emphasizing that he was kind to the Copts and removed many of the unjust practices of the past.[43]

After the dust had settled and Salah al-Din's political career was secure, a calm period prevailed over Egypt and the rest of the area. This was reflected in the peaceful relationship between Copts and Muslims. Salah al-Din restored the country's infrastructure, built schools and hospitals, and allowed the Copts to build and restore churches.

Outside Egypt, Christian–Muslim relations were not so peaceful. The European Crusader campaigns in the Middle East, which had begun during the Fatimid dynasty in 1099, continued to support a Crusader presence along the eastern shores of the Mediterranean for about 250 years. In the Crusader kingdoms of Palestine, some mosques were converted to churches, and parts of the important al-Aqsa Mosque were used for storing ammunition and stabling horses. Muslims were required to pay the *jizya*. Things were not much better for Eastern Orthodox Christians. The Roman Catholic Crusaders considered the Eastern churches to be heretical and could not imagine the presence of large Eastern Christian communities existing in the heart of the Islamic empire.[44] Under the Crusaders, the Copts were forbidden from making their annual pilgrimages to the Holy Land. The presence of Western Christians in Palestine created some of the same difficulties the Copts had encountered with the Byzantines in the fifth century (mentioned in the first chapter). The Muslims distrusted Copts because they shared the Christian faith of the hated invaders; the Christian rulers distrusted them because they held heretical beliefs and shared cultural traits with the Muslim enemy.

When Salah al-Din liberated Jerusalem from the Crusaders in 1187, he ordered that Coptic Church property seized by the Crusaders be returned to the Coptic Church. The tenure of Salah al-Din was largely considered a peaceful time for Copts and Muslims alike.

The Ayyubid dynasty lasted for about eighty years, from AD 1174 to 1250. After Salah al-Din, control of the empire was distributed among his five sons and his brother al-'Adil. Egypt was given to al-'Aziz Salah al-Din, but soon thereafter the brothers began to fight against each other. Al-'Adil Salah al-Din unified the empire and took control of Egypt. After him, four of his descendants ruled in succession from 1218 to 1250, though, in its later years, the dynasty was plagued with internal disputes. The last important sultan was al-Kamil al-Salih Ayyub (reigned AD 1240–49), a transitional sultan whom we will discuss shortly.

Mark Swanson, in his volume on the Coptic papacy in Islamic Egypt, describes the period under al-'Adil Salah al-Din and his son al-Kamil (reigned AD 1200–18) as a peaceful and prosperous time for Egypt. Under their rule, Copts were not allowed to be scapegoated or victimized. Peace and stability brought many benefits. Although it was not yet evident, Swanson notes,

> The Coptic Church stood on the brink of a period of profound cultural flowering, so much so that modern scholars of Copto-Arabic literature speak of an early thirteenth-century renaissance

> or golden age, in which art-historical studies have shown that the cultural flowering was by no means limited to the written word. A number of factors would contribute to this flowering, including generally peaceful and prosperous times; the possibility within the Ayyubid Empire of sharing ideas, texts and artistic styles between Egyptians and other regions, Syria in particular; and the existence of a class of Coptic notables with the capacity of lavish patronage for the arts and for scholars. It should be noted that this class of notables would itself generate a number of scholars in the course of the "renaissance."[45]

The second half of the thirteenth century ushered in significant changes that had a devastating effect on Egypt, as we will see in the next two chapters. The middle of the thirteenth through the fourteenth centuries was a period of turmoil for the Muslim world. The Abbasid Empire was invaded and sacked by the non-Muslim Mongols in 1258. The last Abbasid caliph escaped to Egypt, where he resided as a figurehead for the Muslim world. The Mongols, an army of warriors made up of Mongolian and Turkish tribesmen from the steppes of Central Asia, ruled over Iran and Iraq for about a century and were converted to Islam in the course of that period.

It was Sultan al-Salih Ayyub who first brought slave soldiers to Egypt. Captured by the Mongols and raised as a class of slave warriors, these soldiers eventually came to rule Egypt under the name Mamluks, which means 'owned' or 'slaves.' The Mamluks were not originally Muslims, but they converted to Islam. Many of them did not even speak Arabic in the beginning.[46] We will hear more about them in the next chapter.

Toward the end of the Ayyubid dynasty (1250), the European Crusaders realized that the way to control Palestine was through controlling Egypt. They attempted a campaign against Egypt from the sea, targeting the eastern part of the Delta during the tenure of al-Kamil al-Salih Ayyubi. The French contingent, led by Louis IX, reached Mansura during the Nile flood season. The Egyptians opened the dikes of the Nile, isolating the French king and his army by an impassable pool of water. They became prisoners of the Egyptians and had to pay a heavy ransom for their release.[47]

During this battle with the Crusaders, al-Kamil al-Salih Ayyub, who was seriously ill, died. His son and heir, Turan Shah, was in Syria, so al-Salih's widow, Shajar al-Durr (literally, 'tree of pearls'), took charge. She concealed her husband's death and continued to manage the affairs of Egypt during this difficult time. Shajar al-Durr was a beautiful and clever slave, whom al-Salih had freed and married. She bore him a son (Khalil) and became a close advisor to her husband. The sequence of events that followed proved her to be a shrewd and clever politician. Following al-Salih's death, she appointed a new head of the army, but after he was killed on the battlefield, she successfully led the army herself. She announced the death of al-Kamil al-Salih Ayyub only after his son Turan Shah had arrived from Syria and become the new sultan. The newly appointed sultan did not live up to Shajar al-Durr's (his stepmother's) expectations, so she orchestrated his assassination. The head of the Mamluks and the army then agreed to select Shajar al-Durr as the ruler of Egypt, making her the first female ruler in the Muslim world at that time. One of the important achievements during this period was the expulsion of Louis IX and the Crusader army from Egypt.

Shajar al-Durr had many titles, including Malikat al-Muslimin (Queen of the Muslims) and Sultana (the female version of the Arabic 'sultan'). She was mentioned in the Friday sermon in mosques, and coins were minted with her titles. But her appointment was opposed by the puppet Abbasid caliph in Baghdad, and objections were raised against her because she was a woman. In addition, there was concern about the increasing influence of the Mamluks who supported her.

Under pressure, Shajar al-Durr married a Mamluk leader, 'Izz al-Din Aybak (Aybak means 'the head of the army') and ceded the throne to him. The Mamluk warriors accepted him as sultan; however, Shajar al-Durr was still influential and held significant power. She concealed sultanate affairs from Aybak and prevented him from seeing his other wife. But Aybak needed to form an alliance with a strong amir who could help him ward off a threat from a faction of Mamluks who had fled to Syria. In 1257, he decided to marry the daughter of Badr al-Din al-Lu'lu', the Ayyubid amir of Mosul (four hundred kilometers north of Baghdad). When Shajar al-Durr found out about the plan, she conspired to have Aybak killed. She succeeded in this, but the murder was eventually revealed. Shajar al-Durr was stripped and beaten to death with clogs by servants in her bathroom. Her naked body was found outside the Citadel, and she was buried not far from the historic Ibn Tulun mosque.[48]

5
THE MAMLUK ERA (AD 1250–1517)

The Mamluks originated as an army of Turkish, Circassian, and Georgian slave warriors imported by the Ayyubid Empire to protect its territories in Egypt and Syria from invasions by the Crusaders and the Mongols. As their masters grew weaker, the Mamluks gained strength and influence through their monopoly on military power. Known for their arrogance, cruelty, and treachery, they became a self-perpetuating military elite that managed to rule Egypt for more than two centuries (1250–1517). Their era was characterized by internal power struggles, with rival factions at war with one another. In all, Egypt was ruled by a succession of fifty-five sultans (the terms *sultan* and *malik* (king) were used interchangeably). This large number reflects the frequency with which ambitious leaders were able to depose whoever was on the throne and take his place.

Though the Mamluks had converted to Islam and eventually learned Arabic, many did not know much or care much about religion or culture. However, they knew the significance of Islam to the masses, so they sought support from the leading Muslim clergy by ensuring they had a high standard of living and allowing them to build beautiful mosques and other buildings. Although the buildings were beautiful, they were a façade that covered the impoverished life of most Egyptians. The Mamluk era was a politically turbulent and difficult period for Copts and Muslims alike.

The first Mamluk to rule Egypt was 'Izz al-Din Aybak, who came to power by marrying the sultana Shajar al-Durr in 1250, and died in 1257 when his wife successfully plotted to have him killed, as described in the previous chapter. During his tenure, Aybak appointed the Christian Abu Sa'd Hibat Allah as a minister and continued to employ Copts as administrators and tax collectors. Hibat Allah, to please his sultan, who needed more revenue to continue fighting the Crusaders, imposed a tax for that purpose and doubled the *jizya* on the Copts.[1] After Aybak was killed, his son, al-Mansur Nur al-Din, became the new king. He appointed as minister Hibat Allah al-Fayzi, a Copt who had converted to Islam. He also continued to increase taxes. But when people revolted, the new king deflected their anger by having al-Fayzi crucified on Bab Zuwayla, one of Old Cairo's main gates.

After Baghdad was sacked by the Mongols in 1258, the last caliph, al-Mustansir bi-Allah (reigned 1261–62), escaped to Egypt, where he remained under the protection of the Mamluks. After him, the Mamluk dynasty maintained a succession of twenty-two Abbasid puppet caliphs. On occasion, the Mamluks would kill an uncooperative caliph and replace him with one of his sons. The position of caliph was important as a religious symbol to give the foreign Mamluks legitimacy in the eyes of the people and the Islamic world. In practice, the only time people heard about him was the mention of his name in Friday's sermon.

The third Mamluk sultan, Sayf al-Din Qutuz, defeated the Mongols in battle in 1260, and liberated Syria and Palestine from their control. This battle was a turning point in the history of the region. On his return to Egypt, Sayf al-Din was killed by a group of Mamluk followers of al-Zahir Baybars, one of his own commanders.[2] Baybars seized control and ruled Egypt from 1260 to 1277. He turned out to be one of the best of the Mamluk kings to rule Egypt. He unified the country, rebuilt fortifications, and strengthened the navy. He also managed to control Syria and Palestine, and occupy Antioch—then the richest town in the otherwise deteriorating Byzantine Empire—in 1268.

Although Baybars did much good for the country, relations between Copts and Muslims were strained. According to the Muslim historian Ibn Iyas, some fires took place in Cairo during Baybars's tenure. Rumors spread that the Copts were responsible. The sultan gave the order to round up all the Copts and burn them alive. While the preparations were underway, the head of the army met with the sultan and asked him to forgive the Copts. The sultan agreed, on the condition that the Copts deliver fifty thousand dinars to the treasury and repair all the burned buildings.[3] A similar version of this story was published by the Christian Muffadal ibn al-Fada.[4]

The most mysterious and devastating incident for the Copts during the Mamluk era occurred in AD 1321, at a time of political upheaval. Nasir al-Din Ibn Qalawun (1285–1341), the ninth king of the Mamluk dynasty, succeeded to the throne after his brother was assassinated. He was soon removed, but was able to regain the crown after a short while. This struggle was repeated three times before his power was firmly established. During Ibn Qalawun's tenure, on June 13, 1321, during the Muslims' Friday sermon, about sixty churches and monasteries from Alexandria to Aswan were destroyed. Exactly how this happened remains a mystery, but because this incident occurred during the Friday sermons, it appeared to have been the work of a well-organized Islamic group. It is the first incident of its kind described in Egypt. The sequence of events was mentioned in detail by several historians.[5] A summary by al-Maqrizi, who is widely considered the best Muslim historian in the Middle Ages, describes the events this way:

> The sultan ordered a stable to be built and a lake dug near al-Zuhari church. The workers wanted to destroy the church, but the representative of the sultan ignored their request. On Friday, June 13, 1321, during the Muslim sermon, some members of the crowd shouted, "Allahu Akbar"—"God is the Greatest"—and proceeded to destroy the church. They stole whatever they could put their hands on, and killed whoever was inside the church. The church was reduced to a pile of rubble in a short period. The mob continued their campaign and destroyed Saint Mina's church in the al-Hamra neighborhood. This church was highly regarded by the Copts and had received many gifts from Copts all over Egypt. Whatever was there was stolen. Then the growing mob moved on to two nearby churches. One was a convent with about sixty nuns, who were robbed even of their own clothes. The mob burned these churches while most Muslims were still inside their mosques during the Friday sermon. All this was done in a short period and took the authorities by surprise.
>
> After the Friday sermon, people coming out of the mosques were horrified by the dust and smoke of the burning churches. The looters were in the streets with whatever they had stolen from the churches; some were intoxicated from drinking the wine reserved for communion. The scene was so terrifying that it looked like the end of the world.
>
> The noise of the commotion reached the residence of the sultan in the Citadel. When details of the news reached him, he was very disturbed and became very angry. He asked how the mob had dared do all this without his order. The sultan ordered some of his lieutenants to arrest those responsible, but before they started on their mission, news came from other parts of Cairo that many other churches had also been demolished. Some Copts were trapped inside the Church of al-Mu'allaqa ['Hanging Church'—an important historical site that still exists near the complex of the

Coptic Museum in Old Cairo]. The mob was about to break into the church. At this point, the sultan became furious. He ordered four of his military leaders to kill any members of the mob they found in the streets. The mob near the Hanging Church was so large that the Mamluks could not contain it, so they declared that whoever remained in the street would be killed. Most of the mob dispersed, and only those who were intoxicated from drinking the church wine remained. Some Mamluks kept watch near the Hanging Church until evening, fearing the return of the mob, and some even stayed overnight.

Within a week, news started to reach the sultan that similar attacks had occurred on other churches all over Egypt from Alexandria to Aswan on that same Friday. In some mosques, after the sermon, a member of the Muslim congregation was said to have shouted, "You poor people, get out of the mosque and destroy the churches!" Some did just that. It was a day that was hard to describe or even believe. The sultan was furious. He feared that matters might get even further out of control. The Mamluks close to the sultan tried to calm him by saying that these events could not have happened without God's will—that they were God's retribution for the corruption of the Copts and their misuse of power.[6]

Al-Maqrizi continued his narrative:

Within a month of that horrible Friday, fires sprang up in different places in Cairo. The damage from these fires was much more than that from destroying the churches. Many houses were burned to the ground. The fire was uncontrollable; as soon as it stopped in one place, it started in another. A strong wind fanned the fire; the wind was so strong that it overturned boats in the Nile. It even knocked down some trees. As the fire approached the homes of some Mamluks, Sultan Ibn Qalawun became very concerned. He directed his leaders to make every effort, with the help of the people, to put out the fires. There was great concern and effort from all sides, but the fire continued. During this episode, Copts came under suspicion after someone noticed that the fire was burning mosques and Islamic buildings. Two monks were caught leaving an Islamic school with their hands and clothes contaminated with oil and tar. Rags soaked with oil and tar were also found inside the school. The mob arrested the two monks and handed them and the evidence over to the authorities. The sultan ordered their punishment. Another Copt, dressed like a Muslim, was also caught inside a mosque with some rags soaked with oil and tar. The Copts confessed their deeds to the governor of Cairo. It turned out they were monks from al-Baghl Monastery on Muqattam Mountain [on the outskirts of Cairo]. The Copts in custody admitted that some Copts had collected donations for the purpose of setting fires in Muslim places as retaliation for the destruction of churches and monasteries during the previous month.

The sultan consulted with his leaders regarding this matter and decided to appoint a representative to speak to the Coptic patriarch, John IX (1320–27). Karim al-Din, the ruler of Alexandria and close associate of the sultan, took up this task. The patriarch visited Karim al-Din, who confronted him with the individuals who had been caught and who had confessed. The patriarch wept and he said, "Those are the trash of the Copts, who responded to the trash of the Muslims who destroyed the churches." When the patriarch left Karim al-Din's residence, Karim al-Din accompanied him for his safety. The respect Karim al-Din showed to the patriarch irritated the mob, who shouted at the Mamluk, "You have no right to side with the Copts who burned our homes!"

The fires continued. The Muslim mob was agitated and wanted revenge. The arrested Copts were severely punished. Eventually the truth came out that fourteen monks from al-Baghl Monastery had cooperated in the plan to burn Muslim homes. One monk was an expert at mixing oil and tar to start fires. The fourteen monks had then dispersed to burn different parts of Cairo. The authorities arrested the rest of the monks and some were burned to death; al-Baghl Monastery was razed to the ground. A great number of Muslims gathered to witness the punishment, but events did not end there. A group of Copts who were passing by were badly attacked, and their clothes were torn off. These acts continued. It was a chaotic period. Seeing that things were out of control, the sultan again became angry and wanted to punish the mob. As he rode with his entourage to town on a routine visit, he was surprised to see a large, angry mob yelling, "God protect Islam!" The mob confronted him with two Copts who had been caught burning Muslim homes. They were burned to death on the spot. A

Copt who had a position of status in the administration passed by during this episode, accompanied by others. His presence agitated the mob, and they pulled him off his mule and threw him to the ground. They wanted to burn him, as well, but he declared, "No God but God, Muhammad is the Prophet of God," and became an instant Muslim to save his life.

When the sultan's deputy, Karim al-Din, passed by with his followers, the mob threw stones at him and cursed him for siding with the Copts. The mob was still agitated, and the chaos continued. When Karim al-Din told the sultan what had happened, the sultan became enraged. Some of the sultan's close advisors and associates suggested that all Copts be fired from the administration. But the sultan refused to do this. Instead, he directed some of his military leaders to take troops into the agitated quarters and kill by the sword whomever they saw. He even threatened them: "If you don't catch those who threw stones at Karim al-Din, my deputy, I swear on my head that I will hang you instead." The news of this campaign spread quickly, and most people deserted the streets. Shops were closed, and some people even crossed the Nile to avoid confrontation. About two hundred people were arrested, and some were killed. Some were hanged on Zuwayla's gate, and others had their hands cut off. The fires continued. Three more Copts were arrested after they were found with tar and oil, ready to start another fire. They confessed. The sultan faced a crowd of about twenty thousand holding blue rags with white crosses marked on them, like flags. The crowd shouted, "No religion but Islam, God supports Islam!" They shouted to the sultan, "Support us against the infidels. Don't support the Copts!" The shouting was so loud that it terrified even the sultan and his entourage. When the sultan and his deputies could not control the angry mob, they tried to please them, hoping to calm them down. The Copts became scapegoats so the sultan could pacify the mob. He allowed them to persecute the Copts and rob them of their belongings, saying, "Whoever finds a Copt can take his money, belongings, and even his life." The mob shouted to the sultan, "God give you victory!" It was declared in Cairo that the Copts' money and lives were fair game.

A dress code was imposed on the Copts, making it hard for them even to leave their homes safely. To avoid harassment, they disguised themselves with yellow turbans, the dress code of the Jews. It was

> also declared that Copts could not ride horses or mules, and anyone who rode a donkey must ride it facing backward. Copts could not go to public baths unless they wore a bell around their neck. They could not dress like Muslims. Finally, Copts were fired from public jobs. Under these conditions, many Copts converted to Islam. This was the third great wave of conversion. Officials who converted to Islam without their families were forced to separate from their families and were required to pray five times daily in a mosque.[7]

Al-Maqrizi concluded this account by saying that unprecedented damage and destruction occurred. Many people were killed, and their goods and treasures were destroyed or stolen. Some historians have called al-Maqrizi the first Coptologist because he dedicated a long section of his *Khitat* to a detailed account of the Copts and their lives, churches, and monasteries.[8]

Being warriors and outsiders, the Mamluks were not knowledgeable about Islamic matters; their interest in Islam was limited to their need to preserve their authority. To gain legitimacy, they needed recognition from four Muslim judges, each one representing one of the four Muslim sects within Sunni Islam. Although some Mamluk sultans assumed a narrow Islamic viewpoint that led to discrimination and violence against the Copts, in general they were not anti-Christian for religious reasons. They valued and needed the Copts' knowledge of administrative and financial matters in order to run the country.[9]

But the Mamluks' practical and laissez-faire attitude toward religion left the field open for others of a more devout and ideological bent. One influential Muslim leader of the period was Ibn Taymiya (1263–1326), who surfaced first in Syria and then in Egypt. He issued radical treatises against everything he saw as un-Islamic, including the presence of Christians and their churches in the Muslim world. These fatwas had the potential to agitate the Egyptian masses.[10] Even before Ibn Taymiya reached Egypt, he presented a threat to the ruling class and to other established Muslim leaders. He was jailed in Syria, and sent from Damascus to Cairo for interrogation. He was also jailed in Egypt on three separate occasions, and forbidden from issuing any more fatwas.

In total, Ibn Taymiya issued thirty-seven volumes of Islamic thought and fatwas. Some of these fatwas could be directly or indirectly understood to promote the destruction of churches. Some have speculated that Ibn Taymiya was the brain behind the coordinated destruction of sixty churches in one day, described by al-Maqrizi above. There is evidence to support that notion, but nothing conclusive. Mark Swanson mentions that Ibn Taymiya agitated and wrote enormous treatises against all that he saw as un-Islamic, including Christians playing influential roles in Egyptian society.[11] Exactly how the plan was carried out remains a mystery. However, these events started a chain reaction that led to the Islamization of Egypt, as will be discussed in the next chapter. Ibn Taymiya's writings are still read and are influential in promoting the radical Islamic thought that motivates jihadist Muslims of today.

As al-Maqrizi's *Khitat* makes clear, the persecution of the Copts was worst at a time when the government was weak. Sultan Ibn Qalawun was removed and returned to power three times.[12] In his narrative, quoted at length above, al-Maqrizi describes the administration's inability to control the masses. The sultan's anger at the mob was due, not to what they had done, but to the fact that they dared to do it without his permission. His own inability to control the mobs led him finally to sanction their violence toward Copts, deflecting it away from himself and his followers.

The Coptic Church and papacy offered their own self-serving interpretation of these events. They tried to absolve the Copts of responsibility for starting the fires, by saying that (1) Christianity is against violence, and (2) the monks from al-Baghl Monastery who were arrested for setting fires were Melchites, a sect of Greek origin, and not Copts at all.

During the Ayyubid and Mamluk periods, the Coptic Church was required to make additional payments that were determined by the mood and needs of the ruling class. To meet these financial demands, the patriarchs asked the bishops for donations; the bishops, in turn, collected money from their dioceses. As one example, Ibn Iyas states that Ibn Qalawun decided to confiscate twenty-five thousand acres from the church endowment and distribute it among his Mamluk leaders.[13] As a result, the church became poorer and weaker. At times, the selection of patriarchs was delayed because of government interference. A general atmosphere of corruption plagued the church. Some church posts were sold to the higher bidder, a practice called *al-shartuniya*.[14]

The Mamluks continued to use Copts as administrators and tax collectors. As a result, some Copts became very wealthy and influential. The presence of conspicuously rich Copts raised a problem for the whole community.[15] The misuse of power by some Copts led to collective punishments, as we have seen and will revisit in the next chapter.

Permission from the sultan was required for the restoration of old or destroyed churches. This permission was often difficult to obtain, and even when granted, occasionally led to violence. In 1328, the Copts managed to obtain permission to restore St. Barbara's Church. However, when the Copts restored the church, they also expanded the building. This angered some Muslims. The sultan ordered the destruction of the expanded part, but the whole building was destroyed by a mob. It was subsequently replaced by a mosque, which the sultan then ordered to be destroyed.[16]

During this difficult period, some Copts had little choice but to convert to Islam. As we have noted, this was the third major wave of conversion. (The first was during the Abbasid dynasty, and the second was during the reign of al-Hakim.) After the violence against them diminished, some converts tried to go back to Christianity. However, according to most Islamic views, once a person has converted to Islam, he may not leave it. Furthermore, his descendants would also be Muslims. As an example, there is the case of a man whose father had converted to Islam, but he, the son, wished to remain a Copt. When he refused to embrace Islam, he was jailed. The Copts complained to the ruler, who freed him from jail. This in turn set off protests by some Muslims, leading to violence and the destruction of a nearby church.[17]

The Copts suffered during the Mamluk dynasty, but Muslims also suffered from mistreatment, high taxation, and an ineffective infrastructure. Ibn Iyas tells a story about the revolt by some Arabs and farmers in the south, due to high taxes. They refused to pay the taxes, blocked the roads, and stole grain. However, they were brutally crushed by al-Amir Shikhu, who cut off the head of any farmer or Arab he was able to catch. He used the chopped heads to construct several terraces and some minarets on the banks of the Nile. This was similar to what the Mongols did in Baghdad under Hulagu Khan.[18]

Economic factors outside Egypt contributed to the the Mamluks' decline. After the Abbasid capital, Baghdad, was sacked by the Mongols, trade between India and Europe increasingly followed routes through Egypt. This gave the Mamluks a monopoly of the spice trade, allowing them to raise prices and increase their revenue. In 1498, the Portuguese explorer Vasco da Gama discovered a sea route to India around Africa that was less costly and avoided the disturbed area of the Middle East. As trade shifted to this sea route, Egypt was deprived of important revenue, and the Mamluks' power declined.

The late Mamluk period witnessed a continuation of infighting between various Mamluk factions. These internal power struggles weakened the Mamluks' power and ultimately led to their demise. Their control was also weakened by severe flooding of the Nile, poor water management, worsening of agricultural conditions, and the desertification of some land.[19] Despite these difficulties, the Mamluks managed to hang on to power until the Napoleonic invasion of Egypt in 1798. At that time, Egypt was under Muhammad 'Ali, as will be discussed in the next two chapters.

Husayn Fawzi, the late Egyptian historian, summarized the misery of the Egyptians during the Mamluk era in the following story: Fawzi claimed to have uncovered an important mathematical formula that revealed the status of the Egyptians under the Mamluks. The formula showed an Egyptian pie divided into twenty-four parts: four slices went to the sultan, ten slices went to Mamluk leaders, and ten slices went to the army. The share of the Egyptians, according to this formula, was zero. How did they survive during this period? Fawzi, being a scientist, used a sophisticated computerized search to find the answer, but the computer could not determine the share of the Egyptians, either. Fawzi became depressed. His grandmother noticed his depression and asked about it. After careful thought, she said, "My son, Egyptians survive even if they drink muddy water, eat the grass of the land, and wear rags. Their share is the twenty-fifth slice, and it is found only in the kingdom of heaven."[20]

6

THE ISLAMIZATION OF EGYPT

By the *Islamization* of Egypt, we mean the process by which the majority of Egyptians converted to Islam, and Christians became a minority. This shift in religion also coincided with the period during which the language of the people largely changed from Coptic to Arabic.

Little is known about the speed and extent of conversion to Islam in the early Islamic period because historical evidence is scanty. Naturally, some Christians converted to Islam out of belief; others did so to join the new ruling elites. As the centuries went by, the process of conversion was generally slow except during three periods. The first was during parts of the Abbasid dynasty mentioned in chapter three. The second was during the al-Hakim period mentioned in chapter four. The third and most important period was during the Mamluk era in the thirteenth to fourteenth centuries, as mentioned in chapter five. Most contemporary historians regard the latter period as the time of greatest conversion from Christianity to Islam in Egypt. We have already touched on some of the reasons for this in the previous chapter. Let us now look at the process in greater detail.

The Arabs invaded Egypt in AD 640. Initially, they did not force or even encourage Egyptians to convert to Islam. Those who did convert were still required to pay the *jizya*, so it was not a financial incentive at first. In AD 714, the Umayyad caliph ʻUmar ibn ʻAbd al-ʻAziz ordered that the *jizya* not be collected from those who converted to Islam. He said, "God sent Muhammad to enlighten people, not to collect taxes."[1] This change in policy provided an incentive for Copts, especially the poor, to become Muslims, as the *jizya* represented a significant financial burden. As taxes continued to increase during the Umayyad and Abbasid dynasties, there were thirteen uprisings (see chapter three), which were accompanied by a slow but steady conversion to Islam. During the period of independent rulers of Egypt (see chapter four), the economy improved and taxes did not increase. Except for the period of al-Hakim in the early eleventh century, there was no massive conversion to Islam during the independent dynasties. The number of Christians converting to Islam increased gradually, but no research has determined the exact rate of conversion.

During the two decades of al-Hakim's tenure (1000–21), about three thousand churches were destroyed in Egypt, Syria, and Palestine.[2] Although the effect of al-Hakim was devastating, he reversed his decision and gave permission for the Copts to reclaim and rebuild their churches, before he mysteriously disappeared. Research by the modern Muslim historian Tamer el-Leithy found a positive correlation between the destruction of churches and the rate of conversion to Islam.[3] Some of this destruction was mentioned in the previous chapter. What instigated the massive destruction of churches that continued over the thirteenth and fourteenth centuries? Although many factors came together to influence Coptic conversion to Islam, the factors described in the following sections were most important.

Threats to Islam from Mongols and Europeans

During the Middle Ages, the Islamic world felt threatened by a number of events. Among the most serious were the Mongols' conquest of the Abbasids in Baghdad in 1258, the presence of European Crusaders in southern Syria and Palestine (1095–1291), and the gradual loss of Muslim-controlled territory in the Iberian Peninsula. This last event culminated in the 1492 expulsion of 300,000 to 400,000 Muslims—about 20 percent of the population—who carried with them into exile first-hand experience of injustice at the hands of Christian conquerors, thus confirming and spreading the conviction that Islam was under attack and needed to be defended. These three events together gave rise to militant forms of Islam across the region. Although Christians in the Middle East were not responsible for instigating the Mongol invasions, the Crusades, or the Reconquista in Spain, they nevertheless became scapegoats and suffered considerable damage and losses as a result.

Religious polemics, both Christian and Muslim, have presented arguments in defense of their respective communities. One example, which sheds light on the social and political context surrounding Coptic–Muslim conflict in thirteenth-century Egypt, has recently been edited and translated into English by Luke Yarbrough.[4]

The manuscript which Yarbrough translates and discusses is titled *Tajrid sayf al-himma li-istikhraj ma fi dhimmat al-dhimma (The Sword of Ambition)* by Abu 'Amr 'Uthman ibn Ibrahim al-Nabulsi al-Masri (1192–1262). The title rhymes in Arabic, and Yarbrough suggests a literal rendition in English might be "Unsheathing Ambition's Sword to Extract What the Dhimmis [non-Muslims] Hoard," or "The Sword of Ambition," for short. It is a collection of Islamic legal arguments, historical precedents, anecdotes, and other writings, all in support of al-Nabulsi's contention that Copts, Jews, converts to Islam, and uncultured individuals of any background should be banned from all positions of power or responsibility.

Al-Nabulsi had risen to the high post of auditor of the tax administration for virtually all of Egypt, before falling out of favor with the government and losing his position—a situation he blamed on Copts and Coptic converts to Islam. He was particularly resentful of Coptic administrators and tax collectors whom he saw flourishing economically while his own fortunes declined. Despite the author's need to air his personal grievances at some length, much in his book reflects the cultural climate of its time. For example, the corruption of Coptic tax collectors was a widespread problem, as we have mentioned elsewhere, and was an ongoing source of popular resentment against Copts in particular.

Al-Nabulsi's arguments, often couched in inflammatory language, found a receptive audience among his contemporaries. His examples appealed to those with limited knowledge of Islam who wished to bolster their pre-existing prejudices by citing "religious" authority. For example, he cites many hadiths which condemn non-Muslims, but only one such passage from the Qur'an itself. While the Qur'an contains many examples of interfaith tolerance, al-Nabulsi singles out one passage from Surat al-Ma'ida:

> O you who believe, take not the Jews and the Christians for allies. They are friends of each other. And whoever amongst you takes them for friends, he is indeed one of them. Surely Allah guides not the unjust people. (Surat al-Ma'ida 51)

While this passage is an exception to the general attitude expressed in the Qu'ran as a whole, it is still quoted by Islamists today as justification for discriminating against Jews and Christians.

After al-Nabulsi's death, the sentiments he expressed were elaborated by Ibn Taymiya, an early proponent of jihadist ideology who is often considered the father of modern political Islam. Ibn Taymiya issued numerous fatwas and proclaimed the right of the *umma* (Muslim nation) to overthrow any government that does not rule according to Islamic principles. In the last chapter, we mentioned Ibn Taymiya's possible influence—direct or indirect—on the destruction of about sixty churches on a single day in

1321. Again, in the midst of the harsh conditions of the plague in 1354, Ibn Taymiya issued a fatwa to confiscate the endowments of churches and monasteries. Based on this fatwa, the Mamluk sultan al-Salih ordered the seizure of about 25,000 feddans (one feddan equals about one acre) and distributed the land to senior Mamluks. These actions had serious financial implications for Christian institutions.[5] Ibn Taymiya may have thought he represented the views of Islam, but some of his interpretations of the Qur'an were rigid and disagreed with other Islamic authorities of his time.

Changing Demography in the South of Egypt

While the presence of the Crusaders in southern Syria and Palestine was a threat to Islam, it also threatened trade routes from the East and hindered Muslim pilgrims traveling to Mecca from Egypt and North Africa. As a result, a new route for trade and for pilgrims was established from Egypt to Hijaz (Arabia), by crossing the Red Sea. This route originated in Qus, a town on the east bank of the Nile in southern Egypt, where new Muslim Sufi settlements sprang up.[6] As these Muslim communities evolved and increased in number, they found themselves in an area still dominated by Christians. Small towns in southern Egypt were full of Copts. Asyut had twenty-five churches. Sanbu, north of Asyut, had twenty-seven churches. The town of Akhmim, to the south of Asyut, had no less than seventy churches. Qamula had fourteen churches. There were also many monasteries in the south. The monastery of the martyr Abu Nafar reportedly had an endowment of one hundred feddans of fertile land and twenty-four churches in the thirteenth century.[7]

Some influential Sufis, such as Ibn Nuh, came from North Africa (the Maghreb) and brought to Egypt memories of Muslim defeat and humiliation at the hands of Catholic Spain. Their hostile feeling toward European Christians was transferred to Christians in Egypt, and this attitude in turn rubbed off on some Egyptian Muslims, leading to the destruction of churches and synagogues, some of which were converted into mosques.[8] In 1219, a Coptic bishop described how Muslims—mostly from North Africa—destroyed every church they came upon. The bishop noted that nothing was more hateful to those Maghrebis than Christians. They arrested Copts and Jews and ordered that they be punished until they paid 11,000 dinars. In 1301, a Mamluk sultan, yielding to public pressure and to pressure from the king of Morocco, ordered all churches to be closed on the grounds that they were accumulating too much wealth.[9] Although this reflects the weakness of the Mamluks, it also shows the ability of the

Moroccans to stir up sectarian violence, a pattern that continued until the French occupation of Egypt in 1798.

In the absence of a strong central government, the new Sufi settlements acted as unauthorized moral regulators. They often went against existing laws and undercut the Mamluks' political authority. Because few, if any, churches existed in much of Arabia and North Africa, some Muslims who came from these areas had little experience with mixed religious communities. They thought churches should not be allowed anywhere in the land of Islam. These attitudes were bound to be problematic when holders of these views came to Egypt, a country which still had extensive Christian and monastic cultures. Although the existence of many churches in Egypt was considered by some radical Muslims to demonstrate resistance to Islam, it might better be seen as a reflection of Islamic tolerance. More than five centuries after the Arab invasion, Egypt still had a thriving Christian community and a large number of churches. This would not have been the case if Muslim rulers had pursued a policy of universal and forced conversion in the territories they conquered. In this respect, they showed greater tolerance than many European Christian rulers of the time.

Changes in Egypt's demography had direct effects on interfaith relations. The town of Qus became a center of Sufism that produced well-known Sufis, such as Abu-l Hajjaj (whose tomb is in Luxor) and Abu-l 'Abbas (whose tomb is in Alexandria), as well as radical ones, such as Ibn Nuh, who came from North Africa.

Some Sufi Muslims organized and mobilized anti-Christian feelings. For example, in 1307, in the town of Qus, thirteen churches were destroyed in a period of two hours.[10] In 1321, at least sixty churches were destroyed in one day in various places in Egypt, from Alexandria to Aswan. This wave of destruction continued for many years, with incidents in 1259, 1264, 1279, 1283, 1293, 1301, 1321, and 1354.[11] The year 1354 witnessed some of the most important attacks on Copts, including confiscation of church endowments and prohibition against employment of Copts (even those who had converted to Islam) in public service. When forced to convert to Islam, many Coptic families went through the formalities, but remained covertly Christian, resulting in sham conversions.[12] This was offensive to many Muslims. Under pressure from radical clergies, the government was receptive to accusations that these converts were crypto-Christians who oppressed Muslims with impunity. El-Leithy gives examples of what he calls "alternative conversions."[13] In the thirteenth and fourteenth centuries, the number of conversions increased sharply, as many Copts realized that their social and economic welfare lay in converting to Islam. Overt persecution also played a decisive role, according to the historian Shaun O'Sullivan. He states that in the town of Qalyub alone, about 450 persons converted to Islam in a single day.[14]

Rich Coptic Administrators and Tax Collectors

Some members of the Christian elite in Egypt were socially prominent and held highly visible administrative posts. Coptic tax collectors, in particular, were often very wealthy and were hated due to the nature of their jobs. This antipathy was frequently generalized to include all Copts. Rich Copts were an asset to the churches, and so the wave of conversions deprived the church of important financial resources. Surprisingly, even after the many well-documented mass conversions, some Copts continued to hold high financial positions and still dominated the profitable business of tax collection. This was the case until the British invaded Egypt in 1882. The ratio of Muslim tax collectors (if any) to Coptic tax collectors is not known.

The Coptic and Jewish communities were sometimes targeted for extortion, due to their perceived wealth. In 1265, fires broke out in Cairo. Sultan Baybars I accused the Copts and Jews *(dhimmis)* of arson and ordered a large pit in which to burn them. One of the Mamluk leaders interceded on their behalf and bribed the sultan with the staggering sum of 500,000 gold dinars, payable in annual installments of 50,000 dinars. Although this was extortion, it also shows the power and resources of a wealthy community.[15]

Marriage and Conversion

The Coptic Church allows marriage to only one wife and does not recognize divorce, while Islam has much more relaxed marital customs. As Copts and Muslims continued to live side by side, the wave of conversions began to blur cultural boundaries, especially between the Coptic and Muslim elites. This opened the way for Copts to adopt some of the Islamic customs of marriage, divorce, and concubinage. This started to present a problem for some Copts and for the church. Patriarch John XIII (1484–1524) instructed priests to excommunicate offenders. Due to the difficulties of obtaining a divorce in the Coptic Church, some Copts started to rely on Muslim courts, which weakened the authority of the Coptic Church. Some affluent Copts relied on political pressure. For example, one Mamluk amir wanted to help a Coptic employee obtain a second marriage, and threatened the church itself if the priest did not allow that marriage. The priest still pronounced the excommunication, but did so silently between himself and God.[16]

Marriage laws, too, encouraged the demographic shift from a Christian population to a Muslim one. When a Muslim man married a Christian woman, she was allowed to keep her Christian faith, but the church considered this an Islamic marriage and the children of the mixed marriage were always considered Muslims. A Muslim woman, on the other hand, was forbidden from marrying a non-Muslim under any circumstances. Nor was she allowed to convert to another religion. So in practice, conversions were a one-way street, increasing the number of Muslims and decreasing the number of Copts. Islamic marriage laws had a similar effect on the Jewish community.

The Shift from Coptic to Arabic Language

The ancient Egyptian language of the Nile Valley was initially written in hieroglyphics, a form of sacred pictorial writing. This was followed by the hieratic writing used by priests, which was further simplified to the demotic ("of the people") language. During the Ptolemaic dynasty (third century BC), the demotic language began to be written in Greek letters, with the addition of seven original letters to represent Egyptian sounds not found in Greek. With the arrival of Christianity and the influence of Greek culture, the Greek language progressively infiltrated the ancient Egyptian language, resulting in development of the Coptic language around the second century AD. Twenty-five percent of the Coptic vocabulary was Greek.[17] This percentage was higher in Alexandria and other cities with large Greek populations, but lower in small cities and in the countryside. The Bible was translated from Greek to Coptic in about the fourth century.

By the time the Arabs came to Egypt in the seventh century, the evolved Coptic language was the dominant language, and Coptic Christianity had been the national religion since the fifth century. About sixty years after the Arab conquest, 'Abd al-Malik, the viceroy of Egypt (AD 705), was the first to order that Arabic be the only language used by the government administration. Copts in the government started to learn Arabic and to use it. However, many words did not have an Arabic equivalent and therefore were written phonetically with Arabic letters. A similar adaptation occurred in Persian and the Pakistani languages, when Islam spread to those regions.

As more Egyptians converted to Islam, the Arabic language gained ground and the use of Coptic declined. By the tenth century, the majority of Egyptians knew Arabic. In the thirteenth century, Copts started to write their own theological treatises in Arabic as well as Coptic. The south of Egypt was the slowest to change. Al-Maqrizi noted that during the fifteenth century, women and children in the south still knew almost no other language than Sahidic (southern) Coptic. But by the sixteenth century, the Coptic language was spoken in only a few areas of southern Egypt. It did not completely disappear as a spoken language until the early twentieth century, the last holdouts being some small villages in the south, such as Naqada, Farshut, and Qus.[18] Although no longer a living language today, Coptic is still used to some degree in the Coptic Church liturgy, alongside Arabic.

However, traces of the ancient Coptic language can be found in the spoken Egyptian language of today.[19] Words, phrases, and certain grammatical constructions in modern spoken Egyptian Arabic can be traced through Coptic back to pharaonic times. That is why Egyptians speak a form of colloquial Arabic that is quite different from both the Arabic spoken in other areas of the Middle East and classical written Arabic. Egypt's unique culture is expressed in part through surviving remnants of its ancient language.

Classical Arabic, modeled after the Qur'anic language of the seventh century, has traditionally been the formal language used for writing. But by the beginning of the twentieth century, some writers started to promote a written form of Egyptian Arabic based on the modern spoken language. These writers included Ahmad Lutfi al-Sayyid (the first president of the Egyptian University), Qasim Amin, Salama Musa, Muhammad Husayn Haykal, Jurji Zaydan, and others. In the second half of the century, additional literary work was written in colloquial Egyptian Arabic, including the work of prominent writers such as Ihsan 'Abd al-Quddus and Yusuf Idris, and poets such as Salah Jahin, 'Abd al-Rahman al-Abnudi, and Ahmad Fu'ad Nigm.

Some conservatives regard the language of the Qur'an as holy and think it should be preserved without changes. Nevertheless, language is a living thing. New words are always being invented or borrowed from other languages. This influence works in both directions. Nowadays, modern colloquial Egyptian speech is influencing the wider Arab world. It has infiltrated the formal Arabic language, even outside Egypt, due to the heavy influence of Egyptian culture on cinema, television, and other media.

Both culture and language evolve slowly over time and have ancient roots. Even though Egypt became a Muslim country, some elements of the old pharaonic and Christian religions were retained by Egyptian Islamic culture, particularly in funerary practices and religious festivals *(mulids)*. Egyptian and foreign scholars have done extensive studies of the correspondence between modern behavior and the scenes of daily life depicted on the walls of ancient tombs and on papyri. Examples include folk medicine and religious expressions. To this day, Egyptian farmers still use the ancient Egyptian calendar in their farming operations. These links between past and present enrich our understanding of both ancient and modern eras.[20] Anthropologist Michael Agar and others reveal how deeply our language and cultural values intertwine to define who we are and how we relate to one another.[21] The change from the pharaonic/Coptic language to Arabic was slower and even more gradual than the change of religion from Christianity to Islam. The historian Ahmad Yusuf has listed hundreds of words and phrases still in use today that originated in the ancient Egyptian language. Not only have the words and phrases been retained, but also the grammar and sound.[22] Modern colloquial Egyptian Arabic has been influenced not only by the ancient Egyptian language, but also to a much lesser degree by languages spoken by the Persians, Greeks, Romans, Arabs, Turks, French, and English.

In 1981, the writer Louis Awad wrote a scholarly book on the origin and evolution of the Arabic language. He described colloquial Egyptian Arabic by saying that its spine is Arabic but its meat goes back to the ancient Egyptian language.[23] The book faced a serious challenge from the Islamic Research Center of al-Azhar University, which held the view that the Arabic language—the language of the Qur'an—should not be researched or criticized.[24] As a result, Awad's book was banned on December 15, 1981, by a court order. That ban was not lifted until 1993, when the book was finally republished.

Awad's book used newly available tools to Egyptians for language research and was praised by many intellectuals of the time, including Naguib Mahfouz and Tawfiq al-Hakim.[25] However, some Islamists did not want to recognize that the Arabic language is alive and changing; they wished to freeze it in the form in which it appears in the Qur'an. Criticism of Awad's research was magnified by the fact that he had a Christian name, even though he was not an observant Christian at all. An Islamist university professor wrote an article against Awad's book in which he described Awad as a Western Crusader. Instead of criticizing the contents of the book in a scholarly manner, the author focused on defending the Qur'an and asserting the miracle of its language.[26] The attack on Awad by the Islamists continued throughout his life.

7

EGYPT UNDER THE OTTOMANS (1517–1798)

While the Mamluks' power was declining, a new Islamic power was rising and spreading from northeastern Anatolia. The Ottoman Turks had replaced the shrinking Byzantine Empire by AD 1453. As the Ottoman Empire expanded, it eventually impinged on Mamluk-held territory. The first military confrontation between the Turks and the Mamluks took place in Syria in AD 1516. During the conflict, the Mamluk sultan, al-Ghuri, was killed on the battlefield. Al-Ghuri was replaced by Tuman Bey, who confronted the Turkish army outside Cairo the following year. Tuman Bey was captured alive by the Turkish army under the command of Sultan Selim. Tuman Bey was hanged, and his body remained on Bab Zuwayla for three days, before he was finally buried on April 15, 1517. At this time, all territories under the influence of the Mamluks—including Arabia, the center of Islam—surrendered to the new power without further fighting.

Turkish Rule

The Turkish Ottoman Empire soon became the largest Islamic empire the world had ever seen. It included North Africa, the Middle East, and parts of central Europe, India, and China. On his triumphant return to Anatolia from Egypt, Sultan Selim brought with him many Egyptian and Mamluk treasures, including gold and silver, carried on the backs of a thousand camels. He also brought with him skilled Christian and Muslim craftsmen. The puppet caliph in Cairo was taken by the Turks to Istanbul, but the Turks did not claim the caliphate until their military power had started to decline. Instead, they simply used their control of the position to ensure their leadership in the Muslim world.[1]

The Turks ruled Egypt by controlling three competing centers of power. The first was the official representative of the Turkish sultan (the basha); the second was the head of the occupying Turkish army; and the third was composed of surviving Mamluks who had transferred their loyalty to the Ottomans. These three ruling institutions were supposed to balance each other so none could claim total authority—that remained solely in the hands of the Turkish sultan in Istanbul. This strategy worked for more than two centuries. The Turkish sultan changed his representative periodically so no basha could become too independent. The Turkish army in Egypt was weakened by internal conflict among the troops. However, the remaining Mamluks slowly regained power, finally becoming independent in the seventeenth century as the power of the Turkish sultan was marginalized.

During the Ottoman era, the average Egyptian was subjected to a new system of taxation called *al-iltizam*. Under this system, the principal tax collectors guaranteed and delivered an agreed-upon sum of money to the government. They collected it from the people in whatever way they could. The collectors were able to keep for themselves up to half of what they collected.[2] This system filtered down to the local tax collectors in the villages. The result of this system was harmful to society at large. It led to excessive taxation and to excessive wealth for the class at the top. Farmers who could not pay taxes deserted the land.

The system used for collecting the *jizya* from Copts was also different from what had been done before. Under the original system, one or two dinars were paid by every Copt regardless of his economic status. The new system divided Copts into three categories: rich, middle class, and poor. The wealthier the man, the more he paid. Record-keeping under this system revealed that the majority of Copts were not as well-off as some might have been led to believe. For example, in 1737, of the 120,000 Copts who were paying *jizya*, 10 percent were rich, 20 percent were in the middle class, and 70 percent were poor.[3] Poor Copts who were not able to pay the *jizya* were jailed, or had their children work as servants for those who could pay the *jizya* on their behalf. To guarantee that they would pay their *jizya*, Copts were not allowed to leave their village unless they had paid. If they did leave, they had to show a receipt as proof of payment.

In 1734, the sultan's share of the *jizya* was 15 million bara. As the economic state of the Ottoman Empire declined, the sultan's share of the *jizya* also declined. When the sultan decided to increase the *jizya*, the Copts protested. About a thousand Copts went to the office of the administration in the Citadel, where they faced the government security forces. Two Copts were killed, and the rest dispersed.[4] As the Turkish Empire continued to decline, the sultan's share of the *jizya* decreased further. By 1787, it had stopped completely. At that time, the Turkish sultan's representative, Hassan Dzaerli, left Egypt, marking the end of the Turkish presence, at least until their brief and symbolic return after the French left Egypt in 1801, as we will discuss in the next two chapters. However, Egypt remained formally under the Turkish sultan until the French invaded Egypt in 1798.

We have already mentioned that tax collection was a highly lucrative profession carried out by Copts. Unfortunately, under the Turkish system, it was particularly vulnerable to corruption and extortion. Because tax collectors were committed to delivering a specific sum to the government, there was an incentive to squeeze even more out of the people and keep the extra for themselves. One way to do this was to falsify the census records, making it appear that there were fewer Copts than there really were. Based on the falsely low census numbers, only a portion of the *jizya* collected from Copts needed to be turned over to the government, and the excess could be pocketed. Tax collectors, particularly those in villages where Copts were the majority, made a tidy profit. Collecting taxes from both Copts and Muslims was often accompanied by the use of force. Some poor Copts escaped to the mountains during the collection season to avoid paying the *jizya*. Some rich Copts set up endowments dedicated to paying the *jizya* of those who could not afford it.[5]

The *jizya* was not the only discriminatory tax imposed on the Copts. Other taxes, too, were imposed according to the moods and needs of the ruler. In 1566, when Sultan Sulayman al-Qanuni wanted to conquer Yemen, he ordered that his campaign be financed by the Copts and all foreign merchants.[6] At times, a sum of money was imposed on the Coptic patriarch in exchange for obtaining the sultan's recognition of his post. Under Turkish rule, taxes were high on all Egyptians, but the Copts paid the highest share, due to the *jizya*.

During the latter part of the Ottoman period, anyone with military power could collect taxes by force; some villages were paying taxes twice. If a village did not pay taxes on time, the entire village was penalized and vandalized. To add insult to injury, a new tax was imposed which added the cost of collecting taxes to the taxes people already had to pay. Nelly Hanna, a contemporary historian, cites six demonstrations in Cairo alone against excessive taxation in the period between 1678 and 1738. All shops were closed during the demonstrations.[7]

Coptic–Muslim Relations

By the middle of the eighteenth century, Turkish power had weakened. The Ottoman Empire was being attacked by the Russians along their common border, and outlying territories were beginning to challenge the central authority in Istanbul. In Egypt, the Mamluks started to regain power, and their leader took the title "Ruler of Egypt" *(shaykh al-balad)*. The most important Mamluk was 'Ali Bey al-Kabir (1728–73), a former slave who was freed by his master Ibrahim Katakhda, and elevated to the title of bey. After Katakhda's death al-Kabir became the virtual ruler of Egypt. He continued to use Copts in high administrative posts and as tax collectors. His Coptic secretary, Mu'allim Rizq, attained a position that no other Copt had achieved at the time. Internal struggles with other Mamluks forced al-Kabir to flee Egypt on two occasions—once to Arabia and once to Syria. On another occasion, he fled to the south of Egypt. When he regained power, Syria, Arabia, and Egypt were all under his control. He tried to cooperate with the Russians against the Turks, but the Turks conspired commander, Muhammad Bek Abu-l Dhahab, to have him killed in 1770.

In 1785, the Turkish Kapudan Hassan Basha came to Egypt to reassert Turkish sovereignty over Egypt. During his short stay in Egypt (1785–87), Hassan Basha extorted as much money as possible from the Copts. He ordered a survey of all Coptic homes and imposed taxes according to their wealth. On top of that, an additional sum was collected from all Copts, causing great hardship for many of them. He ordered the Copts not to employ Muslims, not to use animals for transportation, and not to buy slaves. Those who had slaves were ordered to free or sell them. He imposed a dress code and forbade the Copts and the Jews from using the names of Biblical prophets for themselves or their children. Just before leaving Egypt, he rescinded some of his harshest orders after receiving a monetary gift. When the Mamluks were back in power, they imposed their own laws to squeeze money from the Copts as well as the Muslims.[8]

We have previously mentioned that the dress code had nothing to do with original Islamic traditions. Its primary purpose was to single out non-Muslims as visibly different. Often this was done in a manner that was designed to humiliate the Copts and the Jews and to allow Muslim clergy to appear superior—for example, by forbidding non-Muslims from using items of high quality. The dress code not only required Copts and Jews to wear certain colors, but extended to the kinds of shoes they were allowed. They could not wear clothes in the colors preferred by Muslim shaykhs, and their shoes could not be of good quality.[9] Sometimes the dress code was employed as a money-generating scheme; cynical rulers imposed it with the expectation that the affected community would then pay a handsome bribe to have it removed.

The Muslim historian 'Abd al-Rahman al-Jabarti (1756–1825) tells a story that reflects the state of Coptic–Muslim relations at that time. In 1784, the Copts wished to organize a group pilgrimage to Jerusalem, so they bribed a prominent shaykh to issue a fatwa that allowed them to do so. A thousand dinars were given to Shaykh 'Abdullah al-Shabrawi, who prepared a fatwa indicating that Copts could not be prohibited from performing religious visits to sacred places. The Copts started to prepare for their pilgrimage, but another prominent shaykh, Shaykh al-Badri, got wind of the bribe and angrily said to al-Shabrawi, "Now that you have done this, the Copts will start having festivities in preparation for their pilgrimages, just as the Muslims do for theirs." Stung by the rebuke, Shaykh al-Shabrawi then permitted some people, including a student of his from al-Azhar University, to attack the Christians' festivities. The Copts were stoned, beaten, and robbed of their possessions. A church near Damurdash was also plundered. The Copts suffered greatly from that incident, and much of what they had was lost or scattered.[10] Muhammad 'Afifi, the modern historian who investigated many of the original documents of the Turkish period in Egypt, confirmed al-Jabarti's narrative.[11] However, he also uncovered examples in which Copts were allowed to go on pilgrimages after paying heavy taxes to the Turkish authorities.[12] The Turkish Sultan's representative ordered a survey of Copts homes so their assets could be taxed accordingly. He also ordered a large sum of money to be collected from the Copts.[13]

Building churches in Egypt has been a problem right up until the present time. During the Turkish rule, some Islamist clergy interpreted Islamic law to mean that no new churches could be built in any Islamic lands. The only thing that was allowed was the restoration of old or deteriorating churches, and even that was subject to restrictions, such as use of the original building materials and maintaining the size of the original building.[14] Some historians cite an example from the seventeenth and eighteenth centuries, in which the Copts expanded the size of a church. The rulers were supposed to demolish the additional space in the church, but instead the sultan, Ahmed Quara Mohamed, allowed the Copts to keep the expanded building in exchange for paying a monetary penalty. The sum was raised by the Coptic patriarch Yuhannas XVI, who managed to collect it from private donations. In another example, a complaint was made about a second church, but when it proved false, it was ignored.[15] It was customary during this period to inspect all churches for expansions and renovations.[16] While it was difficult for Copts to build or restore their old churches, non-Coptic Christians from other countries—who were often important to foreign trade—enjoyed freedom to build their Protestant and Catholic churches. This reflected the increasing influence of foreigners and European missionaries in Egypt. We will return to this in the chapters that follow.

As the Ottoman Empire declined, its hold over Egypt continued to weaken. The Mamluks were jockeying for power among themselves, and the social order was strained. There was sporadic sectarian violence, and mobs encouraged by some Muslim clergy persecuted the Copts. The modern historian 'Afifi gives the following examples: One Islamic scholar repeated insulting phrases to Copts in public; another beat a Coptic administrator in the street. When the latter reported this to a prominent Mamluk, his answer was, "What do you expect me to do to a great Islamic scholar who has beaten a Copt?"[17] It would be a mistake to assume the Ottoman administration singled out Muslims for better treatment than they gave the Copts; both groups suffered from the results of poor administration. However, the Copts suffered additional mistreatment as a result of being a target against whom the masses could vent their frustration.[18]

Because prominent Islamic scholars gave legitimacy to Turkish Ottoman rulers who knew little about Islam, the rulers and the scholars needed each other. This symbiotic relationship allowed some of the well-known shaykhs to rise on the socioeconomic ladder, with the prominent shaykhs of al-Azhar Mosque often at the very top. Al-Jabarti mentions that one of them, Shaykh Muhammad Abu-l Anwar, built a fancy house with a mosque that overlooked a pond so he did not have to burden himself by going to an outside mosque. According to Hanna, the eighteenth-century shaykh Ahmad al-Damanhuri "found the Ottoman state to be the closest to the early caliphate state on account of the mutual need for and support of the *shari'a* and for *ulama*."[19]

Al-Jabarti, an Azharite shaykh himself, was an eyewitness historian of that time. He listed the excessive wealth of some of those scholars, who possessed gold and silver currency in vast amounts. Shaykh Muhammad Shinin, the head of al-Azhar Mosque, was one of the wealthiest people of his time.[20] Al-Jabarti was also critical of the clergy's poor knowledge of Islam. He quotes a poem, written by another Azharite shaykh of that time, that said in part, "Al-Azhar Mosque, God plagued it with lack of knowledge. Its shaykhs wear large turbans to indicate their status and knowledge. They often carry ninety pamphlets. They lean toward where the money is; maybe they can catch some of it."[21] But the institution of al-Azhar Mosque itself was in turmoil, like the rest of Egypt. Some Azharites held more progressive views: they represented a new and emerging generation of the middle class. They later became influential in resisting Turkish control and French colonization. Among them were al-Jabarti, Shaykh al-'Attar, and al-'Attar's student al-Tahtawi, to name just a few. These individuals and their followers played an important role in the following few decades, including attempts to modernize Islamic thought.

The Decline of the Ottoman Dynasty

The decline of Egypt during the late Turkish period was reflected in the deterioration of Islamic institutions, mentioned by al-Jabarti and others. Near the end of the Turkish era, Sufism attracted many followers. Sufism has a deep history in Egypt, as seen by the many tombs and festivals that survive even today. But the attraction during the Ottoman period was not necessarily based on Sufism's strong mystical tradition. Rather it was often based on the belief that Sufis could perform magic or predict the future and had the ability to change events. For some, this became a means to escape the hard realities of life. In one story, a woman who was having an affair with Amir Yusuf al-Kabir was unsure of his love, so she went to a Sufi who claimed he could provide a love charm by writing some incomprehensible letters on her lower belly. When the amir saw the writing, he became furious and demanded to know the meaning of this. She confessed that a woman friend had suggested visiting the Sufi in order to obtain her heart's desire.[22]

The Coptic Church was also deteriorating during the Ottoman period. A couple of examples will illustrate the chaotic state of affairs within the church. In the seventeenth century, during the tenure of patriarch Mark V (1602–18), a bishop declared that Christianity did not forbid polygamy. This notion found acceptance among some rich Copts who wanted to have more than one wife. The church tried to change the bishop's opinion, but their efforts were in vain. Eventually, the bishop was excommunicated. The supporters of polygamy managed, with the help of the administration, to remove Mark V and install another patriarch. But this did not last long, and Mark V returned to his post, with popular support from his followers. During this period some church posts, such as those of priests and bishops, were sold for money.[23]

In addition to internal decay, the Coptic Church faced external threats as well. Catholic and Protestant missionaries started to convert the Copts—including some Coptic priests—to their churches. The Coptic Church was poorly equipped to withstand this invasion. The level of knowledge among the average Coptic clergy was no better than that of their Muslim counterparts, making it difficult for them to counter the arguments of the foreign missionaries. Efforts to convert Muslims were notably unsuccessful, due to a decree by some Islamic scholars that a Muslim who converted to another religion should be killed. We will revisit the missionaries' activities in chapter nine.

An important early effort to throw off foreign control and establish self-government took place between 1765 and 1769. During this period, Shaykh Hammam bin Yusuf, an Egyptian Bedouin, was able to control the south of Egypt from Minya (241 kilometers south of Cairo) to the border with Sudan. Bin Yusuf managed this area independently of the central government of Egypt. He collected his own taxes and maintained his own defense forces. According to Louis Awad,[24] this movement had some of the features of a revolution in which Egyptian farmers and Bedouins supported Hammam's revolt against the central government. Furthermore, Awad thought this revolution created an experimental republican system of government in which the land was removed from the ownership of the Mamluks and distributed to the farmers. 'Afifi mentions that during the independence of the south, Hammam succeeded in managing the affairs of this huge territory and earned the respect of the people—rich and poor, Copts and Muslims. Hammam used the Copts as administrators and tax collectors. This movement threatened the central government in Egypt, and was crushed in 1769 by military force and by conspiracy.[25] Egypt was weak, unstable, and ready for change, as we will see.

8

THE FRENCH ADVENTURE IN EGYPT (1798–1801)

As a result of the Industrial Revolution and the discovery of the New World, the European countries became dominant economic and military powers. They imported tremendous wealth from their vast colonies and exported some of their internal troubles, in the form of religious dissenters and criminals, to the New World. While Europe was rising and modernizing itself, the Middle East and the Islamic world were stagnating, trapped in archaic traditions. Egypt, a crossroads for trade routes to the Far East and Africa, was a prime target for control by Europe.

In the eighteenth century, ongoing conflict between England and France extended to the Middle East. Napoleon wished to establish a French presence in Egypt in order to control the British route to India and the Far East. His ultimate dream was to link the Middle East to France. He is quoted as saying, "Egypt is the most important country in the world. Whoever controls Egypt can control the world."

The British knew the French had dispatched a huge fleet to the eastern Mediterranean but they did not know its exact destination. A British fleet, under the command of Admiral Horatio Nelson, was sent to search, and narrowly missed catching its quarry on several occasions. On June 28, 1798, the British ships arrived at Alexandria. On being informed that the French were not there and that neither French nor British warships were welcome in the lands of the Turkish sultan, Nelson departed on June 29, 1798. Two days later, the French fleet and Napoleon himself arrived in Egypt with four hundred ships loaded with about 54,000 men. They seized control of Alexandria with little difficulty. Within days, the French army was on its way to Cairo, encountering only minimal resistance from the Mamluks along the way. On July 21, the French were in position outside the capital, ready for what became known as the Battle of the Pyramids. This was the real beginning of Napoleon's adventure in Egypt.[1]

When news of the French arrival in Alexandria reached Cairo, the Mamluks thought they could easily confront them and trample them with their horses.[2] Al-Jabarti described how Egyptians in Cairo prepared for the war:

> The shaykhs prayed for victory, while the mob carried sticks, beat their drums, and chanted religious slogans, as if they were going to win the battle by ritual chanting. In the countryside, the mob searched for weapons in foreigners' and Christians' homes. The search then expanded to include churches and monasteries. Mobs wished to kill all Christians, but the authorities prevented them from doing so.[2]

The news that foreign Christians had invaded Egypt stirred up sectarian violence that continued sporadically throughout the several years that the French stayed in Egypt.[3]

The Battle of the Pyramids was brief and decisive. Before the engagement, Napoleon is said to have exhorted his men, "French soldiers, remember that from the top of these pyramids, forty centuries of history look down on you!" It took only forty-five minutes for the French to crush the Mamluk defenses. Some Mamluks escaped to the south of Egypt, and some Muslim leaders escaped to Istanbul to ask the Turks for help. The French victory was a bitter lesson to the Muslim world. Unlike the Crusaders of past centuries, Napoleon's army was equipped with more advanced weapons and strategy, which gave them a decisive advantage over their opponents. Egypt and the Muslim world had stagnated for centuries. It was time for things to change.

While the French were subduing the Mamluks in Cairo, the British fleet, under Nelson, finally caught up with the French warships anchored east of Alexandria, and destroyed most of them in the Battle of the Nile. The transport ships had already sailed back to France. Napoleon was now trapped in Egypt without his navy, and cut off from home by the British, who controlled the sea. In addition, the British were cooperating with the Turkish sultan, who had his own reasons for wanting to keep France out of Egypt.

But Napoleon was resourceful. Even before he arrived in Cairo, he had arranged for the distribution of pamphlets printed in Arabic (using the first Arabic printing machine). The text began with an Islamic invocation:

> In the name of God the Merciful, the Compassionate. There is no God but God. He has no son and no companion in his sovereignty.

> On behalf of France, which was built on the foundation of freedom and equality—the commander in chief of the French armies, Bonaparte, informs the inhabitants of Egypt that the sancaks who hold sway over the land of Egypt, have for a long time treated the rights of the French nation with disgrace and contempt. . . . Now the hour of their punishment has come. How sad that for centuries this band of Mamluks, procured from Georgia and Circassia, has spread corruption in a most beautiful country, one whose equal is not to be found on the whole globe.

Napoleon's flyer mentioned his respect for Islam and the Turkish sultan, and then concluded with the threat that "all villages resisting the French army will be burned."[4]

Under Napoleonic Rule

Napoleon took control of Cairo on July 23, 1798. To govern the country, he established a national assembly of sixty members, representing all the provinces; the head of this assembly was selected by secret ballot. He quickly set up an advisory council *(diwan)* to participate in running the country, along with local diwans in each province. Cairo's local *diwan* was composed of nine members, while provincial *diwans* were composed of seven. All members were clergy, merchants, or other prominent people. This system later was expanded to include Copts and foreigners. This was a revolutionary system, and Egypt had never seen anything like it before. The French tried to duplicate in Egypt what had been done in France as a result of the French Revolution.[5]

The duties of the central *diwan* included (1) selecting the members of the local *diwans* and determining their salaries, (2) designing the judiciary system, (3) creating the inheritance laws to be used in the land, and (4) proposing reforms to the ownership and tax systems. The French plan was later coupled with a reform plan to unify taxation among Egyptians, and to adjust the land taxes according to soil fertility and availability of water. In addition, the French hoped to see the farmers who worked the earth become owners of their own land. Unfortunately, due to political and military disturbances, this system did not achieve its intended results, although it did leave its mark on Egypt in the years that followed.

From the beginning, Napoleon went out of his way to try to win the trust of Muslims, who viewed the French as hated invaders and ungodly "polytheists," that is, Christians who believed in the Trinity. Within a month after reaching Egypt, Napoleon ordered a day of celebration for the birth of the Prophet Muhammad. He and his entourage attended the celebration in al-Azhar Mosque. They were dressed in beautiful Eastern outfits, and sat on cushions on the floor covered with rugs. The festivity was attended by a hundred shaykhs. Napoleon even appeared to be chanting Islamic phrases and moving his head with the chanting, just as the shaykhs were doing. It was a scene that impressed some of the shaykhs. Napoleon repeated that he was "very convinced of the holiness and the purity of Islam."[6]

Napoleon also attempted to remove the advantages enjoyed by Copts who were tax collectors or administrators. Although he relied on the Copts to collect taxes, he did so reluctantly. In some cases, he had no choice; he still appointed the Copt Girgis al-Guhari to be in charge of all the tax collectors, but he watched him closely. Napoleon's intention was to establish a new tax system in which he would not need to depend on the Copts, whom he considered to be thieves and who were hated in the country. However, he recognized that only the Copts knew how to manage Egypt.[7] Later, the French general Menou (Abdallah de Menou, after he converted to Islam and married a Muslim woman) accused the tax collectors of stealing 1,292,143 pounds. He arrested Abu Takia, a tax collector, and fined him 750,000 pounds.[8] Despite these efforts at reform, Copts continued to dominate the field of tax collecting until the British ended the practice at the end of the nineteenth century.

Girgis al-Guhari wrote to Napoleon asking him to remove the restrictions imposed on the Copts by the Mamluks. The answer he received was "It will be my pleasure to remove inhuman restrictions imposed on Copts or any other minority, as it has happened in Europe." Napoleon added, "I will punish severely the villagers who killed Copts during sectarian violence. I will remove all dress codes imposed on the Copts, and allow them to carry weapons to defend themselves and to ride mules and horses." Jacques Tagher, who researched some of the original documents of this period, concluded that Napoleon tried to win the sympathy of the Muslims, but he did not go so far as to persecute the Copts to please the Muslims. At the same time, he did not indicate sympathy for the Copts, nor did he succeed in removing the hatred from some of the Muslims' hearts.[9] Napoleon had to walk a fine line. He was aware that people had accepted him reluctantly, and that even though some shaykhs had welcomed him during their meetings, their welcomes were insincere.

After four months in Egypt, on October 22, 1798, an unexpected popular uprising erupted against the French. Called the "first revolt against the French," it was instigated by some Mamluks and Turks who opposed the French fiscal policy. The center of the rebellion was al-Azhar Mosque. During the rebellion, some French soldiers who were wandering in the city without their weapons were killed, as was the French governor of Cairo.

The French turned their artillery on the most rebellious locations, including even the venerated al-Azhar Mosque. They carried out further acts of punishment, including execution of some al-Azhar scholars and other individuals deemed responsible for inciting the rebellion or joining it. Many people were killed.[10] During this revolt, French troops entered al-Azhar Mosque with their horses; they even tethered their horses to the *mihrab* (the sacred part of the mosque that points toward Mecca), which greatly offended the Muslims. Many Muslims had doubted Napoleon's good intentions toward Islam, but the attack on al-Azhar Mosque removed any remaining illusions. Some Christians were attacked by the Muslim mob during this rebellion.[11]

A few weeks later, a Turkish fleet attacked the French at Alexandria. It was easily defeated and most of the Turkish troops were drowned, killed, or captured. After this battle, when Napoleon met with some prominent Egyptians who visited to congratulate him on his victory, he noticed they seemed sad that he had defeated the Turks. He told them, "I wonder about your sadness, even though I have repeated to you that I am a Muslim. I believe in one God. I love the prophet and the Muslims."[12] By this time, few believed him. In the eyes of most Egyptians, Napoleon and his army were infidels who favored Christians over Muslims.

A state of turmoil persisted. Some Christians were attacked, along with neighboring Muslims.[13] Al-Jabarti, an eyewitness to the upheavals of this period, mentions that a Moroccan group and a group from Arabia started to spy on the homes of French and Christians. They attacked the inhabitants and killed them, making no distinction between men, women, and children.[14]

Did the position of the Copts justify the hostilities against them? Many Muslims connected the Copts to the French, based on religion alone, so the Copts were considered suspect. But according to Tagher, there was no supporting evidence to connect the Copts to the French, except in the case of Mu'allim Ya'qub, an episode described in the next section. In general, the Copts were inclined to dislike the French. All tax collectors, for example, hated the French because they interfered in what the tax collectors thought was their private domain, thus cutting their profits. With non-Coptic Christians, it was a different story. While the French were in Egypt, some

Christians—in particular, the Syrians, Armenians, and Greeks—sought refuge with them. Especially after mistreating Muslims, certain Christians looked to the French for protection from retribution. During the revolt, the mob attacked their homes and even nearby Muslim homes.[15]

Napoleon extended his expedition as far as Syria. He and his troops advanced with ease until they reached the well-fortified city of Acre. Napoleon laid siege to it for three months, but was unable to capture it, so he decided to go back to Egypt and claim victory. During this campaign, the French took prisoner about three thousand Turkish soldiers. All were killed. Shortly after this, Napoleon returned to France. His campaign in Egypt was falling apart and he hoped to find victory in France, which he initially did.

After Napoleon's departure, General Kléber became leader of the French forces in Egypt. He realized the difficulties that faced him, and wanted to take his troops back to France peacefully and with dignity. However, in March 1800, Mamluks and Turks, supported by the British, attacked the French. But Kléber defeated them in Heliopolis, a suburb of Cairo. This was known as the "second revolt against the French." After suppressing the rebellion, Kléber imposed more taxes on all Egyptians, except the Christians. This action led to more difficulties for the Christians, some of whom began to hope that the French would be in Egypt for a long time. However, in a move planned and financed by the Turks, Kléber was assassinated, in June 1800, by the Syrian Islamist Sulayman al-Halabi.[16] Kléber was replaced by Jacques-François de Menou, a Frenchman who had married a Muslim woman, converted to Islam, and took the name Abdallah. General Menou was eager to evacuate the French troops from Egypt. After difficult negotiations with the Turks and the British, the French surrendered to the British and were transported back to France.

The Coptic historian Ya'qub Nakhla Rufila and the Muslim historian al-Jabarti both recount an episode that occurred during the final days of the French in Cairo. Nosoh Basha, the Turkish sultan's representative who was leading some Turkish troops into Cairo to replace the French, incited the mob to kill all Christians. Many Christians were killed, along with some Muslims, and their shops and homes were looted. A Moroccan man and a gang of followers spied on Christians and killed whomever they found. Some Copts and other Christians escaped to the French camp for safety, leaving their belongings behind. One Copt, by the name of Mu'allim Ya'qub, did not try to escape. He fortified and successfully defended his quarters in the Azbakiya neighborhood, a district where many Copts lived and where the Coptic cathedral was located. We will hear more about him shortly. Sectarian violence continued until the French defeated the Turkish troops and forced them out of Cairo.[17]

Mu'allim Ya'qub: Visionary or Traitor?

Probably the most controversial Copt in the past millennium was Mu'allim Ya'qub (meaning "Master Ya'qub," a title given to a respected and knowledgeable person). During the French invasion, Ya'qub cooperated with the French and was fascinated by them. We will elaborate on some of the events that made him controversial because this will shed light on the rift and lack of confidence between Copts and Muslims—not only during that difficult period, but continuing until the present time.

As a young man, Ya'qub made a fortune serving the Mamluks. But when the French arrived, he quickly appreciated their way of thinking, which was modern compared with that of the Mamluks. Ya'qub served the French with devotion and energy, and learned a lot from them. In this respect, he stood out as different from most Copts, who shied away from dealing with the French.

Ya'qub organized the military's mail service to connect French troops in the south of Egypt with Cairo. He then aided General Louis Desaix's campaign against the fleeing Mamluks in the south. He was so helpful to Desaix during this campaign that he received the Sword of Honor award from the French army. He became friendly with Desaix, who must have acquainted him with the principles of the French Revolution, which had taken place less than a decade earlier. Ya'qub was struck by the disparity between the fossilized worldview of the Mamluks and Turks and the modern European outlook of the French in Egypt.[18]

During the March 1800 confrontation between the French and the Mamluks and Turks in Heliopolis, some Turks and Mamluks slipped into Cairo and roused the population. During the turmoil, some Copts were attacked and fled to the French for protection. However, as mentioned above, Ya'qub stayed in his house near Coptic Lane, close to the Coptic patriarchate, in an area where about three thousand Copts lived. Ya'qub barricaded the area and managed to protect it from the mob for twenty days, until Kléber settled the "second revolt against the French." Kléber ordered all the Copts to remain in their quarters, and those who had fled to return to their homes. As a result of Ya'qub's successful defense, a Coptic legion was formed with Kléber's blessing. Ya'qub was given the title of general and had command of nearly a thousand Copts, who wore uniforms similar to those of the French.[19] This convinced many Muslims that Ya'qub had sided with an external enemy against Egypt. However, it should be noted that some Muslims, including some of the Mamluks, also worked under the French army. In fact, the Copts were the last to join the French.[20]

When the French left Egypt, Ya'qub left with them. The Turks asked him to stay and guaranteed his safety, but he preferred to leave with the French, along with some other Egyptians, as part of what was called the Egyptian delegation. He had a plan in mind, but died at sea in August 1801 before reaching France.

Al-Jabarti, who was a member of the General Assembly *(diwan)* established by Napoleon, felt Ya'qub had betrayed his own country by cooperating with the French. Al-Jabarti looked on Ya'qub with contempt. Most Muslim Egyptians saw the French as infidels who threatened Islam and Muslims, especially after the French shelled al-Azhar Mosque during the "first revolt." The French invasion also reminded Muslims of the Crusades, which had brought foreign Christian armies into Egypt. Copts disliked the French for other reasons. They saw the French as outsiders whose presence stirred up sectarian violence against them, and who interfered in the business of tax collecting, thus reducing the profits of the Coptic elite. Most Copts did not approve of Ya'qub's cooperation with the French.

The impact of Ya'qub's story did not end with his departure and his death en route to Europe. More than a century later, the Muslim historian Muhammad Shafiq Ghurbal (1894–1961) revisited the Ya'qub episode. In 1932, he revealed documents from the British foreign ministry that contained discussions between Ya'qub and a principal naval officer while on their way to Europe. Ghurbal called these discussions the first proposal for the independence of Egypt.[21] As a result of the documents, Ya'qub appeared in a new light. He had hoped for a free Egypt, based on an Egyptian military force that would be trained and equipped according to modern European standards. He wanted to prevent Egypt from sliding back into the chaos and violence that had existed under the Turks and Mamluks. Ya'qub thought any government that might result from European intervention or assistance would be better than the government Egypt had had before the Napoleonic campaign.

Ya'qub is considered by some a traitor and by others a visionary. He never had the chance to pursue his vision because he died on his way to Europe and his vision died with him. What Ghurbal wrote did not attract much attention at the time. But in 1969, Louis Awad, a Copt, included Ghurbal's data when writing a comprehensive historical perspective of political efforts to modernize Egypt. He included a discussion about the role of the French presence in Egypt.[22] In his final analysis, Awad concluded it would be a mistake to consider either Muslims (such as ‘Umar Makram) who sought help from the Turks to liberate Egypt from French occupation, or Copts (such as Mu‘allim Ya‘qub) who wanted help from Europe to liberate Egypt from Turkish colonization, as movements motivated solely by religious affiliation. Awad thought both Makram and Ya‘qub wanted to see an independent Egypt. They represented different schools of thinking and chose different routes, but neither should be considered a traitor. Awad's view, however, raised an outcry along sectarian lines that has continued to the present time. In 2006, Raga' al-Naqqash, a well-known writer and editor, criticized Awad's analysis of Ya‘qub's attempt to liberate Egypt based on European help.[23] Al-Naqqash believed that Ya‘qub was a traitor and that the story of his seeking Egyptian independence had been fabricated. Other writers have also been critical of Awad,[24] reflecting the increasing influence of political Islam.

Ultimately, Egypt's efforts to modernize did come about through contact with Europe. As will be discussed in the next chapter, Muhammad ‘Ali and his descendants used Europeans as consultants and sent many Egyptians to study in Europe. In this way, Muhammad ‘Ali "brought Europe to Egypt." But his efforts were derided by some radical Islamists, who called him Wali (or ally) al-Nassara, meaning 'ruler of the Christians.' Nevertheless, it was under Muhammad ‘Ali that the modernization of Egypt began.

The End of the French Adventure in Egypt and Its Effects

In July 1801, as the British orchestrated the evacuation of the French from Egypt, Turkish forces entered Cairo. People were happy to see the Turkish troops, but they were soon disillusioned. The Turkish troops were a mixture of different Muslim ethnic groups who fought among themselves. The years from 1801 to 1805 were chaotic. Instead of being a liberating force, the Turkish troops turned into something else. They became involved in trade, expelled people from their buildings and took over those buildings, and became just another colonial occupier.

Al-Jabarti described the Turks as "the worst kind of people to have walked the face of the Earth." He preferred the French infidels over the Turks who claimed to be the protectors of Islam. Al-Jabarti was particularly impressed by the French example of justice meted out by law. After being exposed to two cultures and the practice of two religions, he concluded that the concept of justice is not connected to religion. As an example of French respect for the law, he noted that, in 1798, the French had shot to death three Frenchmen because they were stealing from homes.[25] He was also particularly interested in observing the just trial of the Syrian man who was accused of assassinating General Kléber.[26] Awad has mentioned additional examples of French respect for the law.

The French episode in Egypt, and its aftermath, sharpened the conflict between the forces of conservatism and those of modernity. In 1802, when the French ambassador Sebastiani visited the scholars in al-Azhar University, some expressed hopes that the French would return to Egypt.[27] Others felt threatened. Al-Jabarti recognized many of the difficulties Egypt suffered during this chaotic period. He pointed out the antiquated knowledge of Egypt's leaders, in general, and of al-Azhar University, in particular. Al-Azhar was the only institution of higher learning in Egypt at the time, and its leaders resisted new ideas. Their interest was in maintaining their high social status.[28] But a movement to modernize this venerable institution was brewing beneath the surface, as we will see shortly. Not surprisingly, Egypt still suffers from these same fundamental problems today, more than two centuries later.

During chaotic periods, the Copts tended to be targets of mob violence, and the period following the French withdrawal was no exception. After the French left, there was a rumor that the sultan had issued a declaration that Christians must comply with the dress code. In response, a mob started to strip any Christians who appeared in the streets wearing good clothes. Al-Jabarti thought this did not represent a victory for Islam, but rather just took advantage of helpless people. Within a month, the sultan declared that no one should harass the Christians because Christians "are the subjects of the sultan."[29]

In summary, the French adventure in Egypt, though it lasted less than three years, had a profound impact. It brought Egypt face to face with the European Enlightenment. It also made Egypt the subject of intense scientific study. Along with his troops, Napoleon had brought with him to Egypt 167 of France's best scientists, scholars, and artists. While some of them helped the campaign from a military point of view, they also collected much information on the geography, history, and natural science of Egypt. On August 20, 1798, Napoleon inaugurated the Institut d'Egypte, which produced articles on physics, mathematics, economics, medicine, art, literature, sociology, demography, the Nile, and many other topics. The Institut d'Egypte was open to Egyptians who showed an interest in this work, including al-Jabarti and other Azharite shaykhs.[30]

Based on notes, drawings, and samples collected by Napoleon's expedition, France published *La Description de l'Egypte*, a comprehensive set of volumes that examined virtually every aspect of Egypt's natural history, both ancient and modern. The first volume was published in 1809, and the final volume in 1829. *La Description de l'Egypte* is still a good source of information about Egypt at that time.

The Institut d'Egypte survived into modern times. Over the years, many prominent Egyptian scientists have been members. Unfortunately, on December 17, 2011, the Institut suffered a devastating fire, the exact circumstances of which are unknown. The destruction of about 200,000 original manuscripts and rare books was a great loss, reminiscent of that of the ancient Library of Alexandria.

9

MUHAMMAD 'ALI DYNASTY (1805–1952)

After the French left, Egypt once again came under the rule of the Ottomans and the Mamluks. But the Ottoman Empire itself was in turmoil. The war with Austria and Russia had exposed weaknesses in the Ottoman army, which lacked discipline and modern equipment. There was also chaos at the top. During the short-lived French adventure in Egypt, Sultan Selim III held power (1789–1807). He was a well-educated reformer, with an appetite for literature, music, art, and modernity. But he was opposed by the clergy and by a segment of the military. In 1807, he was ousted from power and replaced by his cousin, Mustafa IV. One year later, both Selim and Sultan Mustafa IV were assassinated, and Selim's brother took the throne.

In the midst of this turmoil, an important figure arose in Egypt. Muhammad 'Ali was an Albanian commander who had come with the Ottoman army to reoccupy Egypt during the evacuation of the French. He emerged as an opportunist and a shrewd, visionary politician who was able to take advantage of the power vacuum created by the struggle between the Mamluks and the Ottomans. First, he allied himself with the popular shaykhs of al-Azhar, the most respected and influential Egyptian institution at the time. In 1805, the Azharite shaykhs demanded that Muhammad 'Ali replace the Ottoman governor of Egypt *(wali)* Ahmad Khurshid Basha. They succeeded in persuading or pressuring Sultan Selim III to approve their choice. Muhammad 'Ali agreed to consult with the Azharite shaykhs about the future of the country, but this agreement did not last long.

During this internal power struggle, an external European threat was on the horizon. The Mamluk leader al-Alfi was cooperating with the British to invade Egypt. The British fleet arrived in Egypt in 1807, accompanied by about six thousand troops. However, al-Alfi died before the fleet landed, disrupting the British plan. Ultimately, the British were defeated by the Egyptians, and the 1807–1809 campaign failed.

The Founder of Modern Egypt

By 1809, Muhammad 'Ali's power was on the rise; however, he faced resistance from two sides. The first was from the Azharite shaykhs, who were angered that Muhammad 'Ali had stopped consulting them and was ignoring the commitments he had made to them. Through careful maneuvering, Muhammad 'Ali was able to divide the ranks of the shaykhs. He exiled their leader, 'Umar Makram, in August 1809. Without a united front, the Azharite shaykhs lost much of their power to resist Muhammad 'Ali.

The second and more important resistance to Muhammad 'Ali came from the Mamluks. They posed the greatest threat because, although they only numbered about twenty-five hundred at that time, they were armed and had followers.[1] Muhammad 'Ali was determined to destroy them. First, as with the shaykhs, he used political maneuvers to divide their leadership; then he plotted to kill them. He invited the Mamluk leaders to attend a feast honoring his son, who was about to lead an army to Arabia to put down a Wahhabist rebellion against the Ottoman sultan.[2] On March 1, 1811, 470 Mamluks accepted Muhammad 'Ali's invitation to the well-fortified citadel. There they were surrounded by Muhammad 'Ali's loyal troops, who set upon the Mamluks and slaughtered them in the midst of the festivities. It is said that only one managed to escape, by jumping with his horse over the citadel's wall. Other Mamluks who had not attended the feast were hunted down and killed by Muhammad 'Ali's troops in Cairo and other districts. The total number of Mamluks killed was about one thousand.[3] When Egyptians learned what had happened to the Mamluks, a mob gathered and started to attack the Mamluks' homes, taking whatever they could put their hands on. Many Mamluks were killed by the mob. The rioting continued until the *wali*'s men intervened and took control of the city.[4]

This was the end of nearly six centuries of Mamluk power in Egypt. Although this terrible slaughter rid Muhammad 'Ali and Egypt of the Mamluks, it caused the Egyptians to feel terrified of their new ruler. Few were inclined to challenge him. Now that he had weakened the Azharite shaykhs and disposed of the Mamluks, Muhammad 'Ali had a free hand to remake Egypt as he wished.

Muhammad 'Ali recognized Egypt's potential. He wanted to modernize the country and build a strong army based on the science of the time. The army he created is considered by some historians to be the main achievement that made modern Egypt possible. Though he was born the son of a tobacco merchant from a small town in northern Greece, Muhammad 'Ali had worked as a tax collector and had gained military experience under the Ottomans. He had risen to the rank of commander, leading an Albanian contingent as part of the Ottoman army that had reoccupied Egypt in 1801.[5] With this background, he was well qualified to reorganize both the army and the country. He instituted a number of reforms, applying the same scientific approach he used to build the army, with varying degrees of success.

Strengthening the military was a high priority for Muhammad 'Ali. He introduced a military draft to increase the size of the army; this was the first time in more than two thousand years that a draft had been used in Egypt. Initially, the army was headed by Turks and Albanians, but later the leaders were Egyptians. Copts were excluded from military service because they were paying the *jizya*. When the *jizya* was abolished, during the rule of Muhammad 'Ali's son, Sa'id Basha, Copts joined the army.

Muhammad 'Ali nationalized all the land and monopolized crop production, especially cotton, which had been introduced to Egypt by a French agronomist. He transformed a largely subsistence agriculture into an export-oriented economy, with cotton as one of the promising new cash crops. The country was now trading in important commodities that allowed Muhammad 'Ali to finance a strong army and a modern state. The government bought the wheat from farmers for eighteen piasters per *ardab* (150 kilograms) and sold it to Europe for one hundred piasters. As a result of this policy, the prices of some commodities increased two to three times, and inflation increased.[6]

Muhammad 'Ali employed a forced-labor system (*sukhra* in Arabic; *corvée* in French) for building public works. Young men were rounded up in their villages and sent to work on various projects. Some never returned home; they worked until they died. The *sukhra* system was resented by Egyptians, especially by the helpless poor, who saw middle-class and rich Egyptians paying money in lieu of doing this service.

In his attempt to modernize Egypt, Muhammad 'Ali realized he had to employ European talent and technology not only to build a strong army but also to build schools, barrages, dams, factories, and hospitals. Antoine Barthélémy Clot, a French doctor, founded the first modern medical school in Cairo, which included a teaching hospital of 720 beds. An important road in Old Cairo is named after him. Muhammad 'Ali invited unemployed French officers, who constituted the remains of the defeated Napoleonic army, to stay in Egypt. In addition, Greeks, Italians, and Armenians were employed as administrators, technicians, teachers, foremen, and even skilled laborers.[7]

Although Muhammad 'Ali sought out talented men regardless of their religious affiliation, upper-level positions often went to foreign Christians, who as a result enjoyed a relatively high standard of living. This annoyed many Muslims, and earned Muhammad 'Ali the derogatory title *Wali al-Nassara* (literally, 'The Ruler of the Christians'). Neither the Copts nor the Egyptian Muslims had the training or technical expertise to build modern institutions, or even to compete with European middlemen in the new market for cotton, grains, and other agricultural export products.[8] The influx of Westerners and Western ideas introduced new models of organization, and paved the way for Copts and Muslims to participate in the community and in government in ways they had not done before. The results of these changes became evident in the nineteenth and twentieth centuries, as we will discuss.[9]

To fund his modernization program, Muhammad 'Ali needed to maximize tax revenue. Tax collection under the Ottomans and Mamluks had been chaotic due to the arbitrary taxes levied by different princes at different times. Muhammad 'Ali wanted to standardize the system and implement it efficiently. For this, he had to rely on the Copts, as previous rulers had done. Although the profession of tax collecting was very profitable, the way it was practiced was riddled with corruption. In order to put a stop to these practices, Muhammad 'Ali had the tax collectors arrested on charges of corruption. They were then reinstated after they had paid large fines. In some cases, the tax collectors were able to negotiate how much money they had to pay. This pattern was repeated several times during this period.[10]

As conditions in Egypt became more orderly, Coptic–Muslim relations also improved. Muhammad 'Ali was not a religious fanatic; he was known as a harsh, but just, ruler who was determined to curb abuses regardless of the religious affiliation of those involved. Jacques Tagher, who researched some of the original documents from this period, tells the story of a quarrel between a Copt and a Muslim. The Muslim complained to the governor of Damietta. The governor ordered that the Copt be whipped five hundred times, and then taken on a walk through the Coptic quarters as a humiliating lesson to the Copts. When Muhammad 'Ali learned of this incident, he sent a high-ranking officer to Damietta with an order to imprison the governor in Alexandria for five years and to fine him a large monetary sum.[11]

Throughout history, from the time the Arabs arrived in Egypt to the present time, better Coptic–Muslim relations have often been associated with a stable and orderly central government. Muhammad 'Ali's era was no exception. During his tenure, there were no restrictions on building or restoring churches. The poll tax continued to be collected from Copts, but it is unclear whether Copts were still subjected to a dress code. In a period of just a few years, Coptic–Muslim relations improved significantly.

Muhammad 'Ali founded many vocational schools. To improve the standard of knowledge, he sent educational expeditions to European countries, especially to France. Between 1826 and 1847, he sent nine expeditions, totaling about five hundred students—among them, his own sons. These students studied a number of subjects such as agriculture, chemistry, medicine, mining, and industrial development.[12]

Rifa'a al-Tahtawi was an Azharite shaykh who accompanied one of the expeditions to France as an imam, to give Islamic sermons to the students. Al-Tahtawi stayed in France from 1826 until 1831 and mastered the French language. During this and later periods, he wrote and translated a number of important books. Al-Tahtawi said, "I have seen the ethics of Islam in France, but I haven't seen Muslims. In Egypt, we have Muslims, but we don't have the ethics of Islam." This slogan became well known among Egyptian intellectuals who were trying to reform Egypt. It indicated how far removed Muslims had become from the true spirit of Islam. Al-Tahtawi's many writings are considered an important contribution to the enlightenment of modern Egypt.

Muhammad 'Ali is considered the founder of modern Egypt. In addition to a strong army, he built a new educational system. He not only defended Egypt but expanded its territory. His military campaigns added Sudan, Arabia, Syria, and Palestine and reached as far as Greece and Anatolia, thereby threatening the Ottoman Empire. Eventually, he encountered resistance from Europe. In a conference held in London on May 15, 1840, Great Britain, Russia, Prussia (now part of Germany), and Turkey agreed to allow Egypt to keep only southern Syria (Palestine), Arabia, and Sudan. Muhammad 'Ali was given ten days to accept these terms. He refused. The British responded with military action against Egypt, primarily in southern Syria. Hostilities began in September and continued through November 1840. The Egyptian army and navy were overpowered, Egypt was defeated, and Muhammad 'Ali's territory shrank to what historically had constituted Egypt.[13] Despite this setback, Muhammad 'Ali managed to found a dynasty and secure a legacy for his descendants. Ailing and senile in his last years, he died in 1849, after having ruled Egypt for about half a century.

The Dynasty after the Death of Muhammad 'Ali

Prior to his death, Muhammad 'Ali was succeeded by his eldest and most trusted son, Ibrahim. However, Ibrahim was also ill, and died in 1848.

He was succeeded in turn by Muhammad 'Ali's grandson, Abbas, who ruled until 1854, when he was murdered by two of his slaves. Abbas was a weak ruler who hated all Christians, and expelled many of the European experts Muhammad 'Ali had brought to Egypt. Abbas also wanted to expel all the Copts to Sudan, but the shaykh of al-Azhar, Ibrahim al-Bajuri, refused to issue a fatwa that allowed him to do so. Al-Bajuri told Abbas that the Copts were the original Egyptians and that Islamic views toward them had not changed.[14]

In 1854, the throne went to Muhammad 'Ali's fourth son, Sa'id Basha. Sa'id continued the tolerant policy toward Christians started by Muhammad 'Ali. In 1855, he ended the *jizya* that had been imposed on non-Muslims since the Arab invasion of Egypt. A few years later, the Ottoman Empire also ended the *jizya*, after Europe penetrated the weakened empire and forced them to do so. The Copts welcomed Sa'id's decision, and many named their sons Sa'id in his honor. The ending of the tax removed the last formal obstacle to equality between Copts and Muslims. Copts were now subject to serve in the army under the draft system, as Muslims did.

In 1856, Sa'id selected Arakel Nobar Bek, a Christian Armenian-Egyptian, to rule Sudan. However, Arakel died within two years from a tropical disease.[15] He was the first non-Muslim to rule a large Muslim territory.

An important highlight of Sa'id's tenure was the initiation of the Suez Canal project. Earlier attempts to connect the Mediterranean and the Red Sea can be traced as far back as the thirteenth century BC under the pharaohs. Thirty centuries later, Napoleon, during his short time in Egypt, considered constructing a canal. But the calculations of French engineers in 1799 showed that the discrepancy between the sea levels on each side was too great to allow navigation through the canal, so the project was halted. A few years later, the project was suggested again to Muhammad 'Ali, but he refused to undertake it because he feared it might lead to European intervention in Egypt.

Ferdinand de Lesseps (1805–94), a French diplomat who served in Alexandria and Cairo in 1832–33, was a friend of Sa'id Basha. After Sa'id became the ruler of Egypt, he invited de Lesseps to visit him on November 7, 1854. By the end of this month-long visit, and without even doing a feasibility study, they had signed a contract to construct the Suez Canal. The concession granted to de Lesseps gave him ownership of the land and the company for ninety-nine years. In addition, Egypt was to provide 80 percent of the labor (under the *corvée* system) and would receive 15 percent of the profits from the canal. The cost of the project was estimated by de Lesseps to be about 200 million pounds, with Egypt being responsible for about 45 percent of this amount.[16] This was the beginning of major financial difficulties for Egypt. In addition, the project was plagued by poor management. Sa'id did not pay attention to details, and unchecked European influence in Egypt increased significantly during his tenure; his relationship with de Lesseps is just one example.[17]

Isma'il Basha, Sa'id's nephew and prime minister, succeeded him in 1863. In 1867, the Ottoman sultan granted him the hereditary title of khedive. Under Isma'il, Coptic–Muslim relations continued to improve. While Sa'id had fostered tolerance toward Christians, Isma'il's government promoted full equality. During Isma'il's tenure, the political system was opened up for wider participation by both Muslims and Copts. During her extended visit to Egypt, Lucy Duff-Gordon (1821–69) observed that the town of Biba had selected a Coptic mayor even though the population was overwhelmingly Muslim, with only thirteen Coptic families. She observed that the Muslims and the Copts were very tolerant of each other.[18]

Isma'il encouraged changes in social customs as well. For example, when a Copt converted to Islam, it was traditional to hold a festival honoring the new convert by taking him on a tour of the town, dressed in white. This public demonstration was intended, in part, to humiliate the Copts, so to avoid bad feelings between Copts and Muslims, Isma'il banned this activity. In addition, he ordered that, whenever someone converted to Islam, a meeting be held to ensure that the conversion had been freely chosen and was not the result of outside pressure. Priests and the mayor of the village attended these meetings.[19]

In his attempt to modernize and beautify Cairo, Isma'il suggested the road to the old Coptic cathedral on Clot Bey Street be extended. Since this would entail demolishing the existing cathedral, he consulted the Coptic patriarch Demetrius II (1862–70) and offered to build a new, fancier cathedral as a replacement at government expense. The patriarch objected to Isma'il's proposal because he did not want to tear down a cathedral to build a road. Isma'il respected the patriarch's wish, and the original cathedral remained in place.[20]

Isma'il had been educated in France and Austria. He was fascinated by the European educational system and wanted to copy in Egypt much of what he had seen in Europe. For the first time in Egyptian history, a Muslim ruler supported the church's educational system. Isma'il financed Coptic schools that taught modern science, foreign languages, history, geography, and some engineering principles. He also granted an endowment to these schools of 1500 feddans (equal to about 1500 acres).[21] These schools were founded in Cairo, Alexandria, and other big cities during the tenure of Patriarch Cyril IV (1854–62). There were twelve schools, including two schools for women (the first in Egypt), as well as a vocational school. Isma'il supported these schools financially, and allowed their graduates to be exempt from the military draft. Both Copts and Muslims were allowed to attend all of these schools, and some graduates became ministers and prime ministers in the administration.[22]

In 1866, Isma'il founded the first elected consultative body (Majlis al-Shura). Any native-born Egyptians over the age of twenty-five were allowed to run for this consultative body, which had seventy-five members. Both Copts and Muslims were elected. Some of the elected Copts were mayors and other officials in the administration. The Egyptian thinker and judge Tariq al-Bishri has listed some of the names of the elected Coptic officials.[23] One of the topics discussed in the Majlis was whether to accept Copts in public schools without restriction.[24] Isma'il took pride in showcasing equal treatment of Copts and Muslims; his administration included two Christian prime ministers, Nubar Basha and Boutros Basha, who represented him at high-profile Islamic festivities.[25]

Not everything was so positive, however. Isma'il quickly discovered that the terms of the Suez Canal concession, granted to de Lesseps by his predecessor Sa'id Basha, were not fair or even tenable for Egypt. Therefore, the contract between de Lesseps and the Egyptian government was modified to reduce the labor and land allocated to the company, in exchange for a payment of 4.2 million pounds.[26] Isma'il had to borrow money from European banks to meet this cost, and the banks were happy to lend it to Egypt. Excavation for the canal began in 1859 and was completed in 1869. The inauguration festivities were attended by many European dignitaries, including Empress Eugénie, wife of Napoleon III. Verdi was commissioned to compose the opera *Aida* for this occasion. The opera was first performed at the recently built Opera House in Cairo on December 24, 1871. After the inaugural festivities were over, Isma'il announced, "Egypt is now part of Europe." But modernization came at a high cost.

During his sixteen years in office, Isma'il spent about 200 million pounds on modernization projects. The money was raised through a combination of heavy taxation and by borrowing from European lenders at high interest rates of between 12 percent and 27 percent.[27] Isma'il also borrowed from rich Egyptians. According to Louis Awad, Isma'il spent 46 million pounds to finish the Suez Canal, dredge the many irrigation canals, build bridges and sugar factories, improve harbors, and construct railroads and telegraph lines.[28] In addition, he established 4,817 elementary and secondary schools (his predecessor had built only 185), as well as four schools of higher education.[29] Additional costs went to increasing the army from 18,000 to 95,000. This was done to support numerous military involvements which included extending Egyptian influence into Ethiopia, helping the Turkish sultan in Yemen and Russia, and aiding the French in Mexico. Other expenditures included financing expeditions to discover the source of the Nile, beautifying the big cities and providing them with water and light, building thirty palaces and an opera house, and hosting extravagant festivities to mark the opening of the Suez Canal.[30]

Egypt's debts by the end of Isma'il's reign reached 95 million pounds. The amount Isma'il received from European lenders was 32 million pounds, but the accumulated interest inflated this sum to 95 million.[31] Isma'il is often accused of corruption and mismanagement, but we should judge him in the context of all his many accomplishments. Some of his spending was extravagant and unnecessary, but during his tenure Egypt advanced in modernity more than it had in the several hundred years before.

During the last two years of Isma'il's reign, financial difficulties increased. He commissioned the British judge and paymaster-general Sir Steven Cave to study Egypt's financial problems. On March 23, 1876, Cave attributed the difficulties not to bankruptcy, but to poor management. He concluded that Egypt had the resources to meet its debts if it was better managed.[32] Under pressure from the British and French lenders, Isma'il agreed to allow dual Anglo-French control over Egypt's finances. The Anglo-French controllers became ministers in the administration, with veto power over expenditures. They decided that 66 percent of the government's revenue would go to its creditors and the remaining 44 percent would go to cover the rest of the government's expenses. These included annual payments of about ten million pounds to the Turkish sultan, as well as the cost of maintaining the irrigation system, schools, healthcare system, police, and security forces.[33] The Anglo-French view was that the government's expenditures, including the cost of maintaining the army, had to be significantly reduced. Finally, under pressure from Great Britain and France, Isma'il was forced to abdicate the throne in June 1879. He was replaced by his eldest son, Tawfiq Basha.

The American consul in Cairo, A.E. Farmland, expressed surprise that the European governments had exercised their power over Egyptian's debts, because the liberal trade laws of the nineteenth century did not allow states to intervene to protect private investors in the case of bankruptcy, unless there was proven misrepresentation. Otherwise, investors were allowed to assume the risk. In this case, the European banks were partially responsible because they had lent Isma'il money time and again even though they were aware of his circumstances.[34]

The Coptic Church and Colonialism

During Ottoman rule in Egypt, the Coptic Church, along with the rest of the country, continued to suffer from poor management and an archaic worldview. During that period, most Egyptians, especially in the villages, knew almost nothing about their respective religions beyond their rituals. This left them poorly defended against the influx of new political and religious ideas from the West which began with Napoleon and continued later under British and American influence.

After the Enlightenment and the Industrial Revolution, European countries expanded their power and started to colonize many parts of the world. Often the first toehold of colonization was gained through evangelical missions which were sent to preach Christianity to the native population. Long before actual military colonization of Egypt, Western missionaries tried to convert Egyptians to Catholicism or Protestantism.[35] They also provided schools, orphanages, and medical services. Gradually, the influence of the missionaries expanded. In 1878, the American Presbyterian Church was able to open thirty-five schools.[36] In 1898, the Catholic Church was granted its own head of the church in Egypt, appointed by the Vatican.

The missionaries' inroads on the Coptic Church were an incentive to educate and modernize the archaic Coptic Church itself. Coptic Pope Cyril IV (1854–61) was a reformer, and he saw that the way to resist this invasion was through better education.[37] To further this goal, he purchased a new printing press from Europe—one of the earliest presses in Egypt to be privately owned.[38]

The next patriarch, Demetrius II (1862–70), was also instrumental in resisting the influence of the missionaries. However, he was more active in his resistance than his predecessor had been, with mixed results.[39] Demetrius II continued to get support from Khedive Isma'il, who gave the pope a boat to travel up and down the Nile. The pope made several stops in areas where the missionaries were active, and warned the Copts against sending their children to the missionary schools. He even sent priests to threaten those who did not obey with excommunication. As a result of this campaign, the number of students in missionary schools declined. American missionaries looked to the American and British consulates for help.[40] One missionary, John Hogg, along with the American consul, visited Demetrius II to protest his harsh campaign against the missionaries. They tried to allay his worries by saying, "We just teach the Bible. There is no reason for concern." The patriarch replied, "If you really know the Bible, why don't you teach it to your slave owners? Why don't you teach it to the brother who is fighting his brother in the Civil War? We had the Bible long before America was discovered."[40]

How serious was the Protestant (and, to a lesser extent, Catholic) threat to the Coptic Church? Certainly there were isolated incidents. In one case, evangelical youths broke into a Coptic Church in Asyut and burned and destroyed some of its icons, resulting in some of the youths being arrested and sentenced to prison.[41] But the main threat was demographic. In 1875, there were only six hundred Egyptian Protestants in Egypt. By 1947, this number had increased to 90,967. In 1904, there were about twenty-two thousand Egyptian Catholics. This number had increased to 80,180 by 1947.[42] S.S. Hassan estimated that between 5 and 10 percent of Copts had been converted to other Christian denominations by missionaries prior to 1952, while the number of Muslims converting to Christianity in any form did not exceed a hundred.[43] The Coptic Church was losing members and wanted to stem the outflow.

In addition to the demographic threat, the growing presence of Western denominations had political implications. Pope Demetrius's successor, Cyril V (1874–1927), continued the resistance against the missionaries' activities. He was also a nationalist and a supporter of the Urabi and Zaghlul revolts, which will be discussed in the following chapters. In resisting the missionaries, Cyril V was resisting the growing power of colonial interests. However, Muslims did not always see it that way. As had happened in earlier eras, the presence of Western Christians heightened tensions between Egyptian Muslims and their Coptic neighbors. In her volume on American evangelicals in Egypt, Heather J. Sharkey writes:

> [American missionaries] inadvertently mobilized anti-colonial nationalists and Islamists against a perceived cultural onslaught, galvanizing men like Hassan al-Banna, founder of the Muslim Brotherhood. By associating themselves with British colonial and American consular powers while working closely with local

> Christians, they planted doubts among many Muslims about the likely pro-Western sympathies of Egyptian Christians—doubts that continue to strain Egyptian inter-communal relations today.[44]

The presence of the missionaries did have some positive effects on the Coptic Church, which later implemented many practices copied from the missionaries, including the custom of Sunday schools. The first Egyptian Coptic Sunday school was founded by Habib Girgis (1856–1951), a graduate of the Egyptian Coptic Theology School, which was established in Egypt in 1893. In 1941, a conference of Egyptian Coptic Sunday schools attended by 350 teachers representing fifty branches urged teachers to start Sunday schools everywhere in Egypt. The movement of Coptic Sunday schools was instrumental in creating a new generation of educated Copts who were ready to lead the church half a century later.

10

THE URABI REVOLT (1879–82)

The Urabi revolt was the pretext for Great Britain to occupy and take control of Egypt in 1882. The revolt arose as a response to the growing influence of the British and French, who had taken control of Egypt's finances after the catastrophic debts incurred under Isma'il Basha. When Isma'il protested against foreign intervention, the British had him replaced by his son, Tawfiq, who was more inclined to go along with their wishes. The British in Egypt used their relationship with the Muslims and their relationship with the Copts in different ways to serve their own ends, as we will see in the next chapter. Despite British efforts to divide the communities, the Urabi revolt revealed a strong unity between the Coptic and Muslim leaders as they met the political challenges of their time. It was a pivotal period in Egyptian history, worth looking at in some detail.

As a young man, Ahmed Urabi (1841–1911) learned reading, writing, and mathematics under a Coptic teacher by the name of Michael Ghatas. They both lived in an integrated Coptic and Muslim community.[1] Urabi's early education also included studying at al-Azhar University, where he learned passages of the Qu'ran, an asset that later made him popular among the masses. Urabi was accepted into the armed forces after Sa'id Basha started to include the sons of mayors and distinguished farmers as officers in the army. During his military service, Urabi witnessed discrimination toward Egyptians by non-native Egyptian officers of Turkish, Circassian, and Albanian origin. He himself was forced to remain at the rank of lieutenant colonel for nineteen years, before he was allowed to become a full colonel. This kind of discrimination increased his political awareness and eventually brought Urabi to the forefront of Egyptian political life as a potential leader.[2]

As French and British influence increased, the influx of foreigners into the administration was increasingly resented. Although their membership reached only 2 percent, foreigners received 15 percent of government salaries.[3] Resistance to the increased foreign influence crystallized around the slogan "Egypt for the Egyptians." This slogan was embodied in a new political party called the National Party (al-Hizb al-Watani). The party's manifesto was jointly formulated and presented by Muhammad 'Abduh (a Muslim) and Louis Sabunji (a Christian). The platform of the party was political and not religious. Membership was open to anyone, regardless of religion or social status. The egalitarian principles of the National Party foreshadowed those of the Urabi revolt.[4]

On February 18, 1879, in an effort to cut government expenditures, a number of army officers were forced to retire on half salaries. They had not been paid for eighteen months. About 2,500 officers demonstrated and briefly arrested the prime minister, Nubar Basha, and the British minister, Sir Charles Rivers Wilson.[5] This was the first mutiny in the Egyptian army's modern history. The administration resigned, and the decision to retire the officers was temporarily halted.

The army's unrest continued. The new administration under Tawfiq Basha decided to reduce the size of the army from 95,000 troops—built up under Isma'il—to a mere 12,000. In addition to reducing costs, this step allowed selective retention of Turkish, Circassian, and Albanian officers who were more loyal to Tawfiq. Reducing the size of the Egyptian army was one more step toward eliminating it altogether in preparation for British control of Egypt.

The minister of war at the time was the Circassian Osman Rifki Basha, who was closely related to Tawfiq Basha. Rifki removed some of the high-ranking native Egyptian officers and replaced them with non-Egyptians. The native officers resented this decision. They united under the leadership of Ahmed Urabi, and sent a delegation of three officers, headed by Urabi, to petition Prime Minister Riyad Basha to remove Rifki on the grounds that his policy was discriminatory and unjust. Urabi and two other officers were arrested, but were quickly released in a counter-move orchestrated by some of their compatriots, who had anticipated the arrest.[6] Rifki was removed and replaced by an officer acceptable to Urabi's group. At this point, Egyptians outside the army were becoming reluctant to accept what amounted to a virtual takeover of their government by foreigners. These civilians awaited their opportunity to overthrow Tawfiq and drive his associates back across the Mediterranean.[7]

Urabi made his move on September 9, 1881. Responding to the impotence of Prime Minister Riyad Basha's government in dealing with increasing unrest among the officers, Urabi led a strong representation of the army to the Abdin Palace, the residence of Tawfiq Basha. He demanded removal of the administration, reinstatement of the Parliament, and various changes regarding the army. Tawfiq, surrounded by foreign consuls, met with the demonstrators. After a short but heated exchange, Tawfiq told Urabi and the other officers, "You have no right to make any demands. I inherited this land from my parents and grandparents." Urabi responded by saying, "We shall no longer be inheritable, and from this day on we shall not be enslaved." This was the second and the most serious mutiny by the army.[8]

Tawfiq retreated to his palace and left the foreign consuls to negotiate with Urabi and the rest of the officers. The confrontation ended with a significant achievement by Urabi and his supporters. After some negotiation, Riyad Basha's administration was removed. Urabi's group's recommendation for prime minister was Muhammad Sherif Basha, the head of the National Party and also the head of the Egyptian aristocracy. Tawfiq accepted the new prime minister, but Sherif Basha initially declined the post because the offer came from the army officers. Urabi gathered the members of the consulting Parliament, and they met with Sherif Basha and requested he accept the post of prime minister. Sherif Basha accepted the post on two conditions: (1) that Urabi's officers be removed from Cairo along with their battalions, and (2) that Tawfiq guarantee the safety of the officers. Urabi agreed, and both conditions were accepted. Following this, events snowballed. Sherif Basha's administration was short-lived. Placed in an impossible position between the demands of the dual controllers (the British and the French) and the Parliament, Sherif Basha was forced to resign on February 2, 1882, after less than five months in office.[9] Several changes accelerated the inevitable seizure of control by the British. By February 5, 1882, another administration had formed. Urabi became the minister of war. The Urabi revolt gained the support of various prominent civilian groups, as well as the National Party. There was even discussion of removing Tawfiq altogether.[10]

By this time, Alexandria was ready to explode. On one hand, people felt hemmed in by the presence of the British fleet, which was positioned within sight of the city. On the other hand, they resented the presence of a large number of foreigners, some of whom were armed, exerting control within the city itself. Things came to a head when a Maltese man, who was a British citizen, killed an Egyptian over a dispute about the rental rate of a donkey. The dispute, which some suspect may have been staged, led to what became known as the Slaughter in Alexandria. The number of reported casualties varied from fifty to three hundred, depending on the source. According to Evelyn Baring, Earl of Cromer, who was the British controller general in Egypt, forty-five to fifty foreigners were killed in the violence.[11]

On July 6 and July 10, 1882, the British issued two ultimatums to Tawfiq: (1) exile Urabi from Egypt, and (2) exile the other officers from Cairo within twenty-four hours. Tawfiq supported the ultimatums, but Urabi and his followers rejected them. The British fleet, composed of fifteen warships carrying 5,700 fighting men, was standing by ready to act. After the twenty-four-hour deadline had passed, the British bombarded Alexandria and then entered the city under the pretext of protecting the Christian foreigners from Muslim militants—at least this was the justification reported in Europe.[12] France initially opposed the British military intervention in Egypt.

Great Britain had appointed itself the protector of Christians in Egypt. But apparently this did not include native Egyptian Christians, as there was no hostile action against Egyptian Christians. The conflict was between foreigners and what they represented, and the Egyptian people.[13]

Tawfiq went to Alexandria to seek British protection. Once safely there, he issued a decree removing Urabi on June 20. In Cairo, a different story was unfolding. On June 22, an assembly of roughly five hundred distinguished Egyptians met and decided to refuse to obey Tawfiq's order to remove Urabi. This large assembly included members of the National Party, along with many dignitaries, high officials, and religious leaders, such as the head of al-Azhar Mosque, the Coptic patriarch, the head rabbi, and even some members of the royal family. Louis Awad provides a complete list of the assembly members.[14] A full-scale revolt against Tawfiq and the British was launched, but the balance of power was not in their favor. At this meeting, two prominent Muslim shaykhs issued a fatwa against Tawfiq for supporting the British invasion.[15] This was a de facto deposing of Tawfiq.

The major battle against Urabi's forces took place near a small town called al-Tal al-Kabir in the eastern part of the Nile Delta. The confrontation between the Egyptians and the British did not last long. According to some accounts, Urabi held a *dhikr* (Sufi festival) the night before the battle, and the British attacked very early in the morning.[16] The Battle of al-Tal al-Kabir lasted for only twenty minutes. As had been the case nearly a century earlier—when Napoleon overcame the Mamluks in 1798, in a battle lasting forty-five minutes—Egypt's military defense was no match against a modern European army.

Unrest in Egypt had international ramifications. France wanted to protect the bondholders of the Suez Canal Company, although 89 percent of the ships sailing through the canal were British. Finally, Great Britain and France agreed between themselves to leave Egypt to Great Britain in exchange for allowing France to claim Tunisia.[17] France took over Tunisia in 1881, and Morocco in 1911; Algeria had been colonized by France in 1830. Whatever the claim—whether the British colonized Egypt because of Urabi's actions, or to protect the European Christians, or to collect European banks' debts—the fact that Britain colonized and remained in Egypt for about seventy years reveals its true motives. Egypt and the Suez Canal were on the route to India, and the takeover of Egypt was a necessary cog in the wheels of European colonial power.

Enemies of the Urabi revolt spread rumors that one of its purposes was to take over Coptic assets. Some mobs tried to take advantage of this, but Urabi put a quick end to any potential violence. He informed all governors to stop this rumor and to protect Coptic assets.[18]

The Egyptian army was dismantled by a decree from Tawfiq on September 19, 1882. Twenty-nine thousand people were arrested, including all the leaders of the resistance movement. Urabi and his close officers were sentenced to death, but under pressure from the British this sentence was reduced to exile in Ceylon (now Sri Lanka). The British had finally achieved their long-awaited goal of gaining control of the Suez Canal, and thereby securing their trade route to India. They remained in Egypt until 1954, when a successful army revolt in 1952 removed both the British and King Farouk, the last of Muhammad 'Ali's descendants to rule Egypt.

11

EGYPT UNDER THE BRITISH (1881–1954)

Having secured its route to India, Great Britain settled in for a long stay in Egypt. A central figure in this transition was Evelyn Baring, Earl of Cromer. [Though he did not receive the title until 1909, we will refer to him as Cromer because it is the name under which he wrote and the one by which he is best known.] Cromer played a central role, controlling Egypt for about a quarter of a century. He represented Britain as one of the dual controllers of Egypt's finances in 1879, and was instrumental in removing Isma'il Basha and replacing him with his more amenable son, Tawfiq Basha. After Great Britain colonized Egypt, Cromer governed from 1883 until he resigned in 1907. During his tenure, he turned Egypt into a British dependency in all but name, called the Veiled Protectorate. For the first decade, after years of chaos, Egyptians appreciated stability of any sort.[1] Cromer established a reformed and efficient administration, and introduced a certain measure of justice. The Egyptians respected Cromer for his reforms, but they—especially the nationalists—feared and disliked him.[2]

Let us look first at the influence of Great Britain on the Egyptian economy. Egypt was an important source of superior quality cotton for Britain's textile industry. Egyptian cotton exports to Great Britain from 1878 to 1882 totaled 9.3 million pounds—a figure which grew to 25 million pounds between 1908 and 1912. Britain used its influence on the Egyptian economy in order to support its own textile industry, importing Egyptian cotton and returning a small fraction of it in the form of textiles.[3] Fully half of Egypt's imports from Great Britain were textiles, worth four million pounds. A similar strategy was employed by the British in India.

Government revenues during the first thirty-five years of Egypt's colonization increased by 80 percent, without a significant increase in taxation.[4] This was basically the result of improved management. The Aswan Dam was built in 1899–1902 and was raised twice, in 1907 and 1929, increasing the area of irrigated land by 10 percent (about 600,000 acres). During the first thirty-five years of British control, cotton production increased 145 percent, wheat production increased 50 percent, and corn production increased 75 percent. Exports increased by 140 percent, and imports increased by 219 percent. In the same period, the population increased by 75 percent. It is worth noting that Egypt remained a primarily agricultural economy, without improved industrialization.[5] It is also worth noting that, while the economic figures increased between 1882 and 1919, the overall economy stagnated during this period relative to the increase in population.[6] Egyptian debts were reduced by agreement with the lenders, and a revised repayment schedule was implemented.[7]

Although Cromer improved the economy, achieved stability, and curbed corruption, he ignored the issues of self-rule and education.[8] At heart, he was an autocrat. In his book *Modern Egypt*, he revealed his belief that the only form of government suitable for Egypt was benevolent despotism.[9] Cromer's policies, however, were questioned by even the British at that time. Louis Awad and other intellectual Egyptians have pointed to the racist nature of Cromer's policies. For example, Cromer expressed the view that "to get native Egyptians to rule Egypt is like asking for Canadian Indians to rule Canada."[10]

The British, the Muslims, and the Copts

Before we examine Coptic–Muslim relations in Egypt during the period of British rule, it is necessary to give an overview of some important events that were taking place in the larger Islamic world. One of these was the emergence of a pan-Islamic movement inspired by Jamal al-Din al-Afghani (1838–97) and his disciple Muhammad 'Abduh. This movement cooperated with the colonial powers of the time from behind the scenes, and later cooperated with the United States. Al-Afghani had a magnetism that could rouse his followers. Although the British had mastered the art of manipulating tribal, ethnic, and religious affiliations after they colonized large territories in central Asia, they covertly supported al-Afghani's efforts to start a political Islamic movement. This movement, which continues to the present day in various forms, has had a devastating effect on many parts of the Muslim world, and has had repercussions in Europe and the United States as well.[11]

Jamal al-Din was born a Shiite Muslim in Persia in 1838. He later adopted the name al-Afghani to suggest he had roots in Afghanistan, a stronghold of the predominant Sunni branch of Islam. He traveled widely, spending three years in imperial Russia and four years in Munich. In Persia, the shah appointed him war minister and then prime minister. But after he started to incite the masses against the Persian monarch, he was forced to leave.[12] Al-Afghani also visited Great Britain and India. In India, the British-led colonial authorities welcomed him as an Islamic scholar. He was escorted aboard a government-owned vessel and taken to Suez and then to Cairo. In Cairo, he was adopted by the conservative anti-nationalist prime minister Riyad Basha (1835–1911). Riyad Basha persuaded al-Afghani to take up residence in al-Azhar Mosque, where he taught and received a monthly government stipend. Al-Afghani spent eight years in Egypt, but left when the British colonized the country.[13]

While in Egypt, al-Afghani met and cooperated with Muhammad 'Abduh, an Azharite graduate who was teaching Arabic in a new college (Dar al-'Ulum). 'Abduh subsequently cooperated with the Urabi revolt, was imprisoned, and then was exiled from Egypt. Al-Afghani joined 'Abduh in Paris, where they produced a pan-Islamic newspaper, titled *al-'Urwa al-Wuthqa (The Indissoluble Bond)*, that was addressed to Muslims around the world. The paper had two main messages. The first was that Islam had become corrupt through ignorance. The second was that Muslim countries had been betrayed by their rulers. These messages are still proclaimed by political Islam today.

'Abduh returned to Egypt in 1889 and became a moderate Islamic reformer. He was supported by Lord Cromer.[14] As a result of this support, 'Abduh was named to lead a committee to reorganize al-Azhar. He became an important figure whose opinion was sought and respected. Eventually he became the grand mufti who interpreted Islamic laws. Why did the British support political Islam in Egypt, and why did they continue to do so? In this case, strengthening a religious movement was seen as a means of weakening the nationalist movement. The danger of religious institutions often is not due to the religion itself but to its political application. 'Abduh was a moderate Islamic thinker, but after his death he was replaced by his disciple, Rashid Rida. Rida became radicalized and influenced the Muslim Brotherhood movement as well as its offspring and even more radical jihadist groups.

During their early years in Egypt, the British maintained control through a policy of divide and conquer—a strategy that had proven successful in governing other territories. In addition to strengthening Islam to counter secular nationalist aspirations, the British manipulated the relationship between Copts and Muslims to their own advantage. Between 1882 and 1919, most Copts did not feel they needed the protection of the British. There had been no serious problems between Copts and Muslims since Muhammad 'Ali came to power at the beginning of the nineteenth century. The British found that many Copts and other Christians held high administrative positions without being resented by Muslims. Some Copts were still in control of land surveying and tax collecting, professions they had dominated even before the Arabs came to Egypt in the seventh century. The Copts were reluctant to cooperate with the British in this archaic but profitable system. So in 1929, the government under British guidance started a school for tax collection that was attended by Muslims, including al-Azhar Islamic High School graduates.[15] This quickly brought an end to Coptic domination in this area.

The British were aware of Egypt's significance in the Muslim world due to its large Muslim population and the presence of al-Azhar as a preeminent center of Islamic learning. Appearing to favor the Copts would hurt Great Britain's image in the wider Muslim world. Gradually, the British started to replace some Copts with Muslims, especially in high and visible positions. Reducing the influence of Copts in tax collection was an important objective. The British claimed that by doing this, they protected the Muslim majority from the domination of the Coptic minority. The Copts started to feel discriminated against.[16] Traditionally, they had occupied a greater share of government jobs due to their often higher levels of education. But as Muslims became equally well educated, this situation changed.

When Copts' and Muslims' resistance to the British presence started to pick up momentum in 1908, the British attempted to defuse it by turning around and appointing a Copt, Boutros Ghali Basha, as prime minister. Ghali was subsequently assassinated at the hands of a Muslim—an event which created considerable sectarian tension. In 1919, when opposition to the British intensified, the British again appointed a Copt as prime minister. Awad is of the opinion that selecting a Copt as prime minister was not in itself an issue; its intention was to irritate the Muslim majority and preoccupy Egyptians with sectarian tensions. However, if this was the goal, the policy did not succeed.[17] It should be mentioned that Cromer's policies were determined by political expedience, not personal favoritism. Early in his tenure he stated that there was no significant difference between Copts and Muslims, except that one went to a church while the other went to a mosque.[18]

The failure of the Urabi revolt had led to a national mood of despair. However, it did not suppress nationalist aspirations for long. Within a decade, a resistance movement against the British colonization had begun to organize. Mustafa Kamel (1874–1908), a young Egyptian who had received a law degree in France in 1892, became a prominent leader of this movement. In 1900, Kamel founded an anti-British newspaper called *al-Liwa'*, and in 1907, he established the National Party (al-Hizb al-Watani). Thirty members of this party were elected to the executive committee, including two prominent Copts.[19] The party and newspaper raised people's awareness that the British were in Egypt as a colonial power. Although the movement was anti-British, it did not seek separation from the Turkish Islamic empire. Most Copts shied away from joining the party because they noticed an Islamic undertone to its policies. In addition, the newspaper published some anti-Coptic articles by a Muslim radical.[20] The party garnered the support of the new ruler of Egypt, 'Abbas Hilmi II, who had replaced his father, Tawfiq Basha, after the latter's death in 1892. Kamel also received support from Turkey and from many of the Turks and Circassians in Egypt. The party became weak after its financial support was significantly reduced due to the defeat of Turkey, and the dismantling of its empire, after the First World War.

Another national party, also established in 1907, was called Hizb al-Umma, the People's Party. This party sought to liberate Egypt from the Turks as well as from the British. It did not want an autocratic ruler, such as Isma'il or Tawfiq. Rather, it called for a constitution and parliamentary government similar to modern political systems in Europe. The leaders of Hizb al-Umma thought that Egyptian independence could not be realized with the help of Turkey or France, even though the latter was traditionally the enemy of Great Britain. They believed liberation had to come from within the country itself—from an authentically Egyptian resistance movement. This party was a dominant part of the political scene until 1952. The party stood for freedom of speech, freedom of religion, and the right of Egyptians to participate in the executive and legislative branches of government. Many Copts played an important role in promoting these principles.

Newspapers at the time reflected a wide variety of views from across the political spectrum. Some advocated radical Christian views; others supported Muslim activists. Some supported the British presence in Egypt and had British financial support, while others were nationalist or independent newspapers.[21] The turn of century saw sectarian tensions increase to a degree which had not been seen in Egypt for almost a century. The British discreetly encouraged polarization along religious lines. An incident in 1906 brought things to a head.

On June 11, 1906, some British officers were pigeon shooting in the small village of Dinshaway on the west bank of the Nile Delta, not far from Cairo. The pigeons were not wild; they were owned by farmers and lived in tall dovecotes built by those farmers. The officers were hunting on private land near a threshing floor, which caught fire as a result. The angry farmers tried to drive the officers away. Due to the language barrier, the officers were confused and scared as they tried to flee. One officer ran about eight kilometers on a hot summer day. He later died from a heatstroke, according to the report of a British physician. Several other officers were also injured in the incident. One farmer was killed by the officers, and others were wounded. This incident became a turning point in relations between the colonial power and the Egyptian nationalist movement. It was also a factor in sectarian violence between the Copts and Muslims, as we will see.

A few years before this incident, on February 25, 1895, Cromer had a law passed by the Egyptian government that required Egyptians who attacked members of the British army to be tried by a special tribunal. This tribunal was headed by the minister of justice (an Egyptian) and included a legal advisor to the Justice Department (a British citizen) and a judge from the British army in Egypt.

Cromer wanted to use the Dinshaway incident to teach the Egyptians a lesson. A special tribunal was immediately convened, and ninety-two farmers were put on trial. Four men were sentenced to death, two were sentenced to life in prison, eleven received sentences of one to fifteen years, and eleven were flogged. The capital punishment and flogging were carried out in Dinshaway by British soldiers and in the presence of the villagers. These scandalous sentences, which were supposed to demonstrate colonial justice and induce compliance by the population, had the opposite effect. Like the Amritsar Massacre, which had occurred in British-controlled India a decade earlier, the Dinshaway incident raised general awareness of colonial abuses and galvanized opposition to British occupation. In Great Britain and France, this incident was well covered by the liberal media. As a result, Cromer lost his credentials and was eventually removed from Egypt.

The minister of justice who presided over the tribunal was a Copt, Boutros Ghali Basha. As a result, his name became associated with the Dinshaway incident. Ghali served as prime minister from 1908 until 1910, when he was assassinated by a young Muslim Egyptian. To understand the circumstances, it might be worthwhile to look briefly at Ghali's career.

In 1886, before he became prime minister, Ghali was appointed to head a commission that selected Islamic law (sharia) court judges, a post that obviously should have been held by a Muslim. He was appointed to be minister of finance in 1893, and then foreign minister in 1894. Ghali was seen as sympathetic to the British and to their puppet, Tawfiq Basha.

During his tenure as prime minister, Ghali agreed to British rule over Sudan, which at the time was under Egyptian control. He also agreed to extending the Suez Canal concession by an extra forty-five years beyond the original date of 1968, in return for payment of four million pounds to the Egyptian government between 1910 and 1914, plus 4 percent of annual revenues, which would be increased to 50 percent by 1968.[22] The Egyptian people had resented the Suez Canal since the beginning of the project, because of the forced labor and widespread loss of life incurred during its construction. When the proposed extension of the Suez Canal concession went to the Egyptian assembly, it was rejected by sixty-six votes, with only one vote in favor. Boutros Ghali bore the brunt of the blame for this proposal. It showed his lack of judgment and sensitivity.

On February 20, 1910, Boutros Ghali was assassinated by Ibrahim al-Wardani.

Some Copts defended al-Wardani on the grounds that Ghali was a supporter of British colonial power. Al-Wardani gave the following reasons for the assassination: (1) Ghali's attempt to extend the Suez Canal concession, (2) his agreement with the British about their role in Sudan, (3) his role in the Dinshaway tribunal, and (4) his implementation of rules to limit the freedom of the press. Al-Wardani was sentenced to death.[23]

Ghali's assassination added to sectarian tensions. Newspapers on both the Coptic and the Muslim sides inflamed the situation, leading to the increased polarization of the two communities. This was crystallized in the form of a Coptic conference in Asyut and a Muslim conference in Alexandria, both held in 1911. Within a month of the assassination, on March 11, the Copts held their conference to protest job discrimination. Eldon Gorst, who had replaced Cromer as British consul-general in Egypt, initially objected to the conference on the grounds that the Copts' share of government jobs was much greater than their percentage in the population. The National Party, which was dominated by Muslims, also objected to the Coptic conference on the grounds that if the Copts had grievances, they should direct them to the British rulers, rather than to other groups. The Coptic patriarch had his own concerns about the conference and did not support it, but the Coptic bishop of Asyut, where the conference took place, both supported and attended it. Many prominent Copts, including Ghali's son, sided with the patriarch and opposed the conference.[24] Overall, only about 2 percent of Copts supported the conference.[25] Despite the lack of support from the mainstream Coptic community, some Muslim writers accused the Copts of trying to create their own state in Asyut. This accusation persisted in some Islamic circles, but had no basis in fact. It is important to point out that, in addition to having a sizable Coptic population, Asyut was also a center for Protestant missionaries, some of whom supported the conference. These factors may have influenced events.[26]

What were the Copts' demands at their conference? Initially, they intended to ask for better representation, equal access to civil service positions, the designation of Sunday as a holiday for Copts, equal access to state education, and the provision of Christian religious instruction alongside the mandated Islamic instruction in state schools.[27] When the conference started, those who presided over it were the moderates, and eventually the rhetoric was toned down. By the closing session of the conference, the demands were limited to designating Sunday as a holiday for Copts working for the government, equal access to jobs, equal access to government schools, and government support for all public utilities and organizations. Most of the speakers emphasized the significance of national unity.[28]

As the Coptic conference was being organized, some Muslim leaders planned a separate conference, to be held on April 29, 1911, to represent the views of their community. They called it the Egyptian Islamic Conference, and it was presided over by the conservative Riyad Basha, a former prime minister.[29] From the beginning, the Islamic conference was influenced by moderates. The participants objected to making Sunday a holiday, and thought all job appointments should depend only on the qualifications of the applicant, independent of religious affiliation. With respect to demands for better access to education, it was pointed out that the Copts' level of education was already higher than that of the Muslim population. The conference rejected the proposal to grant a percentage of seats in the parliamentary election to any group.[30] Some speakers mentioned the role of foreign missionaries in planting seeds of division between the Copts and Muslims. Other speakers pointed to the high ratio of Copts in some departments of government. For example, Copts made up 6 percent of the Ministry of Education, 15 percent of the Justice Department, 46 percent of the Treasury Department, and 96 percent of the Ministry of the Interior (the thinker and judge Tariq al-Bishri thinks this last figure was due to the low level of their administrative jobs). Even though Copts were 6.4 percent of the population, they held about 10 percent of the country's assets.[31]

Both conferences marginalized the views expressed by their more extreme attendees, and the rhetoric became less heated. Neither conference directly addressed the issue of British colonial power. At this stage, it was clear to the intelligentsia that cooperation between the Copts and the Muslims was more important than their differences.

Great Britain's stated policy was that it would remain in Egypt until Egypt became stable; then they would withdraw. However, Cromer repeatedly informed the Western world at large that an Egyptian nation did not exist, and that Egypt was a conglomeration of different races living together.[32] European public opinion was starting to change when, in 1904, Great Britain and France reached an agreement called the Entente Cordiale. According to the terms of the agreement, France recognized British control over Egypt, while Britain reciprocated by recognizing French control in North Africa. At the beginning of the First World War in 1914, when the Ottoman Empire sided with the Central Powers, Great Britain unilaterally declared Egypt its protectorate. At the end of the war, the Turkish Empire was dismantled. As a result, the Egyptian national movement shifted from a pan-Islamic movement under the leadership of the Turkish caliphate to an Egyptian nationalist movement. Rejection of pan-Islamism made it possible for Copts to join with Muslims in a joint effort to gain national independence. The British strategy to divide Egyptian loyalties along sectarian lines had failed.[33]

In 1917, Great Britain proposed constitutional reform in Egypt which featured a new legislative assembly with sixty-six elected members and seventeen appointed members. The latter included four Copts and three Bedouins, in addition to Egyptian merchants, physicians, and religious educators. This body also included British ministers, British advisors, and other foreigners. Decisions made by the assembly could not be implemented without the approval of Great Britain's foreign secretary. This proposal was widely resented when it was presented to the Egyptians in 1918. It became clear that the British did not intend to yield control, much less leave the country, any time soon.[34]

12
FROM REVOLT TO REVOLUTION (1919–52)

As popular resistance against the British gained momentum, a new leader, Sa'd Zaghlul, arose to fill the vacuum left by the death of Mustafa Kamel, the leader of al-Hizb al-Watani (the National Party), who had died in 1908 at the young age of thirty-four. Zaghlul was tall, charismatic, and self-confident. Early in his life, he sympathized with the Urabi revolt. As a result, he lost his job with the government, though nothing was proven against him. He obtained a law degree from the University of Paris in 1898, and became a lawyer and then a judge. With the approval of Lord Cromer, Zaghlul advanced to become minister of education in 1906, then minister of justice in 1910. However, he resigned from his post after he had a dispute with Khedive 'Abbas Hilmi II, the son of Tawfiq Basha. In 1913, he was appointed vice president of the Legislative Assembly. Zaghlul married Safiya, the daughter of Prime Minister Mustafa Fahmi Basha.

In November 1918, Zaghlul and three members of the Legislative Assembly (of 1913) met informally with Sir Reginald Francis Wingate, the British high commissioner, to discuss the future of Egypt's independence and its relationship with the British.[1] No Copts were present at this meeting. However, after the meeting became known, the Copts wanted to participate in such discussions, and Zaghlul welcomed them. The group expanded to twelve members, including three Copts, one of whom was Wassef Ghali, the son of the assassinated Boutros Ghali.[2] The group called itself the Wafd, meaning 'the delegation.' Zaghlul's movement was secular and used the slogan "Religion for God, and the nation for all." From that point on, Copts were an important part of the Wafd, which later became a full-fledged political party. Zaghlul, and later his successor, continued to support Copts as they took an active, not merely symbolic, role in Egyptian politics.

When Zaghlul and his colleagues met with Wingate, they asked for Egypt's independence, but were told that Egyptians were not yet capable of self-rule. When this was reported in the Egyptian newspapers, anti-British feeling increased and support for the Wafd grew. Zaghlul and his small delegation realized they were not authorized to represent the country as a whole, so they asked for that authorization from the Egyptian people directly. Petitions to that effect began streaming in, despite difficulties in communication due to British-imposed wartime restrictions during the First World War (1914–18).

At the end of the war, some of the old empires—including the Turkish and Austrian empires—were defeated and dismantled. New boundaries were being drawn and new countries formed, as territories formerly controlled by the defeated Central Powers were parceled out to the victorious allies Great Britain, France, Italy, and the United States. Despite its claims to support principles of self-determination and the rights of minorities, it was clear that the British had no intention of letting Egypt become independent. In 1919, when the Paris Peace Conference was convened at Versailles to set peace terms and decide the fate of former German and Ottoman territories, the Wafd Party wanted to participate to represent Egypt. But the British objected to having an Egyptian delegation at Versailles, even though much smaller countries—including Saudi Arabia, Armenia, Syria, and Lebanon—were allowed to attend the conference.

The popularity of the Wafd Party continued to increase in the face of Great Britain's opposition. In anticipation of further political activities and possible arrests, the Wafd Party's executive committee set up four secret levels of organization; if one level was arrested, the second level could replace it without any loss in momentum or organization. At one point in the struggle, the fourth level of the executive committee was activated after the three levels above it had been arrested.

As the movement against the British became more organized, national unity between the Copts and Muslims took a new turn. By April 20, 1919, during the Coptic Easter celebration, both Copts and Muslims, men and women, turned the day into a national holiday. Muslims turned out in large numbers around the Coptic cathedral to share the day with Copts. This included some Muslims from the Islamic Theology School of al-Azhar. The religious festivity turned into an anti-British political demonstration in addition to a display of national unity. What happened in Cairo was repeated on a smaller scale in other big cities. The same phenomenon was repeated during the Muslims' religious holidays, as well—Copts turned out in joint celebration with their Muslim compatriots. These displays of unity were the first of their kind in modern Egyptian history. Traditionally, Copts and Muslims had greeted each other during religious holidays, but this had been limited largely to neighbors and friends. During this period, religious holidays became national and political holidays. The Zaghlul movement became a strong secular movement. Sectarian tensions were a thing of the past, at least for a few years.

Another new development was the emergence of women as a voice in politics. On April 24, 1919, a delegation of Coptic women went to the mosque of Sayyida Zaynab in the center of Old Cairo to return the visit by Muslim women to the Coptic cathedral. They were very well received by high-profile Muslim women.[3] The women's movement was not limited to symbolic exchange visits, but extended to organized demonstrations against the British in the streets of Cairo. In addition, women signed a petition against the British occupation of Egypt, which was presented to the British high commissioner. This was the first women's demonstration in Egypt's history.[4] Some of those women became leaders of the Egyptian feminist movement. During the revolution and afterward, some Muslim women removed their head covering *(hijab)*. They became advocates for improving the status of women and of political prisoners. There was no difference between Copts and Muslims in these activities.[5]

The movement against the British continued to accelerate. The nationalists used force against the colonial power. Episodes of violence increased and there were casualties on both sides. As the situation began to get out of control, the head of the British army in Egypt, General Watson, threatened to respond with force if needed, but this threat was to no avail. On March 8, 1919, the British arrested Zaghlul and three other heads of the movement. They were exiled to Malta. The next day, demonstrations spread like wildfire in all of Egypt's large cities. Churches and mosques became centers for political activity. Muslim shaykhs delivered anti-British speeches in churches, and priests did the same in mosques, including al-Azhar Mosque. The Egyptian flag became a crescent hugging a cross, with a green background, as a symbol for national unity. Sir Eldon Gorst, the British consul general in Egypt, was sent back to Britain and replaced by Field Marshal Edmund Allenby. Allenby released Zaghlul and his companions from Malta, ending their exile.

The demonstrations and violence continued to escalate. The British minister Lord Curzon downplayed the severity of the situation. He declared that the Foreign Office was dealing with matters of worldwide importance that made the Egyptian question seem but a trivial affair.[6] Lord Curzon described the revolt as the work of some radical students and stated that no Egyptian government employees had participated in or encouraged it. Angered by this false statement, Egyptians employed by the government demonstrated for three days. The government was shut down except for foreign employees. At this point, Allenby, the British high commissioner in Egypt, gave in and permitted the Wafd Party and whoever else wanted to go to the peace conference to do so. Thirteen people—three Copts and ten Muslims—traveled to Paris.[7] When the party arrived in Paris, the American president Woodrow Wilson, who had previously supported the right of the people to self-determination, announced U.S. recognition of the British mandate over Egypt. Thus the doors were closed in the face of the Egyptians. This was a disappointment, but the revolution continued.

The British intensified their efforts to put down the revolt in Egypt. A military court was used to sentence people to death or to life in prison. Responding to deteriorating conditions, the British government sent a commission headed by Lord Milner, the colonial secretary, to investigate the situation and to make recommendations for setting up limited self-government under a continuing British protectorate. Prime Minister Muhammad Sa'id Basha declared he would resign as prime minister if Milner came to Egypt while Zaghlul and the rest of the Wafd Party's executive committee were still in Paris trying to bring international pressure to bear on the British. The Milner Commission wanted to find an Egyptian alternative to the hardline Zaghlul and his Wafd Party.

Milner arrived in Egypt on December 7, 1919. Muhammad Sa'id Basha resigned and was replaced by the Copt Youssef Wahba Basha, an appointment which the British may have thought would cause sectarian division. If this was their hope, they were disappointed. There was strong opposition from all Egyptians, particularly from the Coptic community, who resented the British attempt to split the national unity. An attempt on Wahba's life was made by 'Iryan Yusuf Sa'd, who was also a Copt and a student at Cairo Medical School.[8] Assassination attempts were made on other ministers' lives as well.[9] The Milner Commission returned to Britain in March 1920.

Great Britain then sent a representative to the Paris Peace Conference to invite Zaghlul and the Wafd Party to come to England to negotiate matters regarding Egypt's future. They did so, but no progress was made with the Wafd Party hardliners, who wanted nothing less than full independence.[10] The Egyptian delegation went back to Egypt on April 15, 1921. The demonstrations continued. The British decided to remove Zaghlul and the other prominent Wafd Party leaders from the political scene in order to find more agreeable politicians with whom they could negotiate. On September 29, 1921, Zaghlul and five prominent

Wafd Party members were exiled to the Seychelles Islands, a British colony in the Indian Ocean. The six exiles included three Muslims and three Copts. A new Wafd Party executive committee replaced the original one and called for passive resistance and for a boycott of British products. They were influenced by Gandhi's civil disobedience movement in India. The new Wafd Party executive committee was composed of four Muslims and four Copts. They were arrested, but another executive committee, consisting of four Muslims and two Copts, took their place.[11] The ratio of Copts to Muslims in the Wafd Party was much higher than the ratio in the general population, possibly reflecting an increased awareness of the need for national unity, as well as higher education and standard of living among Copts at this point.[12] The resistance continued, and Great Britain was not able to contain it.

Due to the failure to reach an agreement, political instability and political assassinations increased. Egypt was without any administration for a time, and some administrations were able to stay in power for only a few months. Great Britain decided to try a different strategy; on February 28, 1922, Britain unilaterally ceased to consider Egypt its protectorate. Great Britain asserted its right to retain military force in Egypt to secure the communications of the British Empire, to defend Egypt against foreign aggression, and to protect foreign and minority interests. The status of Sudan, which was a part of Egypt at the time, was to be discussed at a later point.[13]

The overwhelming majority of Egyptians, and the Wafd Party in particular, strongly objected to this one-sided new arrangement. It fell short of the evacuation of British troops that Egyptians wanted to see. Copts also resented Britain's claim that it had a right to remain in order to protect minorities. Wassef Ghali, the Wafd Party secretary and a Copt, declared that Great Britain had no mandate to protect minorities; this was the duty of the League of Nations according to its charter.[14] But this remained part of Great Britain's colonial policy, notably in India, where the emphasis on religious divisions eventually led to the separation of India and Pakistan.

Ending Egypt's status as a protectorate was in reality an empty concession, but it did allow some limited benefits to Egypt. On the one hand, Egypt was now able to have its own foreign policy; its ruler, Ahmad Fu'ad, was given the title of king; and most important, Egypt was allowed its own constitution and a new administration. On the other hand, Great Britain's control of the country remained essentially unchanged, and the resentment of the Egyptians continued until the British finally left Egypt in 1954.

The Wafd Party (1923–52)

The clampdown in Egypt was now loosened. Zaghlul and the rest of the exiled Wafd Party leaders were released from their island imprisonment and returned to Egypt on March 31, 1923. A new national administration was formed and immediately faced the major task of constructing a new constitution. A committee of thirty members was selected, including minority representation (four Copts, one Jew, and one Bedouin). The Wafd Party boycotted the constitution committee on the grounds that members of this committee should have been elected, not appointed.

The most heated debate in the committee was over how to assure the presence of minorities in the parliament. Two views were discussed: to set a quota for minorities, or to leave it to the voters to decide. Opinions were not split along sectarian lines; there were both Copts and Muslims arguing strongly on each side of the issue. One important concern on both sides was not to allow the British to intervene on behalf of minorities. Most Copts were against adding any rules to assure the selection of minority members. This was the position of the Wafd Party.[15] When asked for his opinion, the Coptic patriarch Cyril V stated, "Whatever is in the best interest of Egypt—whether selecting a Copt [by quota] or not—let it be." In other words, the church did not take a position on either side.

The final version of the constitution did not have any quotas for minorities. The constitution was named after that year (1923) and had some liberal features in terms of personal freedom, the right to form political parties, and freedom of speech and of the press. But the king had the right to issue laws and to remove and appoint governments. This, as we will see, weakened the liberal experiment.

The first election, held in September 1923, was conducted without outside tampering. The results showed overwhelming support for the candidates of the Wafd Party, which received 90 percent of the 214 seats in Parliament. Elected Copts accounted for 7.5 percent. After the Wafd Party, the most important party was the Liberal Constitution Party (al-Ahrar al-Dusturiyun), which received only 3 percent of the seats. The Liberal Constitution Party had been highly influential in formulating the constitution, and at one point was considered a moderate version of the Wafd Party. This party had some Coptic candidates, but most Copts voted for candidates of the Wafd Party, as did the majority of Muslims. Between 1923 and 1950, whenever the Wafd Party participated in an election and the voting was not tampered with, the Wafd Party received the majority of the votes and the Copts voted heavily for the party's candidates.

Zaghlul headed the new administration after his landslide victory. The new government was made up of ten appointed members, two of whom were Copts, and one who was a Jew. When King Ahmad Fu'ad objected to choosing two Copts and suggested having only one, Zaghlul responded, "We do not make a distinction between Copts and Muslims."[16] The Wafd Party had both a broad appeal and the financial means to field candidates in almost every constituency. According to the census of 1917, the percentage of seats occupied by Copts exceeded their ratio in the population. A summary of the parliamentary elections from 1923 to 1950 is presented in appendix 2, table 1.[1] The information in this table was obtained from various sources. Vivian Ibrahim's tables covered the number of Copts in the administration. Vivian Ibrahim summarizes the percentage of non-Muslims in government from 1890 to 1954.[18]

From 1923 to 1952, Egypt was controlled by a balance of power among several competing interests: (1) the British, supported by their army and colonial system; (2) the king, who had the formal right to approve or dismiss the government, and who wished to rule autocratically as his ancestors had; (3) the Wafd Party, which was supported by most Egyptians; and (4) minor political parties that had no popular base, but were willing to support the British or the king. Among the latter group, the Liberal Constitution Party (al-Ahrar al-Dusturiyun) stood out as the party of the intellectuals and large landlords. The political system at the time was best described by a British politician as an unstable chair with three legs: one leg represented the British colonial power, the second leg represented the palace, and the third leg represented the wide range of political parties. The historian Raouf Abbas and others considered the 1923 constitution to be an autocratic constitution with only a liberal façade.[19] When the results of an election or the performance of the government did not suit the British or the palace, the elected administration was forced out of office.

Between 1923 and 1952, the Wafd Party was by far the most popular party. Whenever it participated in fairly run elections, it won easily—as it did in 1924, 1925, and 1926. But it was not allowed to stay in power for very long. Despite its majority position, the Wafd Party ruled for only seven years out of these three decades, due to intervention by the British and/or the king. Influential individuals who supported the palace were also able to interfere with the election process or tamper with election results, which is why the Wafd Party did not participate in some later elections (1931, 1936, 1942, and 1945). The election of 1950 was the last one in which the Wafd Party participated. That year, the percentage of parliamentary seats held by Copts declined to only 2.5 percent. From 1952 to the present, fewer than 1 percent of seats in parliament have been held by Copts. This has been concurrent with a deterioration in democratic processes and a rise in political Islam, something we will address in the next chapter.

Even though the Wafd Party won by a landslide due to its strong popularity, it did not reach out to intellectuals or independents from other parties to create a unified front. The party's greatest strength lay in organizing demonstrations and appealing to the public's emotions. Its top priority was to get the British out of Egypt—other goals could wait. Unfortunately, this narrow focus did not achieve its goal and may have prevented the party from building a sustainable democratic foundation for civil society in Egypt.

Zaghlul's first administration did not stay in power for more than ten months. Its downfall was swift, dramatic, and demonstrates the weakness of the elected government in the face of concerted opposition from the British and the king. On November 19, 1924, Sir Lee Stack, a British army officer and governor general of Sudan—whose appointment as head of the Egyptian army was widely resented by Egyptians and had been publicly opposed by Zaghlul—was assassinated by an Egyptian nationalist. Two days later, the British government issued a harshly worded ultimatum, calling for an immediate apology from the Egyptian government and an inquiry into the shooting. They demanded that those responsible be punished, that political demonstrations stop, and that a fine of 500,000 pounds be paid to the British government. In addition, they demanded the withdrawal of all Egyptian officers and army units from Sudan within twenty-four hours. If these demands were not met, His Majesty's government threatened to take immediate and appropriate action to safeguard Britain's interests in Egypt and Sudan.[20] The Egyptian government agreed to investigate the incident, to pay the fine, and to stop the demonstrations. But this was not enough.[21] British troops occupied the port of Alexandria. Zaghlul was forced to resign on November 23, and a new non-Wafdist government was appointed by the king the next day. The new administration complied with the British demands, including the withdrawal of the Egyptian army from Sudan. To show their power, the British arrested some prominent Egyptian officials, including elected officials.[22]

On November 24, 1924, the elected parliament—which was still dominated by the Wafd Party—was suspended for a month. Before the month was out, it was dismantled and a new election was set for March 6, 1925. The new parliamentary elections again resulted in a majority for the Wafd Party (116 seats versus 87), with Zaghlul elected speaker of the house.[23] This result did not suit the palace or the British, so they suspended the newly elected parliament, and continued to recognize the non-Wafdist administration appointed by the king. The newly elected officials held a meeting in the Continental Hotel. At this meeting, the parliament gave a vote of no confidence to the administration.[24] The instability continued until a new election was held in 1926, when the Wafd Party again received the majority of the vote. The assassination of Sir Lee Stack was investigated and a trial was held. One person was sentenced to death. The Wafd government was not held responsible.[25] Zaghlul died on August 27, 1927, at age sixty-nine. He is remembered as a heroic figure during a critical period of the Egyptian struggle for independence.

Mustafa al-Nahhas succeeded Zaghlul as party president, and Makram Ebeid, a Copt, became the party's secretary. Al-Nahhas and Ebeid made a strong team; both had worked closely with Zaghlul and had been exiled with him. Some Wafd leaders who were not pleased with the new leadership split off and formed new parties. But the public remained solidly behind al-Nahhas and Ebeid. The Wafd Party continued to represent liberal democracy.

The Copts heavily supported the secular principles of the Wafd Party and could not see a role for themselves in the pan-Islamic movement or in any of the minor political parties. As a result of Coptic support, the Wafd became a target for criticism by other parties, especially Islamic ones. Islamic slogans against the Wafd Party started to emerge in political campaigns, but the party retained its popularity.

In 1942, during the Second World War, Ebeid and al-Nahhas had a falling-out. Ebeid accused al-Nahhas' wife of corruption and the resulting scandal led to Ebeid being ejected from the Wafd and forming his own political party (al-Kutla), which remained a minor party. The majority of Muslims and Copts stayed with the Wafd Party, under the leadership of al-Nahhas. Al-Nahhas was widely considered to be an honest leader, but he was not as effective as some had hoped he would be. The British were still in Egypt, with their heavy-handed policies, and the palace continued to manipulate all the political parties. King Fu'ad died in 1936 and was succeeded by his son, Farouk.

Even before the 1919 revolt, a cultural renaissance movement *(nahda)* was beginning to be felt in many areas, from art and literature to economics and politics. In literature, many prominent writers appeared, such as Tawfiq al-Hakim, Taha Hussein, al-'Aqqad, Muhammad Husayn Haykal Basha, and many others. In the arts, there were Mahmud Mukhtar, the sculptor, and Umm Kulthum, the best singer Egypt has ever produced. In the media, Egypt saw its first female editor in chief, Rose al-Yusuf, whose well-read magazine still carries her name today. In economics, there was Talaat Harb, who the established the Bank of Egypt (Banque Misr), which supported many industries. Of course, in politics, there was the Wafd Party, with its liberal policies. In the field of Islamic studies, there was Muhammad 'Abduh, who tried to broaden people's understanding of Islamic matters. The Copts participated in this cultural flowering, with no obvious signs of discrimination.

In appendix 1, we profile six prominent individuals—three Copts and three Muslims—whose stories reflect the hopes and disappointments of the *nahda* period. The first three, Taha Hussein, Salama Musa, and Jurji Zaydan, represent intellectuals in education and social thinking. The fourth is Talaat Harb, an economist of the period; the fifth is Rose al-Yusuf, a female actress who turned to publishing magazines and newspapers; and the sixth is Makram Ebeid, a lawyer, politician, and political writer.

New exterior factors started to affect the political landscape within Egypt in the 1920s and 1930s. One factor was the demolition of the caliphate in Turkey, in 1923. This contributed to the rise of political Islam, including the Muslim Brotherhood. A second factor was the Bolshevik Revolution in Russia, after which the ideas of communism and socialism made their way into Egypt. A third factor was the rise of fascism in Italy and Germany—a development which encouraged the emergence of small, semi-militant factions within some Egyptian political parties and within the Muslim Brotherhood. All these factors shaped the political landscape of Egypt in the second quarter of the twentieth century. The rise of a radical strain of political Islam is arguably the most important development during that period.

Political Islam

> Many things were added to Islam for political purposes, that would not have pleased God or the Prophet. These are now considered a core part of Islam. Those who objected to these additions and proposed modern interpretations of Islam were accused of heresy.
>
> — Muhammad Husayn Haykal, literary writer and politician

We mentioned in chapter three that the practice of relying on sayings of the Prophet as an authoritative source was repudiated by the Prophet himself. This opinion was upheld by the first and second caliphs. Abu Bakr, the first successor to the Prophet, gathered five hundred hadiths and found some to be at variance with what he himself had heard the Prophet say. His concern was that if the *hadiths* were not reliable, they could be misused and would mislead others. Abu Bakr and other early caliphs thought the Qur'an was the authority and was sufficient. But people felt a strong need to collect, modify, and even fabricate some *hadiths* to suit their own purposes, such as supporting a ruler's authority or solving community problems. By the time of the Abbasid dynasty, the number of *hadiths* reached the astronomical number of seven hundred thousand.[26] There have always been differences of opinion between Islamic scholars regarding the *hadiths*. Some sects, such as the Hanafi, which has many Egyptian followers, recognize only seventeen hadiths, while the Hanbali sect, common in Arabia, recognizes fifty thousand.[27]

In modern times, with the rapid transfer of information via the Internet, social media, and television, the distinction between the *hadith* and the Qur'an has become blurred. The holiness of the Qur'an has been extended to the *hadith*. Many contemporary Muslims do not know the difference between what God said in the Qur'an, what is attributed to the Prophet in the *hadith*, and what was added by Islamic commentators centuries ago. The difference between the rigid Islam of the Arabian Peninsula (the Hanbali sect) and the more flexible Islam of Egypt (the Hanafi sect) parallels their respective environments. In the harsh, unforgiving desert environment of Arabia an uncompromising, literal interpretation of Islam developed; while in the more stable, cultivated Egyptian landscape a more relaxed allegorical interpretation of the text was allowed. [28]

There are also widespread misconceptions about Islamic history. For many Muslims, a glorified image of the caliphs is associated with the greatness of the Islamic Empire. Some yearn to return to an idealized version of the past, when the caliphate enforced Islamic law over a vast territory. But very few caliphs ruled according to the ethics or the teachings of the Qur'an. The word 'mercy' is mentioned in the Qur'an seventy-nine times, and the word 'justice' also is mentioned many times. However, this generous spirit of Islam was often disregarded in practice. Some caliphs killed their brothers, sons, or fathers so they could take their place. For example, the Turkish caliph Muhammad al-Osmani (1390–1421) killed about a dozen of his brothers and half-brothers to eliminate any competition. The highest Islamic expert in Turkey (mufti) at the time approved this killing to avoid the possibility of a conspiracy, or so he claimed. At one point, there were three separate caliphates which competed with each other: one in Spain, another in Egypt, and a third in Iraq. This was all very different from the early spirit of Islam. In addition, many of the later caliphs enjoyed extravagant lifestyles, in contrast to the Prophet and the first four caliphs, who did not leave any inheritance worth mentioning. Presenting an idealized image of the past and relying on questionable *hadiths* are two effective strategies used by political Islam to garner support from Muslims, particularly those who feel threatened by modernity and who long for a "purer," simpler time.

Another practice that allowed some Islamic scholars to use Islam politically was to ignore selected older verses of the Qur'an, and emphasize later verses that suited their needs. They justified the practice based on the principle that a more recent verse supersedes the previous ones *(al-nasikh wa-l-mansukh)*. Using this principle, the number of verses ignored was anywhere from a few to about five hundred.

The caliphate as an institution was abolished in 1923, when the Turkish army officer Kamal Atatürk declared Turkey a modern republic. The caliphate had been a symbol of Islam in popular culture and served as a symbol of Islamic glory in popular imagination. Abolishing the old system left an emotional vacuum and created disappointment for many Muslims. Some considered it a threat to the religion itself, and wondered if Islam would survive without the caliphate. At that time, most of the Muslim world was either colonized or under the influence of European countries. These foreign powers not only dominated the military and economic spheres, they also introduced modern ideas that challenged the existing social order and worldview. When a society feels threatened, it consolidates its identity around its most stable part. In the Muslim world, this was Islam.

In Egypt, two schools of thought arose in response to the loss of the Turkish caliphate. The first proposed filling the void by having the Egyptian king replace the old Turkish caliph. The second, which appeared a few years later, proposed establishing the Muslim Brotherhood to assume the authority of the caliphate, with the ultimate goal of setting up a government based on Islamic principles. In an effort to establish a new caliphate in Egypt, a fatwa was issued declaring that King Fu'ad of Egypt was a descendant of the Prophet. People recognized and resented this attempt to give the king false religious legitimacy. They demonstrated in opposition to the return of the caliphate.

In 1925, 'Ali 'Abd al-Raziq, an Islamic scholar, published a book on the Islamic rules of governance.[29] He demonstrated that Islam, and more specifically the Qur'an, did not provide a system for ruling the Muslim world *(umma)*; there was no prescription for "Islamic government." The al-Azhar school of theology, backed by the power of the king, responded by putting 'Ali 'Abd al-Raziq on trial and firing him from al-Azhar. This incident had political implications and led to the resignation of the government. The dream of bringing the caliphate to Egypt was shattered, and the stage was set for an alternative, more radical, ideology.

Hassan al-Banna (1906–49), the founder of the Muslim Brotherhood, came from a modest background. He attended Dar al-'Ulum, a college that educated prospective teachers of Arabic, literature, and Islam. He graduated in 1927 and founded the Muslim Brotherhood in 1928. Al-Banna was a charismatic preacher who was influenced by the Wahhabi sect of Islam in Arabia. This sect follows a literal, conservative interpretation of the Qur'anic text. Within a decade, al-Banna and the Muslim Brotherhood had attracted many followers both inside and outside Egypt, eventually receiving financial support not only from Egypt, but from Arabia's petrodollars. The Muslim Brotherhood grew to become a well-organized institution, with newspapers and branches all over Egypt as well as in some other Muslim countries. Initially, the Muslim Brotherhood's message was to promote the correct practice of Islam in daily life.

The rapid rise in popularity of the Muslim Brotherhood encouraged al-Banna to enter politics in order to pursue the dream of reviving the caliphate. He received some support from the palace as well as from minor political parties who saw this as an opportunity to weaken the Wafd Party and its liberal democratic policies. Al-Banna ran for a seat in Parliament but failed to be elected. Seeing that he enjoyed greater popularity than did some of the minor parties that supported him, he revised his strategy. When democracy did not get him to power, he founded a secret underground paramilitary organization to stir up political instability, hoping this would create a political climate that would help the Muslim Brotherhood gain power.[30]

This underground paramilitary wing of the Muslim Brotherhood began a campaign of violence and terror which included the assassination of two prime ministers—Ahmed Maher Basha in 1945 and Mahmud Fahmi al-Nuqrashi in 1948—as well as some judges and police officers.[31] Police stations and other symbols of authority were attacked. When this violent campaign could not be contained, Prime Minister al-Nuqrashi Basha, who had previously supported the Muslim Brotherhood, now banned the organization for resorting to violence.[31] As a result, al-Nuqrashi himself was assassinated by the Brotherhood. His replacement, 'Abd al-Hadi Basha, cracked down even more strongly. Some members of the Muslim Brotherhood were harassed, imprisoned, and brutally treated. By this point, the king was concerned about his throne. It is likely he was the one who ordered the assassination of al-Banna which was carried out in 1949. After that, the Muslim Brotherhood went underground.

The Muslim Brotherhood was not well equipped to deal with the challenges presented by modernity, such as the economic, political, and social changes that were underway—particularly the place of religious minorities in Muslim society. They adhered to earlier and more traditional attitudes that confined non-Muslims to an inferior position. Bolstered by trends toward greater equality in society, Copts had thought these discriminatory ideas were a thing of the past. But despite al-Banna's repeated statements that the Muslim Brotherhood was not hostile to minorities, the Muslim Brotherhood used both mosques and leaflets to spread anti-Coptic messages.[32] The Copts resented this, though some conceded that the problem was not with Islam itself but with those adherents who twisted its teachings.[33]

The Copts and Political Islam

Coptic newspapers, such as *al-Manara al-misriya*, reported little community violence in the 1920s. But violent incidents increased in the 1930s and 1940s.[34] This coincided with a rise in the Muslim Brotherhood's activities. Anti-Coptic outbursts occurred in many places in Egypt. Government officials were not eager to be seen taking vigorous steps against the Brotherhood's activities. By the 1940s, the Muslim Brotherhood had become too powerful for any party, including the Wafd Party, to defy openly. The Muslim Brotherhood emerged as the master of the streets, with an armed underground force and sympathizers estimated in the thousands. The government was willing to allow some violence against the Copts as a convenient safety valve to release the frustrations of the masses, and sometimes it simply was incapable of containing it.

By March 1947, tensions increased, as is evident from several attacks on Coptic churches. A church in the city of Zagazig was burned down, and there were attacks on churches in Cairo and other places.[35] Communal relations had been strained for at least two years, partly due to the Muslim Brotherhood's activities. This happened at the same time as the

Brotherhood was carrying out a number of similar attacks on Jewish homes and shops. The Copts were worried they would meet a fate similar to that of the Jews in Europe.[36]

As the situation worsened, some Coptic newspapers called for the dissolution of the Muslim Brotherhood and all organizations that mixed religion with politics. The government finally, and by mere chance, discovered the secret place the Brotherhood stored their weapons. Realizing the seriousness and the magnitude of the threat, the government moved to dissolve the society in 1949.[37] When the Wafd Party returned to power in January 1950, they allowed the Muslim Brotherhood to return, though some parts of the organization remained underground. The new head of the Muslim Brotherhood was an elderly judge named Hassan al-Hudaybi.

In January 1952, a mob in Suez City destroyed the Coptic church, school, and Benevolent Society building; three Copts were murdered.[38] In the same month, 750 buildings belonging to Muslims, Christians, and Jews were burned and looted, mostly in Cairo. The incident was triggered by the British killing of fifty Egyptian auxiliary policemen in Isma'ilia, a town north of Suez, during the struggle against colonial power. Fingers were pointed at the Muslim Brotherhood and other similar organizations, but nothing was proven. The government could not stop the mob, which was beyond control.

As a result of the burning of their church in Suez, the Copts were frustrated and angry. Under considerable political pressure, the patriarch publicly exonerated the Muslim Brotherhood. He announced that the Coptic Christmas that year would be a time of mourning and not celebration. The government tried to dissuade the church from making a strong public gesture, but failed. The government offered financial compensation to rebuild the church, but the Copts rejected this and demanded an investigation instead. Nahhas Basha, the Wafd prime minister, visited the patriarch twice in an attempt to pacify the angry Copts. Finally, the government had to issue a statement deploring the incident. Also, the palace sent two representatives to the patriarch to express the king's regret.[39] Ebeid visited the supreme guide of the Muslim Brotherhood, al-Hudaybi, and discussed the situation with him and other Brotherhood leaders. Ebeid invited al-Hudaybi to visit the patriarch, and the two men met on January 18, 1952.

This pattern of events has been repeated again and again, with slight variations from one incident to another, up to the present time. The leaders meet and chat, with photo opportunities and media coverage, but without reaching agreement on a long-term policy to remove the sectarian tensions which have continued up to the present day.

Coptic–Muslim Relations among Intellectuals

To understand the political climate and Coptic-Muslim relations among intellectuals at that time, it is helpful to look at Naguib Mahfouz's *Sugar Street*, the third novel in his well-known Cairo Trilogy. In it, two of the major characters, Riyad Qaldas, a Coptic scientist and artist, and his friend Kamal 'Abd al-Jawad, a teacher and philosopher, discuss the political situation as they walk through the old section of Islamic Cairo, near al-Azhar Mosque. Part of the dialogue between them goes as follows:

> Riyad Qaldas was upset that evening. He said passionately, "The constitutional crisis has concluded with the rout of the people. Al-Nahhas's removal is a defeat for the nation in its historical struggle with the palace."
>
> Kamal answered sorrowfully, "It's clear now that [King] Faruq's as bad as his father."
>
> "Faruq's not the only one responsible. The traditional enemies of the people have engineered this debacle. It's the work of Ali Maher and Muhammad Mahmud. Lamentably Ahmad Maher and al-Nuqrashi, these two populist leaders, joined ranks with the enemies of the people. If the nation were cleansed of traitors, the king would not find anyone to help him suppress the rights of the people." After a short silence, he continued: "The English aren't playing an active role now, but the people and the king are at loggerheads. Independence isn't everything. There is also the people's sacred prerogative to enjoy their rights and their sovereignty—to live as free men, not slaves."
>
> Unlike Riyad, Kamal was not deeply engaged in politics, but his doubts had not been able to destroy it for him, as they had so many other interests. It retained an emotional vitality for him. His heart believed firmly in the rights of the people, no matter how divided his intellect was on the subject, espousing at times "the rights of man," and on other occasions proclaiming, "It's all a question of survival of the fittest. The masses are the common herd." It might also wonder, "Isn't Communism an experiment worth exploring?" His heart had not been purged of the populist sentiments with which he had grown up, and these were mixed with memories of Fahmi.
>
> Politics was an essential element of Riyad's intellectual activity. He asked, "Is it possible for us to forget the humiliating reception Makram Ubayd got in the square in front of Abdin Palace or

al-Nahhas's criminal ouster, that insulting calumny, like spit in the face of the nation? Blind hatred makes some applaud it, alas."

"You're just angry because of what happened to Makram Ubayd," Kamal teased.

Without any hesitation Riyad replied, "All of us Copts are Wafdists. That's because the Wafd Party represents true nationalism. It's not a religious, Turkish-oriented bunch like the National Party. The Wafd is a populist party. It will make Egypt a nation that provides freedom for all Egyptians, without regard to ethnic origin or religious affiliation. The enemies of the people know this. That's why the Copts were targeted for barefaced oppression throughout the Sidqy era. Now we'll be experiencing that again."

Kamal welcomed this candor, which demonstrated the depth of their friendship. All the same he felt like teasing Riyad some more: "Here you are, talking about Coptic Christians, when you believe in nothing but science and art . . . ."

Riyad fell silent. They had reached al-Azhar Street, where the cold wind gusted rather fiercely. As they walked along they came to a pastry shop, and Kamal invited Riyad to have some with him. They each got a modest plateful and stepped to the side of the shop to eat. Then Riyad said, "I'm both a freethinker and a Copt. Indeed I'm both a Copt and a man without any religion. I frequently feel that Christianity is my community, not my faith. If I analyzed this feeling, I might entertain some reservations about it. But not so fast . . . isn't it cowardly to ignore my people? There's one thing that can help me overcome this quandary, and that is to devote myself to the kind of sincere Egyptian patriotism envisaged by Sa'd Zaghlul. Al-Nahhas is a Muslim by way of religion, but he's also a nationalist in every sense of the word. He makes us think of ourselves as Egyptians, whether we are Muslims or Copts. I could lead a happy life with an untroubled mind by focusing on thoughts like these, but a real life is at the same time a responsible one."

Kamal's breast was agitated by emotions and his thoughts wandered as he smacked his lips over the pastry. Riyad's appearance, which was so purely Egyptian that it reminded him of a Pharaonic portrait, stirred various reflections: "Riyad's points can't be denied. I'm torn between the dictates of my intellect and of my heart, and so is he. How can a minority live in the midst of a majority that oppresses it? Different sacred scriptures are commonly compared according to the level of happiness they provide to human beings, and that is most clearly represented by the amount of aid they give the oppressed."

Kamal said, "Forgive me. I've never had to deal with racism. From the very beginning my mother trained me to love everyone, and I grew up in the revolutionary atmosphere that was free of ethnic prejudices. So I have had no experience with this problem."

As they resumed their walk, Riyad said, "One would hope there wouldn't be any problem at all. I'm sorry to have to tell you bluntly that we grew up in homes with plenty of gloomy memories. I'm not a Coptic chauvinist, but anyone who neglects human rights, whether at home or at the end of the earth, has neglected the rights of all mankind."

"That's beautifully put. It's not surprising that truly humanitarian manifestos originate frequently in minority circles or with people whose consciences are troubled by the problems of minorities. But there are always some fanatics."

"Always. Everywhere. Men have only recently evolved from animals. Your fanatics consider us cursed infidels. Our fanatics consider you infidel usurpers. They call themselves descendants of the kings of ancient Egypt and people who were able to preserve their religion by paying the poll tax levied on non-Muslims."

Kamal laughed out loud. Then he said, "That's precisely what the two sides say. Do you suppose the origin of this dispute is religion or a human proclivity for dissension? Muslims don't all agree with each other and neither do Christians. You will find that there have long been disagreements between Shi'i Muslims and Sunni Muslims, Hijazi Muslims and Iraqi Muslims, Wafdists and Constitutionalists, students in the humanities and in the sciences, and supporters of the rival Ahli and Arsenal soccer teams. But in spite of this contentious streak in human nature, we are deeply upset when we read newspaper accounts of an earthquake in Japan. Listen, why don't you treat this subject in your stories?"

"The problem of Copts and Muslims . . . ." Riyad Qaldas was quiet for a time. Then he said, "I'm afraid it would be misunderstood." After another period of silence he added, "And don't forget that, in spite of everything, we're enjoying our golden age. At one time Shaykh Abd al-Aziz Jawish suggested that Muslims should make shoes from our hides."

> "How can we eradicate this problem?"
>
> "Fortunately it has been absorbed by the problem of the people as a whole. Today the Copts' problem is the people's problem. We are oppressed when everyone else is. When the people are free, we are."[40]

This dialogue between the two friends continues to touch on other subjects, but does not stray far from Coptic–Muslim relations. The excerpt above reflects the way many Coptic and Muslim intellectuals related to each other and to the political climate of their day. Both Coptic and Muslim intellectuals supported the policies of the Wafd Party—particularly its nationalist aspirations—as being in the best interests of Egypt. But Copts, in addition, saw the Wafd as the only party which offered them equality with Muslims and welcomed them as full participants. Mahfouz suggests this is part of what underlies Riyad's passion for politics. Through the Wafd Party, Copts could gain entry into the political realm in a way that was not available to them through Islamic parties or through the ideology of political Islam. For many Copts at the time, this made political engagement doubly compelling.

However, the passage also reveals, directly or indirectly, some differences between the two friends. Riyad freely states that he is a freethinker and not a religious Copt. For him, Christianity is "my community, not my faith." In a sense, nationalism has, for him, become a substitute for religion. This idea stirs up conflicted thoughts in Kamal, a secular Muslim. He is made uncomfortable, and a bit defensive, when his Coptic friend indirectly alludes to the difficulties faced by the Coptic community at the hands of the Muslim majority. Kamal avows his own lack of prejudice and then shifts to making generalizations. He wonders whether sectarian disagreements simply reflect human nature. It is more comfortable for him to think of the differences between Copts and Muslims in intellectual terms—as being like those between Shi'i and Sunni Muslims, Wafdists and Constitutionalists, or even fans of rival soccer teams. Kamal's discomfort seems deeply human. Naguib Mahfouz's sensitive portrayal of the emotional position of both Copts and Muslims is what makes this novel a great work, and part of what earned him the Nobel Prize for Literature.

The Problem of Building Churches in Twentieth-Century Egypt

Previous chapters have touched on some of the difficulties in building churches. Restrictions on building and repairing churches are an indicator of the level of tension and discrimination between Muslims and Copts.

They may be the cause or the effect of sectarian tensions, linked at times to outbreaks of serious violence. In the early days of Islam, building churches was not difficult. Nothing in the Qur'an prohibits building churches. As the number of Muslims increased and tensions between the two communities rose, Islamic *fiqh* (understanding) was looked to as an authority on issues the Qur'an did not mention.

Islamic *fiqh* has espoused different positions regarding building churches in Islamic lands. In 1980, for example, the mufti of the Muslim Brotherhood held the following views: (1) new cities built by Muslims, even new towns built in contemporary Egypt, should have no churches; (2) areas historically taken in battle by Muslim armies, such as the city of Alexandria in the seventh century and Constantinople in the thirteenth century, should have no churches; and (3) areas that were annexed without war, such the greater part of Egypt, may keep existing churches but not repair them or build new ones, unless specifically mentioned in the surrender agreement.[41] But if we go back to the Turkish period, we see that the building and restoring of churches was approved by the sultan in 1856. The rights of religious minorities to build their own houses of worship, no matter how small those minorities might be, were protected. A request was to be made by the head of the community to the sultan, who gave his approval and protection for the new building.[42] This system not only allowed churches to be built, but provided protection for those churches.

After Egypt became formally independent of the Turkish Empire, following the Second World War, the regulations for building churches changed. There was no longer a sultan to appeal to, but a permit to build or renovate a church still had to be obtained from the highest ruling authority, which was the prime minister after 1923.

After the 1919 revolution, especially in the 1930s and 1940s, obtaining a permit to build or renovate a church was easy. The Wafd Party's policies provided a reasonable degree of separation between state and religion. But even during this relatively liberal period, the principle of equality did not hold up in practice on all occasions. For example, in 1934, under the administration of 'Abd al-Fattah Yahya Basha (not a Wafdist), the under-secretary of the interior, al-Keraby Basha, issued new, more stringent regulations for building and renovating churches. The process allowed wide discretion in determining suitable locations for churches:

1. Is the land not in use? Is it agricultural land? Is it owned by the applicant, and is the ownership legal?

2. How far is the desired location from Islamic sites or a mosque in the area?
3. Is the land in an area dominated by Muslims or Copts?
4. If the land is located in a Muslim neighborhood, do the residents have any objection to building a church there?
5. Is there already another church in the town?
6. If there is not a church in the town, how far is the nearest town with a church?
7. What is the number of people in the Coptic community in the town?
8. Is the location near public buildings? If it is near the banks of the Nile or any public road, the corresponding departments must give consent.
9. An official document indicating the distance between the proposed location desired and any public stores must be sent to the administration.
10. An engineering plan with a scale of 1 to 1,000 must be signed and approved by the head of the church and a certified engineer.[43]

These considerations were far more rigorous than those required under the Turkish Empire in 1856. There were many ways to deny a permit if that was the desired outcome. For example, after an application for a new church was submitted, the official response was often delayed for a long time. During this period, a small mosque would be built near the proposed location; permission for the church would then be denied based on the close proximity to that mosque. In the beginning of the 1940s, as political Islam became more popular with the masses, building churches became more and more difficult. After 1952, a presidential decree was required in order to build or renovate a church.

Though the rules for building churches were relaxed at times, often they were applied in a discriminatory way. As a result, the Copts found ways around the regulatory obstacles. For example, they first obtained a permit to raise a building for a Coptic social organization; later, the completed building would be consecrated as a church. The government then had two choices: either accept the status quo or demolish the building. Often the officials accepted the status quo, but on rare occasions when tensions were high, the church was demolished, leading to sectarian violence. We will see some examples of this in the next chapter.

13

THE 1952 REVOLT AND THE NASSER ERA (1954–70)

By 1951–52, the political climate in Egypt was deteriorating on many fronts: the political parties were corrupt and their popularity had declined; the king was seen as a corrupt leader and a womanizer; the British were still stationed in the Suez Canal and exercised political influence; and political Islam continued to gain in strength. Several administrations came and went, with none lasting for long or achieving much.

This was the condition of the country on July 23, 1952, when a group of young army officers staged a coup d'état. The officers' action was welcomed by many Egyptians, especially after King Farouk, a symbol of corruption and decadence, was removed from the throne. The officers—all of whom were Muslims—came from a variety of different political orientations; some sympathized with the Muslim Brotherhood and others were leftists or communists. But the majority did not have any clear political goals beyond improving the army, expelling the British, and removing the king. Gamal Abd al-Nasser was different; he envisioned a new Egypt based on social justice and industrialization.

The United States initially supported the officers' movement. It hoped the coup would be a stepping stone toward allowing the United States to replace the ailing British imperial interests in Egypt. In June 1953, the officers declared Egypt a republic. Nasser became the president in 1954, after the brief tenure of Muhammad Naguib, who was removed from office after an internal power struggle, and subsequently was put under house arrest.[1]

Within two years, the officers had banned all political parties and were ruling with unilateral authority. They allowed the Muslim Brotherhood to continue operating, claiming it was not a political party, even though in actuality it functioned as one. The Brotherhood remained intact and thought the officers' revolt was of their own doing—or at least that the officers had succeeded as a result of their support. Each saw the other as a potential ally in achieving their own goals.

The honeymoon between the officers and Muslim Brotherhood was short-lived, however. The Muslim Brotherhood wanted veto power over any legislation that did not seem to them Islamic. In addition, they wanted to impose reactionary Islamic views, such as a strict dress code for women. Their demands were ignored by the officers. The rift between the officers and the Muslim Brotherhood started to widen. In 1954, the Brotherhood attempted to assassinate Nasser, but the attempt failed. This led to the arrest and torture of many of the Brotherhood's members, even those who were not involved in any of the organization's militant activities. A military court sentenced seven members of the Brotherhood to death, including the head of the organization, whose sentence later was reduced to life in prison. The Muslim Brotherhood was weakened and again went underground.

In the meantime, Nasser began to implement his plans for broad social reforms. He embarked on a land reform program to break up the large estates of wealthy landowners. The government first confiscated parcels of land larger than two hundred feddans (one feddan equals 1.04 acres) and later confiscated parcels down to one hundred feddans. The confiscated land was then distributed to small farmers who did not own any land.

In the mid-1950s, an important item on Egypt's agenda was the Aswan High Dam project. A new and much larger dam was to be built upstream of the old Aswan dam. It would provide electricity as well as expand the cultivated land by about 15 to 20 percent. Egypt hoped the World Bank and the West would help finance the project and provide technical expertise. But its request was denied because Egypt wanted to keep its political independence and refused to accept conditions that would have replaced British influence with U.S. influence.

Nasser's solution was to nationalize the Suez Canal and finance the High Dam from its revenue. The Egyptians were ecstatic about regaining the canal; they still remembered that the canal had been built by forced labor, and that its construction had led to the colonization of Egypt. The nationalization of the canal and the U.S. refusal to finance the High Dam were highly charged political decisions which led to a sequence of significant events.[2] The Israelis, the British, and the French resented the nationalization of the Suez Canal and the rising power of an independent Egypt. They attempted to overthrow Nasser's regime with military force in 1956. Ultimately, the invasion failed, especially after the United States, the Soviet Union, and most of the world opposed the military intervention. Egypt put up strong resistance and gained support in the Arab world and among Third World countries. Ultimately, the High Dam was built with the help of the Soviet Union, a step which was interpreted in the context of the Cold War; Western propaganda depicted Egypt as part of the Communist bloc, though this was far from the truth. Nasser's foreign policy was based on pan-Arabism and pan-Islamism. Egypt avoided taking sides in the Cold War and was one of the leaders of the non-aligned nations. In 1964, Nasser became the president of the Non-Aligned Movement. The West did not want to see a strong and independent Egypt whose presence might hinder Western policies aimed at accessing the region's large oil reserves, and at maintaining uncritical support for Israel.

After the successful nationalization of the Suez Canal in 1956, Nasser initiated an accelerated industrialization program under the leadership of Dr. Aziz Sedki, a Harvard PhD engineer. The government also instituted major socialist programs, including free health care and an expanded free educational system. The government guaranteed jobs for all graduates.

One criticism of Nasser's regime is that it tried to do too many things too fast. In spite of the government's best intentions, some of its projects failed due to poor planning and poor management, with no self-correcting mechanism. Egypt increasingly became a police state. Many of the officers who were running organizations lacked the talent and background to succeed. In addition to arresting and torturing communists and members of the Muslim Brotherhood, the regime also suppressed dissenting intellectuals, university professors, judges, and writers.

The Muslim Brotherhood attempted to overthrow the Nasser regime again in the mid-1960s. Sayyid Qutb, a Muslim writer and thinker, expounded the idea that Muslims should boycott the country's institutions and resort to jihadist violence. By following this course of action, the Muslim Brotherhood hoped to create chaotic conditions that would allow them to gain power.[3] This was and still is a Muslim Brotherhood strategy. In 1966, Qutb and some of his followers were sentenced to death by a military court. The Copts were relieved and felt safe after the government crackdown on the Muslim Brotherhood—but not for long. Qutb's writings survived him and still provide ideological underpinning for the modern jihadist movement we see today in the Middle East and elsewhere. After Qutb's death, the Brotherhood went underground again. Some members found work opportunities in Saudi Arabia and the Gulf area, where they were welcomed and felt at home with the very conservative Wahhabi sect of Islam. They also received considerable financial help there.

During the Nasser era, policies that supported free and open education and guaranteed employment led to greater equality for Copts and Muslims in many areas. However, although the government expanded the free education system, it enforced teaching religion as a basic subject in school curricula. By contrast, in 1937, the Wafd Party had considered religion an optional subject. The al-Azhar theology school expanded during the 1960s into a modern university with colleges of medicine, engineering, literature, and so on. While this provided good opportunities for Muslim students from Egypt and abroad, it excluded Copts completely.[4]

As conditions for the poor improved, the middle class expanded, and many Egyptians felt hopeful, Coptic–Muslim relations also improved, at least on the surface. Employees were hired and promoted according to their qualifications and experience, independent of their religion. Nevertheless, at the higher levels, promotions were often based on personal selection, allowing religious bias to be a factor. The number of Copts in prominent positions started to decline. In contrast to the masses, wealthy Copts and Muslims were not pleased with the social agenda of the government. Many had lost some or most of their assets due to land redistribution and nationalization of many corporations. In the 1950s and 1960s, many affluent Egyptians, both Copts and Muslims, emigrated from Egypt to the West.

While personal bias often worked against the Copts, sometimes it worked in their favor. One notable example involved obtaining permits to build new churches—something that was still difficult during this period. However, Patriarch Cyril VI (1959–71) was on good personal terms with Nasser; they had mutual respect for each other. After the patriarch visited Nasser to ask about obtaining permits to build churches, Nasser gave permission to build twenty-five churches annually, without the need to follow the archaic procedures described in the previous chapter. The church was pleased, but the root of the problem was not resolved, and the old system was reinstated after Nasser died in 1970.

During the period of dispensation, Cyril VI wished to build a new cathedral to house some of the relics of St. Mark that had come from the Vatican. But he did not have the financial resources to do so, as the church had lost many of its endowments.[5] Moreover, it no longer had the financial support of rich Copts, who now had lost many of their own assets. Despite the church's financial difficulties, the pope refused to seek financial aid from outside Egypt. He used his personal connections with the government to obtain funding toward building the new cathedral. Nasser's confidant, Muhammad Husayn Haykal, was very instrumental on that issue.[6] This was one of the rare times when a Muslim regime actively contributed to building a church. Nasser himself attended the groundbreaking ceremony in 1965. The opening ceremony of the cathedral in 1968 was attended by many dignitaries. This attendance was highly publicized and was appreciated by most Copts, although some radical Muslims no doubt felt differently.

The government under Nasser was a one-party system with a parliament, the Majlis al-Sha'b (literally, 'People's Assembly'). Starting in 1956, several constitutions were adopted or modified, and several elections were held. But it was a sham democracy. The percentage of Copts in these elections was close to zero (less than half of one percent; see appendix 2, table 2). This was due in part to the absence of political parties that could absorb the Copts, but also to the rise of political Islam. To overcome this embarrassment, in 1956 Nasser introduced an amendment to the constitution that gave the president the right to appoint ten members to parliament.[7] The members appointed by Nasser, and later by Sadat and Mubarak, were mostly Copts. This non-democratic policy of appointments did not solve the systemic problem. Instead of finding a political solution similar to the multiparty system which followed the 1919 revolt, the system of appointments has continued until the present time. The church was asked to nominate some candidates so the president could select a representative to the parliament from among them. This gave the church at least some recognized role in the political system. Later, during the era of Cyril VI's successor, Shenouda III, the church started to act as the de facto representative of the Copts with respect to the government. While Shenouda III denied his intervention in politics, most Copts considered him their representative in the absence of a true democracy.

Some of the faults of the Nasser era became apparent to the public, especially after the Six-Day War in 1967, when the Israelis were easily able to defeat the combined forces of Egypt, Jordan, and Syria within that span of time. By the time hostilities ended, Israel occupied Sinai, the West Bank of Jordan, and the Syrian Golan Heights. It controlled territory many times larger than the state of Israel itself. Nasser was caught off guard by this war, which he had not prepared for. He had not anticipated the political consequences of some of his actions. The defeat smashed Nasser's image and his ego. He admitted his responsibility and resigned as president. But people all over Egypt and in many Arab countries rejected his resignation. They poured into the streets immediately after hearing the news, and demanded he stay in office despite the shameful defeat. This emotional outpouring demonstrated the degree of respect and affection given him by the people. In spite of his many mistakes, Nasser had managed to do some good for Egypt's middle class and the poor. He had a vision of a prosperous and independent Egypt, and offered hope for the future after centuries of foreign domination. Nasser stayed in office, but the consequences of his defeat are still unfolding in the Middle East today. Nasser, a diabetic and a heavy smoker, died of a heart attack in September 1970, at the age of fifty-two. As the news of his death reached the streets, the country went into a state of shock and mourning. At least five million people lined the streets for Nasser's funeral procession and the funeral itself was attended by all the Arab heads of states, except King Faisal of Saudi Arabia.

Nasser's legacy is complex. His policies strengthened the power of the army, the intelligence agency, and the presidency. At the same time, they weakened the independent institutions of the country, such as the judiciary, the universities, and the media. His harsh suppression of the Muslim Brotherhood, and the failure to build democratic institutions through which opposition could be expressed, ultimately led to the resurgence not only of the Brotherhood but of other jihadist groups.

Nasser did not build a lasting social-political system. When Sadat, Nasser's successor, came to power, he was able to shift Egypt's policy 180 degrees, neglecting the industrial and public sectors in favor of a liberal economic policy that led to serious corruption, as we will see. But in spite of his regime's shortcomings, Nasser was a towering figure in the Middle East and in Third World countries. Maybe his accomplishments are best summed up by the poet Ahmad Fu'ad Nigm, who said of Nasser, "He achieved miracles, but many of his projects failed."

The Coptic Church in Transition

As Egypt's political and economic direction started to change after Nasser's death, the leadership of the church was also changing. It became younger and more ambitious. These changes in both the state and the church had a major effect on Coptic–Muslim relations. Before we return to the national political scene, it is important to give some background about events taking place within the Coptic Church itself.

From the time Christianity first came to Egypt until the nineteenth century, church leaders had governed its internal affairs. In the thirteenth and fourteenth centuries, as Copts began to be a minority, the government came to consider the church as an official representative of the Coptic community. In the absence of democracy, it was expected that the patriarch and the bishops would play such a role. But the Coptic lay aristocracy (the *arakhina*) who financed the church, and had traditionally played an informal role in its affairs, also wanted to play a larger part, as did a younger generation of educated Copts.

Beginning in the eighteenth and nineteenth centuries, as Egypt's educational system improved, some Copts became more knowledgeable and better educated than the clergy, even in religious matters. By 1877, a Coptic newspaper, *al-Watan*, founded and run by educated young Copts, began providing an independent channel of communication to the Coptic community. Between 1874 and 1892, the *arakhina*, influential and wealthy laymen, formed an organization of Coptic laymen known as the Church Community Council or CCC (al-Majlis al-Milli). Once organized, they tried to expand their influence in church affairs. The CCC's initial agenda included overseeing the church endowment and charitable donations, and improving education among the poor—laymen and priests alike. In addition, the CCC started to look into the church laws governing personal status in matters such as marriage, divorce, and inheritance. The CCC also wanted to be involved in selecting future popes. Regional councils of the organization were to be formed under the presidency of the local bishops. The CCC was officially recognized by khedive decrees in 1874 and again in 1883.[8] Not surprisingly, this lay organization and its agenda was resented by the clergy and church hierarchy as an intrusion on what had been their prerogatives.

When Pope Cyril V and the bishops opposed the CCC, an overt power struggle ensued. Eventually, the new khedive, Abbas II (1892–1914), intervened. Supported by the British, he ordered Pope Cyril banished to the Monastery of al-Baramus, and replaced him with Bishop Athanasius of the Sanbu diocese on September 1, 1892—a move orchestrated largely by the CCC. When Pope Cyril refused to go along with this plan, the Holy Synod supported him by excommunicating Bishop Athanasius.[9] Athanasius, the politically appointed pope, received almost no recognition from the clergy or from Copts at large, who saw his appointment as an outside intrusion into Coptic church affairs. In the end, both the CCC and the government begged Cyril to return to his office on February 4, 1893. The victorious pope and supportive bishops went on running church affairs in the traditional way, and the conflict between influential laymen and the church hierarchy continued to smolder.[10]

In the 1940s, Fu'ad University (now Cairo University) began graduating a new generation of young Christians and Muslims, many of whom were critical of the status quo and dissatisfied with the existing conditions and institutions in the country. Some educated Copts had much to criticize within their own church. They complained that then-patriarch Yusab II (1946–56) was weak and surrounded himself with people who were corrupt; that the selection of priests and bishops was subject to bribery; that many priests and even some bishops were poorly educated; and that churches and monasteries were poorly maintained. To give one example, the Monastery of the Holy Family in Upper Egypt (north of Asyut) was a rich monastery and had only thirty-five monks in 1926. Little of its wealth went toward improving the deteriorated buildings or educating the monks. The monks rose in protest in 1936, 1937, 1939, 1947, and 1959. Some of these mutinies were dealt with by expelling the most rebellious individuals, but the problem was allowed to continue with no significant progress. At one point, the situation became so bad that the corruption of this particular monastery was brought to the attention of the Egyptian parliament and the media.[11]

Sana S. Hassan, who studied the revival of the modern church, describes in her excellent volume the poor living conditions of some priests in Upper Egypt. For example, she visited a priest in Abu Tig (south of Asyut) who lived with his family, including numerous children, in a one-room hotel, without any sanitary facilities. Some chickens and a goat also shared the room. Their only income was in the form of gifts from the congregation whenever a funeral or wedding was held.[12] The status of this priest was not unique in the poor areas of Egypt.

Dissatisfaction with the leaders of the Coptic Church reached a climax in 1954 when a small radical Coptic group called al-Umma al-Qibtiya (the Coptic Nation) kidnapped the aged Pope Yusab II (1946–56) at gunpoint and forced him to abdicate. He was made to sign an order relieving him of his duties, and then was sent to a monastery in the desert at Wadi al-Natrun. The kidnappers were quickly arrested, put on trial, and sentenced to prison. The Holy Synod decided to exile the old patriarch to the monastery of the Holy Family in Asyut. According to Coptic tradition, as long as a pope is alive, the church cannot select a new one, so the patriarch's seat remained vacant until Yusab died in 1956.[13]

The Copts then had to select a new patriarch. Who would it be? One of the educated, ambitious young monks, or one of the old, conservative, traditional monks? According to tradition, clergy and laymen participate in the first phase of the selection process by directly voting for candidates. In the second phase, the names of the three candidates who receive the most votes are placed in a container, and one name is drawn out by a blindfolded child during a special church service. The Copts believe that, in this way, God's hand intervenes to choose the next patriarch from among the three.

It might be noted that there is no provision for a fourth, blank slip—just in case God does not want to select any of the three names.

At the time of the selection in 1956, the majority of the Holy Synod were old, conservative bishops, who had some reservations about the young educated monks. They worried that these young monks might initiate radical changes. Some of the new monks were even accused of being communists. But the young monks had the support of the new generation of educated Copts. Fearing the growing influence of the younger generation, the Holy Synod was able to change the rules for selecting a new pope to include the requirements that a nominee have a minimum of fifteen years as a monk and not be less than forty years old. This excluded all the young monks from consideration. (The reader may remember that the most prominent Egyptian pope in the history of the Coptic Church was Athanasius I, in the fourth century, who was selected at the age of thirty.) Although the young monks were unable to put forward a candidate from among themselves, they supported the eventual selection of Cyril VI (1959–71). Cyril was a kind-hearted, spiritual monk, and most Copts loved him. He used to travel and conduct services all over Egypt, even in remote areas. The door of his cathedral was always open.

Realizing that church reform would have to come from within, many dedicated and well-educated Copts chose to enter either the priesthood or the monastic life in order to serve the community and bring about change. According to Coptic church tradition, priests were required to be married in order to serve their congregations. Monks had to be celibate, but they could rise to become bishops or popes—positions whose influence was much greater than that of a priest.

Pope Cyril VI selected three of the most educated monks for prominent positions—two as bishops and one as an abbot. These three men greatly influenced the church. The first was Nazeer Gayed, who obtained a degree in literature and history, became a bishop, and later became Pope Shenouda III. The second was Yusuf Iskander, a pharmacist, who became a monk and influential scholar under the name of Matta al-Miskin (Matthew the Poor). The third was Saad Aziz, later Bishop Samuel, who held a degree in law from Cairo University and two master's degrees from Princeton University, one in psychology and one in religious studies. Bishop Samuel was an important link to other churches outside of Egypt.

Before Gayed became a monk and took the name Shenouda, he had been in charge of a Sunday school newspaper and was a prolific writer and speaker whose articles were widely read. Eventually he rose to become a bishop. His lectures on Friday evenings in Cairo were very well attended, and some of his talks were printed in booklets or distributed on audio cassettes. He was invited to speak at other churches, and gained wide popularity. The large attendance at his lectures reportedly put the country's security system on alert during Nasser's era. Also, there was friction between Bishop Shenouda and Pope Cyril VI. Despite these difficulties, Shenouda had many followers.

When Nasser died in 1970, Sadat became the new president. When Cyril VI died in 1971, Shenouda became the new patriarch, Shenouda III. Unfortunately, Sadat and Shenouda did not have the warm personal relationship that their predecessors had had. These changes in leadership created a new relationship between the church and the state. When relations between the pope and the president deteriorated, President Sadat found an ally in Matta al-Miskin.

Matta al-Miskin had been a successful pharmacist. After he entered the religious life, his intelligence and discipline earned him respect and promotion within the church. He was selected as the pope's representative in charge of Alexandria, but when he started to ordain young educated priests, he met resistance from the old guard. He decided to retire to the monastery and focus on studying Coptic church history. There he produced many well-researched volumes and was surrounded by younger monks who were of a similar caliber, but who were not accepted by the well-established old monasteries. Although this younger generation brought new knowledge and hope for the future, they were still accused of being left-wing ideologues and were mistrusted by the older monks.

Pope Cyril VI allowed Matta al-Miskin to become the abbot of the old St. Macarius Monastery in Wadi al-Natrun, where he was joined by some of his disciples. At that time, only six elderly monks lived in the monastery, which was in a deteriorated condition. Matta al-Miskin obtained financial grants which allowed the old buildings to be restored and new ones to be built, maintaining the original style. Under his supervision, the monastery started a vigorous land reclamation program in the desert. The green expanse around the monastery attracted the attention of President Sadat on one of his flights over the desert. Sadat and Matta al-Miskin became acquainted and eventually worked together after the relationship between Pope Shenouda and Sadat reached an impasse, as we will discuss.

14
THE SADAT ERA (1970–81)

President Anwar Sadat was a highly controversial figure. Henry Kissinger, President Nixon's secretary of state, called him a clown, but later, when Sadat's policy agreed with that of the United States, he referred to him as the greatest statesman since Otto von Bismarck. Was Sadat a visionary leader or a clown? Of the many books written about Sadat, two are of particular significance because they shed light on Sadat's personality. One was written by Sadat's advisor and speech writer, Ahmad Baha' al-Din, who was also editor in chief of a number of magazines and newspapers.[1] The second book is by David Hirst and Irene Beeson of the *Guardian* newspaper, both well versed in Egyptian politics and Middle East policy.[2]

During Nasser's era, Sadat was known as "Mr. Yes Man." He was the only officer within the ruling military junta who never opposed Nasser on any issue. It is still a mystery how Sadat became Nasser's successor. Some of the officers who worked with Nasser thought their own views were closer to Nasser's policy and therefore they were better qualified to be his successor than Sadat. Moreover, they did not have much respect for Sadat. This group thought they could easily remove him after he replaced Nasser. But Sadat proved to be a more competent and astute politician than most people gave him credit for. He managed to trick his opponents, some of whom ended up in prison for conspiracy against the state, after their telephone conversations were recorded.[3]

In the wider society, too, Sadat had opponents from across the political spectrum. He was not well respected or trusted by the political left and the intellectuals. These groups were disappointed that despite the regime's promises, including freedom of the press, greater freedoms did not materialize. Their hopes for an end to the police state of Nasser's time were short-lived.

But an even more dangerous opposition came from the right. Political Islam had been a problem for the previous regime under Nasser. Some radical Muslim clergy attributed the defeat of 1967 to the fact that Egypt had strayed from God's teachings. They claimed that the Egyptians had become infidels and needed to return to a stricter form of Islam. Egypt had refused to attend the Islamic conference of 1966 which Arabia had organized in an attempt to curb the leftist movement. But later, in an effort to appease the Islamists after the defeat of 1967, Egypt joined the Islamic conference of 1969.[4]

As support for conservative Islam increased, Sadat and some of his close advisors decided to use it to counteract the power of the political left and the Nasserites. The Sadat government promoted its own interests by unleashing the Muslim Brotherhood and other jihadist groups who hated the left, the liberals, and the previous regime's socialist policies. Some members of the new regime financially supported political Islam.[5] Sadat and his advisors underestimated the danger of religion being used as a force in politics, and they underestimated the real capabilities of political Islam, especially the Muslim Brotherhood. Later, when the government was unable to deal with political Islam, Sadat said, "There should be no religion in politics and no politics in religion." But by then it was too late. Sadat played a dangerous game with the Islamists—a game that eventually cost him his life and cost Egypt much more.

Financing and Political Islam

Before discussing the rise of political Islam under Sadat, let us digress for a moment to look at some aspects of its role in the financial system. During Sadat's era, two financial developments had a major effect on the political landscape. The first was an influx of money from the Gulf states; a number of members of the Muslim Brotherhood who had been working in the Gulf returned to Egypt. They brought with them plenty of cash, in addition to the ultra-conservative Wahhabi sect of Islam, whose fundamentalist views were not yet common in Egypt. The second development was the appearance of Islamic banks.

Some Islamic scholars claim that Islam is by its nature supportive of free enterprise or the modern system of capitalism. The Prophet was a merchant and encouraged his followers to work in trade; the leaders of contemporary political Islam also believe in free enterprise. But al-Azhar scholars during Nasser's era in the 1950s and 1960s supported socialism as a good economic model for the Muslim world. During Sadat's era, when economic policy shifted back toward capitalism, al-Azhar supported the new system. Thus we see that Islam has been supportive of both capitalism and socialism at different times and in different circumstances.

Muslims have, of course, always engaged in trade. Over the centuries, various methods of financial transactions were developed in order to comply with principles expressed in sharia. These principles include not borrowing or lending at interest *(riba)*, not engaging in speculative investment *(gharar)*, and not supporting practices that are prohibited to Muslims *(haram)*. It should be noted that Judaism and Christianity also lay down rules of ethical financial dealing for their followers. In each of the three religions, one finds variations of opinion among its scholars, as well as variations in degree of compliance by its adherents—some follow the dictates of their religion strictly, and some not at all. For Muslims who followed a strict interpretation of Islam, conventional Western commercial banking practices posed a problem.

Islamic banks started to emerge in the late 1950s and early 1960s. During this time, the conservative Islamic governments of Saudi Arabia and the Gulf states looked with alarm at the rise of revolutionary, socialist, and secular governments just beyond their borders (Syria, Iraq, and Egypt). These neighboring countries had considerable experience with European banking systems and international finance. It was not always a beneficial collaboration—financing the Suez Canal project was a disaster for Egypt—but they learned. The Gulf countries had less experience. In the end, it was an Iraqi and an Egyptian who started an Islamic banking system that could compete with the established banking systems in the countries with secular governments.

In 1960, a Shiite Iraqi Islamist by the name of Mohamed Bakr al-Sadr laid the foundation for Islamic banking as a financial resource to fight the communists in Baghdad. Al-Sadr was well connected to the Muslim Brotherhood.[6] In 1963, an Egyptian by the name of Ahmed al-Nagar founded Mit Ghamr Bank in Germany. This bank, named after a city in the central Nile Delta, is considered the first Islamic bank. Al-Nagar, the father of Islamic banking, was connected to the Muslim Brotherhood's violent underground movement against the Nasser regime.[7]

The Faisal Islamic Bank of Egypt (FIBE), founded in 1976 during Sadat's era, was owned by Prince Mohammed al-Faisal of Saudi Arabia, a son of King Faisal. This bank played an important role in the growth of political Islam in Egypt and the region. Faisal's group had Islamic banks in most of the Muslim capitals; however, they were independent from the branch in Egypt. These banks gave grants to mosques, Islamist-friendly media, and small Islamic organizations.[8] The FIBE has had on its board many distinguished Egyptians, including former Egyptian prime minister 'Abd al-Aziz Hijazi and the grand mufti of Egypt, who gave the bank Islamic legitimacy. One of its founders was Shaykh ʻUmar ʻAbd al-Rahman, the spiritual leader of Islamic jihad, the fundamentalist group whose members assassinated Sadat. ʻAbd al-Rahman helped the CIA recruit martyrdom-seeking jihadis for the Soviet–Afghan war. In 1993, ʻAbd al-Rahman was convicted for his role in the bombing of New York's World Trade Center. Also associated with the FIBE were the well-known Muslim Brotherhood leaders Shaykh Yusuf al-Qaradawi, Youssef Neda, and ʻAbd al-Latif al-Sharif. These three, in addition to ʻAbd al-Rahman, were removed from the FIBE after the assassination of Sadat. Neda was listed as a terrorist financier by the U.S. Department of the Treasury. Al-Qaradawi is widely known in the Arab world for his militant table-thumping speeches, which were distributed on audio cassettes. Al-Sharif, who was imprisoned by Egypt in the 1990s, was a notorious wheeler-dealer with connections to militant Islamists.[9]

The Islamic banks received support from prominent American and international financial institutions such as Citibank and Chase Manhattan; Goldman Sachs, Fannie Mae and Freddie Mac; Hong Kong and Shanghai banks; and the International Monetary Fund (IMF). These banks and institutions supported the economic and political policies of the West, in addition to pursuing their own profits. After the Arab–Israeli war of 1973 and the ensuing oil embargo, oil revenues in the rich Arab countries increased significantly. As a result, the Islamic banks' business mushroomed. By 2004, there were more than 270 Islamic banks in the world, with assets of $260 billion.[10] Some of these banks support political Islam and the jihadist wars that are devastating many countries in the Middle East today. In the meantime, political Islam, especially the Muslim Brotherhood, has expanded its influence to political organizations and parties in Europe and the United States.[11]

The Rise of Political Islam under Sadat

Political Islam continued to gain influence in Egypt during the Sadat years. Islamists started to control some of the mosques, where they preached radical Islamic views, such as replacing secular law with sharia (Islamic law), which during Sadat's era took a turn toward more right-wing Islamic views imported from Saudi Arabia. For example, some preachers called for the implementation of Islamic law without specifically defining what sharia meant.[12] They used mosques as a breeding ground for radical Islamic views imported from Arabia.

In universities, Islamic student activists began to harass and use violence against liberals, Copts, and unveiled female students. The call to implement sharia law was of particular concern to the Copts, who wanted to know what it would mean for them. Some Islamists spread rumors that the Copts were an obstacle to implementing sharia law, and certain judges started to apply sharia law to the Copts.[13] This was contrary to the interpretation by scholars of Islamic law, who stated sharia law should be applied only to Muslims, allowing Christians to have their own laws, which are basically limited to marriage and divorce issues.

Some radical Muslim groups in Parliament proclaimed that three groups should be considered enemies of Islam: Christians, communists, and Jews.[14] Markers of Islamic identity became more pronounced. Wearing the veil *(hijab)* gained popularity. The media started to refer to Sadat by his Islamic name, Muhammad Anwar al-Sadat, instead of Anwar al-Sadat. They called him al-Ra'is al-Mu'min ('The Believer President') and showed pictures of him praying with Islamic prayer beads in his hands.

This increased Islamization of the culture posed a challenge for the Copts. Not long after becoming patriarch, Pope Shenouda III had his first confrontation with the government. It was over the burning of a church. Due to the difficulty of obtaining building permits, the Copts sometimes resorted to illegally building churches without a permit. Another way around the regulations was to take a building that had been approved for a Christian social organization and slowly convert it into a church. This trick sometimes backfired, as happened on November 6, 1972, in the case of an illegal church in al-Khanka, on the outskirts of Old Cairo. In what was the first incident of its kind in modern history, the police, along with some Islamists, moved in and destroyed part of the church. On the following day, the young Pope Shenouda ordered bishops and priests to go to the site of the ruined church and perform a mass there, even at the risk of being shot and killed. Sadat was dismayed that the pope was willing to resort to such an open confrontation. Sadat often acted on impulse, and in this case, he was determined to have a showdown. He said, "I can't carry on with this time bomb ticking away beneath us."[15] This incident took place shortly before the war with Israel in October 1973, when Sadat had other pressing issues to deal with. Muhammad Haykal, one of Sadat's most important advisors and speech writers in that period, suggested a parliamentary inquiry into the problem. This assuaged Sadat's anger and allowed breathing space for all the parties involved.

The parliamentary investigation was very thorough. It attributed the problem to the difficulties the Copts faced in building churches. Sadat visited both the patriarch and the shaykh of al-Azhar in an effort to relieve the sectarian tension. He was well received by the pope and the synod. This visit took place at noon, which was the Muslim time for prayers. Sadat prayed, surrounded by the pope and the bishops, an event which was shown live on TV. Sadat asked Shenouda how many churches he needed to build each year. Shenouda suggested forty. Sadat said, "I grant you fifty permits without any red tape." But Pope Shenouda later said, "In four years, we got the permits for only half the number allowed for one year."[16] It is interesting to note that the parliamentary inquiry found that according to the Department of the Census, there were 1,442 churches in Egypt, but according to the Interior Ministry, there were only about five hundred. The discrepancy between these two numbers could be due to various reasons, one of which was building churches without the appropriate permits.[17] The sectarian tension was relieved, but only briefly.

From the beginning, Sadat faced another difficult challenge. In addition to opposition from both leftists and Nasserites, he had to deal with the Israeli occupation of Sinai. Three years earlier, Israel had invaded the Sinai Peninsula during the Six-Day War of 1967, and had started to build settlements in the occupied territory as if it intended to stay there. Liberating Sinai was a high priority for Sadat, but it was difficult for Egypt to get sophisticated military supplies and adequate training from the Soviet Union, its only military supplier. The status quo was good for the Soviet Union because it made the Arabs more dependent on them. The Soviets did not think the Egyptians or Syrians were capable of liberating their lands through military force. The United States, too, was happy with the defeat of the Arabs at the hands of Israel, a strong U.S. ally. In light of the Cold War, the status quo suited U.S. policy makers who saw Israel's victory as a victory of democracy over communism. For their part, the Israelis were full of confidence and unwilling to make serious concessions for peace. Instead, they started to build strategic settlements in the territories they had taken, including most of the West Bank and East Jerusalem as well as Sinai and the Golan Heights. Most Egyptians were eager to regain Sinai, but did not welcome the prospect of another war.

When the October 1973 war began, the Egyptian army did much better than it had before. The formidable Bar-Lev line, Israel's defense on the east side of the Suez Canal, was overrun by Egyptian forces, and many Israeli soldiers were taken as prisoners of war. The Israelis were shocked by this unexpected attack by the Egyptians and the Syrians. The United States quickly supported Israel's army by supplying material to make up for its losses. Supplies came directly from the United States to Sinai to fortify the Israelis for battle. U.S. diplomatic efforts managed to halt the fighting, but only after Israel had advanced on the battlefield. No further diplomatic progress was made for about four years. In Israel, the more conservative Likud Party replaced the Labor Party after the war. The Likud Party considered Gaza and the West Bank to be parts of greater Israel. To emphasize their claims, they called the West Bank by the ancient biblical names of Judea and Samaria, which historically had been Hebrew kingdoms for only seventy-five to 150 years.

After the war, Sadat gained the respect of most Egyptians and many world leaders, and emerged as a strong statesman. He introduced several peace proposals, but to no avail. The stalemate was finally broken by Sadat's groundbreaking visit to Israel in 1977, which stunned the world and earned him the Nobel Peace Prize the following year—a prize he shared with Menachem Begin, the founder of the Likud Party. Prior to the creation of Israel, Begin had been the leader of the Irgun, a Zionist group that carried out terrorist attacks against the British and the Palestinians in the 1940s.

Pope Shenouda visited the Egyptian army on the front lines, and liked to publicize the fact that he was a reserve officer. His relationship with Sadat improved, but only temporarily. On Sadat's recommendation, Shenouda visited the United States and met with President Jimmy Carter in April 1977. When Carter asked Shenouda about the Coptic Church's opinion on Israel, Shenouda answered, "The Jewish people are no longer the chosen people. That ended with the coming of Jesus Christ. If they were the chosen people, what would that make you and me?" Shenouda's views on Israel were consistent with views he had expressed before he became pope. He had delivered a well-attended speech on Israel and the Bible to the Egyptian Journalists Syndicate, and had published a booklet on the subject reflecting the Coptic Church's views at the time.[18] Shenouda, like most Egyptians and the rest of the Arab world, was sympathetic to the Palestinian cause.

Sadat's Difficult Years

As political Islam continued to gain power and popularity among the masses, some of the Islamists' activities started to undermine the country. In 1974, Saleh Saria, a Muslim Brotherhood graduate of the Military Academy of Science, attempted a coup d'état to assassinate Sadat and install an Islamic government. The coup quickly failed. The group called themselves Shabab Muhammad (Muhammad's Youth). The participants were given a military trial, and some were sentenced to death. One of those who admired Saria and his forceful, if naive, coup d'état was Ayman al-Zawahiri, who later became one of the leaders of al-Qaeda.

Sadat's policy of using Islam as a political tool backfired in many ways. The Muslim Brotherhood gradually penetrated many areas of Egyptian life, especially the educational system and the media. More and more space in the government media was devoted to religious topics, but often the treatment was shallow and focused on rituals. For example, the most prominent newspaper in Egypt, *Al-Ahram*, addressed the following question from a reader: "Is it appropriate for someone who works at the Cairo Museum to pray next to a statue from ancient Egypt?" The question only arose because some ultra-conservative Islamists promoted the view that any depiction of human form, including great art and ancient statues, is a form of idolatry and must be rejected as anti-Islamic. The destruction of the great statue of Buddha in Afghanistan is an example of this type of narrow thinking.

In this climate, sectarian tensions increased again, often based on false rumors, such as the claim that Pope Shenouda was scheming to increase the number of Copts and decrease the number of Muslims so Egypt would again become a Christian country.[19] Demographics became a subject of debate. The government censuses from 1897 to 1996 showed the Copts to be about 6 percent of the population.[20] The church strongly disputed this figure. Its own estimate, based on its census of Copts, was much higher. Some estimated the proportion of Copts to be as high as 18 percent.[21] As a result of this disagreement, after the 1996 census the government stopped providing figures for the percentage of Copts, in order to avoid conflict with the church.

There were disruptions at the personal level as well. In a well-attended mosque in Cairo, a well-known preacher urged his congregation not to do business with Copts or even greet them socially. There was an immediate outcry, and, as the result of a media campaign against him, the preacher was banned from preaching.[22] But outside Cairo and other big cities, this campaign to segregate Copts from Muslims continued uncensored and started to spread to other radical and popular mosques. During this period, the government failed to actively discourage discrimination against Copts.[23] The Copts became the enemy in the eyes of some preachers and their followers, who preferred to aim their hostility at an "other" rather than address the real political, social, and economic issues facing society.[24]

In 1977, al-Azhar proposed that the death penalty be imposed on any Muslim who changed his or her religion.[25] No significant number of Muslims had ever converted to Christianity; if this happened at all, it was only in a handful of cases. There were more instances of Copts converting to Islam, but although these, too, were few in number, they were highly publicized. The church's concern was what would happen to a Copt who converted to Islam and then wanted to return to Christianity. Al-Azhar's proposed penalty of capital punishment could have been implemented in the case of a former Christian who was accused by a shaykh of deserting Islam.

This was a time of concern for anyone who opposed these radical views. Pope Shenouda protested al-Azhar's proposal. A day of fasting and prayer took place in all churches to protest the proposed law. Prime Minister Mamdouh Salem visited the pope to reassure him that capital punishment was not going to be accepted by the government as law.[26] This incident and others like it reflected the level of mistrust between the Copts and Muslims, as well as between the government and the Islamists.

Sadat was not a fanatic, as those who knew him well attested. In an effort to ease tensions, he sent Musa Sabry—his close associate, advisor, and a Copt—to discuss matters with Pope Shenouda. In these discussions, Shenouda requested that more Copts be appointed as members of parliament, judges, foreign ambassadors, and deans of colleges. This was the first time in modern Coptic history that a Coptic patriarch had made such requests. Sadat refused, saying that if he complied with these demands, Egypt would become a sectarian state, like Lebanon, where each sect has a quota to be filled. Sadat said he had instructed the government not to discriminate among Egyptians based on religion.[27]

But the ratio of Copts in high positions did not reflect that non-discriminatory policy. While Copts made up 25 percent of the membership in professional associations (lawyers, pharmacists, doctors, and journalists), they comprised only 2.8 percent of CEOs of public sector companies. Out of 127 ambassadors, only one was a Copt. In the field of education, there were no Coptic deputy ministers or regional directors of education. Of 166 university presidents and deans, none were Copts.[27]

In the absence of true democracy, the church was under pressure to represent the Copts. Pope Shenouda denied that he tried to intervene in state politics, and claimed that he spoke only as an Egyptian citizen. But this was disingenuous. His position and strong personality naturally gave added weight to his opinions on issues of relevance to the Copts. Whether he was just expressing personal opinions or attempting to intervene in politics is an academic question. Shenouda's position subjected him to serious criticism, particularly by the Islamists.[28] Was Shenouda one of the causes of increased sectarian violence? Some Islamists thought so.

In 1977, many important events took place. In January, the Copts held the first Coptic conference in sixty-six years. The topics discussed included freedom of religion, protection of family values, equal opportunities, parliamentary representation for the Copts, the effect of implementing Islamic laws, and the freedom to build Coptic churches. The conference was to be continued until the government responded to the Copts' grievances. The attendees issued a public statement, which the government refused to publish in its newspapers. The church called for Copts to fast from January 31 to February 2, hoping God would listen to their grievances, since it appeared the government would not. Lacking political representation, the church became at least in part a spokesman for the Coptic community. Many bishops agreed with the policies of Pope Shenouda.

In the mid-1970s, a new factor emerged. Due to increased waves of emigration, more Copts were living abroad than ever before, especially in the United States, Canada, Europe, and Australia. For these emigrants to the West, the Coptic Church was an important focus of religious and social life. Not surprisingly, they paid close attention to events back home and were supportive of the Copts in Egypt. During this period, the number of Coptic churches in the West increased. Copts abroad formed an organization called the American, Canadian, and Australian Coptic Association. Through its political and media connections, this organization exerted pressure on public opinion in Egypt, on the government, and at times on President Sadat. Other Coptic activist organizations abroad went further, inflaming the sectarian situation with distorted facts. For example, claims that a large number of Copts, especially young women, had been kidnapped and forced to convert to Islam were grossly exaggerated if not fabricated outright.

Copts were not the only ones to mobilize from abroad. Some Muslims who emigrated from Egypt were politically active on behalf of political Islam. Political Islamists, especially the Muslim Brotherhood, not only were activists on a grassroots level but formed strong economic enterprises that still wield political power today in Egypt, the Middle East, and the West.[29]

The late 1970s were not good years for Egypt or for Sadat. His economic policy was liberal, but in the absence of strong and fair regulations, it opened the door for corruption. Some people became very rich very quickly. In January 1977, following the removal of food subsidies—a step recommended by the World Bank and the International Monetary Fund—the price of staple foods went up, setting off spontaneous and violent demonstrations from Alexandria in the north to Aswan in the south. The demonstrators chanted angry slogans, such as "The rich live in palaces and the poor live in cemeteries." Some officials' homes were attacked. In Aswan, demonstrations came very close to the presidential residence, where Sadat was staying at the time. The food subsidies were reinstated. The army was sent into the streets, without ammunition, and peace was quickly restored. However, the demonstrations had a devastating effect on Sadat's spirit. He refused to admit the faults of his economic policy, and called the bread riots "the riot of thieves," dismissing the demonstrations as the work of communists and left-wing activists.[30]

In June 1977, a radical Muslim group (al-Takfir wa-l-Hijra, an offshoot of the Gama'a al-Islamiya) kidnapped Dr. Muhammad al-Dhahabi, the previous minister of Islamic religious endowments *(waqf)* and an Islamic scholar who rejected the narrow interpretations of Islam put forth by radical Islamic groups. In exchange for al-Dhahabi's release, the kidnappers demanded an LE 200,000 ransom, the release of their members in prison, an apology from the media for spreading lies about them, and a public confession from the government that it had not been governing according to Islamic principles and would do so from now on. When the government did not acquiesce, the kidnappers killed al-Dhahabi. This radical group considered the rest of the Muslim community to be infidels. It was influenced by the writing of Sayyid Qutb, who had been sentenced to death in the mid-1960s. The person who executed al-Dhahabi was a former officer in the Interior Ministry, who had been fired from his job and thought he had been mistreated. Forty-five members of the group were arrested and tried. Five were sentenced to death, and others were sentenced to time in prison. Despite the ominous implications of occurrences such as this, Sadat persisted in seeing them as isolated incidents.[31]

Sadat wished to be seen as a peacemaker. Even before his historic visit to Israel, he met with the Coptic Holy Synod and listened to the grievances of the church, saying in a televised interview, "I didn't know that your conditions were so bad." When one of Sadat's assistants called his attention to the fact that he was speaking live on air, Sadat answered, "I know that. But people have to know about this." Sadat continued by saying that the grievances of the Copts contradicted the spirit and meaning of the Egyptian constitution regarding equality. But unfortunately his words were not backed up by deeds.[32] In a gesture designed to show his ecumenical desire for peace, Sadat invited the American evangelist Billy Graham to visit Egypt. He also visited Pope Paul VI in the Vatican and received his support for peace.

Sadat visited Israel on November 19, 1977, leading to a new but difficult round of negotiations. Sadat genuinely thought the war between the Arabs and Israelis was largely psychological and could be resolved peacefully. He also thought the United States held 99 percent of the cards in the Arab–Israeli conflict. Events proved both assumptions to be inaccurate. While Sadat's visit broke some of the psychological barriers and brought the Israelis and Egyptians face to face in direct discussions, the negotiation proved much more difficult than expected. When no progress had been made, President Carter invited Sadat and Begin to Camp David in 1978. After very difficult negotiations and significant pressure from Carter, primarily on Sadat, a peace agreement—the Camp David Accords— was finally agreed upon. However, it should be noted that this was a treaty between Egypt and Israel, not the overall treaty between the Israelis and Arabs which Sadat had wanted.

The Camp David agreement enhanced Sadat's prestige in the West, but it antagonized the rest of the Arab world, especially the Palestinians, and was resented by many Egyptians as well. After Camp David, Israel wanted normalization of relations with Egypt that went beyond merely signing an agreement. But a majority of the Egyptian people did not support the treaty and opposed normalizing relations. Those Egyptians who accepted the treaty hoped that peace would bring stability and economic prosperity. This did not happen. Some of Sadat's advisors thought allowing the Copts to visit Jerusalem on pilgrimages would help normalize relations with Israel. However, Pope Shenouda did not agree. He declared that Copts would go on pilgrimages only when there was a consensus about the peace agreement among all Arabs, especially the Palestinians; until then, any Copt who went to Jerusalem would be excommunicated. Shenouda's position stemmed from his longstanding opposition to Israel based on his religious convictions and his view of the humanitarian rights of the Palestinians. Because of his policy on Israel, he was called the Pope of the Arabs.[33] Sadat and his advisors considered Shenouda's statement to be a challenge to the regime, and indeed it was. Pope Shenouda appeared as a leader representing the Copts, and he gained popularity in the wider Arab world for his public criticism of the Camp David Accords and his support of the Palestinians.

The period from 1977 to 1979 was a difficult time, as sectarian tensions continued to increase. The shaykh of al-Azhar, Abd al-Halim Mahmud, convened a conference of Islamic organizations in July 1977. The recommendation of the conference stated that any law or regulation that ran counter to the teachings of Islam should be treated as null and void, and should be rejected by Muslims; and Islamic laws should prevail over parliamentary legislation. The shaykhs' statement attributed the delay in implementing Islamic laws to the regime's wish to appease non-Muslims.[34] Pope Shenouda strongly attacked the attempt to force Islamic laws on non-Muslims, and denounced this as an attempt to replace nationalism with religion. As an act of protest, Shenouda, along with the rest of the bishops, decided not to celebrate Easter that year. Instead, they went to the desert monasteries to pray for deliverance from oppression. Relations between the state and the church had never been so strained.

In May 1979, Sadat and Begin held a press conference in the city of Isma'ilia on the Suez Canal. Sadat's hopes for a comprehensive peace agreement, or even for peace on good terms for Egypt, were shattered. At the press conference, Begin came across as unyielding and arrogant. Egyptians found some of his remarks humiliating. He repeated the myth that Jewish slaves had built the pyramids, a claim refuted by current scholarship (the great pyramid was completed in 2560 BC, centuries before Abraham, and more than a thousand years before Moses). Begin also stated that Sadat admitted to having started the war of 1967. There is no way to confirm or refute what Sadat may have said in private, but even many Israelis reject the claim that Egypt initiated hostilities. Sadat did not respond to any of these statements made by Begin at the press conference.

Sadat was going through the most difficult time of his life. His dream for peace had turned into a nightmare. The peace process had a high risk of failing. U.S. president Carter, British prime minister Callahan, and other dignitaries visited Sadat to boost his deteriorating spirits. Sadat was now forced to accept an unbearable situation and continue his peace efforts, which had started with his visit to Israel.[35]

In a public address to the nation on May 14, 1980, President Sadat declared that he had information that the ambitious Pope Shenouda wished to be the political leader of the Copts. Furthermore, Sadat claimed to have reports that showed Shenouda was working on a plan to establish a Coptic country in the south of Egypt, with its capital in Asyut. He said Shenouda had to know that "I am a Muslim president presiding over a Muslim country." He mentioned that he had been about to make a drastic decision on this matter, but had received a letter from an unnamed young girl which had persuaded him to change his mind. Even though he himself had mixed religion with politics, Sadat proclaimed, "There is no politics in religion, and no religion in politics." The address was published in all the Egyptian newspapers on May 15. The claim that Copts planned to establish a Coptic country was never substantiated, and was emphatically rejected by the Copts and the patriarch, as well as by most Muslims. Sadat's address was received with concern and anger by the Copts, including those abroad. They feared there would be negative repercussions, but fortunately no demonstrations against Shenouda or the Copts materialized after Sadat's address. The majority of Egyptians did not take Sadat's claim about a Coptic state seriously; they were more concerned about the state of the country and where Egypt was headed.

The Islamist challenge to Sadat's regime continued to come from many radical Muslim groups. For example, one group flexed its muscles against the regime when the government refused to permit them to organize a camp in Cairo University during a Muslim holiday (Eid al-Adha in 1980). In response, the group simply went to the other bank of the Nile and occupied a mosque for their activities. They proceeded to give many speeches and sermons through loudspeakers broadcasting twenty-four hours a day. The speeches were directed against the regime, particularly against the treaty with Israel.[36]

Attacks on churches, monasteries, Coptic stores, and students continued. The historical church of Qasriyat al-Rihan was burned down in March 1979. The sectarian climate was charged and ready to explode. In June 1981, Egypt witnessed the worst sectarian violence in many years. In the area of al-Zawiya al-Hamra, in northern Cairo, an argument between neighbors about land for a proposed church turned into an armed battle. Seventeen people were killed, fifty-four were injured, and more than a hundred were arrested. Many illegal weapons were confiscated.[37] The Coptic media and foreign media fanned the flames by exaggerating the number of casualties, claiming that eighty were killed.

In the beginning of August 1981, Sadat visited the United States, which was now under the Reagan administration. He was not received with the same enthusiasm he had experienced from President Carter after his visit to Israel. He was also confronted with hostile demonstrations by Copts in front of the White House in Washington, D.C., and in front of the Metropolitan Museum of Art in New York City, when he visited the newly renovated Egyptian wing. To make matters worse, the Coptic community took out half-page advertisements in both the Washington Post and the New York Times listing the Copts' grievances. Sadat was furious. He accused Pope Shenouda of orchestrating the hostile reception. In fact, in anticipation of a hostile attitude among Coptic emigrants, Shenouda's public relations expert, Bishop Samuel, had gone to the United States in advance of Sadat's visit to ask the community to lie low and not provoke him.[38] But Samuel's visit did not achieve much.

Relations between the head of the church and the state were at a low point. Sadat wanted to fire Pope Shenouda, but this was not within his jurisdiction. The only authority capable of removing a pope was the Holy Synod, which could only do this if the patriarch was found guilty of deviating from the creed of the Coptic Church. The Holy Synod had no grounds or desire to remove Shenouda. However, this did not mean Shenouda was universally popular among Copts. A few church leaders were not pleased with the way Pope Shenouda had dealt with the state since the beginning of his tenure. One of these critics was Matta al-Miskin, the abbot of St. Macarius, whom Sadat had gotten to know as a result of seeing his successful reclamation of desert land near the monastery. Matta al-Miskin tried unsuccessfully to mediate the conflict between the Pope and the president. Sadat hoped he could replace Shenouda with Matta al-Miskin, but this was not possible, nor was it acceptable to Matta al-Miskin or to the Copts. The solution finally came from Matta al-Miskin, who suggested the state could cancel the decree recognizing the pope as the head of the Coptic Church. This was an old tradition; because the pope was considered a high-ranking employee of the state, the state was required to issue a decree recognizing him. If the decree was voided, the pope would not be allowed to deal officially with the state on any matter. Matta al-Miskin suggested that a committee of five bishops—excluding himself—replace the pope. He selected the bishops, and Sadat approved them. By this time, the pope was ensconced in a monastery, which was subsequently surrounded by an army unit, effectively putting him under the equivalent of house arrest. No one was allowed to enter or exit without permission from the security forces. Several lawyers volunteered to take legal action on the patriarch's behalf against the government, but Shenouda declined this offer. He refused to recognize the decree issued by Sadat. He later asserted that the pope is the highest authority of the church, whether he is in his formal residence or in a monastery. Shenouda remained popular among most Egyptians.

Sadat did not stop at removing the pope. He became intolerant of any opposition, and went on the attack. On September 5, 1981, the regime rounded up and arrested more than fifteen hundred people, including many prominent individuals who opposed Sadat's policies but had not violated any laws. The arrests were carried out in the middle of the night, with a large number of troops as if mobilized for a battle. Those rounded up included some of Sadat's previous advisors and ministers, prominent journalists, university professors, religious activists, clergy, and heads of political parties. Anyone opposing Sadat—whether from the right, left, or center—was subject to the roundup.[39] In an address to the nation, Sadat accused his opposition of being infidels and said they "should not have a place in our society, particularly in any position that might affect youth, such as schools and the media. On October 6, a month after rounding up his opposition, Sadat was assassinated by a small group of young jihadist officers during a military parade commemorating the October 6 war with Israel. The head of the group that assassinated him was Khalid Islambouli, a twenty-four-year-old army officer who belonged to a radical Islamic group that had previously condemned Sadat to death. They felt Sadat's death was justified because (1) he did not rule according to Islamic law, (2) he had agreed to the Camp David Accords, and (3) he had ordered the arrest of Muslim leaders. The mission was planned and carried out in less than two weeks. The assasins knew this would be a suicide mission, and wanted it to be as public as possible. Later, under interrogation, al-Islambouli said, "What we have done was for the sake of God. I do not want anything for myself. We want to make Sadat an example to warn all who come after him, and to teach them a lesson."[40]

The only place besides Cairo that saw trouble after the assassination of Sadat was Asyut, where the university was a stronghold of al-Gama'a al-Islamiya. Colonel al-Zumar, a member of the organization that assassinated Sadat, fled to Asyut to escape arrest. Al-Zumar was able to stir up trouble with the police there, and about a hundred police were killed. Al-Zumar was arrested, along with other survivors from the group. The rest of Egypt was more or less calm after the initial shock. Some Islamic scholars from al-Azhar University were supportive of the assassination of Sadat based on their interpretation of Islamic law, while others from the same university considered it a criminal act that should be opposed from an Islamic point of view.[41]

Sadat's funeral was well attended by Western dignitaries, including three former U.S. presidents (Carter, Ford, and Nixon) and Begin, Rabin, Shamir, and Sharon from Israel. Sadly, few Egyptians attended. The assassins of Sadat were tried, and three were sentenced to death. Nineteen others were given sentences ranging from one year to life in prison.

While there was often tension between Copts and Muslims during periods of political and economic hardship, as described in the previous chapters, this was by no means the norm throughout most of Egyptian history. For long stretches of time and in many places, the relationship between Copts and Muslims was that of neighbors and friends who dressed alike, celebrated each other's festivals, engaged in business together, and shared good and bad times. The two communities were culturally very similar. In the early nineteenth century, for example, the British consul-general of Egypt, Lord Cromer, observed that the main difference between a Copt and a Muslim was that one worshiped in a church and the other worshiped in a mosque. Despite the periods of turmoil we have described, relations between the communities were generally harmonious through the centuries.

In the middle of the 1970s, this relationship again took a turn for the worse. After Sadat came to power in 1970, he cooperated with the Islamists to weaken the left and counter the intellectuals who opposed his attempt to shift policies away from those of his predecessor, Nasser. The Islamists agreed to cooperate with the government. In return, the government did nothing to stop Islamist infiltration of the educational system and the professional unions. As a result, the decades since then have witnessed an increasingly strong Islamic imprint on the culture of Egypt, and a deterioration in relations between Copts and Muslims. While Copts and Muslims still live in an integrated society in the big cities, this has become less true in the rural areas. Many Copts have been obliged to move from small towns and villages to the cities in order to escape discrimination and harassment.

One relatively recent cultural change is the widespread adoption of Islamic forms of dress and appearance that now make it easier to identify Muslims at a casual glance. The majority of Muslim women now wear *hijab*. Some cover their faces completely except for the eyes *(niqab)* and even wear gloves in the middle of the hot summer. Since non-Muslim women do not follow any of these practices, they stand out from the majority on the street. Many Muslim men can be identified by styles of beards and long robes that are specifically associated with Islamism. Some cultivate a callus on their forehead as a visible sign that they pray five times a day, touching their foreheads to the ground in submission to God. Unlike the dress codes of past centuries, religious identification by appearance today is not the result of discriminatory laws. However, visible differences do set members of minority communities apart from the majority of their fellow countrymen in a way that was almost unknown just a few decades ago.

Since the 1970s, there has also been a growing Islamic presence in the media. Religious shows on television, radio, and the Internet have multiplied. Qur'an recitation, sermons by Muslim clerics, and religious debates are frequent offerings. Many of these programs are shallow and ignore the serious social, educational, and economic problems of the present day.

Book publishing has experienced a similar shift toward preoccupation with Islamic subjects. A 1988 study by Mahmud Amin al-'Alim reported that out of 7,109 recently published books that year, 36 percent were on religion, 60 percent were in a different area of the social sciences, and only 4 percent were on applied science.[42]

On a personal note, when I (FA) graduated from high school in Alexandria in 1959 there were only a few Islamic books in the school library. Upon revisiting the school in 2015, I looked at their library and was surprised to see that about half of the books now deal with Islamic religious topics. These examples demonstrate the degree to which Islamist influence has infiltrated the educational system and the Egyptian culture at large.

Many specifically Islamic organizations have sprung up. These include banks, supermarkets, schools, and so on, which further separate the two communities from each other in the realm of everyday life. Some Islamists directly or indirectly encourage a rift between Copts and Muslims by asking Muslims to ignore Copts, not to deal with them, and not to share their holidays. The result has been a chilling effect on Coptic–Muslim relations in general, and a recent rise in violence targeting Copts and Coptic institutions.

15
THE MUBARAK ERA (1981–2011)

After Sadat's death, Hosni Mubarak, the vice president, assumed the presidency. With the support of the army behind him, Mubarak's leadership was uncontested and he became the fourth military officer to rule Egypt since 1952.

The first ten years of Mubarak's era were relatively quiet and hopeful years. On gaining control, Mubarak ordered the release of the more than fifteen hundred people who had been arrested by Sadat's regime in the month before his assassination. Some went directly from prison to meet Mubarak for a reconciliation. Other political prisoners were released as well. A number of controversial laws that Sadat had introduced in his final years were quietly shelved, and censorship of the press was relaxed. Under pressure from the World Bank and the International Monetary Fund, the food subsidy program was again scaled back—only this time it was done gradually, so as not to provoke the riots that had resulted from a similar move in 1977. Reducing the food subsidy was a necessary correction to what had been excessively low prices, but it presented an economic burden for the majority of poor Egyptians. The regime's few economic achievements were dwarfed by the suffocating increase in population. What kept the country going was the influx of money from Egyptians abroad, which reached a record level of $15 billion to $18 billion annually.[1]

By the late 1980s, the Muslim Brotherhood's influence was on the rise again. The Brotherhood claimed to reject violence and appeared to distance itself from other jihadist groups. But in reality, these other jihadist groups originated from within the Brotherhood's umbrella—they and the Brotherhood were simply two sides of the same coin, as the minister of the interior, Zaki Badr, described it in 1989.[2] The Muslim Brotherhood's popularity increased after a serious earthquake struck Cairo in 1992. In the ensuing chaos, the Brotherhood was quick to mobilize, going into the streets to help the needy long before the government brought any help. As a result, the Brotherhood gained a reputation as the party of the people, more reliable in a crisis than the government. The Muslim Brotherhood also started to infiltrate and take control of professional organizations, including the powerful teachers', doctors', lawyers', and engineers' associations. The rise of the Brotherhood's popularity began to be of serious concern to the regime. Abd al-Halim Musa, the minister of the interior, complained, "What is going on here? Do we have a state within the state?"[3]

Some have wondered why Mubarak's government was so slow to respond to the Islamist threat. Tarek Osman, a political economist and commentator, offers the following explanation: Mubarak was preoccupied with security—an understandable reaction to having seen his predecessor, Sadat, gunned down before his eyes. His response was to build up the country's security apparatus, which may have given him a false sense of security. Even Mubarak's initial lenient approach toward opposition parties and his relaxation of constraints on the press and other institutions were part of his security-minded orientation. These measures were intended to calm the country without actually allowing real reform. As a military man, Mubarak put great faith in the army and the security forces to maintain his hold on the reins of power. This complacency was soon to be shattered.[4]

What finally spurred the government's efforts to rein in the Brotherhood was a sharp increase in violence by militant Islamists. In 1990, Rif'at al-Mahgoub, a former speaker of the Parliament, was assassinated. In addition, the militants also made attempts on the lives of the minister of information, the minister of the interior, the prime minister, and four police generals. Between 1990 and 1993, as many as 1,164 people were killed or injured in political violence, making it the bloodiest period in Egypt in the twentieth century.[5]

It was not only government officials who were targeted for political assassinations. In August 1992, the liberal political activist and university professor Farag Fouda (1936–92) was assassinated by radical Muslims. Fouda had been critical of some radical Islamic views, and he had exposed areas of Islamic history that the Islamists found unflattering. Because Fouda was objectively critical of certain aspects of Islamic history, he was accused of being an apostate *(murtad)*. Some Islamist leaders excommunicated Fouda and claimed his assassination was justified within Islamic law.[6]

In October 1994, an attempt was made on the life of the well-known Arab novelist Naguib Mahfouz (1911–2006), who was then eighty-three years old. The person who tried to kill him was illiterate and had never read any of Mahfouz's work. His action was motivated by radical Islamic scholars who declared Mahfouz to be an infidel based on their interpretation of Islamic law. Mahfouz's novel *Children of Gebelawi* (also published as *Children of the Alley*) was the main source of the trouble. This book was seen by Islamists as blasphemous because it made allegorical reference to Moses, Jesus, and Muhammad, and placed the authority of modern science above that of religion. The novel was first serialized in the newspaper *Al-Ahram* in 1957, but it did not appear in book form until it was published in Lebanon in 1962. *Children of Gebelawi* received renewed interest after Mahfouz was awarded the Nobel Prize for Literature in 1988. However, due to pressure from many Islamist scholars at al-Azhar University, the novel was not officially published in Egypt until after Mahfouz's death in 2006.

An old and important principle in Islam says that people are free to choose their religion. Some Islamists interpret this to mean that one is free only to accept Islam; once a Muslim, one is never free to leave. According to this restricted view, anyone who renounces Islam becomes an apostate and is subject to the death penalty. Neither Fouda nor Mahfouz ever rejected Islam, but the mere expression of diverse views, even in fiction, was enough to earn them a death sentence.

In 1995, political Islamists backed a failed attempt to assassinate Mubarak in Addis Ababa, while he was attending the Organization of African Unity (OAU) summit. By then, the list of their political victims in Egypt since the 1940s included two prime ministers (while in office), three presidents (while in office), one speaker of the house, and a number of ministers. Not surprisingly, many doubted the sincerity of the Muslim Brotherhood's claimed rejection of violence.

Throughout the Mubarak era, operations carried out by Islamic militants became increasingly complex and sophisticated. Their ability to gather intelligence, to use communications technology, to employ remote controlled devices, and to manufacture explosive devices increased steadily. One factor that contributed to this was the experience and training that some received as volunteer fighters in Afghanistan, where they assisted U.S.-trained and Saudi-financed *mujahidin* ('those who engage in jihad') in the 1979–89 war against Soviet occupation.[7] Eventually these well-trained terrorists came home to roost—not only in Egypt but also in Europe and the United States, where they continue to perpetrate violence against targets they deem un-Islamic.

In Egypt, the choice of targets widened to include cafés, cinemas, cruise ships, and tourists. As part of its war of attrition against the ruling regime, Islamists killed sixty-two tourists on November 17, 1997, at the ancient pharaonic temple of Deir al-Bahari, across the Nile from Luxor.[8] This incident devastated the Egyptian tourist industry for years, causing a loss of at least $3 billion annually. But it was not only the Islamists who were disaffected with Mubarak. The period from 2005 to 2009 witnessed hundreds of riots and demonstrations against the regime, despite the emergency law prohibiting demonstrations.[9]

As the size of the population swelled and its average age grew ever younger, the entrenched authorities were aging in place. Some of the ministers and other high-ranking officials had worked in the administration for twenty years or more. Tahsin Bashir (1925–2002), a diplomat and advisor to Nasser and Sadat, described Mubarak's government as "the regime that mummified Egypt."[10] The government lost touch with the people, and the president removed himself from the crowded, polluted city of Cairo and spent most of his time in the resort of Sharm al-Sheikh on the Red Sea.

A cohort of young capitalist businessmen, appointed to key positions and headed by Mubarak's son Gamal, attempted to rejuvenate the system, but were unable to change a regime which had become debilitated by dysfunction and inertia. The government media paid much attention to Mubarak's son's activities, and tried to bolster his image as the one being groomed to replace his father. But Gamal Mubarak and his capitalist friends knew that in any free election, the people would throw them out.[11]

In 2005, as a result of U.S. pressure, the Muslim Brotherhood participated in the parliamentary election. It did so as an independent party because the Egyptian constitution did not permit religious parties. The representatives of the Brotherhood won eighty-eight out of 444 seats. This relative success gave them hope for the 2010 election, but the government party, the National Democratic Party (NDP), did not want to share power with the Brotherhood or any other party. Before and during the 2010 election, many members of the Brotherhood were arrested. The NDP controlled the outcome of the election by forging votes when necessary, a fraud which was highly publicized in Egypt. In the end, the NDP took 93 percent of the seats in Parliament. The Brotherhood won no seats in that election, but gained the sympathy of many Egyptians as an opposition party to Mubarak's fossilized and autocratic government. No other party was as organized as, or had the financial resources of, the Brotherhood. The situation in the country was untenable. The lines separating power and wealth were blurred; losing power or even sharing it would mean jeopardizing the immense economic interests of the few at the top.

Muhamamd Abu-l Ghar, a university professor, political commentator, and activist, is one of many analysts who have written about the current political scene in Egypt, and its roots in the Mubarak era. The Mubarak era was a prosperous period for the Brotherhood. During that time, it engaged in many activities—both overt and covert—but the most important and dangerous development was their soft penetration of the educational system and their control of important professional associations.[12] Some members of the Brotherhood were arrested and imprisoned, but the organization continued to operate as a highly secretive, well-organized system. Perhaps the Mubarak regime was not aware of the depths of these highly organized efforts; or perhaps it did not know how to deal with them; or perhaps it just continued on the same course due to inertia, thinking it was in control of the situation. At the same time, the regime was reining in other civil and political organizations with a heavy hand. The ultimate policy of the regime—as Abu-l Ghar and other observers saw it[13]—was to show the people they only had two choices: the moderates, represented by the Mubarak regime and heavily supported by the army leadership, or the radical Brotherhood. While the popularity of the Brotherhood was rising in Egypt, they were also expanding their influence to political organizations and parties in Europe and the United States.[14]

The Return of Pope Shenouda

After Sadat's assassination, Pope Shenouda slowly started to resume his duties while still in exile in the monastery. In 1982, lawyers sued the government in an attempt to force a reversal of its decision to remove Shenouda. However, the court rejected the case, citing the fact that it had been a presidential decision.[15] Shenouda was finally reinstated in Cairo in January 1985, about four years after Sadat had removed him from office. Shenouda's delayed return was due, in part, to the high level of sectarian tensions. The political direction of the government had changed after Sadat's assassination, and Shenouda had also changed his policy toward the state. The pope's new relationship with the government was not as confrontational as it had been earlier in his tenure. He set up a committee for national unity to foster better relations between Copts and Muslims.[16] The work of this committee extended to all dioceses, and included efforts to encourage dialogue between Christian and Muslim scholars. In spite of the best intentions, these efforts did not do much to improve relations between the Copts and the Muslims. Some Muslim intellectuals, such as the well-known and influential historian Tariq al-Bishri, were openly critical of church leadership.[17] Political Islamists continued to gain influence and gradually came to dominate the educational system and the professional associations.[18]

During this period, the Copts became increasingly marginalized. As S.S. Hassan describes it, Muslim Egyptians "knew nothing, suspected nothing, and desired to know even less about the Copts' grievances." This is not surprising, since there was very little mention of the Copts or their history in the Egyptian educational system through the high school level. Even ancient Egyptian history was slighted, while Islamic history was selectively emphasized. The difficult or unpleasant events of Islamic history described in the previous chapters were never mentioned. As a result, many Egyptians and Arabs believe that the era of the caliphs and Islamic rule was a rosy and prosperous time, and that the caliphs had ruled according to Islamic principles. This view has been challenged by many historians, but their scholarly views do not find their way into the educational system.

In the absence of democratic representation and in the presence of sectarian tensions, many Copts solidified their identity around the church, just as many Muslims' identities were centered around select Islamic values spread by popular clergy. Many Copts looked to the church because they did not trust that the old Coptic aristocracy—which normally might have provided political leadership for the community—would take a firm stand against the very system which supported its privileged status. Men like Boutros Ghali and Magdi Wahba, both grandsons of former prime ministers and members of elite families, were not eager to challenge a system which had allowed them to rise to positions of wealth, power, and influence despite their religious affiliations.[19] As a result, the strong, charismatic, and highly visible Pope Shenouda III became, by default, the most prominent and outspoken representative for the Copts. This presented a problem for radical political Islam because it called attention to the sizable Coptic community, which could be an obstacle to implementing Islamic laws.[20]

Shenouda wrote articles and granted interviews to the media. His activities and opinions were covered by a few liberal writers, but mainly he drew criticism from Islamists who accused him of seeking to be a political leader, alluding to Sadat's inaccurate and inflammatory claim that Shenouda wanted to set up a Coptic state. Shenouda was denounced openly in certain mosques, especially during Friday sermons, which were attended by a large number of worshipers. Some well-known, well-educated Islamists went so far as to ask their audiences not to greet their Coptic neighbors or wish them happiness on Christian holidays.[21] Others accused Shenouda of trying to interfere in the political system through his control over the church.[22] Generalized criticism of Christians and Christianity began to be heard in mosques.

A Changing Political, Social, and Economic Climate

In *The Coptic Question in the Mubarak Era*, Sebastian Elsässer points out that openly promoting sectarianism and engaging in religious polemics are fairly recent phenomena in Egyptian public culture. Since throwing off the colonial yoke, Egyptians had tended to refrain from expressing divisive sectarian opinions, in the interest of promoting national unity. But under Sadat and Mubarak, taboos against expressing offensive religious speech began to erode.[23] During the Mubarak era, tension between Copts and Muslims began to infiltrate the public sphere to an unprecedented degree. Through satellite television and the Internet, the views of extremists in both communities gained a wide audience. Religious activities also began to get much more coverage in the state media. Perhaps the government did not see any danger in allowing increased reporting on religious topics or increased incorporation of religion in the schools. A more cynical interpretation is that this was a deliberate strategy to divert public attention away from the government's failure to improve the economic, educational, and social status of the people.

How did the Copts respond to the growing hostility from certain segments of society? On the individual level, many affirmed their religious identity through increased personal piety and the outward display of religious symbols. On an institutional level, the church relied primarily on defending its own doctrines without attacking Muslims or Islam. However, as changes in the cultural climate made anti-Coptic polemics more publicly acceptable, some Coptic extremists began to respond with anti-Muslim polemics of their own.

One well-known example was Zakariya Butrus, a Coptic priest in Cairo who became known for his outspoken preaching. Butrus's criticism of government policy toward Copts and his efforts to convert Muslims to Christianity put him in conflict with both the state security forces and Pope Shenouda. Between 1979 and 1988, the church forbade Butrus from carrying out priestly functions or preaching. He was eventually reinstated and assigned to a parish in Australia in 1989. By the 2000s, he was living in the United States, where he became the first Coptic televangelist, starring in a satellite TV channel that proselytized to Muslims and depicted Islam in a negative light.[24] Though the Coptic Church condemned his activity, it was unable to completely silence it.

Modern communications technology, increased freedom of expression outside Egypt, and reduced inhibitions about expressing offensive views formed a new and dangerous combination. Inflammatory rhetoric, together with growing Salafi influence from the Gulf, contributed to a rise in violence within Egypt. In the early 1990s, Islamists had expanded their violent activities to target tourists, government security forces, and the country's infrastructure in an effort to weaken the government.

Muslims who came back from the Arabian Peninsula heavily influenced by the severe Wahhabi sect began to look at Copts as an alien group in the Arab world. Having little government protection, Copts were harassed, especially in the south, where Islamists bombed churches and shops owned by Copts. There were incidents in Sanbu, Tima, Deir Mawas, Abu Qirqas, and al-Kush, to name just a few. Many rich and middle-class Copts—those who could afford to sell their land—moved from southern towns and villages to the large cities for better protection. Pope Shenouda did not organize any demonstrations to protest these incidents, as he had done early in his tenure when a church was destroyed in 1972.[25] Events and politics were different in the late 1990s from what they had been in the early 1980s. Shenouda was now a state ally and not in a position to do much.[26] In some respects he was as helpless as the government was.

The shaykh of al-Azhar, 'Ali Gad al-Haq, further inflamed the situation by issuing a fatwa that declared Copts and Jews were infidels.[26] Some prominent Muslim scholars echoed the same opinion in the media.[27] As a result of this highly charged message, fewer Copts were promoted to high and visible administrative positions in the government. They also were increasingly excluded from the public sector and the universities. For example, there was not a single Copt among 274 university deans and presidents. Muhammad Mujahid mentions many other examples of Copts being excluded from prominent positions.[28] Mustafa Mashhour, a past president of the Muslim Brotherhood, claimed that the Copts should again pay the *jizya* and should not serve in the army.[29] This reflected political Islam's attempt to bring back the past instead of looking toward the future. Rather than work toward improving the problems in society, the Brotherhood directed people's attention toward blaming the Copts. While this was no doubt politically expedient, singling out the Coptic community as a troublesome "other" also had psychological utility. In *The Need to Have Enemies and Allies*, Vamik Volkan discusses the important psychological functions that are served when one community identifies another as an enemy in order to defend against its own internal problems.[30]

The degree to which things had changed since the first half of the twentieth century was reflected in the parliamentary election of 1995, when not a single Copt was selected to run. The secretary-general of the NDP, Kamal al-Shazly, claimed that he could not nominate Copts to represent the party in Parliament because they had no chance of winning. The fact was that the NDP did not have popular support; it was a party on paper, with no real power base.[31] In contrast, the Wafd Party of the 1920s and 1930s had nominated Copts who won even in districts dominated by Muslims. At that time, the Wafd had a strong popular base. Under its umbrella, Copts and Muslims came together to form a united front against the perceived "enemy" of the day, the British. In the 1990s, in the absence of such unity, and in the presence of growing sentiment that Copts were the source of the country's problems, the NDP was impotent.

In 1998 and 1999, a widely publicized incident reflected the charged sectarian atmosphere. A simple dispute between a Copt and a Muslim in the village of al-Kush, 440 kilometers south of Cairo, led to the deaths of twenty people and the injury of twenty more. All of the casualties were Copts, a fact which attracted the attention of Egyptian Copts abroad. The police interrogated about a thousand people, sixteen public prosecutors were involved, and eventually four of the accused were found guilty and sentenced to prison. One received a ten-year sentence because he owned an unlicensed gun, while the other three were sentenced to one or two years in prison. The government paid between 2,000 and 6,000 Egyptian pounds (about $200 to $600) to compensate each family in which someone had died or been injured. The sentences disappointed many Copts, including Pope Shenouda, who felt the court's judgment was disproportionately mild compared to the number of Copts killed, including children and elderly people. There were charges and countercharges. The judge blamed a bishop and three local priests for inciting the Copts. Some Copts claimed to have been tortured by police, but nothing was proven. Copts living abroad managed to generate further publicity around the incident, which led to written accounts that were critical of the government. Public opinion was largely split along sectarian lines, with Copts and Muslims interpreting events quite differently. In much the same way that the 1995 O.J. Simpson trial had exposed the depth of the racial divide in the United States, the al-Kush incident exposed the bitterness and mistrust between the religious communities in Egypt.

Other high-profile incidents followed. In 2004, a Coptic woman by the name of Wafaa' Constantine allegedly converted to Islam in order to obtain a divorce from her husband, who was a priest. This incident was blown out of proportion. The church intervened, claimed her back, and placed her in a convent. In spite of the relative insignificance of one person converting to Islam, this incident annoyed many Muslims on two grounds: (1) the church's interference limited the freedom of Copts to convert to Islam, and (2) the government had complied with the church's demands. In 2010, a woman by the name of Camellia had a similar problem, and the state again allowed the church to intervene. As a result of all the attention these two incidents received from the media, sectarian tensions rose.[32] The professor and political analyst Galal Amin feels the disproportionate attention these cases received indicated a weakening in the fabric of society; the rumors surrounding these cases could only gain traction in an unhealthy social climate.[33]

In addition to changes in the position of Copts in the political and social spheres, their role in the economic sphere was changing as well. From the end of the eighteenth century until 1952, Copts had played an important role in the economic development of Egypt. More than forty of the one hundred richest families in the country were Christians. In the south, the ratio was even higher.[34] Between 1952 and the 1970s, Egypt under Nasser moved toward a socialist economy. Land redistribution and nationalization of companies reduced the wealth of rich Copts and Muslims alike. Liberalization of the economy during Sadat's era (the "open door policy"), under pressure from the World Bank and the International Monetary Fund, brought extreme wealth into the hands of a few. A new class emerged, supported by a few individuals in the government.

Starting in the late 1970s—without adequate Egyptian laws to control it—the open door policy led to unprecedented corruption for the benefit of the few at the top. This increased significantly during Mubarak's era. In one case, high-ranking Egyptian officials were involved in selling off a public sector company, valued at $107 billion, to a few individuals for only $9.6 billion.[35]

Just as growing Islamist influence affected political life, it also played a role in financial matters. One development that revealed weakness and corruption at high levels was a scandal involving so-called Islamic investment companies (Sharikat Tawzif al-Amwal). In the previous chapter we discussed the rise of an Islamic banking system which allowed observant Muslims to conduct financial transactions according to a strict interpretation of sharia. As conservative Islamic practices became more widespread, Islamic banks also became more popular. To capitalize on this trend, unscrupulous individuals formed new "Islamic investment companies" which they claimed would be both highly profitable and in accordance with Islam. Unrealistically high rates of return of as much as 20 percent were promised. Promoted by some Islamic clergy as well as businessmen, "Islamic investment companies" absorbed much of the savings of the Egyptian middle class inside and outside Egypt. These companies operated remarkably free from any government regulations: because high-ranking officials had been involved in these companies and recognized Islamic scholars had endorsed the system, there was little oversight. In fact, the whole system was a classic pyramid scheme. It relied on the continuous flow of incoming funds from new investors to generate payments to its clients and to pay for advertisements to keep the money rolling in. When the flow of investors dried up, the companies collapsed. This hit the society like an earthquake. By the time the government woke up to the scam in 1988, many Egyptians had lost some or all of their life savings.[36]

Political Islam made its influence felt in the legal system as well. When the renowned Islamic scholar Nasr Hamid Abu Zayd wrote critically of how Islam was being misused in politics and in the economy for the benefit of a few, he was denied a promotion to professorship and was accused of being an apostate. Some Islamist lawyers filed a lawsuit to force him to divorce his wife—Ibthal Younis, a professor of French at Cairo University—on the grounds that Abu Zayd was no longer a Muslim and therefore was not permitted to be the husband of a Muslim woman.[37] The court ordered the couple to divorce, but because there was no means to enforce this ruling on people who refused to accept it, the couple stayed together. Although Abu Zayd was not fired, his books were removed from the university library, he was not allowed to teach, and his life was threatened. He accepted a professorship at Leiden University in Holland, where he continued his research and continued to publish in Arabic and English. His wife joined him there and traveled back and forth to Egypt, where she continued to teach. Abu Zayd's story was well covered in the Egyptian and international media. It reflected the deterioration of the educational and judiciary systems, as well as the increased power of political Islam.

The increasing penetration of Islamist influence had a repressive effect on cultural and intellectual life. In chapter twelve we described the vibrant cultural renaissance in Egypt during the first half of the twentieth century, when a number of outstanding individuals, both Copts and Muslims, flourished in the atmosphere of political and social openness (see appendix 1). In the second half of that century, Coptic and Muslim intellectuals continued to enrich the cultural life of Egypt, but their contributions were often limited by repressive political and religious forces within society. Galal Amin, Muhammad Haykal, Louis Awad, Nasr Abu Zayd, Ghali Shukri, Rushdi Said, and many others witnessed and described the deterioration of the educational system that accompanied the rise of political Islam.

The increased use of an Islamic dress code was a visible sign of the growing power of radical Islam over the masses. This was a new phenomenon in Egypt. Some men began to wear beards and short tunics. Women, especially young educated women, began to wear the *hijab*. Within a decade or two, the custom had spread to the majority of women. The women's dress code varied from a fashionable headscarf to a garment that covered the entire body, including gloves for the hands, that was worn even in the heat of summer, similar to the *burka* used in Saudi Arabia, Afghanistan, and Pakistan. The dress code for women was sometimes enforced in the schools; in one case, a teacher cut the hair of a young girl because she would not wear the *hijab*.[38]

The cultural change in dress was strongly supported in the media by some Islamist scholars, while other Islamic scholars denounced it as having nothing to do with Islam. Some complained that the obsession with a dress code reduced Islam to outward appearance and rituals, and missed its true essence. When Farouk Hosni, an influential minister under Mubarak for about twenty years, made offhand comments about the ubiquity of the Islamic dress code, he was harshly criticized not only by the Muslim Brotherhood and Salafists but also by prominent members of the NDP as well as some government officials.[39] The veil, Hosni said, was an indication of the penetration of political Islam among the masses. Preoccupation with the dress code took energy away from parliamentary debates about more important issues such as the economy, education, healthcare, and other pressing political concerns. Sometimes, wearing the hijab was a political statement in itself. Since the president's wife, Suzanne Mubarak, never wore a hijab, the campaign to enforce its use was interpreted by some as an indirect criticism of the president.

The increased use of the Islamic dress code made non-Muslims stand out as different from Muslims, and resulted in greater segregation in society. In his book about the conflict between religion and the secular world, Amin gives many examples and analyzes the impact of the radical Islamic influence that has overtaken Egypt in modern times. Some Islamists believe girls should cover their heads as early as age five, depriving them of some of the freedom of childhood. Lord Cromer remarked during his rule that there were no significant differences between the Copts and the Muslims except that one went to a church while the other went to a mosque.[40] This continued to be true until the mid-1970s. But now, a century after Cromer's remark, visible distinctions in dress between the Copts and the Muslims are strikingly evident, especially for women. Today, Coptic women stand out and are labeled as non-Muslims, along with a few liberal Muslim women who choose not to wear the hijab.

In spite of its difficulties, the Mubarak regime kept power within its own grip. In 1995, a thirty-six-year-old Muslim engineer named Abu-l 'Ila Madi left the Muslim Brotherhood and attempted to start a centrist Islamist political party, Hizb al-Wasat. This party represented the middle ground between the rigid defense of the old Islamic tradition and the wholesale adoption of values and institutions imported from the West.[41] The government refused to grant the proposed party a permit because its platform demanded that Islamic law should take precedence over civil law. Madi, along with other educated Islamists, such as Salim al-'Awwa and Tariq al-Bishri, twice made changes to the proposed platform, but it was still rejected.[42] Some intellectual non-Islamists, including some women and a few Copts, joined the proposed party, but to no avail. The government insisted it would not share power with any party. It refused to learn from the experience of Turks, Jordanians, and Moroccans, who had made room for the Islamists in their own political systems.

In addition to the Islamists, other forms of opposition to the Mubarak regime developed over time. In 1995, Said al-Naggar, a former high-ranking official in the World Bank, started the liberal New Civic Forum, which opposed implementing Islamic sharia law. Al-Naggar received some attention from the media and was even mentioned as a potential prime minister, but he was largely ignored by the government. Another important organization that opposed Mubarak called itself Kefaya (literally, 'Enough'), implying that they had had enough of Mubarak and it was time for him to go. Kefaya emerged in 2004 and became the country's most vocal and inspiring grassroots non-Islamist opposition group. One of its founders was George Ishak, a Copt and an activist. The group gained the support of many Copts and women. The Egyptian Movement for Change (al-Gabha al-Wataniya li-l-Taghyir, or AAL, known as 'Kefaya'), was another organization that drew support from across the Egyptian political spectrum. Not surprisingly, the Muslim Brotherhood distanced themselves from both Kefaya and AAL. In the spring of 2008, another group surfaced which called itself April 6. This movement initially supported a workers' strike in a government-owned textile company in the town of al-Mahalla al-Kubra, an important industrial center in the central Nile Delta.

Opposition to the regime continued, and it seemed that the political system was deadlocked. By this time, Mubarak was in his eighties and had been in power for thirty years. He did not seem to be in good health, and his wife and son Gamal had increasing influence. The Mubarak family denied that they were interested in founding a dynasty—Egypt was not like Syria, they said—but many pointed to evidence that Gamal was being groomed to take his father's place.

Haykal suggested a way out of this deadlock. His proposal was to keep Mubarak as a figurehead, and to have the country governed by a presidential council for a transitional period of about three years. During this transition, the country would be run by an administration of technocrats, while a new constitution was written and voted on. Haykal suggested some candidates for this transitional presidential council, two of whom were Nobel Prize recipients living outside of Egypt. He also suggested including representatives from the army and others with good standing among Egyptians. In 2009, Haykal warned that Egypt was on the brink of chaos if something was not done.[43] His warning was very serious, but it was ignored by the Mubarak regime.

Although its façade remained the same, the Mubarak government had been decaying from the inside for more than a decade. Mohamed ElBaradei, the Egyptian who received the Nobel Prize for his work at the International Atomic Energy Agency (IAEA), said that if one million Egyptians demonstrated against the government, the government would collapse. He announced he might, himself, run for the presidency of Egypt.

The Mubarak regime was ideologically bankrupt, and there was no positive alternative in sight. Mubarak was known for being stubborn. For thirty years, he had refused to appoint a vice president. Instead, he relied on a few elderly advisors who had lost touch with the reality in the streets. Ineffectual political parties were financed by the government to give the false appearance of democracy. The Egyptian constitution had never allowed political parties to be based on religion, so the Muslim Brotherhood was effectively excluded from legitimate channels of political expression. Although the Brotherhood had strong popular appeal and a strong organization, it offered little in the way of practical guidance on how to run the country. Empty slogans and hollow rhetoric, such as "Islam is both the religion and the state" *(al-Islam din wa dawla)* and "Islam is the solution," had popular appeal, but no content; not a single verse in the Qur'an prescribes a form of government or a specific political system.[44]

On Coptic Christmas Eve, January 6, 2010, three men opened fire on worshipers leaving a church in the town of Nag Hammadi, in southern Egypt. Fifteen people were injured or killed, including a Muslim guard. The attackers claimed they were retaliating for the rape of a Muslim child by a Copt. However, one of the three attackers had a known criminal record, and may have been hired to stir up trouble.[45] In less than ten days, the government concluded that the accused had acted on their own, but many did not believe that. Nearly a year later, on December 31, 2010, while Copts were celebrating New Year's Eve, a similar attack was made on a church in Alexandria. This incident left twenty-three people dead and about a hundred injured, and saddened not only Egyptian Christians, but many Muslims as well.[46] In an act of solidarity, some Muslims participated in Coptic Christmas celebrations a few days after the attack. They even guarded other churches from possible attacks. The interior minister declared that the attack was the work of Hamas, the Palestinian Muslim Brotherhood organization, although he did not present any proof. No arrests were made; the perpetrators were never found. Some pointed a finger at the interior minister himself, accusing him of trying to divert attention from the deteriorating conditions in the country. Pope Shenouda accepted condolences from many Egyptians, foreign ambassadors, and dignitaries. While the patriarch's relationship with the government was good on a personal level, the government was impotent when it came to protecting the Christian minority. Amin questioned what the Copts had done to deserve such treatment.[47] As it turned out, these outbreaks of violence against Copts were symptoms of a government about to collapse. Egyptians were tense and fearful of what would happen next. They did not have long to wait. The youth of Egypt had already begun to mobilize for what became the revolution of January 25, 2011.

On June 6, 2010, a twenty-eight-year-old educated man by the name of Khalid Said was killed by two plainclothes policemen near an Internet café for no obvious reason. Most reports claim that he died in police custody. The police tried to fabricate a story that the man died after attempting to swallow a packet of hashish, but the story was not believable. The incident was highly publicized as an example of police brutality. A picture of Said's mutilated head caused a large outcry when it went viral on the Internet. Wael Ghoneim, a thirty-year-old marketing executive at Google who worked in Dubai and had never met Said, created a Facebook memorial page called "We Are All Khaled Said" *(Kolona Khaled Said)*. Other young people did the same on their Facebook pages. These Internet activities quickly drew hundreds of thousands of followers, making this Egypt's biggest dissident Facebook page, and attracting international attention.[48] Other stories similar to that of Said were taking place in Egypt but did not get as much attention—often only a few lines in the newspaper, without any follow-up—but Said's story galvanized young people. The Mubarak regime was on its last legs.

16

THE JANUARY 25 REVOLUTION AND ITS AFTERMATH

By January of 2011, anger against the Mubarak regime had reached a boiling point. In a historic move, the youth of Egypt used social media to organize a massive, nonviolent demonstration against the regime. The call went out to thousands of Egyptians to assemble in Tahrir Square in downtown Cairo on January 25, the day of the annual Police Day celebration. The police tried unsuccessfully to break up the demonstration with their usual brutality, but they were overwhelmed by the large numbers of people pouring into Tahrir Square. First there were thousands and then hundreds of thousands, coming from all directions. Many ordinary Egyptians responded to the youths' call in a way that surprised the regime and the rest of the world. The movement quickly expanded to many other cities in Egypt. The chanting in Tahrir Square was thunderous—calling for bread, freedom, and social justice. A number of people were injured or killed by the police or by thugs on behalf of the regime, but the people held their ground.

Mubarak tried to subdue the people's anger by granting some concessions. He announced on television that he was not going to run for another term (he was then eighty-three years old), and that his son Gamal had no intention of running. For the first time in thirty years, Mubarak appointed a vice-president. He chose seventy-four-year-old Omar Suleiman, his trusted ally and the head of the army intelligence agency. Mubarak claimed he only wanted to finish his term in office. But this was too little, too late. The masses in Tahrir Square accelerated their demands: they wanted Mubarak to leave immediately. Mubarak tried to use the army to end the demonstration by force, but the army refused to comply. The high-ranking army officers were not pleased with the idea of a Mubarak family succession.

After eighteen days, on February 11, Mubarak resigned and appointed the Supreme Council of the Armed Forces (SCAF) to replace him. Mubarak's last order in office was to appoint seventy-year-old General Ahmad Shafiq as prime minister. Shafiq had been a minister in the Mubarak administration. The army took the final step of removing Mubarak and his son, and took the lead in making the important decisions that followed.

Although the people were happy that Mubarak was gone, they quickly realized that General Shafiq was simply a continuation of the old regime with a new face. Under pressure from the street, the newly appointed prime minister was forced to resign within a month. This was the beginning of a chaotic period, which many had feared and predicted. To calm the public, the military spokesmen declared that the army supported the legitimate demands of the people, and would not use force against them.[1] The news that the army was siding with the people was met with jubilation. Demonstrators cheered and embraced soldiers in the streets, and civilians climbed on top of tanks to greet the military personnel.

But the honeymoon with the SCAF did not last long. Essam Sharaf, a university professor with a previous connection to Gamal Mubarak, was appointed prime minister, but he lasted only nine months. He could not achieve much while some of the high-ranking ministers from the Mubarak regime remained in power. The SCAF assumed responsibility for governing the country for six months or until new parliamentary and presidential elections could take place; it ended up staying in power for a period of sixteen months. To put this in context, it is helpful to understand a bit more about the Egyptian military as an institution.

The Egyptian army is made up of about half a million servicemen on active duty and one million reservists. Since the 1952 revolution, it has achieved a high degree of economic power and political independence. In addition to its conventional military duties, the army engages in many non-military activities, such as road construction and managing factories that produce a variety of products, ranging from cement to macaroni and bread. The Egyptian army has been likened to an octopus, with tentacles reaching into many sectors of society. According to the BBC's *Frontline*, the Egyptian army controls about 40 percent of the Egyptian economy.[2] Even within the private sector, influential businessmen often have connections with the government, the military, and the intelligence agency. Moreover, many governors and some city mayors were originally military personnel.[3] The true figures for the army's budget are not shared with the Egyptian people; the figures have not been discussed openly in Parliament since the 1950s. Foreign assistance from the United States in 2014 was $1.5 billion, of which $1.3 billion was for military aid.[4] The Egyptian army's relationship with the United States has been strong. So, while many welcomed the short-term stability brought by the military, no one could predict what the longer-term ramifications would be for the country as a whole. How would this transitional period of military control affect Egypt's economy, foreign policy, and sectarian tensions?

Despite the Coptic Church's opposition, Coptic youth joined the revolution with the same enthusiasm as Muslim youth. Pope Shenouda had been supportive of the Mubarak regime. In 2009, he had even supported Gamal Mubarak's run for office.[5] On January 23, the church asked Copts not to participate in the January 25 demonstration.[6] The youth ignored this request. Thousands of Copts flocked to Tahrir Square, along with their Muslim compatriots. This created a distinctly national secular atmosphere. Repeating a gesture that had been used during the 1919 revolt, the Qur'an and the Bible together were raised high during the initial part of the January revolt as a symbol of national unity. This gesture represented solidarity, while also acknowledging the presence of two religious communities and the significance of religion in Egyptian society.

Egyptians were pleased that Mubarak had been removed. They hoped they would soon have greater freedom to express political views and participate in government. But events soon began to take a different turn. The SCAF announced it would form a committee to amend the constitution (of 1971) as a temporary solution. The new constitution would be voted on by the people. The person appointed by the SCAF to head the committee was Tariq al-Bishri, a prominent and respected retired judge who was known for his Islamist leanings. The committee also included Subhi Salih, a lawyer who was a member of the Muslim Brotherhood.[7] Some welcomed this as evidence of a more inclusive political process; others feared the Islamists were positioning themselves for a takeover. Whatever negotiations may have taken place between the Brotherhood and the SCAF were not formally revealed.

Negotiations with the Brotherhood had started during the last days of the Mubarak regime and were continued by the SCAF. Within days of Mubarak's resignation, the Islamist shaykh Yusuf al-Qaradawi, an old and influential member of the Brotherhood, arrived in Egypt from his home in Qatar. He delivered the Friday sermon on February 19, 2011, to a crowd of hundreds of thousands in Tahrir Square. On March 4, the then newly appointed prime minister Sharaf addressed the large crowds that were still assembled in the square. Next to him was Muhammad al-Biltagi, a leading figure in the Brotherhood.

At the time, political Islamists, represented by the Muslim Brotherhood and the Salafists, were the only organized factions with financial resources and a presence in the street; other parties did not have these advantages. Money was pouring into the country to support both political Islam and other non-governmental organizations. This evidence of outside interests trying to control events in Egypt was disturbing to the nationalists and intellectual Egyptians. On July 29, 2011, many Egyptians were surprised and upset to see the large number of flags from Saudi Arabia, and that of al-Qaeda, filling Tahrir Square.

The events of January 25 took the leadership of the Brotherhood by surprise, as well. They did not expect the revolt to be on such a grand scale or to happen with such speed, and they were caught unprepared. In spite of the Brotherhood's popularity, its top leaders remained largely isolated from their own base as well as from the broader political movement. They were viewed with suspicion by other political groups and parties. Some of their leaders were still in jail, but were freed shortly after the January revolt, in a suspicious and unclear sequence of events.[8] The Brotherhood leaders were cautious and self-restrained, for good reason, because most had been jailed for many years. But the younger members of the Brotherhood were willing and eager to confront the Mubarak regime head on, as were some other young Egyptians. Some students in the Brotherhood were convinced they could be more effective as part of a wider coalition than they would be if acting alone. A coalition would provide them with a measure of protection from the police, and it would encourage young people who were reluctant to associate themselves with the Brotherhood to join the movement.[9] Finally, on January 28, three days after the beginning of the revolt, the Muslim Brotherhood's leading office, Maktab al-Irshad, approved the participation of the youth on the condition that they not attack any government officials by name. The young Brotherhood members worked with students from other groups, including Nasserite and socialist students.[10] But after Mubarak's resignation, the Muslim Brotherhood withdrew from Tahrir Square, and instead dealt with the SCAF through different channels.

The Constitution Committee appointed by the SCAF made some minor changes in the Constitution of 1971, and called for a referendum on March 19, 2011, one month after Mubarak's departure. The referendum was reduced to two options for how to proceed: (1) approve a constitution first, then elect a president and members of parliament; or (2) hold presidential elections first, followed by approving a constitution. Most intellectuals and secularists favored the first option, writing a new constitution prior to holding elections. Many would have recommended putting the government in the hands of a temporary presidential council of technocrats for two or three years while a new constitution was being drawn up. This would give political parties time and freedom to gather resources and organize. But the SCAF and the Islamists rejected that option. Islamists favored early elections to install a new leadership which would then oversee writing the final constitution. The only group that would benefit from a speedy election was the Muslim Brotherhood and its allies, who already had support in the street, considerable financial resources, and a strong organization.

The younger generation of Egyptians had achieved a miracle by removing Mubarak peacefully within eighteen days. But they did not have a representative or unified leadership capable of wielding power or of participating in future planning. There were also strong external powers who opposed significant change, the most important being the United States and Israel and their allies within Egypt.[11] Outside influence was a concern, as the Egyptian borders were quite open, and money was pouring into Egypt through transactions that could not be traced.

Before the March 19 referendum was put to the people for a vote, the Islamists waged a fierce campaign in support of holding an early presidential election. In addition to getting their message out by radio and television advertisements, a number of mosques influenced by the Brotherhood and the Salafists became political campaign centers. Some Islamists declared that voting to hold the parliamentary election first was tantamount to a vote against Islam. They claimed that only the Copts would vote against holding the presidential election first. Naturally, the Copts had serious concerns; they feared political Islam would gain too much power, so most Copts joined those who favored writing the constitution first. The result of the vote on March 19 was disappointing to them and to many intellectuals and nationalists: 77 percent of voters approved holding the presidential election first. This represented a high approval rating for the Islamists, even though most people did not really know what the Islamists stood for. Back in the November 11, 2009, issue of *al-Musawwar Magazine*, the journalist and screenwriter Osama Anwar Okasha had written, "It is impossible for the Brotherhood to rule Egypt via a truly free election. Their only chance to gain power is during a chaotic period after a political vacuum." Now his prediction had come true.

No sectarian violence took place for about a month after the January 25 revolution. However, on March 5, it began to appear. In Itfeh, on the outskirts of Cairo, a church was attacked. The Copts demonstrated, requesting an investigation and justice. Tension between the Copts and the Muslims increased. In the absence of a strong government, some strange

Islamic rulings were handed down, such as making ear-cutting a form of legal punishment. The violence against Copts continued for the next few years, but why it happened and who was behind it were unclear.

Galal Amin and others asked some important questions regarding the sequence of events that followed the January revolution. Why and how did the security forces disappear as demonstrations progressed, thus creating a chaotic period? What incited thugs and undercover agents to terrorize citizens in some neighborhoods, including the revolutionaries in Tahrir Square? Why did the SCAF appoint one weak government after another, including ministers from the Mubarak regime, who achieved little or nothing? Mubarak had been a strong ally of the United States for thirty years, but after the revolt, President Barack Obama and Secretary of State Hillary Clinton announced emphatically that Mubarak had to go, and quickly. What motivated the sudden reversal? Amin asked why there was such a rush to hold a new election even though the political parties (other than the Islamists) were not prepared for it. He also questioned why some of those who had participated in Sadat's assassination had been freed from jail and were allowed to appear on national television shows.[12]

During the SCAF era, demonstrations were everywhere. The country's normal operations seemed to be paralyzed. It was as though people believed that demonstrating, in itself, would solve the country's complex problems. Having waited so long for things to change, they could wait no longer. People began to take matters into their own hands. Muslims as well as Copts were kidnapped for ransom. All this happened in the virtual absence of security; the laws were not enforced.[13] The SCAF started to use force. The number of people who were killed or injured was much greater now than it had been during the first days of the revolution or even under the Mubarak regime. Many of the young revolutionaries in Tahrir Square were harassed and put in jail. Some young women were also arrested and were subjected to humiliating virginity examinations. These incidents were widely covered by the local and international media. The youth chanted, "Down with the military!" and wrote this slogan on walls near Tahrir Square.

In this chaotic post-revolutionary period, many sectarian incidents took place in Egypt, especially in the south. Some Copts were expelled from their communities, especially in small villages; others were attacked, and no investigations were made. Two important examples illustrated the difficulties experienced by Copts, due to the absence of law and order. The first involved the SCAF's appointment of a Coptic governor in Qena province. The second involved violence against churches.

On April 15, 2011, the SCAF appointed twenty new governors. A Coptic general, Emad Shehata Mikhail, was appointed governor of Qena province (455 kilometers south of Cairo), one of the poorest governorates in Egypt. His predecessor had also been a Copt, but Mikhail's appointment created strong opposition due to his religious affiliation. Salafists in Qena organized massive rallies against him and shut down trains running through the province. They argued that their province had been singled out for Coptic governors. After unsuccessful negotiations, a Muslim governor was appointed.[14]

In September and October 2011, an old church in the village of Marinate in Aswan province was destroyed, along with the burning or destruction of three Coptic houses. Different versions of what had happened quickly spread among Copts and Muslims, both inside and outside Egypt. Some said the church deserved to be torn down because they claimed it had been built without permission. Documentation was a problem for many old churches. Official records disagreed on how many churches there were; the building census identified 1,442 churches, while the interior ministry claimed there were only five hundred. Part of the discrepancy was due to a number of old churches having been built without permits.[15] In fact, the church in question was falling apart, and a new one was in the process of being built with the appropriate permits. However, the new church towers were higher than those shown in the architectural drawing. As a result of the publicity about this church, and without knowing all the facts, Copts in Cairo started to demonstrate in front of the radio and television building in the center of the city. They demanded that the governor of Aswan be removed from office, the church be rebuilt, and those responsible for the sectarian violence be arrested and brought to trial. The demonstrators gave the SCAF forty-eight hours to comply.[16] A confrontation between some army units and the demonstrators ensued, leading to the death of about twenty-five people and injuring 257 others. This became known as the Maspero massacre.[17] The demonstrators denounced the SCAF and accused it of being complicit in anti-Christian violence. An alternative explanation claimed that, under pressure, the driver of an armed vehicle panicked and drove through the demonstrators to escape the angry crowd, killing many people, most if not all of whom happened to be Copts. Although this could account for some of those killed, it does not explain the injury of 257 people. The question of who was responsible was not investigated. For many, this incident demonstrated that the Copts were even more vulnerable than they had been before the revolution.[18]

Morsi and the Muslim Brotherhood initially declared that the latter would not seek more than 30 percent of the seats in Parliament and would not put up a candidate for president. However, given the political vacuum and their success in the March 19 referendum, they decided to run candidates for 50 percent of the seats in Parliament as well as a presidential candidate. During 2011 and 2012, political Islam achieved stunning victories. They won the presidency and controlled 66 percent of the seats in Parliament. The victory of the Islamists triggered a significant pushback from high-ranking Egyptian officials, especially in the army. Even before the presidential election, the SCAF implemented a Supreme Court ruling which dissolved Parliament on the grounds of election irregularities. The SCAF also issued a supplement to the temporary constitution of 2011. The terms of this supplement delegated legislative authority to itself, deprived the president of control over matters of national defense and security, and gave the military and the judiciary veto power over the terms of the new constitution. These rulings were intended to prevent the Muslim Brotherhood from obtaining unilateral power over all three branches of government.[19]

The first round of the presidential election included many candidates. The four who obtained the most votes were Hamdeen Sabbahi, a civilian; Ahmad Shafiq, a retired general; Muhammad Morsi, a member of the Muslim Brotherhood; and 'Abd al-Mun'im Abu-l-Futuh, a former member of the Brotherhood who had resigned after the revolution so he could participate (against the wishes of the Brotherhood) in the presidential election. The run-off election in 2012 was between Morsi and Shafiq. For many voters, it was a dilemma; neither candidate was appealing. The question was not whom to vote for, but rather whom to vote against. Morsi won with 51.8 percent of the vote, while Shafiq received 47.8 percent.[20] Many of those who voted for Morsi did so because they did not want another military officer at the helm; many of those who voted for the general did so because they mistrusted the Brotherhood. It was a democratic election in form, but not in substance.

Many felt that Morsi and the Muslim Brotherhood rushed to take office before they were prepared for it—that Morsi blundered his way into politics, without the experience or the necessary staff to govern well. Mubarak's dictatorship had relied on an extensive bureaucracy which Morsi could not replace overnight. In addition, for many years Morsi had belonged to the Muslim Brotherhood—a rigid, hierarchical institution based on obedience. As president, Morsi followed Mubarak's autocratic style, keeping power for himself and making unilateral decisions. He initially overruled the Supreme Court's decision to dissolve parliament due to election irregularities, but then he backtracked and upheld the court's ruling.

Morsi then assigned total authority to the president, giving himself even more power than Mubarak had had. On November 21, 2012, he issued several laws that he called revolutionary. The most important of these made all presidential decisions final and not subject to any future ruling—even by the Supreme Court—until a new parliament was elected and had taken up its duties. He effectively neutralized the checks and balances provided by the judiciary and Parliament. This decision was opposed by many Egyptians and caused demonstrations that continued until December 9, when Morsi was forced to retract his decision.

Morsi's plan for the first one hundred days included regulating traffic, cleaning the cities, improving security, and relieving the fuel shortage. None of these things were done. Difficulties running the country continued, due in part to Morsi's preference for relying on trusted Brotherhood functionaries rather than recruiting competent people from outside the circles he knew. The Brotherhood's hierarchical organization and culture of obedience did not prepare him for working within a complex democratic system.[21]

As resentment grew, demonstrations against Morsi and his Brotherhood-affiliated government increased, especially in the big cities. Egypt was dominated by a mood of anger, discontent, and disappointment. The country was fragmented. Many who had voted for the Brotherhood began to see its limitations when it came to actually running the country. By June, things were reaching a crisis. An organization of young people called Tamarod (meaning 'rebellious') collected signatures for a petition requesting that Morsi hold early presidential elections. Their target was 15 million signatures by June 30, 2013, the first anniversary of Morsi's taking office. Whether Tamarod was truly an independent grassroots movement or was supported by others was not clear, but they garnered wide support. The demonstrations against Morsi and the Brotherhood were much larger than the demonstrations against Mubarak had been. The government tried to impose a curfew, but it was largely ignored. In Port Said, not only was the curfew ignored, but the youth defiantly played soccer in the streets at night. Morsi's government seemed powerless. Muhammad Habib—who had been the second in command of the Brotherhood but resigned during an internal power struggle after the revolution—described the Brotherhood leaders during this critical period as fighting on a modern battlefield using wooden swords. He later said that the Brotherhood leadership had made it inevitable that the Egyptians would revolt against them; anyone who wished to destroy the image of the Brotherhood could not have done a better job than what the leadership did themselves.[22]

Where Egypt was headed worried many Egyptians. Pope Tawadros II, the Coptic patriarch who had succeeded Shenouda, and Shaykh Ahmad al-Tayyib, the head of al-Azhar, were deeply concerned. On June 18, 2013, they requested a meeting with Morsi to express their concern about the state of the country and its future. Morsi said he appreciated the visit. He assured them that nothing would happen to the country as a result of the youths' rebellious movement—that after June 30, there would be July 1 and 2 and so on. According to Pope Tawadros, this response was not reassuring.[23] In a public speech a few days later, Morsi was critical of Pope Tawadros and said their relationship had cooled.

By June 30, 2013, Egypt was still without a parliament. Tamarod claimed they had collected 22 million signatures in support of an early presidential election. The majority of Egyptians no longer supported the Muslim Brotherhood, and the youth did not have leadership capabilities themselves. At this point, the army emerged to take control. General 'Abd al-Fattah al-Sisi was the defense minister and head of the army. On July 3, under his leadership, the army intervened and removed Morsi by force. The head of the Supreme Constitutional Court, Judge Adly Mansour, was declared acting president for one year, starting on July 4. During that year a new constitution was to be proposed and voted on, followed by presidential and parliamentary elections. The announcement of this plan was attended by the heads of the army, the Coptic patriarch, the shaykh of al-Azhar, and other dignitaries, including the head of the Salafist Party and Mohamed ElBaradei. ElBaradei was appointed temporary vice-president in charge of implementing this road map. Though the Western press tended to depict these events as a deplorable coup against a democratically elected president, many Egyptians saw it as an effort to save democracy from a dictator who was trying to undermine the system itself. There were large demonstrations in support of the army's intervention.

The Islamists were shocked at the speed with which events unfolded. After Morsi was removed on July 3, 2013, the supporters of the Brotherhood set up armed encampments and began ongoing demonstrations at two centers in Cairo: one in al-Nahda and the other in Rab'a. For more than a month, the newly appointed government attempted to peacefully dismantle these encampments, but failed. The Islamists waged a campaign of violence in an effort to destabilize the new government. Many attacks targeted the police force, army personnel, government buildings, and electrical power lines. This campaign did not bring down the government, but it caused many random civilian casualties and terrorized the Egyptian people.

Copts, in particular, were targeted, continuing a pattern of systematic discrimination and violence which had been evident for many years. The activist and writer Professor Muhammed Mujahid compiled data on discrimination against the Copts between 2007 and 2014. Between 2011 and 2013, in particular, violence against Copts increased.[24] Mujahid and others consider this period one of the worst in modern Egyptian history with respect to sectarian discrimination and violence.[25] For example, there were seventy attacks on churches and Coptic schools. Fifty-one additional churches were closed due to inadequate protection.[26] Tawadros showed understanding for the critical period Egypt was passing through when he declared it was important to protect the nation first, not the churches.[27] He said the churches were under the protection of God and the Muslim people.[28]

On August 14, 2013, the government finally resorted to force to clear the encampments at al-Nahda and Rab'a. Security forces were sent in and were met with armed resistance. By some estimates, casualties totaled six hundred dead and four thousand injured. This included women, children, and innocent bystanders, as well as members of the government forces and armed Islamists. The exact numbers will never be known.

Field Marshal al-Sisi resigned his post as head of the army on March 14, 2014, and ran for president. He won the election in May 2014, receiving 97 percent of the vote. It was really a referendum. Al-Sisi did not have an organized political campaign and did not promise much, but people voted for him because they hoped for stability which they believed only the army could provide. The army was the only strong organization that remained largely intact in Egypt.

Egypt has embarked on another difficult period, with many serious problems ahead. The violence continues, though at a declining rate. As of the time of this writing (2016), Coptic–Muslim relations have improved, at least on the surface. Whether this trend continues over the long term will depend on whether the economy, education, and living conditions in Egypt improve.

It is said that history repeats itself. Egypt has a long history, and the turmoil of the post-Mubarak period is nothing new. The historian Selim Hassan recounts an episode from the First Intermediate Period (2082–2055 BC):

> Pharaoh Bibi II ruled for many decades. A wise man informed him of the poor state of the country and suggested what should be done about it, but his closest advisers fed him lies, and told the ruler only what he wanted to hear. Nothing was done. Bibi II died in his nineties with no strong hand to take the reins of government. A long chaotic period followed. Egypt was miserable. People were terrified and revolted against the public officials. They were like a flock of sheep in the presence of wolves, with no shepherd around to protect them. That chaotic period lasted for about a century.[29]

Let us hope things improve more quickly this time around.

EPILOGUE

The past isn't dead. It isn't even past.
—William Faulkner

We have looked at the complexity of Coptic–Muslim relations over the centuries in the larger context of what was happening in Egypt at the time. A couple of general observations are worth noting.

First, and most important, Islam as a religion has generally been tolerant of minorities. The fact that a large Coptic community has persisted in Egypt after fifteen centuries of Islamic rule is evidence of this. While the Copts suffered significantly under some rulers, this was the exception. Today, the Copts comprise about 10 percent of the total population, or around eight to ten million people. This is still a sizable number, especially considering the fact that the birth rate of Muslims is higher than that of Copts, in part due to the ease of divorce and the effect of polygamy.

Second, the condition of the Copts has often reflected the condition of the population as a whole. In the history of Egypt, it is hard to find a ruler who discriminated against the Copts without also hurting the Muslims, though in bad times, it was often the minority who bore a disproportionate share of the suffering.

Where do things stand and where is Egypt headed? In June 2013, Egyptians revolted against their leadership for the fifth time since the 1880s. This time the army acted to remove Morsi and the Muslim Brotherhood. There were many casualties among the Islamists, the police, and ordinary citizens, in addition to retaliation against the Copts by the Islamists and unknown forces. Since the army's intervention, political and social upheaval has stabilized and sectarian violence has declined, but continues at a lower level. Was the army's intervention a military coup or was it an expression of the people's will? Although the army's removal of Morsi received welcome support from the people, the sight of an army officer at the head of government is a warning sign for many who wish to see a genuine democratic process established.

The struggle for democracy has been an ongoing challenge in Egypt for the past century. Modernity and social progress can also be reflected in the relationship between the majority and minority. Mahatma Gandhi said, "How the majority treats its minority is a measure of civility." Majority and minority relations are a challenge in the world today, not only in the developing world but also in the developed world. As far as Egypt is concerned, the future of Coptic–Muslim relations is uncertain. The first half of the twentieth century was a hopeful period. In the second half of that century, in the absence of political parties and democracy, political Islam gained momentum—sometimes underground and at other times overtly, as we have seen recently.

Modernity and Islamization do not seem to go hand in hand at present, especially when we see what is happening in the Middle East at large. The rise in political Islam in the form of ISIS (the Islamic State of Iraq and al-Sham), al-Qaeda, and the like represents a setback to modernity and the values of the Enlightenment. Prejudice and intolerance have become the norm in some communities. The best hope for change may be to educate people at a young age. In the current political climate, this is a difficult and long-term challenge. Autocratic governments, struggling economies, the population explosion, and unfair distribution of wealth are some of the problems from which the entire region suffers. Solving these difficult problems will require political will and a long-term policy—something which is currently absent.

Given this background, what is the future of Coptic–Muslim relations in Egypt? A book by Gerard Russell, published in 2014, describes how formerly prominent cultures can completely vanish.[1] The book also identifies currently existing cultures that are in danger of disappearing, with an entire chapter devoted to the precarious situation of the Copts. Russell quotes Mahdi Akef, the past head of the Muslim Brotherhood, as saying "tuz fi Masr," meaning roughly 'to hell with Egypt.' As an Islamist, Akef rejected the nation state in favor of the restoration of an Islamic caliphate, or Islamic empire. Could the rise in political Islam—in the style we currently see in Syria or Iraq as ISIS—prevail and lead to the disappearance of Christianity from the Middle East, and particularly the disappearance of the Copts from Egypt? For the moment, the Sisi government is providing a tenuous stability. But if the economy and the educational system do not improve, political Islam will likely return, possibly taking the form of ISIS or something similar. This will be harmful to Egypt and to the Muslims, and devastating to the Copts.

APPENDIX 1

Six Outstanding Individuals of the Egyptian Enlightenment Period

The first half of the twentieth century witnessed a remarkable flowering of cultural and political activity during a period that has become known as the Egyptian Enlightenment *(al-nahda)*. In spite of the presence of British colonial power and an autocratic monarchy, there was an upsurge of liberal ideals that allowed a number of remarkable individuals—both Copts and Muslims, men and women—to develop their talents and contribute to society. Here are a few examples of those whose lives demonstrate the achievements and limitations of that unique period in Egyptian history.

Taha Hussein (1889–1973)

The legendary Taha Hussein was born the seventh of twelve siblings in a poor family. His father was a guard at a sugarcane factory. At the age of five, Hussein got sick, and his eyesight dimmed. The family could not afford to take him to a doctor. Instead, they sought help from the village barber, who treated his eyes with something that caused complete blindness. However, loss of sight did not take away Hussein's inner vision, and he grew up to be a unique and influential figure who enlightened generations of Egyptians and Arabs. He earned a doctoral degree from the Sorbonne University, and later became a minister of education, receiving many awards, including five honorary doctoral degrees from international universities. How was this possible?

Hussein went to a small Islamic elementary school *(kuttab)* that was run out of a garage. The teacher was a large, blind shaykh whose primary task was to teach his pupils to memorize the 6,236 verses (about 78,000 words) of the Qur'an. In addition to teaching the Qur'an, this shaykh wrote verses on paper amulets and told people to swallow them to receive protection. While some believed in this magical tradition, the young Hussein did not. He did, however, succeed in memorizing the Qur'an—a feat which encouraged his parents to send him to Cairo to study Arabic and Islamic subjects at al-Azhar. In Cairo, he stayed with his older brother, who was studying to be a judge of Islamic law. This was an austere life for the young Hussein. His room was small and filthy. His food often was limited to sprouted fava bean soup for breakfast, and molasses mixed with tahini for dinner. He was granted four loaves of pita bread from al-Azhar. Hussein described in detail his life during this period in his memoir, *al-Ayyam (The Days)*, which was translated into many languages including English.[1]

Hussein had the fine mind of a critical thinker. He respected a few of his teachers, but despised many others for their narrow understanding of Islam. During his late teens, he was introduced to a number of Egyptian intellectuals who encouraged him to write articles for the Cairo newspapers. Some of his articles were critical of al-Azhar's educational system. This did not sit well with the old-fashioned, conservative institution. After spending eight years at al-Azhar, Hussein was well prepared to pass the final exam, but the institution refused to grant him a diploma because of his critical attitude. The conflict between Hussein and the Azharite shaykhs is an example of the struggle between modernity and conservatism that continues up until the present day.

In 1908, Egypt established its first national university, the Egyptian University. Hussein was allowed to attend some lectures and eventually enrolled to obtain a degree. Hussein was very impressed with the modern knowledge he was exposed to there. In particular, the lectures on Islamic civilization were like poetry to his ears, compared with what he had encountered at al-Azhar. Hussein took his studies very seriously. Many people saw the talent and dedication of this blind young man, and were moved to help him—first in Egypt and later abroad. In 1914, at the age of twenty-five, Hussein received the first diploma granted by the Egyptian University. His research thesis was on an old, blind literary Arab of the eleventh century, Abu-l 'Ala' al-Ma'arri, who, like Hussein, was critical of the magical and narrow-minded thinking that had infiltrated Islam. Upon graduation, Hussein was awarded twenty Egyptian pounds and was honored by the khedive as the first person to obtain a degree from the national university. But his ambitions did not stop there. He started to study French in order to further his education by studying philosophy and history in France.

As a blind person at that time, Hussein had many obstacles to overcome. But the stubborn young man did not take no for an answer. Finally, he obtained the formal approvals he needed. His parents wanted him to get married before he left for France, but he refused. While in France, he met a young French woman, Suzanne Bresseau, whose studies had been interrupted by the Second World War, so she had taken a job escorting and reading for the blind graduate student, Hussein. She was a great help to him and recognized his talent. The two fell in love, married, and had two children. They had a happy family life in spite of the later difficulties Hussein faced in Egypt. Suzanne's autobiography has been published in Arabic and French.[2]

After five years in France, Hussein obtained a bachelor's degree and a graduate diploma. He passed the highly competitive examination for university teachers and was awarded a doctoral degree from the Sorbonne for his work on the Arab historian Ibn Khaldun (1332–1406), who is regarded as one of the founding fathers of modern sociology and historiography. During his studies, he mastered French and familiarized himself with Greek and Latin.

On returning to Egypt, Hussein became a professor of Arabic history and literature at Cairo University. He was elected dean of the faculty of letters. Due to his uncompromising principles, he was forced to leave his position on three occasions. In 1932, he was fired from the university after he refused to grant an honorary doctoral degree to a politician who had been recommended by the autocratic prime minister, Isma'il Sidqi Basha. This period, which lasted for about three years, was financially difficult for Hussein and his family, but he stood by what he believed to be right. After Sidqi left the administration in 1936, Hussein was reelected dean. In 1942, he became president of the university. While president, he founded Farouk University (now Alexandria University). This was during the Second World War, when the German general Rommel was near Alexandria, threatening the British and Egypt. But this did not deter Hussein, and the work of establishing the new university went on.

Hussein was an educator and prolific writer. He produced forty-two books on history and literature, wrote nineteen novels, and translated eleven books, in addition to writing 1,481 newspaper and magazine articles. Some of his work is available in languages other than Arabic. Subjects he wrote about include early Islamic history, Arabic literature, Greek mythology, politics, democracy, and the constitution. Three of his literary novels were turned into Egyptian movies, and a documentary was made about his life.

Some of Hussein's books and other writings were controversial; his book on pre-Islamic poetry, published in 1926, is an example. In it, he made the claim that "pre-Islamic" poetry really dated from after the time of the Prophet, basing his argument on the analytical principles of Descartes, which did not accept stories as factual without supporting evidence.

In his introduction to that book, Hussein said, "We shouldn't accept, for example, the story of Abraham in the Bible and Qur'an as fact because we have no evidence of it." This naturally was not well received in conservative religious circles. The book was criticized by some Azharite shaykhs and others, who claimed in court that the book was offensive to Muslims. The court did not find evidence that Hussein had intentionally offended Muslims. Nevertheless, pressure from conservative elements forced the coalition government—which had supported academic rights and freedom of expression—to resign. The book was pulled from the shelves, and republished after some minor changes. This book and some of Hussein's other writings reflected the struggle between the old and the new, as well as the social changes he and others wanted to achieve by encouraging independent thinking.

In 1950, Hussein was appointed minister of education in the last Wafd Party administration, even though he was not a member of the Wafd. In this role, he was instrumental in establishing a free educational system—something he felt should be the right of every Egyptian. During his tenure, he founded the University of Ibrahim (now Ain Shams University) in Cairo and proposed another university in Asyut. He was also instrumental in promoting education for women. Despite difficulties, he managed to have women admitted to the university, and to provide scholarships to allow both men and women to study abroad. Some of these young scholars became prominent contributors in their various fields of study.

In 1952, Hussein met the legendary Helen Keller, who was both blind and deaf. Their meeting was widely reported by the news media in Egypt and abroad, inspiring many, particularly those with disabilities. Hussein's remarkable accomplishments have established him not only as one of Egypt's great intellectuals but as a man whose life exemplifies the ability of the human spirit to triumph over adversity.

Salama Musa (1887–1958)

> My worst nightmare is that we succeed in ridding Egypt of colonial power and internal enemies, but are not able to free our own minds from the mentality of the Middle Ages.—Salama Musa, *The Renaissance*, 1934

Salama Musa came from an upper-middle-class Coptic family. His father died when he was about two years old, leaving Musa to be raised by four older sisters and a mother to whom he was extremely close. He received his earliest education in both Coptic and Islamic religious schools, where the emphasis was on memorizing verses of the Bible and the Qur'an, respectively. He finished high school in 1907 at a government school in Cairo, but was behind most of his classmates in his studies. He did not do well in a rigidly structured educational environment.

While Musa was in Cairo, he was exposed to some of the European advances in science, literature, and the social sciences. His early reading included Alexander Dumas's book on the French Revolution, writings by Nietzsche and Tolstoy, and Arabic books, such as Farah Antone's *al-Din wa-l-'ilm wa-l-mal.*

He read many articles and books on science, including Darwin's theory of evolution, and came to believe that the new science was in conflict with traditional religion. Musa's early reading shaped his subsequent intellectual career.[3] At a young age, he became convinced that social change in Egypt was imperative, and that social reform should take precedence over nationalist movements. Musa became a radical critic of his society.[4]

At the age of eighteen, after finishing high school, Musa could have earned a good income working for the government. Instead, he decided to expand his knowledge and to pursue his fascination with Europe. Fortunately, a small inheritance was sufficient to support him in this endeavor. In 1907, he traveled to France for two years. There, he was free to read and learn without enrolling in a formal degree program. While in France, he discovered Egyptology and was embarrassed not to have learned about this subject in his Egyptian education.

In 1909, he went to Britain, where he spent the next four to five years studying a wide variety of topics on his own. He rented a flat near the British Museum so he could visit it frequently and explore the museum's Egyptian collection. At one point, he enrolled to study law, but found it tiresome and quickly dropped his classes.[5] He chose not to seek a degree and preferred to study independently so as to be free to follow his own wide-ranging interests. These included learning about many aspects of modern life in Europe, such as democracy, freedom of the press, scientific developments, socialism, industrialization, literature, anthropology, philosophy, Darwinism, the rights of women, and the origins of religion. In the back of his mind, he was wondering how he could best transmit this knowledge to Egypt. Although Musa was fascinated by European learning, he was not uncritical. He hated the ugly side of European colonialism, and spoke and wrote against it.

While in England, Musa joined the Fabian Society and was influenced greatly by its socialist policy, which laid the foundation for the British Labour Party. At the Fabian Society, Musa met many distinguished British thinkers, such as George Bernard Shaw and H.G. Wells. Another organization that attracted Musa's interest was the Rationalist Press Association (RPA), which debated Darwinism, socialism, and the rights of women. While in Britain, Musa published some articles in Egyptian publications, including one on socialism, and another that reflected his encounter with Darwinism. His focus was on science and social issues, which he felt were important for Egyptians to know about.

Musa returned to Egypt at the end of 1913. In 1914, he started a new magazine, called *al-Mustaqbal (The Future)*. The first issue included articles on Nietzsche and the East; acting and theater; a new society that translated the classics; Tolstoy; Akhenaten; and the need to translate poems by Ahmed Shawki, in order to give him exposure that might recommend him for the Nobel Prize.[6] Egyptians found the publication new and fascinating. Sixteen issues were published before the magazine was discontinued due to British opposition and a rise in the cost of paper during the First World War. In the middle of 1914, Musa accepted the post of editor in chief for the well-known *al-Hilal* magazine, after the sudden death of its owner and editor, Jurji Zaydan.

While Musa opposed unscientific religious dogma and resented the influence of the clergy on people's lives, he did not condemn any one religion. This was demonstrated in 1920, when Musa read an article by Sir Harry Johnson in the well-known British magazine, *New Statesman*. In it, Johnson asked the British authorities to close down al-Azhar's Islamic school of theology because he claimed it contradicted scientific facts and discriminated against Copts. Musa responded to Johnson's article by saying that, as a Copt living among Muslims in Egypt, he did not find that Muslims disliked non-Muslims. Authentic Islam, he said, taught tolerance and brotherhood, just as Christianity did. Islam did not ban freedom of expression, as the British authorities were doing in Egypt; nor did Islam hinder scientific research, as the Catholic Church did. Musa's response was published in *New Statesman* in 1920.[7] Later, in an interview published in *al-Hilal* magazine, Musa spoke with the head of al-Azhar, Shaykh Murtada al-Maraghi, regarding the modernization of that old institution. Musa suggested an appropriate millennial celebration for al-Azhar almost half a century before it was due, pointing out that al-Azhar was older than both Cambridge and Oxford and should be well honored.[8]

Musa was impressed by Mahatma Gandhi, contacted him, and wrote a book about him in 1934. Influenced by Gandhi, Musa suggested using Egyptian products whenever possible, in order to support Egyptian industries. A prominent businessman, Talaat Harb (see the next section), adopted the idea and started several branches of a department store called Sharikat Bay‘ al-Masnu‘at, which sold domestic products. The stores met with great success and are still found in Egypt today.

In 1929, Musa founded two magazines, one a weekly and the other a monthly called *al-Majalla al-jadida* (The New Magazine). Both published articles by well-known writers. Taha Hussein was a regular contributor. But the magazines also published work by young, unknown writers. Musa had a talent for discovering and fostering promising writers.[10] Naguib Mahfouz was one of them. Mahfouz's first novel, *'Abath al-aqdar* (Mockery of the Fates) was published in Musa's magazine. The novel is set in ancient Egypt and deals with free will and predestination. It was later made into an Egyptian TV soap opera *(al-Aqdar)*. In his well-known Cairo Trilogy, Mahfouz refers to Musa's magazine under the pseudonym *al-Insan al-jadid* (The New Person). In an interview, Mahfouz cited Musa as his greatest teacher.

After 1936, Musa began to slow down. By then, he owned a publishing house and was writing for two magazines and one newspaper; he had spread himself too thin. When the government cut its financial support for his magazines, sales declined and he began to lose money. Many of Musa's ideas were ahead of their time. Prior to 1943, Musa had written about such topics as industrialization of the countryside, growing vegetables and fruits for consumption and export, a system of mandatory and free primary education, limited working hours, and pensions for farmers at the age of sixty-five. To fight communism, Musa urged the government to adopt socialist policies. He thought taxes should be increased to correspond with incomes. In 1930, he asked the government to educate Egyptians about birth control. At that time the population of Egypt was only 14 million; it is now (2016) almost 90 million. He thought the popular Wafd Party should include candidates who were workers or farmers. He wrote about the bleak future of the Palestinians in light of increasing Jewish immigration. Some of his ideas, especially about socialism, were adopted by the revolution of 1952.

In 1937, the problem of religious education in government schools was being debated. The Copts wanted an education equal to that of Muslims. Musa was critical of offering any religious education in state schools and urged the complete secularization of education.[11] He never defended the

Copts out of blind loyalty; he defended them as he would have defended any minority. He preferred to advocate on behalf of societal changes that would benefit both Copts and Muslims. But from the mid-1930s to 1952, the Wafd Party weakened and political Islam increased in strength. This trend was accompanied by growing discrimination against Copts, such as restricted employment opportunities and incidents of church burning, described in the Coptic press.[12] During this period, Musa started to write articles critical of political Islam—including the Muslim Brotherhood and Shabab Muhammed (Muhammed's youth)—which were published in Coptic newspapers, such as *Misr* and *al-Manara al-misriya*. The Coptic patriarch asked these newspapers to stop criticizing the Brotherhood, otherwise they would lose church support. So the campaign stopped.[13] Musa asked readers of the Coptic press to organize societies to help Copts find employment and to start Coptic banks that would provide services similar to what the Brotherhood offered to Muslims.[14]

By the late 1940s and early 1950s, the social and political climate had started to change. After 1952, Musa's writing was limited by censorship. He was unable to write about topics such as the separation of religion and state, nationalization of the Suez Canal, and peace with Israel. After 1951, Musa believed it would be better to have peace with Israel; he thought leaving the problem unresolved would only benefit some politicians and was not in the best interests of either the Palestinians or the Arabs.[15] Events proved him right.

Though not a political activist himself, Musa contributed to the political discussion. In 1913, he had written a small book on socialism, which was translated into English in 1969.[16] This book influenced many thinkers in the Arab world. The last Arabic edition was published in 1962, when Egypt and many Arab countries attempted to adopt a socialist economic system. Musa believed socialism, democracy, and education went hand in hand. In 1921, he and others started a socialist political party. However, Egypt was not ready for it, and the government dismantled the party in 1924.[17]

Musa was arrested and jailed twice because of his writing, even though he was not involved in any acts of violence. During the political instability of 1946, while the constitution was abandoned under the rule of Isma'il Sidqi, Musa was jailed along with two hundred other intellectuals. He was accused of conspiring with others to overthrow the government, but there was no foundation for the allegation. During this period, there was sectarian violence against the Copts, and Musa carried out a campaign critical of the government for not protecting minorities. It is possible this was the real reason for his arrest.[18]

In addition to Musa's many articles in various newspapers and magazines, he published some forty-five books. Compared to Taha Hussein—who influenced large numbers of people through his writings and the establishment of two modern universities—Salama Musa had a more restricted audience. His writing was read primarily by members of the intellectual class. Nevertheless, he had an enormous influence, opening Egypt and the Arab world to ideas from the West.

Muhammad Talaat Harb (1867–1941)

Talaat Harb was born in the old Islamic quarter of Cairo as the son of a railroad employee. Like Taha Hussein, he memorized the Qur'an at a young age. Harb went through the formal educational system to earn a high school diploma, followed by a law degree in 1889. Early in his career, he worked as a wealthy man's business manager; then as manager of a land reform company in the south near Aswan; and, in 1905, as manager of a real estate company.

In 1911, Talaat Harb wrote a book in which he suggested a solution to problems in the Egyptian economy. He proposed the establishment of an Egyptian bank to support Egyptian industrial, social, and cultural projects, with an emphasis on industry. Harb challenged the British colonial view that Egypt could never be anything other than an agricultural society. Although he was sympathetic with the 1919 revolt against the British and knew its leaders well, his vision had a different emphasis. He thought economic independence was the way to bring about political independence. His idea for an Egyptian bank was accepted and supported by a number of wealthy and middle-class Egyptians. While the British disliked the concept of an Egyptian bank, they did not prevent it.

In 1920, Harb achieved his dream. He founded Banque Misr (Egypt Bank) with capital of 200,000 Egyptian pounds, and invited a German banker to help establish its administrative organization. He sent young employees to study banking in various European countries. They then returned to become executives in the bank. Before long, there were thirty-seven branches of the bank all over Egypt, each easily recognizable by the same standardized building façade. Harb was the general manager, but chose not to be the CEO.

Between 1920 and 1940, the bank supported companies representing twenty-seven industries.[19] These included publishing, cotton processing, pharmaceuticals, petroleum products, tobacco, shipping, paper, mining, tourism, film, airlines, and, most important, the textile industry. The degree of success these companies achieved varied depending on the industry and the world market.[20]

Banque Misr became the first multinational corporation in the Middle East. It opened branches in Syria and Lebanon, and established some joint ventures with foreign companies.[21] In its first ten years, the bank's capital increased from 201,000 pounds in 1920 to 7.25 million in 1929.[22] The bank's growth during the early years was aided by a series of protective tariffs enacted by the Egyptian government. Although the prime minister at the time, Isma'il Sidqi, was a political reactionary, he followed an economically progressive policy. He initiated broad changes in economic policy and at the same time confronted any unfavorable reactions by Britain or other foreign powers.[23]

The most successful Banque Misr group was the one related to the cotton textile industry. In 1925, Britain controlled 72 percent of the cotton piece-goods market in Egypt. This dropped to 42 percent in 1933, and to 27 percent in 1936. This trend was due mainly to the growth of Egypt's own textile industry; however, there was also competition from Japan, Germany, and Italy prior to the Second World War.[24] The British were not pleased with the activities of the Banque Misr group because they challenged British economic interests in Egypt. The British foreign office, along with the British textile industry, objected to Egypt's protective tariffs policy. But rather than attempting to coerce Banque Misr into adopting policies approved by Britain, they preferred to co-opt the Banque Misr group by encouraging British companies to produce their piece goods in Egypt.[25]

After its initial success, Banque Misr showed signs of weakening in the late 1930s. It lost its fluidity, and signs of poor management began to appear. As Harb's health deteriorated during this period, political considerations affected many of his decisions.[26] The Bank, in an attempt to save itself, terminated some employees and reduced the salaries of many. But this did not help much. The outbreak of the Second World War had a negative effect on the world market.[27]

What happened during the bank's difficult years is debated. The bank faced opposition and competition from some prominent Egyptians, including the previous prime ministers Isma'il Sidqi Basha and Serri Basha, as well as the Egyptian economic tycoon Ahmad 'Abbud Basha. To defend his empire, Harb exerted political power in Parliament by giving prominent elected officials easy loans; in reality, these loans were political bribes.[28] Al'Afifi Basha was well connected with the British until he was put under house arrest a few days after the revolt of 1952.

The political and economic pressure started to increase on Banque Misr, funds in the Bank declined. Stockholders had to be placated to maintain confidence in the bank. To be able to continue paying dividends, the Bank was forced to dip into its capital funds. The situation was further aggravated when the bank found itself obliged to support the national defense fund for expanding the army during the Wafd Party's rule, after the 1936 treaty with Britain. In 1938, Banque Misr reached a critical point. It sought to obtain a three-million-pound loan from the National Bank of Egypt (NBE). The director of the NBE, Sir Edward Cook, was reluctant to agree to the loan because Banque Misr had used its money to obtain a government tariff that favored its own operations at the expense of the NBE. But under pressure from the finance minister, Ahmed Maher, Cook finally agreed to the loan.

While the bank continued to have difficulties, Harb's health further deteriorated. He and the bank became the targets of a number of conspiracies. Many envied Harb's position as managing director of the bank. One of these was Hafiz 'Afifi Basha, a pediatrician who had no training in financial matters but was well connected with the British. In Egypt, he was considered to be "more British than the British themselves." In 1934, Harb appointed 'Afifi manager of Misr Insurance Company and made him a member of the boards of four other companies in order to offset British fears of a pro-Axis or anti-British bias on the part of the Bank Misr group.[29]

The bank's financial situation continued to deteriorate. In 1939, some investors withdrew their savings. These included the Post Office Savings Bank and other small depositors, which together accounted for 75 percent of all deposits in the bank. The liquidity of the bank dropped to only 108,000 pounds. Cook refused to extend the bank any additional credit. The Egyptian government under Hussein Sirri Basha pressured Cook to grant Banque Misr an additional two million pounds credit on the condition that Harb resign his post.[30] Sirri Basha was closely associated with Ahmad 'Abbud Basha and Isma'il Sidqi Basha. Hafiz 'Afifi Basha took over as bank president, and the Egyptian government gained the right to veto appointments to the bank. Under 'Afifi's tenure, unsuccessful companies were dismantled. Bank Misr was saved at this juncture because many influential politicians held large portfolios that included its shares. The new leadership of the bank removed all the directors who had served with Harb, did nothing to expand the Banque Misr group, and concentrated solely on extracting as much profit as possible. Rather than lessening corruption, the new management caused it to become even more pervasive as competition for directorships increased.[30] Despite all the difficulties, many of the industries supported by Banque Misr have managed to survive until today. Banque Misr currently supports about two hundred projects in various fields that are aimed at serving the national economy.

In addition to his financial and industrial activities, Harb authored a number of books on topics as varied as the Suez Canal, the history of the Arabs and Islam, and the education of women. He thought improvement in the situation of women would not be accomplished by removing headscarves or by dressing in Western fashions, but rather through good education.

Harb retired from public life and spent his remaining years in a small village. He died in 1941 at the age of seventy-four. Today he is considered one of the great figures of modern Egyptian history, ranking with Muhammad 'Ali, Sa'd Zaghlul, and Gamal Abd al-Nasser as one whose legacy has shaped the Egypt we see today. He is commemorated by a statue in the center of a major square in Cairo which bears his name.

Rose al-Yusuf (1888–1958)

Rose al-Yusuf was born in Tripoli, Lebanon. She came to Egypt in her early teens, and began a career in acting in 1910. Initially, she worked for pennies (50 piasters) a day, but she quickly rose to become a popular leading actress who performed in well-known plays of the time, such as *La Dame aux Camélias*. After a dispute, in 1925, with director and leading actor Yusuf Wahbi, she resigned and left the theater to start a career in journalism. She said she thought it was better to leave the theater before the theater left her. She returned to the theater only once; for two days in 1934, she performed in a benefit show to raise money for the small village of Mahallat Ziyad, which had burned down.

Al-Yusuf's early life was difficult. She learned how to read and write early during her career as an actress. As a teen, she gained considerable strength and independence. In 1925, she started a magazine that carried her name. Just as she had excelled as an actress, she also excelled as a journalist, writer, and political activist. Her magazine attracted some of the best writers of the time. It also became a school for young writers, and many who started at the magazine became prominent writers and editors in chief at other journals and newspapers. The magazine introduced the cartoon character of al-Masri Effendi, who reflected the life and difficulties of ordinary Egyptians.

Although al-Yusuf's magazine—and later her newspaper—became popular, her career in journalism was quite rocky because of her independent views. When she criticized the government, the magazine was harassed and banned. She was sentenced to jail on one occasion, but she was persistent. Whenever one of her magazines or newspapers was shut down, she immediately started another with a different name. This was repeated many times.

Al-Yusuf was politically active and used her publications to further the causes she believed in. For example, she supported the 1919 revolution and was one of the young women who demonstrated against British colonial power in Egypt. The writers and editors of her publications supported the growing nationalist movement. She was also supportive of the Wafd Party, but when she harshly objected to some of its policies regarding the need to return to the constitution of 1923, the party stopped supporting her magazine. At a large demonstration against the magazine, Wafd Party supporters began throwing stones at the building. Against the advice of her staff, al-Yusuf went outside to debate with the demonstrators and managed to disperse them peacefully. Later, when the Wafd Party canceled the 1936 treaty with the British, she defended the party. Her magazine predicted the 1952 revolution.

She and the editors and writers of *Rose al-Yusuf* said that most of the difficulties she faced in journalism were not caused by work difficulties or financial hardship, but by the fact that she was a woman. She not only published magazines and newspapers, but also had her own book publishing house with a modern printing press. Al-Yusuf represented a new breed of modern women. A documentary about her was aired on television, and a soap opera was made about her life.

Makram Ebeid (1889–1961)

Makram Ebeid came from an upper-middle-class Coptic family. He attended primary school in Qena, a government school in Cairo, and then the American School in Asyut. In 1905, after he had finished the equivalent of high school at the age of sixteen, his family sent him to Britain to further his education. In 1908, Ebeid obtained a law degree from Oxford and then went to France for two years of further law studies at Lyon University. In France, he was exposed to liberal arts and social studies, which clearly influenced his thinking.

After returning to Egypt, Ebeid joined the Justice Department in 1913 as an advisor and secretary to British officials in the Egyptian government. He resigned this post in 1918 because he disagreed with the government's policies. Ebeid became increasingly involved in the nationalist movement, which sought independence from British control. In a symbolic gesture, Ebeid renounced the English first name he had been given at birth—William—and took the name Makram. His writings—including his open letter of resignation to the Justice Department—attracted the attention of Sa'd Zaghlul, the man who was to become the leader of the 1919 revolt against the British.[31]

Ebeid started teaching law at the Royal Law School in Cairo, but was dismissed in 1921 after he participated in a banquet honoring Zaghlul. Later that year, Ebeid was exiled, along with Zaghlul and other leaders of the national resistance movement. During their time in exile, he became very close to both Zaghlul and Mustafa al-Nahhas, who later succeeded Zaghlul as president of the Wafd Party. Ebeid became known as a faithful and staunch supporter of Zaghlul and his political ideology. Zaghlul did not have any children, and considered Ebeid as his adopted son in spite of their different religions.

Ebeid represented the Wafd Party in Britain on at least three occasions. When involved in negotiations with the British, he proved to be a very tough negotiator. Thanks to his Oxford education, not only had he mastered the English language, but he also had acquired friends and sympathizers in the media as well as in the British Labour Party.

In 1931, Ebeid visited Syria, Lebanon, and Palestine and delivered many speeches on the significance of Arab unity with Egypt at its center. He called for the establishment of a league of Arab nations. In that regard, he was ahead of his time. It was more than a decade later that the Arab League was founded in Cairo in 1945.[32]

Freedom, justice, and equality were important themes throughout Ebeid's life. As a minister of finance and supply in 1936 and 1942, he emphasized the need for a more equitable distribution of wealth. He stated that one percent of Egyptians owned nearly 46 percent of the country's assets, while 90 percent of Egyptian farmers were employed at very low wages, under close-to-slavery conditions, in the service of the wealthy.[33] Ahmad Baha' al-Din, editor-in-chief of several magazines and newspapers, quoted Ebeid as asking the Egyptian Parliament, "What is the good of liberating poor Egyptians from colonial domination if they are not also freed from domestic exploitation?" Ebeid asked for an increase in the minimum wage and removal of taxes on poor farmers.[34]

As a lawyer, Ebeid was well recognized. He defended high-profile political and civilian cases that attracted attention. On several occasions he served as the head of the powerful lawyers' syndicate. One of Ebeid's assets as a politician was his charismatic and dynamic personality. He was proficient in three languages, as well as in the art of public speaking, which distinguished him from other political speakers of the time. His public speeches and writings in Arabic are considered literary works of art. Some nationalist students memorized his words, which were often quoted. He was able to influence the masses through his use of language, choosing words and using a rhythmic cadence to reach the hearts of his listeners.

Although a Copt, Ebeid was never accused of acting unfairly in the interests of the Coptic minority, even when the Copts were experiencing difficult times. Personally, he was not particularly involved with religion. He often quoted the Qur'an in his speeches as a gesture of unity.

Ebeid was highly energetic, intelligent, and ambitious. As secretary of the Wafd Party, he greatly influenced Nahhas Basha, the head of the party. Some felt he dominated Nahhas, especially in terms of taking an extreme position against the British and insisting on achieving the Wafd Party's most ambitious goals.[35] His presence in the cabinet and his influence over Nahhas contributed to a growing resentment. As a result, some prominent members of the Wafd Party split off to form their own party. In 1937, al-Nuqrashi and Ahmed Maher formed the Sa'dist Party, and later both became prime ministers. However, their party was always a minor one that never gained much popularity among the people.[36]

In the early 1940s, the relationship between Nahhas and Ebeid became strained for a number of reasons, leading eventually to the expulsion of Ebeid from the Wafd Party as well as from Parliament. The details of this split have been debated by many.[37] A number of factors—both personal and international—were significant. The trouble may have begun in 1934 when, at the age of fifty-five, Nahhas Basha married a beautiful, young, and ambitious woman who was roughly half his age. Her name was Zaynab al-Wakil.[38] Ebeid was the matchmaker for this marriage. Al-Wakil quickly began to resent Ebeid's influence over Nahhas, and over time she started to influence Nahhas's policies.

Meanwhile, the Second World War brought increased political instability to Egypt. With the German army on Egypt's northwestern border, the British wanted a strong and popular government to rule Egypt at this critical point. Despite its disagreements with the Wafd Party, Britain felt the Wafd was in the best position to fulfill this role. The king hoped for a coalition government headed by the Wafd. But the Wafd Party declined to join because of its bad experience with coalition governments in the past. On February 4, 1942, the British intervened; their forces surrounded the palace and presented an ultimatum to the king: if Nahhas did not form a new Wafd government, the king would be forced to abdicate. The king reluctantly surrendered and appointed Nahhas Basha as prime minister. This incident eroded some of the Wafd Party's credibility because they came to power under the influence of the British.

The Wafd Party was still popular among the people, but it had been out of power for a number of years. When the Wafd finally came to power, a number of its followers, including Nahhas' wife and some of her wealthy relatives, started to ask for favors. Ebeid, the minister of supply and finance, resisted or rejected these requests. As the relationship between Nahhas and Ebeid became strained, some of this information leaked to the public.

The palace—and particularly the chamberlain, Ahmed Hassanein Basha—hated the Wafd Party's policies and resented that the Wafd had agreed to head the government after Britain's ultimatum to the king. Hassanein Basha's long-term plan was to drive a wedge between Nahhas and Ebeid, hoping to weaken the Wafd Party and to undermine the Copts' support for the Wafd. To that end, the king and Hassanein Basha met with Ebeid privately, and encouraged him to expose the corruption in his own administration. Ebeid spoke out strongly and publicly against his own government, headed by Nahhas. The rift between Nahhas and Ebeid, which had been unthinkable a few years before, became a drama unfolding in the public eye. The relationship between these old friends had reached a point of no return. Ebeid claimed he had offered his resignation three times but each time it had been rejected by Nahhas.[39] Finally, Ebeid was dismissed from the government, from his post as secretary of the Wafd Party, and from Parliament.

When Ebeid was fired from the Wafd government, eighteen members of Parliament also left—ten Copts and eight Muslims. The Copts who left were relatives or close friends of Ebeid. But the majority of Copts continued to support the Wafd. When Ebeid ran for the next Parliament and the lawyers' syndicate, he lost both elections by very small margins.

After Ebeid was fired from the government, he exposed the leadership of the Wafd Party. Religion played a very minor role in splitting Ebeid from the Wafd Party.[40] During the Second World War, all publication was under censorship, but Ebeid was able to secretly publish what came to be known as the Black Book on March 29, 1943. Copies of this book, documenting the corruption of the government and attacking Nahhas and his wife, were distributed to all politicians and to the king. The king demanded an explanation from Nahhas and it became a public scandal. Ebeid formed a new political party called al-Kutla al-wafdiya that same year. Even though Ebeid became minister of finance in the next non-Wafd government, his party, al-Kutla al-wafdiya, remained small and insignificant compared with the Wafd.

Ebeid thought he was better qualified to be prime minister than were other political leaders.[41] But the window of opportunity for Copts to aspire to such high office was already closing; political Islam was gaining influence. Both the Wafd Party and Ebeid were stifled in this political climate. When Ebeid died in 1961, his funeral was attended by a large number of people, including President Nasser's representative, Anwar Sadat.

Jurji Zaydan (1861–1914)

Jurji Zaydan, like Salama Musa, was an autodidact; both men became prolific writers who aimed to inform and educate their readers about the modern world, especially with respect to scientific and social developments. But there were differences between the two. While Musa depended on his family's wealth to promote his ideas, Zaydan was a self-made businessman. Zaydan was considered a promoter of Arab nationalism almost half a century before it became an official policy in some countries, including Egypt, Syria, and Iraq.

Zaydan was born an Orthodox Christian in Beirut, Lebanon, where his father owned a modest restaurant. At the age of twelve, Zaydan helped his father in the restaurant. His father believed that any education beyond reading, writing, and basic arithmetic was a waste of time. But his mother wanted her son to have a better career, so she encouraged him to become a salesperson in a textile shop and to take lessons in English from a private teacher, whose fee was a meal in the father's restaurant.

Zaydan was accepted as a student of medicine at the Syrian Protestant College. There he hoped to improve his economic and social status, but fate took him on a different course. At the school, he was exposed to Darwin's theory of evolution, which fascinated him. But the teaching of Darwin at that time was a source of contention between the liberal and conservative teachers. At a young age, Zaydan noticed that the clergy and elites exploited religious beliefs for their own purposes. Cornelius van Dyck, who taught Darwin's theory, was fired from the Syrian Protestant College, along with other liberal teachers. When students demonstrated in support of the liberal teachers, Zaydan and some other students were expelled for involving themselves in college politics. At this stage in his life, Zaydan started to write articles aimed at increasing readers' awareness of Western ideas during this time of Egyptian enlightenment.

In 1883, Zaydan borrowed six pounds to travel to Egypt, where he was welcomed, along with many Syrians, Palestinians, Lebanese, and Armenians who were escaping the Turks' harsh rule and discriminatory policies. Many of these immigrants were Christians, but some were Muslims. Among them was the reformist Muslim scholar Shaykh 'Abd al-Rahman al-Kawakibi (1855–1902), who was assassinated by Turks in Egypt.[42] Some of these immigrants developed interests in business, theater, literature, and newspapers. Many became prominent in their respective fields. They considered Egypt a second home and contributed to the period of *al-nahda*.

Zaydan became a translator for the British campaign to put down the Mahdi's revolt in Sudan. After that, he traveled to London, where he was exposed to the rich cultural life and visited many libraries and museums. Back in Egypt, he undertook a long and very fruitful career in writing and publishing. At that time in Egypt, attempts were being made to modernize Islamic thought, an effort led by the reformer Muhammad 'Abduh (1849–1905), an enlightened Azharite shaykh. 'Abduh argued that religion could be exploited for political gain because the masses were ignorant about their true religion. He wrote extensively on the subject. Zaydan, as a Christian, did not shy away from writing about the sensitive subject of religion, including Islamic thought.[43] He addressed the issue of religion and science in many articles, and argued that true science did not contradict true religion. He thought religion had to adjust to accommodate modern science in areas where science provided proof.[44] Zaydan made the observation that while Europeans rejected religious fanaticism, they indulged in nationalistic fanaticism.

In his writings, Zaydan reflected on society and on laws that might determine its structure, consistency, and patterns of change. He applied some of the principles of Darwin's theory of evolution to the evolution of society and language in his book *The Arabic Language as a Living Being*. Contrary to the prevailing attitudes of the time, he did not consider the Arabic language of the Qur'an to be sacred, and did not think it should be preserved in a form unchanged from the time of the Prophet. Zaydan thought evolutionary change is what keeps language alive and relevant. In any case, observation reveals that spoken language is always evolving, which is why spoken Arabic is different from written Arabic.[45] Zaydan also thought that the written Arabic language should be simplified and should avoid a meaningless, flowery style. Many of Zaydan's intellectual contemporaries shared his views.

Zaydan, together with another Lebanese Christian, Najib Mitri, obtained a printing press and started a small publishing house. After a year, Zaydan became the sole owner. He used the press to produce the first issues of *al-Hilal* (The Crescent) magazine in 1892. Najib Mitri founded another publishing house, called Dar al-Ma'arif (The House of Knowledge), which became a very important press. *Al-Hilal* quickly became a well-read magazine, not only in Egypt but also in other Arab countries. It continues to be a popular cultural magazine today.

In 1910, as a result of his extensive writings on Islam and Arabism—especially his five volumes on the history of Islamic civilization (*Tarikh al-tamaddun al-islami*, 1902–1906). Zaydan was invited to teach Islamic history at the newly founded Egyptian University. However, before he started teaching, the appointment was canceled by the university under pressure from the Islamists, who object to Zaydan because he was a Christian. This was a humiliating episode for Zaydan, and left a stain of bitterness in his heart.[46]

Zaydan is best remembered as one of the pioneer writers of historical novels. He wrote twenty-one historical novels that are still popular today. These novels cover an extensive period of Arab history, including the rise of Islam and the Ottoman Empire. Many of his novels were translated into a dozen languages.[47]

By the end of the nineteenth and the beginning of the twentieth century, Arab nationalism was on the rise in Egypt, Syria, and Iraq. Zaydan and others started to promote Arab nationalist ideas, which are reflected in many of his writings. To Zaydan, Arabic language, history, and religion were the foundation of Arab nationalism, and he wrote extensively on each topic. He saw the establishment of an Arab national identity as his personal mission. His preoccupation with Arabic language and literature was an attempt to make Arab society aware of its cultural heritage and to make that heritage fit the modern world.[48]

Zaydan married and settled in Egypt, where he lived until his sudden death in 1914, at the age of fifty-two.

APPENDIX 2

Summary of Parliamentary Elections

Table 1. Parliamentary Election Results, 1923–50

Year	% of seats held by the Wafd Party	Number of Copts elected	Total number of seats	% of seats won by Copts
1924	90	16	214	7.5
1925	58	13	214	6.1
1926	75	16	214	7.5
1929	90	20	235	8.5
1931	boycotted by the Wafd	4	150	2.6
1936	boycotted by the Wafd	20	232	2.3
1942	boycotted by other parties	23	264	8.8
1945	boycotted by the Wafd	12	264	4.5
1950	71	8	320	2.5

Sources: Carter, *The Copts in Egyptian Politics, 1918–1952*, 143; al-Bishri, *al-Muslimun wa-l-Aqbat fi itar al-jam'a al-wataniya*, 252.

Table 2. Copts Elected during Nasser's Era

Year	Number of parliament seats	Number of Copts elected	Number of Copts appointed	Total % seats held by Copts (elected + appointed)
1957	350	0	0	0
1964	360	1	8	2.5
1969	348	2	7	2.6

Table 3. Copts Elected during Sadat's Era

Year	Number of parliament seats	Number of Copts elected	Number of Copts appointed	% total Copts
1971	360	3	9	3.3
1976	370	0	8	2.2
1969	360	4	10	3.9

Table 4. Copts Elected during Mubarak's Era

Year	Number of parliament seats	Number of Copts elected	Number of Copts appointed	% total Copts
1984	468	4	5	1.9
1987	458	6	4	2.2
1990	454	1	6	1.5
1995	454	0	6	1.3
2000	454	3	3	1.3
2005	454	1	5	1.3
2010	518	3	7	1.9

NOTES

Introduction

1. Hassan, S.S. *Christians versus Muslims in Modern Egypt: The Century-Long Struggle for Coptic Equality* (Cambridge, MA: Harvard University Press, 2003).
2. Vivian Ibrahim, *The Copts of Egypt: The Challenges of Modernization and Identity* (New York: Tauris Academic Studies, 2011).
3. Sebastian Elsässer, *The Coptic Question in the Mubarak Era* (New York: Oxford University Press, 2014).
4. Jacques Tagher, *Christians in Muslim Egypt: A Historical Study of the Relation Between Copts and Muslims from 640 to 1922*, trans. Ragia N. Makar (Altenberge: Oros Verlag, 1998).
5. Al-Ghazali's book, *al-Ta'assub wa-l-tasamuh bayn al-masihiya wa-l-Islam*, is about tolerance and intolerance between Christianity and Islam. It is no longer in print, but it can be downloaded from the Internet, https://www.alarabimag.com/books/14132-%D8%A7%D9%84%D8%AA%D8%B9%D8%B5%D8%A8-%D9%88%D8%A7%D9%84%D8%AA%D8%B3%D8%A7%D9%85%D8%AD-%D8%A8%D9%8A%D9%86-%D8%A7%D9%84%D9%85%D8%B3%D9%8A%D8%AD%D9%8A%D8%A9.html.
6. See Muhammad 'Afifi's introduction to the Arabic version of Tagher's second edition of *Aqbat wa-'il Muslimun* (Cairo: General Egyptian Book Organization, 2010), 27.

   7. Fikry Andrawes, *al-Muslimun wa-l-aqbat fi-l-tarikh* (Cairo: Dar al-Thaqafa al-Jadida, 2017).

Chapter 1

1. Sawiras ibn al-Muqaffa', *Tarikh al-batarika*, ed. Samuel al-Suriany (Cairo: Ma'had al-Dirasat al-Qibtiya, 1984), 25. See also 'Abd al-'Aziz Jamal al-Din, *Tarikh Misr min bidayat al-qarn al-awwal hatta nihayat al-qarn al-'ishrin min khilal Tarikh al-batarika li-Sawiras Ibn al-Muqaffa'* (Cairo: Maktabat Madbuli, 2006), 1:166. This book includes the tenth-century writings of Severus ibn al-Muqaffa' (also called Severus of Ashmunayn),

who compiled accounts from earlier writers. For more information about Ibn al-Muquaffa‘, see Aziz S. Atiya, “Sawiras ibn al-Muqaffa‘,” in *The Coptic Encyclopedia*, 7:2100.

2. ‘Abd al-‘Aziz Jamal al-Din, *Tarikh Misr min makhtotet tarikh al-Batarka li-Sawiras ibn al-Muqaffa‘*)Cairo: Maktabet Madbouli, 2006(, 1:179.
3. ‘Abd al-‘Aziz Jamal al-Din, *Tarikh Misr min makhtotet tarikh al-Batarka li-Sawiras ibn al-Muqaffa‘*, 180.
4. Ra’fat ‘Abd al-Hamid, *al-Dawla wa-l-kanisa*, 2nd ed. (Cairo: Dar al-Ma‘arif, 1983), 3:25. See also Roger S. Bagnall, *Early Christian Books in Egypt* (Princeton, NJ: Princeton University Press, 2009).
5. *Madrasat al-Iskandariya ma‘ sirat wa kitabat Athenagoras wa Pantaenus* (Cairo: Filbatrun li-l-Tarjama wa-l-Nashr, 1996), 51.
6. R.B. Tollinton, *Clement of Alexandria: A Study in Christian Liberalism* (London: Williams and Norgate, 1914), 1:178–239.
7. Samir S.J. Khalil, “Origen in the Copto-Arabic Tradition,” in *The Coptic Encyclopedia*, Atiya, ed., 6:1851–2. See also Aziz S. Atiya, “Origen’s Writings,” in *The Coptic Encyclopedia*, 6:1952–5; and Tollinton, *Clement of Alexandria*, 1:178–239, cited in note 6 above.
8. Atiya, “Origen’s Writings,” 6:1852–55. See also R.B.C. Hanson, “Origen,” in Atiya, *The Coptic Encyclopedia*, 6:1846.
9. Yusabbius al-Qaysari, *Tarikh al-kanisa min al-Masih hatta Qustantin*, trans. Archpriest Murqus Dawud, 2nd ed. (Cairo: Maktabat al-Mahabba, 1979), 294. See also al-Abb Matta al-Miskin, *al-Rahbana al-qibtiya fi ‘asr al-qiddis Anba Maqar* (Cairo: al-Shirka al-Misriya li-l-Tiba‘a wa-l-Nashr, 1972), 240; Tadrus Ya‘qub Malti, *Aba’ madrasat al-Iskandariya al-awa’il* (Alexandria: St. George Sporting Church, 1980), 293.
10. Donald B. Spanel, “Theophilus,” in Atiya, *The Coptic Encyclopedia*, 7:2249.
11. Iris Habib al-Masri, *The Story of the Copts* (The Middle East Council of Churches, Cairo, 1978).
12. Tadros Y. Malaty, *Aba’ madrasat al-Iskandariya al-awa’il* (Alexandria: published by the Coptic Church, 1980), 271. Also see Ra’fat ‘Abd al-Hamid, *al-Dawla wa-l-kanisa* (Dar al-Ma‘arif, 1983), vol. 3, 25.
13. Malaty, *Aba’ madrasat al-Iskandariya al-awa’il*, 293.
14. Layton, *Richard A. Didymus the Blind and His Circle in Late-Antique Alexandria* (Champaign: University of Illinois Press, 2004), 135–38.
15. Layton, *Didymus the Blind*, 159–61. See also M.P. Poncaglia, “Didymus the Blind,” in *The Coptic Encyclopedia*, 3:900.
16. Aziz S. Atiya, “Patriarchs, Dates and Succession of,” in *The Coptic Encyclopedia*, 6:1913.
17. Naphtali Lewis, *Life of Egypt under Roman Rule* (Oxford, UK: Clarendon Press, 1983), 29.
18. Otto F.A. Meinardus, *Monks and Monasteries of the Egyptian Deserts* (Cairo: AUC Press, 1992).

19. For more information about St. Antony's Monastery, see *Monastic Visions*, edited by Elizabeth S. Bolman (New Haven, CT: Yale University Press, 2002).
20. Samuel Rubenson, *Letters of St. Antony* (Minneapolis: Fortress Press, 1995), 60.
21. Athanasius, *Life of Saint Antony* (Red Sea, Egypt: St. Antony Monastery, 1992).
22. Philip Rousseau, *Pachomius: The Making of Community in Fourth-Century Egypt* (Berkeley: University of California Press, 1999).
23. Personal interview with the late Father Matthew the Poor, head of St. Macarius Monastery. He elaborated by saying that the Pachomian system was based on rules rather than spirituality, and required leaders of high caliber, such as Pachomius, who are rare to find. However, some aspects of the Pachomian tradition still survive in Egypt.
24. Rousseau, *Pachomius*.
25. Jean Doresse, *The Secret Books of the Egyptian Gnostics* (New York: MJF Books, 1986). See also Giovanni Filoramo, *A History of Gnosticism* (Oxford and Cambridge, MA: Blackwell, 1992), 170, 183; Rodolphe Kasser, Marvin Meyer, and Gregor Wurst, eds., *The Gospel of Judas: From Codex Tchacos* (Washington, DC: National Geographic Society, 2006).
26. Fikry Andrawes, "Masihiyyat Misr fi quruniha al-ula," *Wijhat Nazar* (Cairo: al-Sharika al-Misriya li-l-Tiba'a wa-l-Nashr, 2005), 37.
27. Gawdat Gabra and Hany N. Takla, eds., *Christianity and Monasticism in Upper Egypt*, vol. 1, *Akhmim and Sohag* (Cairo: American University in Cairo Press, 2008). This 350-page volume is dedicated mostly to St. Shenoute and his monasteries. See also Banub Habashi, *Safha min tarikh al-Qibt* (Cairo: Matbu'at Marimina al-'Ajayibi, 1950), 111–67.
28. J.F. Kelley, "British Isles, Coptic Influences," in Atiya, *The Coptic Encyclopedia*, 2:416.
29. *Matta al-Miskin* (Matthew the Poor), *Monastic Life in the Time of St. Macarius* (Cairo: al-Sharika al-Misriya li-l-Tiba'a wa-l-Nashr, 1972), 542.
30. Watterson, Barbara, *Coptic Egypt* (Edinburgh: Scottish Academic Press, 1988).
31. 'Umar Sabir 'Abd al-Jalil, *Tarikh Misr li-Hanna al-Niqyusi: ru'ya qibtiya li-l-fath al-islami* (Cairo: 'Ayn li-l-Dirasat wa-l-Buhuth al-Insaniya wa-l-Ijtima'iya, 2003), 5.
32. Samuel al-Suriany, *Patriarchs*, 55.
33. Eusebius, *The History of the Church from Christ to Constantine*, vol. 1. Translated by G.A. Williamson (London: Penguin Books, 1965), 330.
34. W.H.C. Frend, "Diocletian," in Atiya, *The Coptic Encyclopedia*, 3:904. See also al-Masri, *The Story of the Copts*, 71.
35. 'Abd al-Jalil, *Tarikh Misr li-Hanna al-Niqyusi*, 91.
36. Aelred Cody, "Coptic Calendar," in Atiya, *The Coptic Encyclopedia*, 2:433.
37. Jill Kamil, *Christianity in the Land of the Pharaohs* (New York: Routledge, 2002), 10.
38. René-Georges Coquin and Maurice Martin, "Diocletian," in Atiya, *The Coptic Encyclopedia*, 3:907.

39. Frend, "Diocletian," 3:906.
40. Frend, "Diocletian," 3:906.
41. David L. Dungan, *Constantine's Bible* (Minneapolis: Fortress Press, 2007), 9, 94.
42. Philip Schaff and Henry Wace, *A Select Library of Nicene and Post-Nicene Fathers of the Christian Church* (Grand Rapids, MI: Wm. B. Eerdmans, 1952), 1:490.
43. Eusebius, *Church History, Life of Constantine the Great* (Grand Rapids, MI: Wm. B. Eusebius), *The History of the Church from Christ to Constantine*, trans. G.A. Williamson (London: Penguin Books, 1952), 1:490. See also Randall Stewart, "Constantine I," in Atiya, *The Coptic Encyclopedia*, 2:588; Stephen J. Davis, *The Early Coptic Papacy* (Cairo: American University in Cairo Press, 2004), 43.
44. Dungan, *Constantine's Bible*, 99.
45. Dungan, *Constantine's Bible*, 111.
46. Dungan, *Constantine's Bible*, 124.
47. Schaff and Wace, *A Select Library of Nicene and Post-Nicene Fathers*, 1:490. See also Davis, *The Early Coptic Papacy*, 50; Karen Torjesen, "Council of Nicaea," in Atiya, *The Coptic Encyclopedia*, 6:1790.
48. Dungan, *Constantine's Bible*, 142.
49. The Egyptian church counts five ecumenical councils between 325 and 451, as cited by Archpriest Kirullus al-Antuni, *'Asr al-majami'* (Cairo: Maktabat al-Mahabba, 1991). However *The Coptic Encyclopedia* (2:512) and *Encyclopedia Britannica* (2:711) count the total number of ecumenical councils during this period as four. See also Janet Timbie, "Melitian Schism," in Atiya, *The Coptic Encyclopedia*, 5:1584.
50. Timothy D. Barnes, *Athanasius and Constantius* (Cambridge, MA: Harvard University Press, 1993), 1.
51. Davis, *The Early Coptic Papacy*, 56.
52. al-Abb Matta al-Miskin, *al-Qiddis Athansius al-Rasuli* (Wadi al-Natrun: Matba'at Deir al-Qiddis Anba Maqar, 1981), 74.
53. Matta al-Miskin, *al-Qiddis Athansius al-Rasuli*, 74–77.
54. Matta al-Miskin, *al-Qiddis Athansius al-Rasuli*, 66.
55. Barnes, *Athanasius and Constantius*, 18.
56. Barnes, *Athanasius and Constantius*, 18.
57. Matta al-Miskin, *al-Qiddis Athansius al-Rasuli*, 758.
58. Barnes, *Athanasius and Constantius*, 1.
59. Matta al-Miskin, *al-Qiddis Athansius al-Rasuli*, 759. See also Barnes, *Athanasius and Constantius*, 8.
60. Salah 'Abd al-'Aziz Mahjub, trans., *Iohannis Ephesini Historiae Ecclesiasticae Pars Tertia* (Cairo: al-Maglis al-A'la li-l-Thaqafa, 2000), 40.
61. David Brakke, *Athanasius and Asceticism* (Baltimore, MD: Johns Hopkins University Press, 1998), 8.
62. al-Matta al-Miskin, *al-Qiddis Athansius al-Rasuli*, 769.

63. Brakke, *Athanasius and Asceticism*; Barnes, *Athanasius and Constantius*; Davis, *The Early Coptic Papacy*; and to some degree, the Arabic book of Matta al-Miskin, *al-Qiddis Athanasius al-Rasuli*.
64. Davis, *The Early Coptic Papacy*, 43.
65. Davis, *The Early Coptic Papacy*, 63. See also Spanel, "Theophilus," 7:2250.
66. Davis, *The Early Coptic Papacy*.
67. Davis, *The Early Coptic Papacy*, 65.
68. Davis, *The Early Coptic Papacy*, 43.
69. Davis, *The Early Coptic Papacy*, 43; see also Spanel, "Theophilus," 7:2249.
70. Davis, *The Early Coptic Papacy*, 43. Also see Matta al-Miskin, *al-Rahbana al-qibtiya*, 239.
71. Davis, *The Early Coptic Papacy*, 70.
72. "Hypatia," *Encyclopedia Britannica*, 5:251. See also Davis, *The Early Coptic Papacy*, 71, and Aziz S. Atiya, "Cyril I, Saint," in Atiya, *The Coptic Encyclopedia*, 3:672.
73. Davis, *The Early Coptic Papacy*, 71.
74. Davis, *The Early Coptic Papacy*, 76.
75. Youssef Ziedan, *'Azazil* (Cairo: Dar El Shorouk, 2008), 110, 178, 183, 348, 362.
76. Tagher, *Christians in Muslim Egypt*, 3.
77. Davis, *The Early Coptic Papacy*, 83.
78. Davis, *The Early Coptic Papacy*, 83.
79. al-Masri, *The Story of the Copts*, 9.
80. Davis, *The Early Coptic Papacy*, 89.
81. Secretarial Committee, *al-Qararat al-mujma'iya fi 'ahd sahib al-qadasa wa-l-ghabta al-Baba Shenouda al-Thalith* (Cairo: al-Markaz al-Thaqafi al-Qibti al-Urthuduksi, 1996), 104.

Chapter 2

1. Alfred J. Butler, *The Arab Conquest of Egypt and the Last Thirty Years of the Roman Dominion* (New York: Oxford University Press, 1998), 39.
2. Butler, *The Arab Conquest of Egypt*, 60.
3. Butler, *The Arab Conquest of Egypt*, 70.
4. Butler, *The Arab Conquest of Egypt*, 72–3.
5. Taqi al-Din Abu-l 'Abbas al-Maqrizi, *Kitab al-mawa'iz wa-l-i'tibar bi-dhikr al-khitat wa-l-athar* (Cairo: Maktabat al-Adab, 1996), 4:392. See also Butler, *The Arab Conquest of Egypt*, 73.
6. Davis, *The Early Coptic Papacy*, 114.
7. Butler, *The Arab Conquest of Egypt*, 119.
8. Davis, *The Early Coptic Papacy*, 115.
9. Butler, *The Arab Conquest of Egypt*, 127.
10. al-Maqrizi, *al-Khitat*, 4:392.
11. W.H.C. Frend, "Monothelitism," in Atiya, *The Coptic Encyclopedia*, 5:1678.
12. Butler, *The Arab Conquest of Egypt*, 191–92. See also Davis, *The Early Coptic Papacy*, 117–20.

13. Butler, 192. See also Ibn ʻAbd al-Hakam, *The History of the Conquest of Egypt, North Africa, and Spain* (The Netherlands: Leiden University, 1930), 61; Abu-l Hassan al-Balazri, *Futuh al-buldan* (Beirut: Maktabat al-Hilal, 1988), 210; John of Nikiou, *Majallat Sahyun* (Zion Magazine), Cairo, 1948, 135.
14. Amr's campaign started with only 4,000 fighters, then increased to between 12,000 and 15,000. Butler, *The Arab Conquest of Egypt*, 226 and 229.
15. Butler, *The Arab Conquest of Egypt*, 222–4. See also John of Nikiou, *Majallat Sahyun*, 137.
16. Butler, *The Arab Conquest of Egypt*, 226.
17. John of Nikiou, *Majallat Sahyun*, Cairo, 1948, 141. See also, "The Treaty of Misr in Tabari," 5–83. This is a separate essay found after the index in *The Arab Conquest of Egypt and the Last Thirty Years of the Roman Dominion*. The copy we used is a special edition for Sandpiper Books Ltd., 1998.
18. Butler, 274.
19. Ibn Hisham, *al-Sira al-nabawiya*, ed. Taha ʻAbd al-Ra'uf Saʻd (Beirut: Dar al-Jil li-l-Tabʻ wa-l-Nashr wa-l-Tawziʻ, 1990), 6:94. Also available online at http://library.islamweb.net/newlibrary/display_book.php?idfrom=5211&idto=5212&bk_no=52&ID=1824.
20. John of Nikiou, "Yohan b'Nikiou," in *Majallat Sahyun*, Cairo, 1948, 144–150.
21. Butler, *The Arab Conquest of Egypt*, 256.
22. Butler, *The Arab Conquest of Egypt*, Appendix, 5–83. See also John of Nikiou, *Majallat Sahyun*, 149; ʻAbd al-Rahman bin ʻAbdallah al-Misri al-Qurashi, *Futuh Misr wa akhbaraha* (Leiden: Leiden University, 1930), 84–90; Muhammad ibn Jarir al-Tabari, *Tarikh al-umam wa-l-muluk*, ed. Muhammad Abu al-Fadl Ibrahim (Cairo: Dar al-Maʻarif, 1967), 4:109.
23. John of Nikiou, *Majallat Sahyun*, 144–145.
24. al-Maqrizi, *al-Khitat*, 1:77.
25. Butler, *The Arab Conquest of Egypt*, 256.
26. John of Nikiou, *Majallat Sahyun*, 143.
27. John of Nikiou, *Majallat Sahyun*, 142. See also Butler, *The Arab Conquest of Egypt*, 439.
28. Butler, *The Arab Conquest of Egypt*, 439.
29. Fahmi Huwaydi, *Muwatinun la dhimmiyun* (Cairo: Dar El Shorouk, 1985), 203. See also Ibn ʻAbd al-Hakam, *The History of the Conquest of Egypt, North Africa and Spain* (The Netherlands: Leiden University, 1930), 84–90. The book's title is in both Arabic and English title.
30. Ibn ʻAbd al-Hakam, 84–90.
31. ʻAli ibn al-Husayn al-Masʻudi, *Muruj al-dhahab* (Beirut: Dar al-Andalus, 1965), 420. See also Butler, *The Arab Conquest of Egypt*, 368.
32. al-Masʻudi, 1965, 1:420.
33. Butler, 389. Also see al-Masʻudi, 2:414.
34. Butler, 372. Also see al-Masʻudi, 2:414.
35. Butler, 372.

36. Butler, 401 and 410. See also Mustafa al-'Abbadi, *Maktabat al-Iskandariya al-qadima* (Cairo: Maktabat al-Anglo al-Misriya, 1977), 22; S.S. Hassan, *Christians versus Muslims in Modern Egypt*, 27.
37. Butler, 403.
38. Ibn 'Abd al-Hakam, *The History of the Conquest of Egypt, North Africa, and Spain*, 158. See also Butler, *The Arab Conquest of Egypt*, 447–50. However, some of these restrictions on Copts were introduced at a later period, as mentioned by Huwaydi, *Muwatinun la dhimmiyun*, 203.
39. Butler, *The Arab Conquest of Egypt*, 448–53.
40. Taha Hussein, *al-Fitna al-kubra*, vol. 1 (Cairo: Dar al-Ma'arif, 1984), 107–109. Also see Ibn Sa'd Besinda, *al-Tabaqat al-kubra* (Beirut: Dar Sadir, n.d.), 3:110. Also, Fahmi Huwaydi, *Muwatinun la dhimmiyun* (Cairo: Dar El Shorouk, 1985), 83.
41. Muhammad ibn Ahmad ibn Iyas, *Badi' al-zuhur fi waqai' al-duhur*, ed. Muhammad Mustafa (Cairo: al-Hay'a al-Misriya al-'Amma li-l-Kitab, 1982), 117.
42. Muhammad ibn Ahmad ibn Iyas, *Badi' al-zuhur fi waqai' al-duhur*, ed. Muhammad Mustafa (Cairo: al-Hay'a al-Misriya al-'Amma li-l-Kitab, 1982), 117.
43. Butler, 452–3.
44. Taha Hussein, *al-Fitna al-kubra*, Othman, 108–9.
45. Muhammad ibn Ahmad ibn Iyas, *Badi' al-zuhur fi waqai' al-duhur*, 117.
46. Muhammad ibn Ahmad ibn Iyas, *Badi' al-zuhur fi waqai' al-duhur*, 117.
47. Ahmad Baha' al-Din, *al-Muthaqqafun wa-l-sulta* (Kuwait: al-Kitab al-'Arabi, 1999), 38:167.

Chapter 3

1. al-Tabari, *Tarikh al-umam wa-l-muluk*, 100.
2. Jamal al-Din, *Tarikh Misr*, 2:1212, 1218.
3. Ibn Iyas, *Badi' al-zuhur fi waqai' al-duhur*, 1:134.
4. Ibn 'Abd al-Hakam, *The History of the Conquest of Egypt, North Africa, and Spain*, 1930, 161.
5. Abi 'Umar Muhammad bin Yusuf, *al-Kindi al-Misri* (Leiden: Leiden University Edition, 1912), 73.
6. Jamal Himdan, *Shakhsiyat Misr* (Cairo: 'Alam al-Kitab, 1980), 2:541.
7. Tagher, *Christians in Muslim Egypt*, 49.
8. Tagher, *Christians in Muslim Egypt*, 113.
9. al-Maqrizi, *al-Khitat*, 159.
10. al-Maqrizi, *al-Khitat*, 159.
11. Huwaydi, *Muwatinun la dhimmiyun*, 129.
12. Dennett, *al-Jizya wa-l-Islam*, 139.
13. Jamal al-Din, *Tarikh Misr*, 2:152.
14. al-Maqrizi, *al-Khitat*, 1:159.

15. Tagher, *Christians in Muslim Egypt*, 64.
16. Ya'qub Nakhla Rufila, *Tarikh al-umma al-qibtiya* (Cairo: Mu'assasat al-Qiddis Murqus, 2000), 69.
17. Tritton, A.S., *Ahl al-dhimma fi-l-Islam*, trans. Hassan Habashi (Cairo: Dar al-Ma'arif, 1967), 81.
18. Farag Fouda, *al-Haqiqa al-gha'iba* (Cairo: Dar al-Fikr li-l-Dirasat wa-l-Nashr wa-l-Tawzi', 1986), 56.
19. Jamal al-Din, *Tarikh Misr*, 2:165.
20. al-Maqrizi, *al-Khitat*, 4:394.
21. al-Maqrizi, *al-Khitat*, 395.
22. Jamal al-Din, *Tarikh Misr*, 170, 172.
23. Jamal al-Din, *Tarikh Misr*, 150.
24. Muhammad ibn Ahmad ibn Iyas, *al-Hanafi* (Cairo: al-Hay'a al-Misriya al-'Amma li-l-Kitab, 1982), 1:125.
25. al-Kindi al-Misri, *al-Hukkam wa-l-qudah fi Misr* (*Governors and Judges of Egypt)*, Beirut, 1908, 76.
26. Jamal al-Din, *Tarikh Misr*, 2:94.
27. al-Maqrizi, *al-Khitat*, 4:395.
28. Jamal al-Din, *Tarikh Misr*, 2:390–98.
29. al-Tabari, *Tarikh al-umam wa-l-muluk*, 5:494.
30. al-Maqrizi, *al-Khitat*, 4:395.
31. Muhammad Sa'id al-'Ashmawi, *al-Islam al-siyasi* (Cairo: Dar Sina li-l-Nashr, 1987), 18.
32. al-Tabari, *Tarikh al-umam wa-l-muluk*, 7:492.
33. al-Mas'udi, *Muruj al-dhahab*, 3:270.
34. Hassan Ahmad Mahmud and Ahmad Ibrahim al-Sharif, *al-'Alam al-islami fi-l-'asr al-'abbasi* (Cairo: Dar al-Fikr al-'Arabi, n.d.), 83.
35. Mark N. Swanson, *The Coptic Papacy in Islamic Egypt 641–1517* (Cairo: American University in Cairo Press, 2010), 33. See also al-Kindi al-Misri, *al-Hukkam wa-l-qudah fi Misr* (*Governors and Judges of Egypt)*, Beirut, 1908, 139.
36. Swanson, *The Coptic Papacy in Islamic Egypt 641–1517*, 33.
37. al-Maqrizi, *al-Khitat*, 3:396.
38. al-Kindi, *al-Hukkam wa-l-qudah fi Misr (Governors and Judges of Egypt)*, Beirut, 1908, 90.
39. Rufila, *Tarikh al-umma al-qibtiya*, 87.
40. Muhammad Isma'il, *al-Muhammashun fi-l-tarikh al-islami* (Cairo: Ru'ya li-l-Nashr wa-l-Tawzi', 2004), 31–61.
41. Swanson, *The Coptic Papacy in Islamic Egypt 641–1517*, 38.
42. Swanson, *The Coptic Papacy in Islamic Egypt 641–1517*, 34.
43. Jamal al-Din, *Tarikh Misr*, 3:380.

Chapter 4

1. Jamal al-Din, *Tarikh Misr*, 3:380.

2. Mahmud and al-Sharif, *al-'Alam al-islami fi-l-'asr al-'abbasi*, 83. See also Jamal al-Din, *Tarikh Misr*, 3:381–88.
3. Tagher, *Christians in Muslim Egypt*, 89.
4. al-Maqrizi, *al-Khitat*, 89.
5. al-Maqrizi, *al-Khitat*, 4:39; see also, Jamal al-Din, *Tarikh Misr*, 3:310.
6. al-Maqrizi, 4:36.
7. Watterson, *Coptic Egypt*, 1988, 121.
8. Huwaydi, *Muwatinun la dhimmiyun*, 67.
9. Sayyida Isma'il Kashif, *Misr fi 'asr al-Ikhshidiyyin*, 1st ed. (Cairo: Dar al-Nahda al-'Arabiya, 1992), 17–19.
10. al-Mas'udi, *Muruj al-dhahab*, 91.
11. Kashif, *Misr fi 'asr al-Ikhshidiyyin*, 253.
12. Huwaydi, *Muwatinun la dhimmiyun*, 72.
13. Kashif, *Misr fi 'asr al-Ikhshidiyyin*, 27.
14. Salam Shafi'i Mahmud, *Ahl al-dhimma fi Misr fi al-'asr al-fatimi al-awwal* (Cairo: al-Hay'a al-Misriya al-'Amma li-l-Kitab, 1995), 27.
15. Jamal al-Din, *Tarikh Misr*, 3:511.
16. Mahmud, *Ahl al-dhimma*, 27.
17. Mahmud, *Ahl al-dhimma*, 323.
18. Jamal al-Din, *Tarikh Misr*, 3:511. See also Tagher, *Christians in Muslim Egypt*, 97.
19. Mahmud, *Ahl al-dhimma*, 223.
20. 'Ali Hosni al-Kharbutli, *Islam and ahl el-dhimma* (Cairo: al-Majlis al-Islami al-A'la, 1969), 170. See also al-Maqrizi, *al-Khitat*, 4:36.
21. Huwaydi, *Muwatinun la dhimmiyun*, 72.
22. Mahmud, *Ahl al-dhimma*, 31.
23. Ibn Iyas, *al-Hanafi*, 1:198–206. See also al-Maqrizi, *al-Khitat*, 4:399; Taqi al-Din Abu-l- 'Abbas al-Maqrizi, *A Short History of the Copts and Their Churches*, trans. S.C. Malan (Whitefish, MT: Kessinger Publishing, 1873), 88.
24. Jamal al-Din, *Tarikh Misr*, 3:576.
25. Atiya, "Patriarchs, Dates and Succession of," 6:1916.
26. al-Maqrizi, *al-Khitat*, 4:399.
27. al-Abb Matta al-Miskin, *al-Qiddis Athansius al-Rasuli* (Cairo: Matba'at Deir al-Qiddis Anba Maqar, 1972), 480. See also Jamal al-Din, *Tarikh Misr*, 3:576.
28. Jamal al-Din, *Tarikh Misr*, 3:556–87.
29. Jamal al-Din, *Tarikh Misr*, 3:576.
30. Ayman Fu'ad Sayyid, *al-Dawla al-fatimiya fi Misr* (Cairo: al-Dar al-Misriya al-Libnaniya, 2000), 594.
31. There is an Arabic documentary film on al-Hakim; it can be seen at https://www.youtube.com/watch?v=SFTL7j9SoVQ.
32. Sayyid, *al-Dawla al-fatimiya fi Misr*, 179.
33. Mahmud, *Ahl al-dhimma*, 23.
34. Ibn Iyas, *Badi' al-zuhur fi waqai' al-duhur*, 1:216.
35. Mahmud, *Ahl al-dhimma*, 23.

36. Sayyid, *al-Dawla al-fatimiya fi Misr*, 262.
37. Swanson, *The Coptic Papacy in Islamic Egypt 641–1517*, 69.
38. Swanson, *The Coptic Papacy in Islamic Egypt 641–1517*, 69. See also Sayyid, *al-Dawla al-fatimiya fi Misr*, 259.
39. Sayyid, *al-Dawla al-fatimiya fi Misr*, 259.
40. Sayyid, *al-Dawla al-fatimiya fi Misr*,161.
41. Sayyid, *al-Dawla al-fatimiya fi Misr*,182.
42. Mahmud, *Ahl al-dhimma*, 261.
43. Jamal al-Din, *Tarikh Misr*, 3:1475.
44. Alastair Hamilton, *The Copts and the West, 1439–1822* (New York: Oxford University Press, 2006). The entire book is dedicated to this topic; however, see in particular pp. 1, 24, 30, 31.
45. Swanson, *The Coptic Papacy in Islamic Egypt 641–1517*, 83.
46. Albert Hourani, *History of the Arab People* (Cambridge, MA: Harvard University Press, 1991), 85.
47. Aziz S. Atiya, "Ayyubid Dynasty, and the Copts," in Atiya, *The Coptic Encyclopedia*, 1:315.
48. Qadri Qal'aji, *Salah al-Din* (Beirut: Dar al-Kitab al-'Araby, 1966), 162. See also Wikipedia, "Shajar al-Durr," https://en.wikipedia.org/wiki/Shajar_al-Durr.

Chapter 5

1. al-Maqrizi, *al-Khitat*, 3:392.
2. Ibn Iyas, *Badi' al-zuhur fi waqai' al-duhur*, 1:307–308.
3. Ibn Iyas, *Badi' al-zuhur fi waqai' al-duhur*, 1:324.
4. Tagher, *Christians in Muslim Egypt*, 144.
5. See Rufila, *Tarikh al-umma al-qibtiya*, 222; al-Maqrizi, *Khitat*, 4:425–33; Tagher, *Christians in Muslim Egypt*, 152.
6. al-Maqrizi, *al-Khitat*, 4:425–33.
7. al-Maqrizi, *al-Khitat*, 4:425–33.
8. al-Maqrizi, *al-Khitat*, 4:425–33.
9. Tagher, *Christians in Muslim Egypt*, 152.
10. Aziz S. Atiya, "Mamluks and the Copts," in Atiya, *The Coptic Encyclopedia*, 5:1517.
11. Swanson, *The Coptic Papacy in Islamic Egypt 641–1517*, 102.
12. Ibn Iyas, *al-Hanafi*, 1:378, 401, 431.
13. Ibn Iyas, *al-Hanafi*, 1:564.
14. Ibn al-Muqaffa', *Tarikh al-batarika*, 1:20. See also al-Maqrizi, *Khitat*, 2:199.
15. Abu Sayf Yusuf, *al-Aqbat wa-l-qawmiya al-'arabiya* (Cairo: Markaz Dirasat al-Wihda al-'Arabiya, 1987), 176. See also Tagher, *Christians in Muslim Egypt*, 160.
16. al-Maqrizi, *al-Khitat*, 3:4–5.
17. Tagher, *Christians in Muslim Egypt*, 160.

18. Ibn Iyas, *al-Hanafi*, 1:55.
19. Fikry Hassan, "Extreme Nile Floods and Famines in Medieval Egypt (AD 930–1500) and Their Climatic Implications." In *Quarternary International* 173–174 (2007), 101–112.
20. Husayn Fawzi, *al-Sindbad al-misri* (Cairo: Dar al-Ma'arif, 1990), 206.

Chapter 6

1. Tagher, *Christians in Muslim Egypt*, 68.
2. al-Maqrizi, *al-Khitat*, 2:497.
3. Tamer el-Leithy, "Coptic Culture and Conversion in Medieval Cairo, 1293–1524" (PhD diss., Princeton University, 2004). See also Tamer el-Leithy, "Sufis, Copts, and the Politics of Piety: Moral Regulation in Fourteenth-Century Upper Egypt," in *Le développement du soufisme*, eds. Richard McGregor and Adam Sabra (Institut Français d'Archéologie Orientale, 2006), 92.
4. 'Uthman ibn Ibrahim al-Nabulsi, *The Sword of Ambition*, trans. Luke Yarbrough (New York: New York University Press, 2016).
5. Thomas J. Draper, "Ibn Taymiyyah: The Struggles of a Mujtahid under the Bahri Mamluk Sultans" (master's thesis, Ball State University, 2013), 106. See also Ibn Iyas, *al-Hanafi*, 1:564.
6. el-Leithy, "Sufis, Copts, and the Politics of Piety," 92.
7. el-Leithy, "Sufis, Copts, and the Politics of Piety," 104.
8. el-Leithy, "Sufis, Copts, and the Politics of Piety," 86.
9. el-Leithy, "Sufis, Copts, and the Politics of Piety," 106.
10. M. Wassermann, "The Process of Islamization in Egypt" (master's thesis, School of Oriental and African Studies, University of London, 1992).
11. el-Leithy, "Sufis, Copts, and the Politics of Piety," 76.
12. Shaun O'Sullivan, "Coptic Conversion and Islamization of Egypt," *Mamluk Studies Review* (2006): 65–79.
13. The Jews and Muslims did the same under pressure during the Inquisition: for Jews, it was called *conversos*; for Muslims, it was called *taqiya*.
14. el-Leithy, "Coptic Culture and Conversion in Medieval Cairo, 1293–1524 A.D" (PhD diss., UMI Microsoft, 2005), 66.
15. O'Sullivan, "Coptic Conversion and Islamization of Egypt," 67.
16. el-Leithy, "Sufis, Copts, and the Politics of Piety," 96.
17. el-Leithy, "Coptic Culture and Conversion in Medieval Cairo," 362.
18. Samuel Rubenson, "The Transition from Coptic to Arabic," *Égypte/Monde Arabe*, 1st series, 27–28 (1996): 77. Available online at http://journals.openedition.org/ema/1920.
19. Emil Maher Ishaq, "Coptic Language, Spoken," in Atiya, *The Coptic Encyclopedia*, 2:604.
20. Wilson B. Bishai, "Coptic Lexical Influence on Egyptian Arabic," *Journal of Near Eastern Studies* 23, no. 1 (1964): 39–47; see also Emil Maher Ishaq, "Coptic Language, Spoken." In *The Coptic Encyclopedia*, Atiya, ed., 2:60.

21. Agar, Michael H. *Language Shock: Understanding the Culture of Conversation* (New York: William Morrow, 1994). Also see Samuel Rubenson, "The Transition from Coptic to Arabic," 1996, 77–92, and 'Abd al-'Aziz Jamal al-Din, *Lughatuna al-misriya al-mu'asara, Manshurat misriya, Nahw thaqafa wataniya dimuqratiya*, Cairo, 2011.
22. Ahmed Abdel-Hamid Youssef, *From Pharaoh's Lips: Ancient Egyptian Language in the Arabic of Today* (Cairo: American University in Cairo Press, 2003), xi.
23. Louis Awad, *Muqaddima fi fiqh al-lugha al-'arabiya* (Cairo: Dar Sina li-l-Nashr, 1993), 42.
24. Louis Awad, *Muqaddima fi fiqh al-lugha al-'arabiya*, 466.
25. Louis Awad, *Muqaddima fi fiqh al-lugha al-'arabiya*, 11, 469.
26. Nasim Megalli. See his introduction to the second printing (1993) of Awad's *Muqaddima fi fiqh al-lugha al-'arabiya* (Dar Sina), 5–22.

Chapter 7

1. Ahmad Husayn, *Mawsu'at tarikh Misr* (Cairo: Matbu'at Dar al-Sha'b, 1972), 3:817.
2. Muhammed 'Afifi, *al-Aqbat fi al-'asr al-'uthmani* (Cairo: al-Hay'a al-Misriya li-l-Kitab, 1992), 37.
3. Jamal al-Din, *Tarikh Misr*, 4:1089.
4. 'Afifi, *al-Aqbat fi al-'asr al-'uthmani*, 41.
5. Jamal al-Din, *Tarikh Misr*, 4:1089. See also 'Afifi, *al-Aqbat fi al-'asr al-'uthmani*, 39.
6. Jamal al-Din, *Tarikh Misr*, 4:1099.
7. Nelly Hanna, *In Praise of Books: A Cultural History of Cairo's Middle Class, Sixteenth Through the Eighteenth Century* (Syracuse, NY: Syracuse University Press, 2003), 145.
8. Tagher, *Christians in Muslim Egypt*, 169–70.
9. 'Afifi, *al-Aqbat fi al-'asr al-'uthmani*, 54.
10. 'Abd al-Rahman al-Jabarti, *Al-Jabarti's History of Egypt*, ed. Jane Hathaway (Princeton: Markus Weiner Publisher, 2009), 73. See also 'Abd al-Rahman al-Jabarti, *'Aja'ib al-athar fi-l-tarajim wa-l-'athar* (Cairo: Matba'at al-Anwar al-Muhammadiya, 1986), 1:246.
11. 'Afifi, *al-Aqbat fi al-'asr al-'uthmani*, 65.
12. 'Afifi, *al-Aqbat fi al-'asr al-'uthmani*, 48.
13. al-Jabarti, *'Aja'ib al-athar fi-l-tarajim wa-l-'athar* (Cairo: Matba'at al-Anwar al-Muhammadiya, 1986), 2:175.
14. 'Afifi, *al-Aqbat fi al-'asr al-'uthmani*, 83.
15. 'Afifi, *al-Aqbat fi al-'asr al-'uthmani*, 83. See also Jamal al-Din, *Tarikh Misr*, 4:1112.
16. Jamal al-Din, *Tarikh Misr*, 4:1112.
17. 'Afifi, *al-Aqbat fi al-'asr al-'uthmani*, 93.
18. 'Afifi, *al-Aqbat fi al-'asr al-'uthmani*, 97.
19. Hanna, *In Praise of Books*, 141.

20. Hanna, *In Praise of Books*, 141.
21. Jane Hathaway, ed., *Al-Jabarti's History of Egypt* (Princeton, NJ: Markus Weiner, 2009), 1:97, 107.
22. 'Ali Barakat, *Ru'yat al-Jabarti li-azmat al-hayah al-fikriya* (Cairo: al-Hay'a al-Misriya al-'Amma li-l-Kitab, 1987), 52.
23. 'Afifi, *al-Aqbat fi al-'asr al-'uthmani*, 275.
24. Louis Awad, *Tarikh al-fikr al-misri al-hadith* (Cairo: Dar al-Hilal, 1994), 20. See also Jane Hathaway, ed., *Al-Jabarti's History of Egypt*, 97.
25. Jane Hathaway, ed., *Al-Jabarti's History of Egypt*, 97.

Chapter 8

1. For the details about the military campaign, see J. Christopher Herold, *Bonaparte in Egypt* (New York: Harper & Row, 1962), 64.
2. al-Jabarti, *'Aja'ib al-athar fi-l-tarajim wa-l-'athar*, 3:8–9.
3. al-Jabarti, *'Aja'ib al-athar fi-l-tarajim wa-l-'athar* (Cairo: Matba'at al-Athar al-Muhammadiya, 1986) 3:4–9.
4. al-Jabarti, *Al-Jabarti's History of Egypt*, Jane Hathaway, ed., 179–81.
5. Louis Awad, *Tarikh al-fikr al-misri al-hadith*, 77.
6. Herold, *Bonaparte in Egypt*, 145.
7. Tagher, *Christians in Muslim Egypt*, 179.
8. Tagher, *Christians in Muslim Egypt*, 181.
9. Tagher, *Christians in Muslim Egypt*, 187.
10. Tagher, *Christians in Muslim Egypt*, 180.
11. al-Jabarti, *Al-Jabarti's History of Egypt*, 186.
12. al-Jabarti, *Al-Jabarti's History of Egypt*, 188.
13. Tagher, *Christians in Muslim Egypt*, 183.
14. al-Jabarti, *'Aja'ib al-athar fi-l-tarajim wa-l-'athar*, 3:36.
15. al-Jabarti, *'Aja'ib al-athar fi-l-tarajim wa-l-'athar*, 3:132.
16. Jane Hathaway, ed., *Al-Jabarti's History of Egypt*, 202.
17. Rufila, *Tarikh al-umma al-qibtiya*, 291.
18. Louis Awad, *Tarikh al-fikr al-misri al-hadith*, 132.
19. al-Jabarti, *'Aja'ib al-athar fi-l-tarajim wa-l-'athar*, 3:132. See also Anwar Louca, "General Ya'qub," in Atiya, *The Coptic Encyclopedia*, 7:2349.
20. al-Jabarti, *'Aja'ib al-athar fi-l-tarajim wa-l-'athar*, 3:231.
21. Louis Awad, *Tarikh al-fikr al-misri al-hadith*, 146.
22. Louis Awad, *Tarikh al-fikr al-misri al-hadith*, 146, 150.
23. Raja' al-Naqqash, *Lewis 'Awad fi al-mizan* (Cairo: Dar al-Hilal, 2006).
24. 'Ayda al-Sharif, *Muhammad Mahmud Shakir* (Cairo: Dar al-Hilal, 1997), 93.
25. Ahmad Hassan al-Sawi, *al-Mu'allim Ya'qub bayn al-ustura wa-l-haqiqa* (Cairo: Dar al-Fikr li-l-Dirasat wa-l-Nashr, 1986), 137.
26. Louis Awad, *Tarikh al-fikr al-misri al-hadith*, 193–96.
27. Jane Hathaway, ed., *Al-Jabarti's History of Egypt*, 204.
28. Jamal al-Din, *Tarikh Misr*, 4:1199–1201.

29. Barakat, *Ru'yat al-Jabarti li-azmat al-hayah al-fikriya*, 48.
30. Jane Hathaway, ed., *Al-Jabarti's History of Egypt*, 190.

Chapter 9

1. ʻAbd al-Rahman al-Rafiʻi, *ʻAsr Muhammad ʻAli* (Cairo: Dar al-Maʻarif, 1982), 104.
2. The Wahhabi movement led to the strong political Islam that prevails in parts of the Muslim world today.
3. al-Rafiʻi, *ʻAsr Muhammad ʻAli*, 113.
4. al-Jabarti, *ʻAja'ib al-athar fi-l-tarajim wa-l-'athar*, 3:4–8.
5. ʻAbd al-Rahman al-Rafiʻi, *Tarikh al-haraka al-qawmiya wa tatawwur nizam al-hukm* (Cairo: Dar al-Maʻarif, 1981), 289.
6. Hassan, S.S. *Christians versus Muslims in Modern Egypt*, 32.
7. Hassan, S.S. *Christians versus Muslims in Modern Egypt*, 33.
8. Hassan, S.S. *Christians versus Muslims in Modern Egypt*, 33.
9. B.L. Carter, *The Copts in Egyptian Politics, 1918–1952* (New York: Routledge, 2013), 2.
10. al-Jabarti, *ʻAja'ib al-athar fi-l-tarajim wa-l-'athar*, 1986, 4:175.
11. Jacques Tagher, *Christians in Muslim Egypt*, 199.
12. al-Rafiʻi, *ʻAsr Muhammad ʻAli*, 407.
13. al-Rafiʻi, *ʻAsr Muhammad ʻAli*, 297.
14. Tariq al-Bishri, *al-Muslimun wa-l-Aqbat fi itar al-jamʻa al-wataniya* (Beirut: Dar al-Wihda, 1982), 40.
15. Nubar Pasha, *Mudhakkirat Nubar Pasha*, ed. Latifa Muhammad Salim, trans. Garo Robier Tabakian (Cairo: Dar El Shorouk, 2009), 247.
16. Nubar Pasha, *Mudhakkirat*, 240.
17. Nubar Pasha *Mudhakkirat*, 253–55.
18. Tagher, *Christians in Muslim Egypt*, 208, 19–21.
19. Tagher, *Christians in Muslim Egypt*, 205.
20. Tagher, *Christians in Muslim Egypt*, 206.
21. Tagher, *Christians in Muslim Egypt*, 206.
22. Zakhari al-Antuni, *Kirullus al-Rabiʻ: Abu-l islah* (Cairo: Deir al-Anba Antonios, 1994), 62.
23. al-Bishri, *al-Muslimun wa-l-Aqbat*, 32.
24. Tagher, *Christians in Muslim Egypt*, 207.
25. Tagher, *Christians in Muslim Egypt*, 209.
26. Louis Awad, *Tarikh al-fikr al-misri al-hadith: min ʻasr Ismaʻil ila Thawret 1919* (Cairo: al-Hay'a al-Misriya li-l-Kitab, 1980), 1:52.
27. ʻAbd al-Rahman al-Rafiʻi, *ʻAsr Ismaʻil* (Cairo: Dar al-Maʻarif, 1982), 52.
28. Louis Awad, *Tarikh al-fikr al-misri al-hadith: min ʻasr Ismaʻil ila Thawret 1919*, 1:67.
29. al-Rafiʻi, *'Asr Ismaʻil*, 1:201. These schools included Engineering, Law, Science, and Medicine and Gynecology.

30. Carol Zeman Rothkopf, *The Opening of the Suez Canal, November 1869: A Water Gateway Joins East and West* (New York: Franklin Watts Inc., 1973). This small book (76 pages) covers the history of the Suez Canal, and contains old pictures.
31. Louis Awad, *Tarikh al-fikr al-misri al-hadith: min ʻasr Isma'il ila Thawret 1919*, 1:67.
32. Louis Awad, *Tarikh al-fikr al-misri al-hadith: min ʻasr Isma'il ila Thawret 1919*, 1:129.
33. Louis Awad, *Tarikh al-fikr al-misri al-hadith: min ʻasr Isma'il ila Thawret 1919*, 1:163.
34. Louis Awad, *Tarikh al-fikr al-misri al-hadith: min ʻasr Isma'il ila Thawret 1919*, 1:130.
35. Febe Armanios, *Coptic Christianity in Ottoman Egypt* (New York: Oxford University Press, 2011), 117; see also Heather J. Sharkey, *American Evangelicals in Egypt: Missionary Encounter in an Age of Empire* (Princeton, NJ: Princeton University Press, 2008); Hamilton, *The Copts and the West 1439–1822*.
36. Hassan, S.S. *Christians versus Muslims in Modern Egypt* (2003), 71.
37. Magdi Guirguis and Nelly van Doorn-Harder, *The Emergence of the Modern Coptic Papacy: The Popes of Egypt*, (Cairo: American University in Cairo Press, 2011), 74.
38. Zakhari al-Antuni, *Kirullus al-Rabi'*, 65, 184; see also Guirguis and van Doorn-Harder, *The Emergence of the Modern Coptic Papacy*, 74.
39. Magdi Guirguis and Nelly van Doorn-Harder, 78.
40. al-Bishri, *al-Muslimun wa-l-Aqbat*, 36.
41. Sharkey, *American Evangelicals in Egypt*, 38.
42. al-Bishri, *al-Muslimun wa-l-Aqbat*, 37.
43. Hassan, *Christians versus Muslims in Modern Egypt*, 73.
44. Sharkey, *American Evangelicals in Egypt*, 1.

Chapter 10

1. Samira Bahr, *al-Aqbat fi-l-hayah al-siyasiya* (Cairo: Maktabat al-Anglu al-Misriya, 1984), 27–29.
2. Afaf Lutfi al-Sayyid, *Egypt and Cromer: A Study in Anglo-Egyptian Relations* (London: John Murray, 1968), 9.
3. Lutfi al-Sayyid, *Egypt and Cromer*, 5.
4. Bahr, *al-Aqbat fi-l-hayah al-siyasiya*, 27. See also *al-Tali'a magazine*, Cairo, 1965, 148.
5. Louis Awad, *Tarikh al-fikr al-misri al-hadith al-khalfiya al-tarikhiya* (Cairo: Dar al-Hilal, 1994), 164. See also Salim, *Mudhakkirat Nubar Pasha*; Evelyn Baring, Earl of Cromer, *Modern Egypt* (New York: Macmillan, 1908), 1:74.
6. Louis Awad, *Tarikh al-fikr al-misri al-hadith min ʻasr Isma'il ila Thawret 1919* (Cairo: al-Hay'a al-Misriya al-ʻAmma li-l-Kitab, 1980), 1:180. See also Earl of Cromer, *Modern Egypt*, 1:74.

7. Zeman Carol Rothkopf, *The Opening of the Suez Canal*, 62.
8. Samir Muhammad Taha, *Ahmad 'Urabi wa dawruh fi al-hayah al-siyasiya al-misriya* (Cairo: al-Hay'a al-Misriya al-'Amma li-l-Kitab, 1986), 103. See also Louis Awad, *Tarikh al-fikr al-misri al-hadith min 'asr Isma'il ila Thawret 1919*, 1:185.
9. Thomas Mayer, *The Changing Past: Egyptian Historiography of the Urabi Revolt, 1882–1983* (Gainesville: University Press of Florida, 1988), 73.
10. Baring, *Modern Egypt*, 1:176.
11. Louis Awad, *Tarikh al-fikr al-misri al-hadith min 'asr Isma'il ila Thawret 1919*, 1:226.
12. Louis Awad, *Tarikh al-fikr al-misri al-hadith min 'asr Isma'il ila Thawret 1919*, 1:227.
13. Baring, *Modern Egypt*, 1:287. There are different versions of the confrontation between Urabi and Khedive Tawfiq. See the details given by Louis Awad, *Tarikh al-fikr al-misri al-hadith min 'asr Isma'il ila Thawret 1919*, 1:178–86. In addition to the version by Lord Cromer and that in 'Abd al-Rahman al-Rafi'i, *al-Thawra al-'urabiya wa-l-ihtilal al-injilzi*, 4th ed. (Cairo: Dar al-Ma'arif, 1983), 185.
14. Louis Awad, *Tarikh al-fikr al-misri al-hadith min 'asr Isma'il ila Thawret 1919*, 1:236. See also al-Rafi'i, *al-Thawra al-'urabiya wa-l-ihtilal al-injilzi*, 144.
15. Louis Awad, *Tarikh al-fikr al-misri al-hadith min 'asr Isma'il ila Thawret 1919*, 1:251–55.
16. Louis Awad, *Tarikh al-fikr al-misri al-hadith: min 'asr Isma'il ila Thawret 1919*, 1:250.
17. Lutfi al-Sayyid, *Egypt and Cromer*, 2.
18. Bahr, *al-Aqbat fi-l-hayah al-siyasiya*, 27–29.

Chapter 11

1. Lutfi al-Sayyid, *Egypt and Cromer*, 196.
2. Lutfi al-Sayyid, *Egypt and Cromer*, 196.
3. Louis Awad, *Tarikh al-fikr al-misri al-hadith min 'asr Isma'il ila Thawret 1919*, al-Hay'a al-Misriya al-'Amma li-l-Kitab (Cairo: Dar al-Hilal, 1980), 1:288.
4. Louis Awad, *Tarikh al-fikr al-misri al-hadith min 'asr Isma'il ila Thawret 1919*, 1:292.
5. Louis Awad, *Tarikh al-fikr al-misri al-hadith min 'asr Isma'il ila Thawret 1919*, 1:292.
6. Louis Awad, *Tarikh al-fikr al-misri al-hadith min 'asr Isma'il ila Thawret 1919*, 1:305–7.
7. Baring, *Modern Egypt*, 2:443.
8. Lutfi al-Sayyid, *Egypt and Cromer*.
9. Baring, *Modern Egypt*, 1:152. In this reference, Cromer quotes Sir Frank Lascelles in his discussion with Khedive Tawfiq. Most likely, Lascelles's opinion reflected Cromer's opinion.

10. Louis Awad, *Tarikh al-fikr al-misri al-hadith min 'asr Isma'il ila Thawret 1919*, 1:159.
11. Robert Dreyfuss, *Devil's Game: How the United States Helped Unleash Fundamentalist Islam* (New York: Henry Holt, 2005), 19.
12. Dreyfuss, *Devil's Game*, 25.
13. Dreyfuss, *Devil's Game*, 25.
14. Lutfi al-Sayyid, *Egypt and Cromer*, 92.
15. al-Bishri, *al-Muslimun wa-l-Aqbat*, 256.
16. Bahr, *al-Aqbat fi-l-hayah al-siyasiya*, 46.
17. Louis Awad, *Tarikh al-fikr al-misri al-hadith min 'asr Isma'il ila Thawret 1919*, 1:114.
18. Baring, *Modern Egypt*, 2:203.
19. 'Abd al-Rahman al-Rafi'i, *Mustafa Kamel* (Cairo: Dar al-Ma'arif, 1984), 286. See also Bahr, *al-Aqbat fi-l-hayah al-siyasiya*, 136.
20. Bahr, *al-Aqbat fi-l-hayah al-siyasiya*, 137.
21. Carter, *The Copts in Egyptian Politics 1918–1952*, 11.
22. Louis Awad, *Tarikh al-fikr al-misri al-hadith min 'asr Isma'il ila Thawret 1919*, 1:116.
23. al-Bishri, *al-Muslimun wa-l-Aqbat*, 47, 64.
24. Bahr, *al-Aqbat fi-l-hayah al-siyasiya*, 57. See also Carter, *The Copts in Egyptian Politics 1918–1952*, 13.
25. Bahr, *al-Aqbat fi-l-hayah al-siyasiya*, 13, 63.
26. Bahr, *al-Aqbat fi-l-hayah al-siyasiya*, 62.
27. Carter, *The Copts in Egyptian Politics 1918–1952*, 13.
28. Bahr, *al-Aqbat fi-l-hayah al-siyasiya*, 62.
29. Bahr, *al-Aqbat fi-l-hayah al-siyasiya*, 64.
30. Bahr, *al-Aqbat fi-l-hayah al-siyasiya*, 65.
31. al-Bishri, *al-Muslimun wa-l-Aqbat*, 87.
32. Lutfi al-Sayyid, *Egypt and Cromer*, 157.
33. Lutfi al-Sayyid, *Egypt and Cromer*, 193.
34. Bahr, *al-Aqbat fi-l-hayah al-siyasiya*, 72.

Chapter 12

1. Fakhri 'Abd al-Nur, *Mudhakkirat thawra 1919* (Cairo: Dar El Shorouk, 1992).
2. Carter, *The Copts in Egyptian Politics 1918–1952*, 60.
3. Bahr, *al-Aqbat fi-l-hayah al-siyasiya*, 74.
4. Bahr, *al-Aqbat fi-l-hayah al-siyasiya*, 77.
5. Bahr, *al-Aqbat fi-l-hayah al-siyasiya*, 99.
6. George A.L. Lloyd, *Egypt since Cromer* (New York: Howard Fertig, 1969), 291.
7. 'Abd al-Nur, *Mudhakkirat thawra 1919*, 71.
8. 'Abd al-Nur, *Mudhakkirat thawra 1919*, 78. See also Bahr, *al-Aqbat fi-l-hayah al-siyasiya*, 85.

9. Tariq al-Bishri, *Sa'd Zaghlul yufawwid al-isti'mar 1920–1924* (Cairo: al-Hay'a al-Misriya al-'Amma li-l-Kitab, 1977), 30.
10. Tariq al-Bishri, *Sa'd Zaghlul yufawwid al-isti'mar 1920*–1924, 11.
11. Bahr, *al-Aqbat fi-l-hayah al-siyasiya*, 96.
12. Bahr, *al-Aqbat fi-l-hayah al-siyasiya*, 100.
13. Tariq al-Bishri, *Dirasa fi-l-muhadathat al-baritaniya al-misriya 1920–1924* (Cairo: Dar al-Hilal, 1997), 57.
14. al-Bishri, *al-Muslimun wa-l-Aqbat fi itar al-jam'a al-wataniya*, 164.
15. Bahr, *al-Aqbat fi-l-hayah al-siyasiya*, 111.
16. Yunan Labib Rizq, *Tarikh al-wizarat al-misriya* (Cairo: Markaz al-Dirasat al-Istiratijiya bi-l-Ahram, 1975), 265.
17. Carter, *The Copts in Egyptian Politics 1918–1952*, 143. Also see al-Bishri, *al-Muslimun wa-l-Aqbat fi itar al-jam'a al-wataniya*, 252.
18. Ibrahim, *The Copts of Egypt*, 185.
19. Raouf Abbas, *Thawrat Yulyu: ijabiyatuha wa salbiyatuha* (Cairo: Dar al-Hilal, 2003), 27. See also 'Abd al-Rahman al-Rafi'i, *Fi a'qab al-thawra al-misriya: thawrat 1919* (Cairo: Dar al-Ma'arif, 1984), 144.
20. George A. L. Lloyd, *Egypt since Cromer*, 2:96.
21. al-Rafi'i, *Fi a'qab al-thawra al-misriya*, 233.
22. al-Rafi'i, *Fi a'qab al-thawra al-misriya*, 255.
23. al-Rafi'i, *Fi a'qab al-thawra al-misriya*, 271.
24. al-Rafi'i, *Fi a'qab al-thawra al-misriya*, 300.
25. al-Rafi'i, *Fi a'qab al-thawra al-misriya*, 322.
26. Husayn Ahmad Amin, *Dalil al-Muslim al-hazin* (Dar al-'Ayn li-l-Nashr, 2007). This book deals with different aspects of the sayings of the Prophet (hadith) and how these were used politically. In 1983, the book received the distinguished prize at the Egyptian Book Fair as the best book of the year.
27. Rif'at al-Sa'id, *al-Irhab al-muta'aslim* (*Akhbar al-Youm*, Qita' al-Thaqafa, 2004), Cairo, 1:31. See also Ibn Khaldun, *al-Muqaddima* (Cairo: al-Matba'a al-Bahiya al-Misriya, n.d.), 311.
28. Rif'at al-Sa'id, *al-Irhab al-muta'aslim* (*Akhbar al-Youm*, Qita' al-Thaqafa, 2004), Cairo, 1:31.
29. 'Ali 'Abd al-Raziq, *al-Islam wa usul al-hukm* (Cairo: al-Hay'a al-Misriya li-l-Kitab, 1993).
30. Rif'at al-Sa'id, *Hassan al-Banna: al-shaykh al-musallah* (Cairo: al-Hay'a al-Misriya li-l-Kitab, vols. 1 and 2, 2004). See also Hilmi al-Namnam, *Hassan al-Banna al-ladhi la ya'rifuhu ahad* (Cairo: Maktabat Madbuli, 2013).
31. Rif'at al-Sa'id, 55.
32. Carter, *The Copts in Egyptian Politics 1918–1952*, 274.
33. Carter, *The Copts in Egyptian Politics 1918–1952*, 274.
34. Carter, *The Copts in Egyptian Politics 1918–1952*, 274.
35. Hassan, *Christians versus Muslims in Modern Egypt*, 53.
36. Hassan, *Christians versus Muslims in Modern Egypt*, 53.

37. Carter, *The Copts in Egyptian Politics 1918–1952*, 276.
38. Carter, *The Copts in Egyptian Politics 1918–1952*, 277.
39. Carter, *The Copts in Egyptian Politics 1918–1952*, 278.
40. Naguib Mahfouz, *The Cairo Trilogy*: *Palace Walk*, *Palace of Desire*, *Sugar Street*, trans. William Maynard Hutchins, Loren M. Kenny, Oliver E. Kenny, and Angele Botros Samaan (New York: Alfred A. Knopf, 1992), 1127–30.
41. 'Abd al-Rahman 'Ali, *al-Ikhwan al-Muslimun: fatawa fi-l-aqbat: al-dimuqratiya, al-mar'a wa-l-fann* (Cairo: Markaz al-Mahrusa li-l-Nashr wa-l-Khadamat al-Sahafiya wa-l-Ma'lumat, 2005), 24.
42. Ghali Shukri, *al-Aqbat fi watan mutaghayyir*, Kitab al-Ahali 29 (Cairo: *al-Ahali* newspaper, 1990), 201.
43. Shukri, *al-Aqbat fi watan mutaghayyir*, 231.

Chapter 13

1. Khalid Muhyi al-Din, *Al'an atakallam* (Cairo: al-Hay'a al-Misriya al-'Amma li-l-Kitab, 2014). This book details how the revolution evolved and the power struggle within the officers' rank and with the Brotherhood.
2. Muhammad Husayn Haykal, *Cutting the Lion's Tail: Suez Through Egyptian Eyes* (London: Corgi, 1988). See also Donald Neff, *Warriors at Suez: Eisenhower Takes America into the Middle East* (New York: Linden Press/ Simon Schuster, 1981); Anthony Nutting, *I Saw for Myself: The Aftermath of* Suez (New York: Doubleday, 1958), 94.
3. al-Sa'id, *Hassan al-Banna*. See also Hilmi al-Namnam, *Sayyid Qutb wa thawrat Yulyu* (Cairo: Maktabat Madbuli, 2013).
4. Saad Eddin Ibrahim, *The Copts of Egypt* (London: Minority Rights Group, 1996), 16. Today, al-Azhar University is a big institution, with about fifty-five colleges, but its standard of education is not high. Egypt has seventeen universities, but their quality of education is poor. Cairo University, the best of Egypt's seventeen universities, is ranked number 452 by the Center for World University Rankings out of 1,000 universities surveyed worldwide in 2018; its quality of education is ranked 569. See the Center for World University Ranking (CWUR) at http://cwur.org/2018-19.php.
5. The church lost much of its endowment as a result of the land reform law that allowed confiscation of land greater than a hundred acres owned by a person or institution.
6. Muhammad Husayn Haykal, *Autumn of Fury: The Assassination of Sadat* (New York: Random House, 1983), 158.
7. al-Bishri, *al-Muslimun wa-l-Aqbat*, 644.
8. Guirguis and van Doorn-Harder, *The Emergence of the Modern Coptic Papacy*, 125.
9. Guirguis and van Doorn-Harder, *The Emergence of the Modern Coptic Papacy*, 125.
10. Guirguis and von Doorn-Harder, *The Emergence of the Modern Coptic Papacy*, 125.

11. Hassan, *Christians versus Muslims in Modern Egypt*, 67.
12. Hassan, *Christians versus Muslims in Modern Egypt*, 129.
13. Guirguis and van Doorn-Harder, *The Emergence of the Modern Coptic Papacy*, 125.

Chapter 14

1. Ahmad Baha' al-Din, *Muhawarati ma' al-Sadat* (Cairo: al-Hay'a al-Misriya al-'Amma li-l-Kitab, 2013).
2. David Hirst and Irene Beeson, *Sadat* (London: Faber and Faber, 1982).
3. Muhammad Husayn Haykal, *The Road to Ramadan* (New York: Quadrangle/ The New York Times Book Co., 1975), 122.
4. Muhammad Sa'id al-'Ashmawi, *al-Islam al-siyasi* (Cairo: Dar Sina li-l-Nashr, 1987), 154.
5. Ghali Shukri, *al-Thawra al-mudadda*, Kitab al-Ahali 15 (Cairo: *al-Ahali* newspaper, 1987), 75.
6. Dreyfuss, *Devil's Game*, 176.
7. Dreyfuss, *Devil's Game*, 178.
8. Dreyfuss, *Devil's Game*, 166.
9. Dreyfuss, *Devil's Game*, 164. Shaykh 'Umar 'Abd al-Rahman (PhD from al-Azhar University) is an important jihadist. He issued a fatwa that deleted five hundred *aya*s based on the *al-naskh wa-l-mansukh* principle. Other Islamic scholars deleted far fewer *aya*s. (The Qu'ran is divided into *sura*s [chapters], which are in turn divided into *aya*s [verses].) Shaykh 'Umar 'Abd al-Rahman was sentenced to jail for life in the United States for his role in encouraging the attack on the World Trade Center in 1993.
10. Dreyfuss, *Devil's Game*, 175.
11. Dreyfuss, *Devil's Game*, 72.
12. al-'Ashmawi, *al-Islam al-siyasi*, 183.
13. Shukri, *al-Aqbat fi watan mutaghayyir*, 175–76.
14. Ghali Shukri, *al-Thawra al-mudadda*, 15: 75–76.
15. Haykal, *Autumn of Fury*, 162.
16. Saad Eddin Ibrahim, *The Copts of Egypt* (Cairo: Ibn Khaldun Center for Development Studies, Cairo, 1995), 18. It is now out of print, but it can be downloaded from the internet, http://minorityrights.org/publications/the-copts-of-egypt-january-1996/. See also Ghali Shukri, *al-Aqbat fi watan mutaghayyir*, Kitab al-Ahali 29 (Cairo: *al-Ahali* newspaper, 1990) 89.
17. Gamal Badawi, *al-Fitna al-ta'fiya fi Misr githuriha* (Cairo: al-Markaz al-'Arabi li-l-Sahafa, 1997) 74.
18. Ghali Shukri, *al-Aqbat fi watan mutaghayyir*, Kitab al-Ahali 29, 23, 68.
19. Saad Eddin Ibrahim, *The Copts of Egypt*, 17.
20. Saad Eddin Ibrahim, *The Copts of Egypt*, 6. See also Abu-l 'Ila Madi, *al-Mas'ala al-qibtiya wa-l-sharia wa-l sahwah al-islamiya* (Cairo: Safir al-Dawliya li-l-Nashr, 2007), 37; Usama Salama, *Masir al-Aqbat fi Misr* (Cairo: Dar al-Khayal, 1998), 27.

21. Saad Eddin Ibrahim, *The Copts of Egypt*, 6.
22. Salama, *Masir al-Aqbat fi Misr*, 9. Also see Saad Eddin Ibrahim et. al, *The Copts of Egypt*, 21.
23. Salama, *Masir al-Aqbat fi Misr*, 127.
24. Vamik D. Volkan, *The Need to Have Enemies and Allies: From Clinical Practice to International Relationships* (Northvale, NJ: Aronson, 1988).
25. Bahr, *al-Aqbat fi-l-hayah al-siyasiya*, 156.
26. Salama, *Masir al-Aqbat fi Misr*, 140.
27. Saad Eddin Ibrahim, *The Copts of Egypt*, 23. See also Salama, *Masir al-Aqbat fi Misr*, 127.
28. Tariq al-Bishri, *al-Dawla wa-l-kanisa* (Cairo: Dar El Shorouk, 2012), 22–25. See also Madi, *al-Mas'ala al-qibtiya*, 56.
29. Dreyfuss, *Devil's Game*, 162.
30. Baha' al-Din, *Muhawarati ma' al-Sadat*, 119.
31. Haykal, *Autumn of Fury*, 131. See also 'Abd al-Rahman Abu al-Khayr, *Qissati ma' al-jama'at al-islamiya* (Cairo: Dar al-Buhuth al-'Ilmiya, 1980).
32. Shukri, *al-Aqbat fi watan mutaghayyir*, 29:100.
33. Sana' al-Sa'id, *al-Anba Shunuda al-Thalith: dunya wa din* (Cairo: al-Hay'a al-Misriya li-l-Kitab, 2004), 224.
34. Abu-l Khayr, *Qissati ma' al-jama'at al-islamiya*, 218.
35. Baha' al-Din, *Muhawarati ma' al-Sadat*, 172.
36. Haykal, *Autumn of Fury*, 221.
37. Haykal, *Autumn of Fury*, 221.
38. Haykal, *Autumn of Fury*, 230.
39. Haykal, *Autumn of Fury*, 232.
40. Baha' al-Din, *Muhawarati ma' al-Sadat*, 131.
41. Haykal, *Autumn of Fury*, 253. See also Salah Abu Isma'il, *al-Shahada: shahadat al-shaykh Salah Abu Isma'il fi qadiyyat tanzim al-jihad* (Cairo: Dar al-I'tisam, 1984).
42. Mahmud Amin al-'Alim, *al-Hilm wa-l-waqi' wa-l-mustaqbal* (Nicosia: IBAL Publishing Institution L.T.D.), 286.

Chapter 15

1. https://www.middleeastmonitor.com/20140205-egypts-central-bank. See also https://www.middleeastmonitor.com/20140208-egyptians-living-and-working-abroad-transfer-19-billion/.
2. Carrie Rosefsky Wickham, *The Muslim Brotherhood* (Princeton, NJ: Princeton University Press, 2013), 76.
3. Wickham, *The Muslim Brotherhood*, 77.
4. Tarek Osman, *Egypt on the Brink* (New Haven: Yale University Press, 2013), 186.
5. Saad Eddin Ibrahim, *Egypt, Islam, and Democracy* (Cairo: American University in Cairo Press, 1996), 73.
6. 'Abd al-Ghaffar 'Aziz, *Man qatal Farag Fuda?* (Cairo: Dar al-I'lam al-Dawli, 1992). See also Fouda, *al-Haqiqa al-gha'iba*.

7. Ibrahim, *Egypt, Islam and Democracy*, 73.
8. Osman, *Egypt on the Brink*, 106, 201–206.
9. Osman, *Egypt on the Brink*, 201–206.
10. Tahsin Bashir, "I Support You but I Do Not Endorse You," an article in *al-Wafd*, September 1992. We no longer have the article in Arabic, but it is referred to in the *New York Times* by its English title as written here. See URL: https://www.nytimes.com/2002/06/14/world/tahseen-bashir-urbane-egyptian-diplomat-dies-at-77.html.
11. Osman, *Egypt on the Brink*, 204.
12. Osman, *Egypt on the Brink*, 204. See also Dreyfuss, *Devil's Game*, 168.
13. Muhammad Abu-l Ghar, "Qabilat al-Ikhwan al-Muslimin," *al-Masry al-youm* (January 8, 2010). https://www.almasryalyoum.com/news/details/213820.
14. Dreyfuss, *Devil's Game*, 181.
15. Mohamed Omara, *Fi al-mas'ala al-qibtiya: haqa'iq wa awham* (Cairo: Dar El Shorouk, 2001), 117.
16. Hassan, *Christians versus Muslims in Modern Egypt*, 117.
17. al-Bishri, *al-Dawla wa-l-kanisa*, 55–64.
18. Shaykh Wagdy Ghoneim and other radical Islamists preached that it was un-Islamic to give holiday greetings to Christians during their religious holidays. See "*Hal yajuz tahni'at al-aqbat bi-a'yadihim*," https://www.youtube.com/watch?v=ZxZ1S0A3LXM. Other well-known Islamic scholars, such as Zaghlul al-Nagar and Mohamed Omara, were critical of Christianity and Christians. Their widely popular writings were offensive to many, and contributed to Muslim hostility against Christians. See Muhammad Munir Mujahid, *al-Aqbat bayn thawratayn*, ed. Solomon Shafiq (Cairo: Mubadarat al-Dirasat al-Naqdiya li-Masihiyyi Misr wa-l-Sharq, 2014), 359–68.
19. Hassan, S.S. *Christians versus Muslims in Modern Egypt*, 111–12, 118.
20. Elsässer, *The Coptic Question in the Mubarak Era*, 190.
21. Shaykh Wagdy Ghoneim, *al-Watan* newspaper, January 6, 2013. A great deal of information about Wagdy Ghoneim is available in Arabic on the Internet.
22. Mujahid, *al-Aqbat bayn thawratayn*, 365.
23. Mujahid, *al-Aqbat bayn thawratayn*, 365. See also Elsässer, *The Coptic Question in the Mubarak Era*, 190.
24. Elsässer, *The Coptic Question in the Mubarak Era*, 203.
25. S.S. Hassan, *Christians versus Muslims in Modern Egypt*, Oxford University Press, 2003, 118.
26. Saad Eddin Ibrahim, *Egypt, Islam, and Democracy* (Cairo: American University in Cairo Press, 1996), 69.
27. Muhammad Sa'id al-'Ashmawi, "Fatwa wa-Maqalla," *al-Ahaly* (April 10, 1996).
28. Mujahid, *al-Aqbat bayn thawratayn*, 365.
29. Carrie Rosefsky Wickham, *The Muslim Brotherhood* (Princeton, NJ: Princeton University Press, 2013), 70. Similar remarks surfaced by other leaders of the Brotherhood and other jihadists.

30. Volkan, *The Need to Have Enemies and Allies.*
31. Salama, *Masir al-Aqbat fi Misr*, 24.
32. al-Bishri, *al-Dawla wa-l-kanisa*, 17.
33. Galal Amin, *Madha hadatha li-l-thawra al-misriya* (Cairo: Dar El Shorouk, 2012), 207.
34. Osman, *Egypt on the Brink*, 165.
35. James V. Grimaldi and Robert O'Harrow Jr., "In Egypt, Corruption Cases Had an American Root," an article published in *The Washington Post* on October 19, 2011. Available online at https://www.washingtonpost.com/investigations/in-egypt-corruption-had-an-american-root/2011/10/07/gIQAApWoyL_story.html?noredirect=on&utm_term=.9ed036bf853a
36. Sami Zubaida, "The Politics of the Islamic Investments Companies in Egypt," *British Journal of Middle Eastern Studies* 17, no. 2 (1990): 152.
37. Nasr Hamid Abu Zayd, *al-Tafkir fi zaman al-takfir* (Cairo: Dar Sina li-l-Nashr, 1995).
38. Galal Amin, *Mihnat al-din wa-l-dunya* (Cairo: Dar El Shorouk, 2013), 128, 174.
39. Amin, *Mihnat al-din wa-l-dunya*, 14, 172, 128.
40. Baring, *Modern Egypt*, 2:206.
41. Wickham, *The Muslim Brotherhood*, 82–83, 86.
42. Wickham, *The Muslim Brotherhood*, 82–83, 86.
43. Muhammad Haykal, interview in *al-Masry al-youm*, October 21, 2009.
44. al-'Ashmawi, *al-Islam al-siyasi*, 166.
45. Amin, *Madha hadatha li-l-thawra al-misriya*, 194.
46. Amin, *Madha hadatha li-l-thawra al-misriya*, 194.
47. Amin, *Madha hadatha li-l-thawra al-misriya*, 198.
48. Wael Ghoneim, *Revolution 2.0: The Power of People Is Greater Than the People in Power* (New York: Houghton Mifflin Harcourt, 2012), 82–125. This chapter deals with how the young people prepared for January 2011 using electronic media.

Chapter 16

1. Wickham, *The Muslim Brotherhood*, 164.
2. *BBC Frontline*, September 17, 2013.
3. 'Abd al-Halim Qandil, *al-Ayyam al-akhira* (Cairo: Dar al-Thaqafa al-Gadida, 2008), 51.
4. William Wan and Ernesto London, "Egypt's aid from U.S. in peril amid crackdown on pro-democracy groups," an article in *The Washington Post*, February 4, 2012, https://www.washingtonpost.com/world/national-security/egypts-aid-from-us-in-peril-amid-crackdown-on-pro-democracy-groups/2012/02/03/gIQAp5GQqQ_story.html?utm_term=.92d73b784b53.
5. *Al-Ahram* newspaper, November 13, 2009.
6. *al-Masry al-youm* newspaper, January 23, 2011.
7. Wickham, *The Muslim Brotherhood*, 170.

8. The cases of Muslim Brotherhood leaders escaping from jail immediately after the January 25 revolt included Muhammad Morsi, who later became President of Egypt. An investigation into Morsi's escape from jail began while he was Egypt's president.
9. Wickham, *The Muslim Brotherhood*, 155.
10. Wickham, *The Muslim Brotherhood*, 156.
11. The United States has a long history of preventing democracy in Egypt; see Jason Brownlee, *Democracy Prevention: The Politics of the U.S.–Egyptian Alliance* (New York: Cambridge University Press, 2012).
12. Amin, *Madha hadatha li-l-thawra al-misriya*, 160.
13. Hani Samir, *Madhbahat Maspero* (Cairo: Dar wa Maktabat al-Hurriya, 2013), 52. This reference documented in great details what happened during this period. See also Mujahid, *al-Aqbat bayn thawratayn*, 341.
14. Jason Brownlee, *Violence Against Copts in Egypt* (Austin: Carnegie Endowment for International Peace, 2013), 14. This publication can be accessed on the internet using the title of this reference.
15. Shukri, *al-Aqbat fi watan mutaghayyir*, Kitab al-Ahali 29, 231.
16. Samir, *Madhbahat Maspero*, 65.
17. Samir, *Madhbahat Maspero*, 154.
18. Brownlee, *Violence Against Copts in Egypt*, 15.
19. Wickham, *The Muslim Brotherhood*, 248.
20. Fikry Andrawes, *al-'Aql wa-l-siyasa* (Cairo: Dar al-Thaqafa al-Gadida, 2014), 53.
21. Nelly van Doorn-Harder, a talk on Morsi at Duke University, February 13, 2013. URL: https://www.youtube.com/watch?v=gynwrDFHXnU.
22. Muhammad Habib, in *al-Masry al-youm* (newspaper), December 20, 2014.
23. Interview with Pope Tawadros conducted by Zina Yazgi from Sky News Network on January 5, 2015.
24. Mujahid, *al-Aqbat bayn thawratayn*, 341.
25. Report issued by Shabab Maspero li-l-Tanmiya wa Huquq al-Insan, Cairo, 2013.
26. Mujahid, *al-Aqbat bayn thawratayn*, 346, 26. See also appendix on page 421 of the same reference.
27. *Al-Ahram* newspaper, December 27, 2014.
28. *Al-Watan* newspaper, September 12, 2014.
29. Salim Hassan, *Mawsu'at Misr al-qadima* (Cairo: al-Hay'a al-Misriya al-'Amma li-l-Kitab, 1992), 1:398.

Epilogue

1. Gerard Russell, *Heirs to Forgotten Kingdoms* (New York: Basic Books, 2014).

Appendix 1

1. Taha Hussein, *The Days* (Cairo: AUC Press, 1932). This is his autobiography in three parts. It was also published in Arabic as *al-Ayam* (Cairo: Dar al-Ma'arif, 1979).

2. Suzanne Taha Hussein, *Ma'ak* (Cairo: Dar al-Ma'arif, 1982). See also Suzanne Taha Hussein, *Avec toi de la France à l'Egypte: un extraordinaire amour, Suzanne et Taha Hussein, 1915–1973* (Paris: Le Cerf, 2011).
3. Ra'uf Salama Musa, *Salama Musa Abi* (Cairo: Dar wa Matabi' al-Mustaqbal, 1992), 33.
4. Vernon Egger, *A Fabian in Egypt: Salama Musa and the Rise of the Professional Class in Egypt, 1909–1939* (Lanham: University Press of America, 1987), 16.
5. Egger, *A Fabian in Egypt*, 21.
6. Ra'uf Salama Musa, *Salama Musa Abi*, 69.
7. Musa, *Salama Musa Abi*, 74.
8. Musa, *Salama Musa Abi*, 92.
10. Musa, *Salama Musa Abi*, 118.
11. Carter, *The Copts in Egyptian Politics, 1918–1952*, 2:223.
12. Carter, *The Copts in Egyptian Politics*, 211.
13. Musa, *Salama Musa Abi*, 145.
14. Musa, *Salama Musa Abi*, 146.
15. Musa, *Salama Musa Abi*, 146.
16. Sami A. Hanna and George H. Gardener, *Arab Socialism* (University of Utah Press, 1969), 55, 275.
17. Musa, *Salama Musa Abi*, 75.
18. Musa, *Salama Musa Abi*, 160.
19. Eric Davis, *Challenging Colonialism: Bank Misr and Egyptian Industrialization, 1920–1941* (Princeton: Princeton University Press, 1983), 145, 20, 117.
20. Davis, *Challenging Colonialism*, 117.
21. Jacques Berque, *Egypt: Imperialism and Revolution* (New York and Washington: Praeger, 1967), 448.
22. Davis, *Challenging Colonialism*, 142.
23. Davis, *Challenging Colonialism*, 142, 90, and 139
24. Davis, *Challenging Colonialism*, 206.
25. Davis, *Challenging Colonialism*, 162.
26. Davis, *Challenging Colonialism*, 164.
27. Davis, *Challenging Colonialism*, 166–7.
28. Davis, *Challenging Colonialism*, 90 and 139.
29. Davis, *Challenging Colonialism*, 166 and 209.
30. Davis, *Challenging Colonialism*, 166 and 209.
31. Mostafa el-Feki, *Copts in Egyptian Politics, 1919–1952* (Cairo: General Egyptian Book Organization, 1991), 63–4.
32. el-Feki, *Copts in Egyptian Politics, 1919–1952*, 97–99.
33. el-Feki, *Copts in Egyptian Politics, 1919–1952*, 99.
34. Ahmad Baha' al-Din, "al-Faris al-Zahaby li-l-haraka al-watania," in *Kalemat wa-mawakef*, edited by Mona Makram Ebeid (Cairo: al-Hay'a al-Misriya al-'Amma li-l-Kitab, 1990) 17.
35. el-Feki, *Copts in Egyptian Politics, 1919–1952*, 93.

36. Yunan Labib Rizq, *al-Wafd wa-l-kitab al-aswad* (Cairo: Markaz al-Dirasat al-Siyasiya wa-l-Istiratijiya, Mu'assasat al-Ahram, 2005). See also el-Feki, *Copts in Egyptian Politics, 1919–1952*, 115; Berque, *Egypt: Imperialism and Revolution* (Praeger Publishers, 1972), 559.
37. el-Feki, *Copts in Egyptian Politics, 1919–1952* (1991), 117.
38. el-Feki, *Copts in Egyptian Politics, 1919–1952*, 129.
39. el-Feki, *Copts in Egyptian Politics, 1919–1952*, 144.
40. al-Bishri, *al-Muslimun wa-l-Aqbat*, 556. Also see el-Feki, *Copts in Egyptian Politics, 1919–1952*, 554.
41. Muhammad Husayn Haykal, *Mudhakirat fi al-siyasa al-misriya* (Dar al-Ma'arif, 1977), 2:250.
42. 'Abd al-Rahman al-Kawakibi, *Taba'i' al-istibdad wa masari' al-isti'bad*, 1st ed., 1902; (Cairo: Dar El Shorouk, 2009). Al-Kawakbi was a Syrian Islamic reformer who wrote one of the most important Arabic books of the nineteenth century on the nature of autocratic rulers and how they enslaved their people; he tried to modernize the archaic Islamic teachings, which threatened the Turkish rulers. He escaped to Egypt, but the Turkish managed to assassinate him in Egypt.
43. Thomas Philipp, *Jurji Zaydan and the Foundations of Arab Nationalism: A Study* (New York: Syracuse University Press, 2010).
44. Philipp, *Jurji Zaydan*, 37.
45. Philipp, *Jurji Zaydan*, 58.
46. Philipp, *Jurji Zaydan*, 34.
47. Philipp, *Jurji Zaydan*, 420.
48. Philipp, *Jurji Zaydan*, 100.

BIBLIOGRAPHY

Sources in English

'Abd al-'Aziz Mahjub, Salah, trans. *Iohannis Ephesini Historiae Ecclesiasticae Pars Tertia.* Cairo: High National Council for Culture, 2000, 40.

Agar, Michael H. *Language Shock: Understanding The Culture Of Conversation.* New York: William Morrow, 1994.

Armanios, Febe. *Coptic Christianity in Ottoman Egypt.* New York: Oxford University Press, 2011.

Atiya, Aziz S. *The Coptic Encyclopedia.* New York: Macmillan, 1991.

Athanasius. *Life of Saint Antony.* Red Sea, Egypt: St. Antony Monastery, 1992.

Atiya, Aziz S. "Ayyubid Dynasty and the Copts." In Atiya, *The Coptic Encyclopedia,* 1:315.

———. "Cyril I, Saint." In Atiya, *The Coptic Encyclopedia,* 3:671–675.

———. "Origen's Writings." In Atiya, *The Coptic Encyclopedia,* 6:1852–1844.

———. "Patriarchs, Dates and Succession of." In *The Coptic Encyclopedia,* 6:1913–1920.

Bagnall, Roger S. *Early Christian Books in Egypt.* Princeton, NJ: Princeton University Press, 2009.

Baring, Evelyn, Earl of Cromer. *Modern Egypt.* New York: Macmillan, 1908.

Barnard, Leslie W. "Clement of Alexandria." In *The Coptic Encyclopedia,* 2:262, 263.

———. "Athanasius and the Melitian Schism in Egypt." In *Journal of Egyptian Archaeology* (1973) 59:181–189.

Barnes, Timothy D. *Athanasius and Constantius.* Cambridge, MA: Harvard University Press, 1993.

Berque, Jacques. *Egypt: Imperialism and Revolution.* Translated by Jean Stewart. New York and Washington: Praeger Publishers, 1967.

Bishai, Wilson B. "Coptic Lexical Influence on Egyptian Arabic." In *Journal of Near Eastern Studies* 23, no. 1 (1964), 39–47.

Bolman, Elizabeth S., ed. *Monastic Visions.* New Haven, CT: Yale University Press, 2002.

Brakke, David. *Athanasius and Asceticism.* Baltimore, MD: John Hopkins University Press, 1995.

Brownlee, Jason. *Democracy Prevention: The Politics of the U.S.–Egyptian Alliance*. New York: Cambridge University Press, 2012.

———. *Violence Against Copts in Egypt*. Austin: Carnegie Endowment for International Peace, 2013. http://carnegieendowment.org/files/violence_against_copts3.pdf.

Butler, Alfred J. *The Arab Conquest of Egypt and the Last Thirty Years of the Roman Dominion*. New York: Oxford University Press, 1998.

Carter, B.L. *The Copts in Egyptian Politics, 1918–1952*. New York: Routledge, 1986.

Cody, Aelred. "Coptic Calendar." *The Coptic Encyclopedia*, Atiya, ed., 2:433.

Coquin, René-Georges, and Maurice Martin. "Diocletian." In *The Coptic Encyclopedia*, Atiya, ed., 3:907.

Davis, Eric. *Challenging Colonialism: Bank Misr and Egyptian Industrialization, 1920–1941*. Princeton: Princeton University Press, 1983.

Davis, Stephen J. *The Early Coptic Papacy*. Cairo: American University in Cairo Press, 2004.

Doresse, Jean. *The Secret Books of the Egyptian Gnostics*. New York: MJF Books, 1986.

Draper, Thomas J. "Ibn Taymiyyah: The Struggles of a Mujtahid under the Bahri Mamluk Sultans." Master's thesis, Ball State University, 2013.

Dreyfuss, Robert. *Devil's Game: How the United States Helped Unleash Fundamentalist Islam*. New York: Henry Holt, 2005.

Dungan, David L. *Constantine's Bible*. Minneapolis: Fortress Press, 2007.

Egger, Vernon. *A Fabian in Egypt: Salama Musa and the Rise of the Professional Classes in Egypt, 1909-1939*. Lanham: University Press of America, 1986.

Elsässer, Sebastian. *The Coptic Question in the Mubarak Era*. New York: Oxford University Press, 2014.

Eusebius. *Church History, Life of Constantine the Great*. Translated by G.A. Williamson. London: Penguin Books, 1952, 1:490.

el-Feki, Mostafa. *Copts in Egyptian Politics, 1919–1952*. Cairo: General Egyptian Book Organization, 1991.

Frend, W.H.C. "Diocletian." In Atiya, *The Coptic Encyclopedia*, 3:904–908.

———. "Monothelitism." In Atiya, *The Coptic Encyclopedia*, 5:1678.

Gabra, Gawdat. *Coptic Monasteries*. Cairo: American University in Cairo Press, 2002.

Gabra, Gawdat, and Hany N. Takla, eds. *Christianity and Monasticism in Upper Egypt*. Vol. 1: *Akhmim and Sohag*. Cairo: American University in Cairo Press, 2008.

Ghoneim, Wael. *Revolution 2.0: The Power of People Is Greater Than the People in Power*. New York: Houghton Mifflin Harcourt, 2012.

Guirguis, Magdi, and Nelly Van Doorn-Harder. *The Emergence of the Modern Coptic Papacy: The Popes of Egypt*. Cairo: American University in Cairo Press, 2011.

Hamilton, Alastair. *The Copts and the West 1439–1822*. New York: Oxford University Press, 2006.

Hanna, Nelly. *In Praise of Books: A Cultural History of Cairo's Middle Class, Sixteenth Through the Eighteenth Century*. Syracuse, NY: Syracuse University Press, 2003.

Hanna, Sami A., and George H. Gardener. *Arab Socialism*. Utah: University of Utah Press, 1969.

Hanson, R.B.C. "Origen." In Atiya, *The Coptic Encyclopedia*, 6:1846–1851.

Hassan, Fikry. "Extreme Nile Floods and Famines in Medieval Egypt (AD 930–1500) and Their Climatic Implications." In *Quaternary International*, 2007, 173–174. https://www.researchgate.net/publication/223718671_Extreme_Nile_Floods_and_Famines_in_Medieval_Egypt_AD_930-1500_and_Their_Climatic_Implications.

Hassan, S.S. *Christians versus Muslims in Modern Egypt: The Century-Long Struggle for Coptic Equality*. Oxford: Oxford University Press, 2003.

Hathaway, Jane, ed. *Al-Jabarti's History of Egypt*. Princeton, NJ: Markus Weiner, 2009.

Haykal, Muhammad Husayn. *Autumn of Fury: The Assassination of Sadat*. New York: Random House, 1983.

———. *Cutting the Lion's Tail: Suez Through Egyptian Eyes*. London: Corgi, 1988.

———. *The Road to Ramadan*. New York: Quadrangle/The New York Times Book Co., 1975.

Herold, J. Christopher. *Bonaparte in Egypt*. New York: Harper & Row, 1962.

Hirst, David, and Irene Beeson. *Sadat*. London: Faber and Faber, 1982.

Hourani, Albert. *History of the Arab People*. Cambridge, MA: Harvard University Press, 1991.

Hussein, Suzanne Taha. *Avec toi. de la France à l'Egypte: un extraordinaire amour, Suzanne et Taha Hussein, 1915–1973*. Paris: Le Cerf, 2011.

Hussein, Taha. *The Days*. Cairo: AUC Press, 1932.

Ibn 'Abd al-Hakam. *The History of the Conquest of Egypt, North Africa, and Spain*. The Netherlands: Leiden University, 1930.

Ibrahim, Saad Eddin. *The Copts of Egypt*. London: Minority Rights Group, 1996.

———. *Egypt, Islam, and Democracy*. Cairo: American University in Cairo Press, 1996.

Ibrahim, Vivian. *The Copts of Egypt: The Challenges of Modernization and Identity*. New York: Tauris Academic Studies, 2011.

Ishaq, Emil Maher. "Coptic Language Spoken." In Atiya, *The Coptic Encyclopedia*, 2:604–607.

al-Jabarti, 'Abd al-Rahman. *Al-Jabarti's History of Egypt*. Edited by Jane Hathaway. Princeton: Markus Weiner Publisher, 2009.

John of Nikiou. "Yohan b'Nikiou." *Majallat Sahyun*. Cairo, 1948, 135–150.

Kamil, Jill. *Christianity in the Land of the Pharaohs*. New York: Routledge, 2002.

Kasser, Rodolphe, Marvin Meyer, and Gregor Wurst, eds. *The Gospel of Judas: From Codex Tchacos*. Washington, DC: National Geographic Society, 2006.

Kelley, J.F. "British Isles, Coptic Influences." In Atiya, *The Coptic Encyclopedia*, 2:416.

Khalil, Samir S.J. "Origen in the Copto-Arabic Tradition." In Atiya, *The Coptic Encyclopedia*, 6:1851–1852.

Layton, Richard A. *Didymus the Blind and His Circle in Late-Antique Alexandria*. Champaign: University of Illinois Press, 2004.

el-Leithy, Tamer. "Coptic Culture and Conversion in Medieval Cairo, 1293–1524." PhD diss., Princeton University, 2004.

———. "Sufis, Copts, and the Politics of Piety: Moral Regulation in Fourteenth-Century Upper Egypt." In *Le développement du soufisme*, edited by Richard McGregor and Adam Sabra. Cairo: Institut Français d'Archéologie Orientale, 2006, 75–119.

Lewis, Naphtali. *Life of Egypt under Roman Rule*. Oxford, UK: Clarendon Press, 1983.

Lloyd, George A.L. *Egypt since Cromer*. New York: Howard Fertig, 1969.

Louca, Anwar. "General Ya'qub." In Atiya, *The Coptic Encyclopedia*, 7:2349–2353.

Lutfi al-Sayyid, Afaf. *Egypt and Cromer: A Study in Anglo-Egyptian Relations*. London: John Murray, 1968.

Mahfouz, Naguib. *The Cairo Trilogy*: *Palace Walk*, *Palace of Desire*, *Sugar Street*. Translated by William Maynard Hutchins, Loren M. Kenny, Oliver E. Kenny, and Angele Botros Samaan. New York: Alfred A. Knopf. Cairo: American University in Cairo Press, 1992.

al-Maqrizi, Taqi-al-Din Abu-l 'Abbas. *A Short History of the Copts and their Church*. Translated by S.C. Malan. Whitefish, MT: Kessinger Publishing, 1873.

al-Masri, Iris Habib. *The Story of the Copts*. Cairo: The Middle East Council of Churches, 1978.

Mayer, Thomas. *The Changing Past: Egyptian Historiography of the Urabi Revolt, 1882–1983*. Gainesville: University Press of Florida, 1988.

Meinardus, Otto F.A. *Monks and Monasteries of the Egyptian Deserts*. Cairo: AUC Press, 1992.

Nabulsi, 'Uthman ibn Ibrahim. *The Sword of Ambition*. Translated by Luke Yarbrough. New York: New York University Press, 2016.

Neff, Donald. *Warriors at Suez: Eisenhower Takes America into the Middle East*. New York: Linden Press/Simon & Schuster, 1981.

Nigosain, Solomon A. "Armenians and the Copts." In Atiya, *The Coptic Encyclopedia*, 1:234–235.

Nutting, Anthony. *I Saw for Myself: The Aftermath of Suez*. New York: Doubleday, 1958.

Osman, Tarek. *Egypt on the Brink*. New Haven: Yale University Press, 2013.

O'Sullivan, Shaun. "Coptic Conversion and Islamization of Egypt." *Mamluk Studies Review* X, no. 2 (2006): 65–79. http://mamluk.uchicago.edu/MSR_X-2_2006-OSullivan.pdf.

Philipp, Thomas. *Jurji Zaydan and the Foundations of Arab Nationalism: A Study*. Syracuse, NY: Syracuse University Press, 2010.

Poncaglia, M.P. "Didymus the Blind." In Atiya, *The Coptic Encyclopedia*, 3:900.

Rousseau, Philip. *Pachomius: The Making of Community in Fourth-Century Egypt*. Berkeley: University of California Press, 1999.
Rubenson, Samuel. *Letters of St. Antony: Monasticism and the Making of a Saint*. Minneapolis: Fortress Press, 1995.
———. "The Transition from Coptic to Arabic." *Égypte/Monde Arabe*, 1st series, 27–28 (1996): 77–92. https://journals.openedition.org/ema/1920.
Russell, Gerard. *Heirs to Forgotten Kingdoms*. New York: Basic Books, 2014.
Schaff, Philip, and Henry Wace. *A Select Library of Nicene and Post-Nicene Fathers of the Christian Church*. Grand Rapids, MI: Wm. B. Eerdmans, 1952.
Sharkey, Heather J. *American Evangelicals in Egypt: Missionary Encounter in an Age of Empire*. Princeton: Princeton University Press, 2008.
Spanel, Donald B. "Theophilus." In Atiya, *The Coptic Encyclopedia*, 7:2247–2253.
Stewart, Randall. "Constantine I." In Atiya, *The Coptic Encyclopedia*, 2:588–590.
Swanson, Mark N. *The Coptic Papacy in Islamic Egypt 641–1517*. Cairo: American University in Cairo Press, 2010.
Tagher, Jacques. *Christians in Muslim Egypt: A Historical Study of the Relation Between Copts and Muslims from 640 to 1922*. Translated by Ragia N. Makar. Altenberge: Oros Verlag, 1998.
Timbie, Janet. "Melitian Schism." In Atiya, *The Coptic Encyclopedia*, 5:1584–1585.
Tollinton, R.B. *Clement of Alexandria: A Study in Christian Liberalism*. London: Williams and Norgate, 1914.
Torjesen, Karen. "Council of Nicaea." In Atiya, *The Coptic Encyclopedia*, 6:1790–1792.
Volkan, Vamik D. *The Need to Have Enemies and Allies: From Clinical Practice to International Relationships*. Northvale, NJ: Aronson, 1988.
Wassermann, M. "The Process of Islamization in Egypt." Master's thesis, School of Oriental and African Studies, University of London, 1992.
Watterson, Barbara. *Coptic Egypt*. Edinburgh: Scottish Academic Press, 1988.
Wickham, Carrie Rosefsky. *The Muslim Brotherhood*. Princeton: Princeton University Press, 2013.
Youssef, Ahmed Abdel-Hamid. *From Pharaoh's Lips: Ancient Egyptian Language in the Arabic of Today*. Cairo: American University in Cairo Press, 2003.
Zeman Rothkopf, Carol. *The Opening of the Suez Canal, November 1869: A Water Gateway Joins East and West*. New York: Franklin Watts, 1973.
Zubaida, Sami. "The Politics of the Islamic Investments Companies in Egypt." *British Journal of Middle Eastern Studies* 17, no. 2 (1990): 152.

Sources in Arabic

al-'Abbadi, Mustafa. *Maktabat al-Iskandariya al-qadima*. Cairo: Maktabat al-Anglo al-Misriya, 1977.
Abbas, Raouf. *Thawrat Yulyu: ijabiyatuha wa salbiyatuha*. Cairo: Dar al-Hilal, 2003.
'Abd al-Hamid, Ra'fat. *al-Dawla wa-l-kanisa*. Cairo: Dar al-Ma'arif, 1983.
'Abd al-Jalil, 'Umar Sabir. *Tarikh Misr li-Hanna al-Niqyusi: ru'ya qibtiya li-l-fath al-islami*. Cairo: 'Ayn li-l-Dirasat wa-l-Buhuth al-Insaniya wa-l-Ijtima'iya, 2003.

'Abd al-Nur, Fakhri. *Mudhakkirat thawra 1919*. Cairo: Dar El Shorouk, 1992.
'Abd al-Rahman, 'Umar. "Mawqif al-Qur'an min khusumuh kama tusawirruh surat al-Tawba." PhD diss., al-Azhar University, 1972.
'Abd al-Raziq, 'Ali. *al-Islam wa usul al-hukm*. Cairo: al-Hay'a al-Misriya li-l-Kitab, 1993.
Abu al-Khayr, 'Abd al-Rahman. *Qissati ma' al-jama'at al-islamiya*. Cairo: Dar al-Buhuth al-'Ilmiya, 1980.
Abu Isma'il, Salah. *al-Shahada: shahadat al-shaykh Salah Abu Isma'il fi qadiyyat tanzim al-jihad*. Cairo: Dar al-I'tisam, 1984.
Abu Zayd, Nasr Hamid. *al-Tafkir fi zaman al-takfir*. Cairo: Dar Sina li-l-Nashr, 1995.
'Afifi, Muhammad. *al-Aqbat fi al-'asr al-'uthmani*. Cairo: al-Hay'a al-Misriya li-l-Kitab, 1992.
al-'Alim, Mahmud Amin. *al-Hilm wa-l-waqi' wa-l-mustaqbal*. Nicosia: IBAL Publishing Institution L.T.D. 280–294.
'Ali, 'Abd al-Rahman. *al-Ikhwan al-Muslimun: fatawa fi-l-Aqbat: al-dimuqratiya, al-mar'a wa-l-fann*. Cairo: Markaz al-Mahrusa li-l-Nashr wa-l-Khadamat al Sahafiya wa-l-Ma'lumat, 2005.
Amin, Husayn Ahmad. *Dalil al-Muslim al-hazin*. Dar al-'Ayn li-l-Nashr, 2007.
Amin, Galal. *Madha hadatha li-l-thawra al-misriya*. Cairo: Dar El Shorouk, 2012.
———. *Mihnat al-din wa-l-dunya*. Cairo: Dar El Shorouk, 2013.
Andrawes, Fikry. *al-'Aql wa-l-siyasa*. Cairo: Dar al-Thaqafa al-Gadida, 2014.
———. "Masihiyyat Misr fi quruniha al-ula." *Wijhat nazar*. Cairo: al-Sharika al-Misriya li-l-Tiba'a wa-l-Nashr, 2005.
———. *al-Muslimun wa-l-aqbat fi-l-tarikh*. Cairo: Dar al-Thaqafa al-Jadida, 2017.
———. *Salama Musa: al-halim fi 'asr al-qalaq*. Cairo: Dar al-Thaqafa al-Jadida, 2014.
al-Antuni, Kirullus. *'Asr al-majami'*. Cairo: Maktabat al-Mahabba, 1991.
al-Antuni, Zakhari. *Kirullus al-Rabi': Abu-l-islah*. Cairo: Deir al-Anba Antonios, 1994.
al-'Ashmawi, Muhammad Sa'id. *al-Islam al-siyasi*. Cairo: Dar Sina li-l-Nashr, 1987.
Awad, Louis. *Muqaddima fi Muqaddima fi fiqh al-lugha al-'arabiya*. Cairo: Dar Sina li-l-Nashr, 1993.
———. *Tarikh al-fikr al-misri al-hadith*. Cairo: Dar al-Hilal, 1994.
———. *Tarikh al-fikr al-misri al-hadith min 'asr Isma'il ila thawrat 1919*. Cairo: al-Hay'a al-Misriya al-'Amma li-l-Kitab, 1980.
'Aziz, 'Abd al-Ghaffar. *Man qatal Farag Fuda?* Cairo: Dar al-I'lam al-Dawli, 1992.
Baha' al-Din, Ahmad. *Muhawarati ma' al-Sadat*. Cairo: al-Hay'a al-Misriya al-'Amma li-l-Kitab, 2013.
———. *al-Muthaqqafun wa-l-sulta*. Kuwait: al-Kitab al-'Arabi, 1999.
Bahr, Samira. *al-Aqbat fi-l-hayah al-siyasiya*. Cairo: Maktabat al-Anglu alMisriya, 1984.
Bakr, Salwa. *al-Bashmory*. Cairo: al-Maglis al-A'la li-l-Thaqafa, 2002.

al-Balazri, Abu-l Hassan. *Futuh al-buldan*. Beirut: Maktabat al-Hilal, 1988.

Barakat, 'Ali. *Ru'yat al-Jabarti li-azmat al-hayah al-fikriya*. Cairo: al-Hay'a al-Misriya al-'Amma li-l-Kitab, 1987.

al-Bishri, Tariq. *al-Dawla wa-l-kanisa*. Cairo: Dar El Shorouk, 2012.

———. *Dirasa fi-l-muhadathat al-baritaniya al-misriya 1920–1924*. Cairo: Dar al-Hilal, 1997.

———. *al-Muslimun wa-l-Aqbat fi itar al-jam'a al-wataniya*. Beirut: Dar al-Wihda, 1982.

———. *Sa'd Zaghlul yufawwid al-isti'mar 1920–1924*. Cairo: al-Hay'a al-Misriyaal-'Amma li-l-Kitab, 1977.

Dennett, Daniel. *al-Jizya wa-l-Islam*. Translated by Fawzi Fahim Jad-Allah. Beirut: Dar Maktabat al-Hayah, 1960.

Ebeid, Mona Makram. *Kalimat wa mawaqif*. Cairo: al-Hay'a al-Misriya al-'Amma li-l-Kitab, 1990.

Fawzi, Husayn. *al-Sindbad al-misri*. Cairo: Dar al-Ma'arif, 1990.

Fouda, Farag. *al-Haqiqa al-gha'iba*. Cairo: Dar al-Fikr li-l-Dirasat wa-l-Nashr wa-l-Tawzi', 1986.

al-Ghazali, Muhammad. *al-Ta'assub wa-l-tasamuh bayn al-masihiya wa-l-Islam*. Available online at: https://www.alarabimag.com/books/14132-%D8%A7%D9%84%D8%AA%D8%B9%D8%B5%D8%A8-%D9%88%D8%A7%D9%84%D8%AA%D8%B3%D8%A7%D9%85%D8%AD-%D8%A8%D9%8A%D9%86-%D8%A7%D9%84%D9%85%D8%B3%D9%8A%D8%AD%D9%8A%D8%A9.html.

Habashi, Banub. *Safha min tarikh al-Qibt*. Cairo: Matbu'at Marimina al-'Ajayibi, 1950.

Hassan, Salim. *Mawsu'at Misr al-qadima*. Cairo: al-Hay'a al-Misriya al-'Amma li-l-Kitab, 1992.

Haykal, Muhammad Husayn. *Mudhakirat fi al-siyasa al-misriya*. Cairo: Dar al-Ma'arif, 1977.

Himdan, Jamal. *Shakhsiyat Misr*. Cairo: 'Alam al-Kitab, 1980.

Husayn, Ahmad. *Mawsu'at tarikh Misr*. Cairo: Matbu'at Dar al-Sha'b, 1972.

Hussein, Suzanne Taha. *Ma'ak*. Translated from the French by Badr al-Din al-'Arduki. Cairo: al-Markaz al-Qawmi li-l-Tarjama, 2009.

Hussein, Taha. *al-Fitna al-kubra*. Vol. 1. Cairo: Dar al-Ma'rifa, 1984.

Huwaydi, Fahmi. *Muwatinun la dhimmiyun*. Cairo: Dar El Shorouk, 1985.

Ibn al-Muqaffa', Sawiras. *Tarikh al-batarika*. Edited by Samuel al-Suriany. Cairo: Ma'had al-Dirasat al-Qibtiya, 1984.

Ibn Hisham. *al-Sira al-nabawiya*. Edited by Taha 'Abd al-Ra'uf Sa'd. Beirut: Dar al-Jil li-l-Tab' wa-l-Nashr wa-l-Tawzi', 1990.

Ibn Iyas, Muhammad bin Ahmad. *Badi' al-zuhur fi waqai' al-duhur*. Edited by Muhammad Mustafa. Cairo: al Hay'a al-Misriya al-'Amma li-l-Kitab, 1982.

Ibn Khaldun. *al-Muqaddima*. Cairo: al-Matba'a al-Bahiya al-Misriya, n.d.

Ibn Sa'd Besinda. *al-Tabaqat al-kubra*. Beirut: Dar Sadir, n.d.

'Imara, Muhammad. *Fi al-mas'ala al-qibtiya: haqa'iq wa awham*. Dar El Shorouk, 2001.

———. *Tayyarat al-fikr al-islami*. Cairo: Dar al-Hilal, 1982.

Isma'il, Muhammad. *al-Muhammashun fi-l-tarikh al-islami*. Cairo: Ru'ya li-l-Nashr wa-l-Tawzi', 2004.

al-Jabarti, 'Abd al-Rahman. *'Aja'ib al-athar fi-l-tarajim wa-l-'athar*. Cairo: Matba'at al-Athar al-Muhammadiya, 1986.

Jamal al-Din, 'Abd al-'Aziz. *Tarikh Misr min bidayat al-qarn al-awwal hatta nihayat al-qarn al-'ishrin min khilal Tarikh al-Batarika li-Sawiras ibn al-Muqaffa'*. Cairo: Maktabat Madbuli, 2006.

Kashif, Sayyida Isma'il. *Misr fi 'asr al-Ikhshidiyyin*, 2nd ed. Cairo: Dar al-Nahda al-'Arabiya, 1970.

al-Kawakibi, 'Abd al-Rahman. *Taba'i' al-istibdad wa masari' al-isti'bad*, 1st ed., 1902. Cairo: Dar El Shorouk, 2009.

al-Kharbutli, 'Ali Hosni. *al-Islam wa ahl el-dhimma*. The Supreme Islamic Council, 1969.

al-Kindi al-Misri, Abi 'Umar Muhammad bin Yusuf. *al-Hukkam wa-l-qudah fi Misr*. Beirut, 1908.

Madi, Abu-l 'Ila. *al-Mas'ala al-qibtiya wa-l-sahwa al-islamiya*. Cairo: Safir al-Dawliya li-l-Nashr, 2007.

Madrasat al-Iskandariya ma' sirat wa kitabat Athenagoras wa Pantaenus. Cairo: Filbatrun li-l-Tarjama wa-l-Nashr, 1996.

Mahjub, Salah 'Abd al-'Aziz, trans. *Iohannis Ephesini Historiae Ecclesiasticae Pars Tertia*. al-Maglis al-A'la li-l-Thaqafa, 2000.

Mahmud, Hassan Ahmad, and Ahmad Ibrahim al-Sharif. *al-'Alam al-islami fi-l-'asr al-'abbasi*. Cairo: Dar al-Fikr al-'Arabi, n.d.

Mahmud, Salam Shafi'i. *Ahl al-dhimma fi Misr fi al-'asr al-fatimi al-awwal*. Cairo: al-Hay'a al-Misriya al-'Amma li-l-Kitab, 1995.

Malaty, Tadrus Ya'qub. *Aba' madrasat al-Iskandariya al-awa'il*. Alexandria: Coptic Church, 1980.

al-Maqrizi, Taqi al-Din Abu-l 'Abbas. *Kitab al-mawa'iz wa-l-i'tibar bi-dhikr al-khitat wa-l-athar*. 2 vols. Beirut: Dar Sadir, n.d.

———. *Kitab al-mawa'iz wa-l-i'tibar bi-dhikr al-khitat wa-l-athar*. 4 vols. Cairo: Maktabat al-Adab, 1996.

al-Mas'udi, 'Ali ibn al-Husayn. *Muruj al-dhahab*. Beirut: Dar al-Andalus, 1965.

Mikha'il, Fayiq. *Suwar min tarikh al-Qibt*. Cairo: Matbu'at Jam'iyyat Mari Minaal-'Ajaybi, 1950.

al-Miskin, al-Abb Matta. *al-Qiddis Athansius al-Rasuli*. Wadi al-Natrun: Matba'at Deir al-Qiddis Anba Maqar, 2002.

———. *al-Rahbana al-qibtiya fi 'asr al-qiddis Anba Maqar*. Cairo: al-Shirka al-Misriya li-l-Tiba'a wa-l-Nashr, 1972.

Muhyi al-Din, Khalid. *Al'an atakallam*. Cairo: al-Hay'a al-Misriya al-'Amma li-l-Kitab, 2014.

Mujahid, Muhammad Munir. *al-Aqbat bayn thawratayn*. Edited by Solomon Shafiq. Cairo: Dar Amaly, 2014.

Musa, Ra'uf Salama. *Salama Musa Abi*. Cairo: Dar wa Matabi' al-Mustaqbal, 1992.

Nakhla, Kamel Saleh. "Hanna al-Niqyusi." *Majallat Sahyun*, July/August 7/8, 1948:8.

al-Namnam, Hilmi. *Hassan al-Banna al-ladhi la ya'rifuhu ahad*. Cairo: Maktabat Madbuli, 2013.

———. *Sayyid Qutb wa thawrat Yulyu*. Cairo: Maktabat Madbuli, 2013.

al-Naqqash, Raja'. *Lewis 'Awad fi al-mizan*. Cairo: Dar al-Hilal, 2006.

Nubar Pasha. *Mudhakkirat Nubar Pasha*. Edited by Latifa Muhammad Salim, translated by Garo Robier Tabakian. Cairo: Dar El Shorouk, 2009.

Omara, Mohamed. *Fi al-mas'ala al-qibtiya: haqa'iq wa awham*. Cairo: Dar El Shorouk, 2001.

Qal'aji, Qadri. *Salah al-Din*. Beirut: Dar al-Kitab al-'Arabi, 1966.

Qandil, 'Abd al-Halim. *al-Ayyam al-akhira*. Cairo: Dar al-Thaqafa al-Gadida, 2008.

al-Qaysari, Yusabiyus. *Tarikh al-kanisa min al-Masih hatta Qustantin*. Translated by Murqus Dawud. Cairo: Maktabat al-Mahabba, 1997.

al-Qurashi, 'Abd al-Rahman bin 'Abdallah al-Misri. *Futuh Misr wa akhbaraha*. Leiden: Leiden University, 1930.

al-Rafi'i, 'Abd al-Rahman. *'Asr Isma'il*. Cairo: Dar al-Ma'arif, 1982.

———. *'Asr Muhammad 'Ali*. Cairo: Dar al-Ma'arif, 1982.

———. *Fi a'qab al-thawra al-misriya: thawrat 1919*. Cairo: Dar al-Ma'arif, 1984.

———. *Mustafa Kamel*. Cairo: Dar al-Ma'arif, 1984.

———. *Tarikh al-haraka al-qawmiya wa tatawwur nizam al-hukm*. Cairo: Dar al-Ma'arif, 1981.

———. *al-Thawra al-'urabiya wa-l-ihtilal al-injilzi*. 4th ed. Cairo: Dar al-Ma'arif, 1983.

Rizq, Yunan Labib. *Tarikh al-wizarat al-misriya*. Cairo: Markaz al-Dirasat al-Istiratijiya bi-l-Ahram, 1975.

———. *al-Wafd wa-l-kitab al-aswad*. Cairo: Markaz al-Dirasat al-Siyasiya wa-l-Istiratijiya, Mu'assasat al-Ahram, 2005.

Rufila, Ya'qub Nakhla. *Tarikh al-umma al-qibtiya*. Cairo: Mu'assasat al-Qiddis Murqus, 2000.

al-Sa'id, Rif'at. *Hassan al-Banna: al-shaykh al-musallah*. Cairo: al-Hay'a al-Misriya li-l-Kitab, 2004.

———. *al-Irhab al-muta'aslim*. Cairo: al-Hay'a al-Misriya li-l-Kitab, 2004.

al-Sa'id, Sana'. *al-Anba Shunuda al-Thalith: dunya wa din*. Cairo: al-Hay'a al-Misriya li-l-Kitab, 2004.

Salama, Usama. *Masir al-Aqbat fi Misr*. Cairo: Dar al-Khayal, 1998.

Samir, Hani. *Madhbahat Maspero*. Cairo: Dar wa Maktabat al-Hurriya, 2013.

al-Sawi, Ahmad Hassan. *al-Mu'allim Ya'qub bayn al-ustura wa-l-haqiqa*. Cairo: Dar al-Fikr li-l-Dirasat wa-l-Nashr, 1986.

Sayyid, Ayman Fu'ad. *al-Dawla al-fatimiya fi Misr.* Cairo: al-Dar al-Misriya al-Libnaniya, 2000.

Secretarial Committee, *al-Qararat al-mujma'iya fi 'ahd sahib al-qadasa wa-l ghabta al-Baba Shenouda al-Thalith.* Cairo: al-Markaz al-Thaqafi al-Qibti al-Urthuduksi, 1996.

al-Sharif, 'Ayda. *Muhammad Mahmud Shakir.* Cairo: Dar al-Hilal, 1997.

Shukri, Ghali. *al-Aqbat fi watan mutaghayyir.* Kitab al-Ahali 29. Cairo: *al-Ahali* newspaper, 1990.

———. *Aqni'at al-irhab.* Cairo: al-Hay'a al-Misriya al-'Amma li-l-Kitab, 1992.

———. *al-Thawra al-mudadda.* Cairo: Kitab al-Ahali, 1987.

al-Tabari, Muhammad ibn Jarir. *Tarikh al-umam wa-l-muluk.* Edited by Muhammad Abu al-Fadl Ibrahim. Cairo: Dar al-Ma'arif, 1967.

Tagher, Jacques. 1951. *Aqbat wa-'il Muslimun.* Reprinted Cairo: al-Hay'a al-Misriya al-'Amma li-l-Kitab, General Egyptian Book Organization, 2010.

Taha, Samir Muhammad. *Ahmad 'Urabi wa dawruh fi al-hayah al-siyasiya al-misriya.* Cairo: al-Hay'a al-Misriya al-'Amma li-l-Kitab, 1986.

Tritton, A.S. *Ahl al-dhimma fi-l-Islam.* Translated and annotated by Hassan Habashi. Cairo: Dar al-Ma'arif, 1967.

Yusabbius al-Qaysari. *Tarikh al-kanisa min al-Masih hatta Qustantin.* Translated by Archpriest Murqus Dawud. 2nd ed. Cairo: Maktabat al-Mahabba, 1979.

Yusuf, Abu Sayf. *al-Aqbat wa-l-qawmiya al-'arabiya.* Cairo: Markaz Dirasat al-Wihda al-'Arabiya, 1987.

Ziedan, Youssef. *'Azazil.* Cairo: Dar El Shorouk, 2008.

INDEX

Italicized page numbers refer to tables.

1919 revolution 153–55, 177, 239, 243; Egyptian flag 153; *see also* Zaghlul, Sa'd

1952 revolution 6, 139, 173, 218, 237, 243; Muslim Brotherhood and 173–74; *see also* al-Nasser, Gamal Abd

1967 Six-Day War 6, 177, 183–84, 188, 195; *see also* Israel; Nasser period

1973 Arab-Israeli war 6, 186, 188–89; Camp David Accords 6, 194, 196; United States and 188–89, 194; *see also* Sadat, Anwar; Sadat period

2011 revolution (25 January revolution) 7, 215; the army 217–19; Coptic Church's opposition to 219; Coptic youth 219; foreign interests and support 219–20; Muslim Brotherhood 7, 219–20; national secular atmosphere 219; national unity between Copts and Muslims 219; police 217, 220; political Islam 221; Salafism 219; social media 217; Tahrir Square, Cairo 217, 219, 222; United States 221, 222; *see also* 2011 revolution aftermath; SCAF

2011 revolution aftermath 229; 2011 March referendum 220–21, 224; 2012 presidential election 224; the army 226, 227, 229–30; attacks on Copts 7, 221–23, 227, 229; chaotic post-revolutionary period 222, 227–28; demonstrations 222, 225, 226; early presidential election 220, 221, 226; Muslim Brotherhood and 224–27, 229; sectarian violence 221–23, 227, 229; Tamarod 225, 226; *see also* 2011 revolution; Morsi, Muhammad; SCAF; al-Sisi, 'Abd al-Fattah

AAL (Egyptian Movement for Change/ al-Gabha al-Wataniya li-l-Taghyir) 213

Abbas (Prophet Muhammad's younger uncle) 57, 68

Abbas II (khedive, Muhammad 'Ali dynasty) 145, 151, 179

Abbas, Raouf 157

Abbasid dynasty 3, 50, 51, 56, 57–62, 68, 91, 161; conversion to Islam during 62, 91, 93; Coptic–Muslim relations 59–62, 67, 72; Egypt recovered from Tulunid dynasty 65–66; equality and justice 57, 59; Mongol invasion 81; Persians and 57, 58, 59; poor policies of 62, 63; puppet caliphs 84; revenue decline 45, 62; revolt 59, 60, 62; succession war 59–60; Sunni Islam 67, 68; tax collection 3, 51, 52, 59, 60, 61–62, 63, 67, 93; Turks and 58

'Abd al-Hadi Basha 164

'Abd al-Hamid, Ra'fat 10

'Abd al-Quddus, Ihsan 100

'Abd al-Rahman, 'Umar (shaykh) 186

'Abd al-Raziq, 'Ali: *al-Islam wa usul al-hukm* 163

'Abduh, Muhammad (shaykh) 136, 142, 143, 160, 248

'Abdullah ibn 'Umar 42

al-Abnudi, 'Abd al-Rahman 100

Abu-l Anwar, Muhammad (shaykh) 108
Abu Bakr (first caliph) 72, 161
Abu-l Faraj 43
Abu-l-Futuh, 'Abd al-Mun'im 224
Abu-l Ghar, Muhamamd 205
Abu Takia 114
Abu Zayd, Nasr Hamid 211, 212
al-'Adid li-Din Illah (Fatimid caliph) 77–78
al-Afdal (Armenian ruler) 76–77
al-Afghani, Jamal al-Din 142–43
Afghanistan 142, 190, 203, 212
'Afifi, Muhammad 2, 107, 108
Agar, Michael H. 101
ahl al-dhimma (protected people) 43
Akef, Mahdi 230
Alexandria 29–30, 42, 111, 130, 215; British military occupation of 137–38, 158; Diocletian 19–20; early Christianity in Egypt 9, 15; French adventure in Egypt 111; lighthouse 42; Museum of Alexandria 11, 12; Persian invasion of 34; revolt 19–20; the Slaughter 137–38; *see also* Library of Alexandria; School of Alexandria
'Ali ibn Abi Talib (fourth caliph) 12, 45, 46–47, 67
al-'Alim, Mahmud Amin 200
Allenby, Edmund (Field Marshal, British high commissioner in Egypt) 153, 154
Amalric I (Crusader King of Jerusalem) 78, 79
American, Canadian, and Australian Coptic Association 192
Amin, Galal 210, 212, 215, 222
Amin, Qasim 100
Ammonius 12
'Amr Ibn al 'As *see* Ibn al 'As, 'Amr
Andrawes, Fikry: *al-Muslimun wa-l-aqbat fi-l-tarikh* 2, 3
April 6 movement 213–14
al-'Aqqad, Abbas Mahmud 160
Arab invasion 3, 31, 36–41, 93; Arab colonization of Egypt 49; Arab fascination with Egypt 41–42; the army and 38–39; Coptic–Muslim relations 36, 40–41; Egypt's surrender treaty with Ibn al-'As 39–40, 41, 45, 55; monasticism and 18; *see also* Ibn al 'As, 'Amr
Arab League 244
Arabic language 3, 17, 50, 100, 248, 249; as alive and changing language 101, 248; Arabic sources 3, 26; classical Arabic 100; colloquial Egyptian Arabic 100, 101; from Coptic to Arabic 3, 93, 99–101; as official language in Egypt 66, 99
Arakel Nobar Bek 128
Arius/Arianism 22, 23, 24, 25
Armenian church 15, 22, 30, 77
Armenian rulers in Egypt 76–77
the army 218, 241; 2011 revolution and aftermath 217–19, 226, 227, 229–30; *ahl al-dhimma* 43; Arab invasion of Egypt 38–39; budget 218; Copts in 5, 79, 125, 128, 135; discrimination against Copts 135, 208; dismantled by Tawfiq Basha 139; economic power and political independence 218; Fatimid dynasty 76; Ibn Tulun and 64; Isma'il Basha and 131; military class 6, 45; Mubarak period 7, 201, 205; Muhammad 'Ali dynasty 124–25, 131, 136; Muslims 38; mutiny 136, 137; Nasser period 6, 178; prayer amir 50; United States and 218
Assad al-Din Shirku 78
Aswan Dam 141, 174
Aswan High Dam project 174–75
Asyut 24, 96, 133, 180, 195, 198, 234, 243; 1911 Conference 147–48
Atatürk, Kamal 49, 162
Athanasius I (Coptic patriarch) 16, 17, 18, 181; exile 25, 26; selection as Patriarch 24–25; separation of the Coptic Church from the Roman church 24; unifying the Coptic Church of Egypt 25; *see also* Coptic patriarch
Atiya, Aziz S. 73
al-'Attar (shaykh) 109

Awad, Louis 110, 118–19, 120, 130–31, 138, 142, 144, 212; *Fiqh al-lugha al-'arabiya* 101
al-'Awwa, Salim 213
Aybak, 'Izz al-Din (Mamluk sultan) 82, 83
Ayyubid dynasty 4, 78–82, 83, 90
Azgor the Turk 63
al-Azhar Mosque/University 2, 50, 68, 69, 107, 108, 114, 120 135, 143, 232; 1960s expansion 176; death penalty for conversion into Christianity 190–91; 'first revolt against the French' 115, 118; Islamic Research Center 101; modernization 120, 232, 236; politics and 6, 152; School of Theology 152, 163, 176, 236; *see also* Islamic scholar
al-'Aziz (Fatimid caliph) 69–70, 71

Badr, Zaki 201
al-Badri (shaykh) 107
Baghdad 59–60, 63, 65, 66, 67, 68, 78, 79, 82, 185; conquest and sack by the Mongols 84, 91, 94; foundation of 58
Baha' al-Din, Ahmad 46, 47, 183, 244
Bahram (Armenian ruler) 76–77
al-Bajuri, Ibrahim (shaykh) 128
al-Banna, Hassan 133, 163, 164
banking 185; *see also* Islamic banking/financing
Banque Misr (Bank of Egypt) 160, 239, 240–42; cotton textile industry and 240; difficult years 240–1; as first multinational corporation in the Middle East 240; *see also* Harb, Muhammad Talaat; Islamic banking/financing
Baring, Evelyn (Earl of Cromer) *see* Cromer, Earl of
Barnes, Timothy D. 25
Bashir, Tahsin 204
Bashmur 60; Bashmuric Revolt 56, 59
Battle of al-Harra 57
Battle of the Nile 112
Battle of the Pyramids 111, 112, 138
Battle of al-Tal al-Kabir 138
Battle of Zab River 58
Baybars, al-Zahir (Mamluk sultan) 84, 98
Bayt al-Hikma (the House of Wisdom) 58
BBC Frontline 218
Bedouins 37, 110, 149, 156
Beeson, Irene 183
Begin, Menachem 189, 194, 195, 198
Bibi II, Pharaoh 228
Bible 133, 219, 234, 235; allegorical interpretation of 3, 15; Gospels 13; Old Testament 12; translation of 11, 99
al-Biltagi, Muhammad 219
Bin Yusuf, Hammam (shaykh) 110
al-Bishri, Tariq 130, 148, 205–206, 213, 219
Bonaparte, Napoleon 4, 51, 111–16, 118, 128, 130, 132, 138; *La Description de l'Egypte* 121; Institut d'Egypte 120, 121; *see also* French adventure in Egypt
Britain 111; 1807–1809 campaign 123; Battle of the Nile 112; British Labour Party 236, 244; Fabian Society 236; French surrender to the British 116; *see also* British occupation
British occupation 5, 141–49, 173, 231; 1954 British withdrawal 155; Alexandria 137–38, 158; British colonization of Egypt 5, 139, 141; British influence on Egyptian economy 141–42; British school for tax collection 144; constitutional reform in Egypt 149; Coptic–Muslim relations 5, 143–48, 152–54; Dinshaway incident 145–46, 147; 'divide and conquer' policy 143, 144, 145, 149; Egypt as Protectorate 141, 149, 154, 155; Egyptian nationalist movement 143, 144, 146, 149, 153, 243; Egyptian resistance against 6, 144, 146, 151–55; Egyptian self-determination 6, 152, 154; end of Copts as tax collectors 44, 52, 98, 114, 144; Entente Cordiale 149; political Islam and 143; sectarian tension/violence 144, 145, 146, 147–48; Suez Canal 5, 139;

taxation 141, 143; Urabi revolt and 5, 135, 137–39; *see also* 1919 revolution; 1952 revolution; Britain
Burjuwan al-Siqilli 71, 73
Butler, Alfred 35, 36, 37–38, 39–40, 42, 43, 45
Butrus, Zakariya 207
Byzantine Empire/Byzantines 19, 31, 33, 36, 38, 57, 73, 84, 103; Arab invasion 36–40; Byzantine church 11; Coptic persecution by Byzantines 3, 80; Egypt's surrender treaty 39–40, 41, 45, 55; Persian invasion of 33–34; Syria and 67, 69; tax system 46, 51, 53; victory over the Persians 34–35

Cairo 68, 72, 129, 130; 1992 earthquake 201; fire in 86–88, 90, 98; French adventure in Egypt 112, 113, 119; *see also* Old Cairo
Cairo Museum 190
Cairo University 179, 181, 196, 211, 233
caliph/caliphate 63, 67, 78, 161–63, 206; abolition of the caliphate in Turkey 160, 162; descendants of the Prophet/*ahl al-bayt* and 57; first four caliphs 67, 162; Friday prayer/sermon and 63, 78, 84; puppet caliph 84, 103
capitalism 184, 204
Carter, Jimmy 189, 194, 195, 196, 198
Catholicism 107–108, 132, 133; Coptic/Catholic churches reconciliation 31; demographics 133; Egyptian Catholics 133; monasticism 17; Paul VI, Pope 193; Roman Catholic Pope 14, 18; Spain 4, 96; *see also* Christianity; missionary
CCC (Church Community Council/al-Majlis al-Milli) 179
census 53, 54, 55, 105, 188, 190, 223; 1917 census 157; 1996 census 190
Chalcedonian Church 30, 35, 41; *see also* Melchite Church
Chosroes, Persian Emperor 34
Christian–Muslim relations 79–80; *see also* Coptic–Muslim relations
Christianity: church/state relationship 21–22, 23, 26; Muslims' conversion to 133, 190–91, 207; as official religion of Roman Empire 18, 22, 23, 26; People of the Book/*ahl al-kitab* 71; separation of Eastern churches from Roman/Byzantine church 11, 15, 22, 30; *see also* Catholicism; Christianity in Egypt; Coptic Church; Protestantism
Christianity in Egypt 3, 9–31, 97; Alexandria 9, 15; Diocletian and the persecution of Christians 19–21, 24, 25; early Christianity in Egypt 9–10, 14, 178; *see also* Chalcedonian Church; Coptic Church; Copts; Melchite Church; monasticism; School of Alexandria
church (Coptic) 96, 97; attack on/destruction of 4, 7, 34, 54, 55, 61, 65, 68–69, 70, 73, 74, 76, 79, 94, 96, 97, 164, 165, 187, 196, 208, 215, 221, 223, 227; attacks during the Friday sermon 84–86, 87, 89–90; the Caesarion church 42; Church of the Holy Sepulcher 69, 74; Church of al-Mu'allaqa/Hanging Church 85–6; Church of St. Mark 42; confiscation of belongings and endowments 73, 90, 96, 97; construction of 27, 29, 41, 44, 69, 77, 79, 107, 126, 169–71, 187–88, 223; converted into mosque 29, 74, 91, 96; Coptic cathedral 117, 129, 152, 153, 176–77; Ibn Taymiya and destruction of churches 89–90, 95–96; Islamic tolerance 65, 69–70; mosque converted into 80; Nasser period 176–7; political Islam and 171; Qasriyat al-Rihan church 196; Qur'an and 170; restoration/renovation of 41, 44, 61, 69, 70, 79, 90–1, 94, 107, 126; Sadat period 187–88; St. Barbara's Church 91; St. Mina's church/complex 65, 85; St. Shenouda's church 74; vandalization of 65, 73, 74, 85; in the West 192; al-Zuhari church 85

church council 13, 22–23, 28; Council of Chalcedon 30; Council of Constantinople 15; Council of Ephesus 28, 30; ecumenical church council 14–15, 23, 30; separation of the Coptic Church 23–24; *see also* Nicene Council
Clement of Alexandria (Titus Flavius Clemens) 11–12, 15; *Paedagogus* 12; *Protrepticus* 12; *Stramata* 12; *see also* School of Alexandria
Clinton, Hillary 222
Clot, Antoine Barthélémy 125
Cold War 175, 188
communism 160, 166, 175, 181, 185, 188, 193, 237
Constantine I, Emperor 18, 21–22
Constantinople (Byzantium) 13, 29, 33; Cathedral of St. Sophia 33; Persian siege of 34
Constitution (national constitution) 6, 155, 177, 193, 204, 214; autocratic constitution 157; 1923 Constitution 156, 157, 243; 1971 Constitution, amendments to 219, 220; 2011 temporary Constitution 224; constitutional reform 149
Cook, Edward, Sir 241
Coptic calendar 20
Coptic Church (Egypt) 3, 6, 178–82; 2011 revolution 219; autonomy 31; Catholic/Coptic churches reconciliation 31; CCC and 179; as the Church of Egypt 41; church leadership 6, 206; Coptic school 129–30, 227; corruption 90, 109, 180; cultural flowering 80–81; fasting and prayer 191, 192, 195; festivities 66, 69, 73, 74, 107, 152–53, 195, 215; history of 2, 10; Holy Synod 179, 180, 181, 193, 197; leadership changes 178, 180; modernization of 5, 132; Ottoman period 109, 132; politics and 6, 22, 24, 177, 191–92; priesthood 181; separation from the Western church 3, 11, 15, 22, 24, 25–26, 27, 30, 31; *al-shartuniya* 90; St. Mark the Evangelist and 9, 55; state and 5, 195–96, 197; Sunday school 134; theological differences over the nature of Jesus 3, 23–4, 25–26, 27, 28, 29–31; wealth 64; *see also* Christianity in Egypt; church; Coptic patriarch
Coptic Conference: 1911 Conference 147–49; 1977 Conference 192
Coptic culture and heritage 18, 31, 59; in danger of disappearing 230
The Coptic Encyclopedia 11
Coptic language 3, 31, 50; Coptic alphabet 11; Coptic sources 3, 26; decline of 66, 99; from Coptic to Arabic 3, 93, 99–101; origins of 99; Saidi dialect 17, 100
Coptic migration/diaspora 176, 192, 209; Coptic activist organization 192; from villages to cities 199, 208; Sadat's visit to United States and 196–97
Coptic Museum, Cairo 17, 86
Coptic–Muslim relations 4, 50, 198–200, 227, 229–30; 1919–1921 national unity between Copts and Muslims 152–55, 209, 219; 2011 revolution aftermath 7, 221–23, 227, 229; Abbasid dynasty 59–62, 67, 72; among intellectuals 166–9; Arab invasion and conquest 36, 40–41; Ayyubid dynasty 80–81; Baybars's tenure 84; British occupation 5, 143–48, 152–54; cultural differences/similarities 50, 199; extreme brutality suffered by Copts 72, 75–76, 88; Fatimid dynasty 4, 68–69, 75–76; French adventure in Egypt 114, 115, 117, 120; government and 90, 126; Ikhshidi dynasty 66–67; majority/minority relationship 230; Mamluk dynasty 4, 72, 83–90, 96; Mubarak period 7, 205–10, 215; Muhammad 'Ali dynasty 5, 126–27, 128, 129, 133–34, 143–44; Ottoman dynasty 105–109; Sadat period 190–92, 194, 196, 199; Salah al-Din's

tenure 79, 80; segregation 190, 200, 206, 212–13; tax collection 3, 51, 52, 56; tolerance 2, 65, 66, 68, 69, 97, 229; Tulunid dynasty 64, 65; Umayyad dynasty 52, 53–57; unity of Copts and Muslims women 153; *see also* Christian–Muslim relations; sectarianism

Coptic patriarch 9, 15; Ibn Tulun and 64–65; jailing and ransom 55, 56, 64–65, 73, 74, 77; 'Pope' title 14; selection of 53, 90, 179, 180–81; *see also* Coptic Church; Coptic patriarchs

Coptic patriarchs: Alexander I, Pope 24; Alexandros II 54; Anianus 9; Athanasius, politically appointed Pope 179; Benjamin I 35–36, 40, 44, 45; Cyril the Great 26, 28, 29, 40–41, 43; Cyril IV, Pope 130, 132; Cyril V, Pope 133, 156, 179; Cyril VI, Pope 14, 176, 181, 182; Demetrius I 9–10, 12, 13, 14; Demetrius II 129, 132–33; Dioscorus 26, 29–30; Gabriel 77; Heracles, Pope 14; Jacob 60; John IX 87; John XIII 98; Khail I 56, 59; Marcos II 59, 60; Mark V 109; Peter I 20, 24; St. Mark the Evangelist as first Patriarch 9; Tawadros II, Pope 226, 227; Theophilus 13, 14, 26, 27–28, 43; Yuhanna/John 25–26; Yulianus/Julian 10; Yusab I 60; Yusab II 180; Zakharias 73, 74; *see also* Athanasius I; Shenouda III

Copts 1; as administrators 44, 66, 69, 70, 71, 73, 75, 79, 83, 90, 98, 106, 114; *arakhina*/Coptic lay aristocracy 178–79; the army and 5, 79, 125, 128, 135; Cairo fire and 86–88, 90; civil service 148; class division 104; conversion to Islam 36, 40, 49, 53, 54, 61, 74, 75, 88, 89, 91, 129, 190–91, 209–10; corruption 95, 105; education 179, 181; exile 74, 75; as infidels 208; as majority group 53, 65; as minority group 1, 36, 148, 155, 178, 190, 229; persecution of 3, 4, 36, 68–69, 73–74, 90, 108; pilgrimage to Jerusalem 78, 107, 194; political Islam and 164–65, 186–87; reduction in population 4, 69, 74; religious identity 31, 206, 207; as tax collectors 3, 44, 52, 69, 70, 83, 90, 95, 98, 105, 114, 118, 126, 144; wealth 52, 90, 98, 104, 148, 210; *see also* Coptic migration/diaspora; Copts, discrimination against; political system and Copts

Copts, discrimination against 2, 6, 44, 54, 74–75, 88–89, 106, 227, 238; the army 135, 208; 'blue bones' 74; Bonaparte, Napoleon and 114; British occupation 144; building and repairing churches 169; civil service/administration 61, 89, 97, 144, 191, 208; dress code 61, 73, 77, 79, 88, 106, 114, 120; dress code as a money-generating scheme 106; education 176, 191; job discrimination 147, 191, 208, 238; Mubarak period 206, 208; Sadat period 190, 191; tattoo 55; wearing a bell 89; wearing a cross 74

coup d'état 173, 189

Cromer, Earl of (Evelyn Baring, British consul-general in Egypt) 138, 141, 143, 147, 149, 151, 199, 212–13; Dinshaway incident 146; *Modern Egypt* 142; policies 142, 144

Crusades/Crusaders 4, 69, 77, 81, 94, 96, 118; Coptic antipathy toward the Crusaders 78, 80; defeat by the Syrian army 78; expulsion from Egypt 82; Fatimid dynasty 80; *jizya* on Muslims 52, 80

Curzon, Lord 153–54

Cyrus (Byzantine patriarch of Alexandria and imperial commander in Egypt) 35–36, 39

al-Damanhuri, Ahmad (shaykh) 108

Darwin, Charles/Darwinism 235, 236, 247, 248

Davis, Steven J. 28
democracy 188, 226, 233, 235, 238; absence of 178, 191, 206, 230; false/sham democracy 177, 214; liberal democracy 159, 163; Muslim Brotherhood and 163; struggle for 230; *see also* election
Desaix, Louis (French General) 117
al-Dhahabi, Muhammad 193
Didymus the Blind 14–15; *Discourse Against Arius and Sabellius* 15; *On the Holy Spirit* 15; *On the Trinity* 15; *see also* School of Alexandria
Dinshaway incident 145–46, 147
Diocletian (Roman Emperor) 19–21, 24, 25; abdication 21
Dirgham (Fatimid minister) 78
divorce 98, 179, 187, 209–10, 211, 229; *see also* marriage
the Druze 75
Duff-Gordon, Lucy 129
al-Duruzi, Muhammad 75

Eastern churches 11, 30, 80
Ebeid/Ubayd, Makram 159, 160, 165, 166–67, 243–47; Black Book on March 29, 1943: 246; al-Kutla al-Wafdiya 159, 246–47; nationalist movement 243, 244; personality 244–45; Wafd Party 244, 245, 246
education 70, 230; Coptic culture/history in school curriculum 1, 206; Coptic school 129–30, 227; Coptic Sunday school 134; Copts 179, 181; Copts, discrimination against 176, 191; free educational system 234; Islamic elementary school/*kuttab* 231; Islamic influence in the educational system 6, 199, 200, 206; Islamism/political Islam and 206, 211, 212; Isma'il Basha and 129–30, 131; missionary school 132–3; Muhammad 'Ali dynasty 5, 127, 129–30, 131; Muslim Brotherhood and 190, 199, 205; Nasser period 6, 175–76; religion as subject in curricula 176, 207; secularization of 237; teaching of history in Egypt 1, 2, 206; vocational school 127, 130; women 130, 234, 242
Egypt 2, 6; ancient Egyptian language 99, 101; ancient Egyptian religion 23, 26, 29, 100–101; autonomy 63, 65, 66; class division 45, 49, 104; colonization/colonialism 132, 133; as Coptic Christian country 1; cultural life 211–12; Egyptian calendar 20, 101; Egyptian Islamic culture 100–101; European control of 111; government 51; independence of 118, 119, 145, 149, 151, 154; modernization of 5, 119, 124–27, 130–31; Persian invasion of 34, 35; Roman Empire and 20, 36; social inequality 49; tourist industry 204; *see also* Arab invasion
Egyptian Enlightenment *see al-nahda*
ElBaradei, Mohamed 214, 226
election 157, 159, 177, *251–52*; 1923 election 156; 1925 election 159; 1926 election 159; 1950 election 158, 165; 1995 election 209; 2005 election 204; 2010 election 204; 2011 election 224; 2012 presidential election 224; 2014 presidential election 227; early presidential election 220, 221, 226; tampered election 157; *see also* democracy
Elsässer, Sebastian: *The Coptic Question in the Mubarak Era* 2, 207
Enlightenment (Europe) 13, 120, 132, 230
Europe 5, 130
Eusebius of Caesarea 13; *The History of the Church* 19, 21
Eutychius 29
Evagrius Ponticus 15

Facebook 215–16
al-Faggani, Sa'd ibn Katib 65
Fahd ibn Ibrahim 71, 73
Faisal (King of Saudi Arabia) 178, 185
Farmland, A.E. 131–32
Farouk I (King of Egypt, Muhammad 'Ali dynasty) 139, 159, 166, 173

fascism 160
Fatimid dynasty 4, 58, 67–78; the army 76; Cairo 68, 72; Coptic–Muslim relations 4, 68–69, 70, 75–76; Crusades 80; destruction of Coptic churches 4, 68–69, 70, 73, 74, 76; famine 76; Shi'a Islam 67, 68, 69; tax collection 72; violent infighting 77
Fatma (Prophet Muhammad's daughter and 'Ali ibn Abi Talib's wife) 68
Faulkner, William 229
Fawzi, Husayn 92
al-Fayiz (Fatimid caliph) 77
Fayum 37
al-Fayzi, Hibat Allah 83–84
First Intermediate Period 227–28
food subsidy program 192–93, 201
Ford, Gerald 198
Fouda, Farag 202, 203
France 139, 145; Entente Cordiale 149; *see also* French adventure in Egypt
French adventure in Egypt 4, 92, 97, 111–21; Alexandria 111; Battle of the Pyramids 111, 112, 138; Cairo 112, 113, 119; Coptic–Muslim relations 114, 115, 117, 120; *diwan* 113, 118; effects of 120–21; end of 116, 119; 'first revolt against the French' 114–15; French respect for the law 119–20; French Revolution and 4, 113; Mamluks and 112, 115, 116, 117; Napoleon's flyer 112–13; non-Coptic Christians 115–16; 'second revolt against the French' 116, 117; sectarian violence and 112, 114, 115, 117, 118; surrender to the British 116; tax system 113, 114, 116; Turks and 115, 116, 117, 118, 119, 120; withdrawal from Egypt 120, 123; *see also* Bonaparte, Napoleon; Ya'qub, Mu'allim
Fu'ad I (King of Egypt, Muhammad 'Ali dynasty) 49, 155, 157, 158, 159, 163; false religious legitimacy 162
al-Fustat 68

Gad al-Haq, 'Ali (shaykh of al-Azhar) 208
Galerius (Roman Emperor) 21
al-Gama'a al-Islamiya 193, 198
Gandhi, Mahatma 155, 230, 237
Gayed, Nazeer *see* Shenouda III
Ghali, Boutros 144, 146–47, 206
Ghali, Wassef 151, 155
Ghatas, Michael 135
al-Ghazali, Muhammad 2
Ghurbal, Muhammad Shafiq 118
al-Ghuri (Mamluk sultan) 103
Gibbon, Edward 24, 25
Girgis, Habib 134
Gordon, Cyrus 30
Gorst, Eldon (British consul-general in Egypt) 147, 153
Graham, Billy 193
Greek philosophy 11–12, 13, 16, 58
al-Guhari, Girgis 144

al-Habhab, 'Abdullah 54, 55
Habib, Muhammad 225–26
hadith 95, 161, 162
al-Hafiz, 'Abd al-Majid (Fatimid caliph) 77
al-Hakim, Tawfiq 101, 160
al-Hakim bi-Amr Illah (Fatimid caliph) 4, 69, 71–72; conversion to Islam under 75, 91, 93–94; Dar al-Hikma/House of Wisdom 75; disappearance 75, 76; extreme brutality suffered by Copts and Jews 72, 73–76; Mas'ud, al-Hakim's slave 72; personality 72–73, 75
al-Halabi, Sulayman 116
Hamas 215
Hanafi school 161
Hanbali school 161
Hanna, Nelly 105, 108
Hanzala ibn Safwan 55
Harb, Muhammad Talaat 160, 237, 239–42; Sharikat Bay' al-Masnu'at 237; *see also* Banque Misr
Hassan, Sana S.: *Christians versus Muslims in Modern Egypt* 2, 133, 180, 206
Hassan, Selim 227–28
Hassan Basha, Kapudan 106
Haykal, Muhammad Husayn 100, 160, 176, 187, 212; transition proposal 214

Heraclius (Emperor) 33, 34–35, 36, 38, 39; monothelitism 35
Heraclius the Small (Emperor) 38, 39
Hibat Allah, Abu Sa'd 83
Hijazi, 'Abd al-Aziz 185
al-Hilal magazine 236, 249
Hirst, David 183
Hizb al-Umma (the People's Party) 145
Hizb al-Wasat 213
Hosni, Farouk 212
al-Hudaybi, Muhammad 2, 165
Hulagu Khan 91
Hussein, Taha 160, 231–34, 237, 239; *al-Ayyam (The Days)*, 232; Bresseau, Suzanne 233; *al-Fitna al-kubra* 47; works by 233–34
Hypatia 28

Iberian Peninsula 94
Ibn 'Abd al-Hakam 37–38, 41, 44, 50–51
Ibn 'Abd al-Malik, Hisham (viceroy and Umayyad caliph) 54–55, 57, 66
Ibn al 'As, 'Amr 36–37, 38, 40–41, 42, 43, 51; early administration under 44–47; Egypt's surrender treaty 39–40, 41, 45, 55; wealth 46, 47
Ibn Bishr, Hassan 70
Ibn al-Fada, Muffadal 84
Ibn Issak al-Dabbi, Enbesa 61
Ibn Iyas, Muhammad bin Ahmad 55, 73, 84, 90, 91; *Badi' al-zuhur fi waqai' al-duhur* 47
Ibn Khakan, al-Hassan 70
Ibn al-Khattab, 'Umar (second caliph) 36, 41, 42, 43, 44, 45, 49, 50, 75; Islamic tolerance 65
Ibn Killis, Ya'qub 69, 70
Ibn Marwan, 'Abd al-'Aziz 53
Ibn Marwan, 'Abd al-Malik 54, 56
Ibn al-Mudabbir 61–62
Ibn al-Muqaffa', Sawiras *see* Severus of Ashmunayn
Ibn Nuh 96, 97
Ibn Qalawun, Nasir al-Din (Mamluk sultan) 72, 84–86, 87, 90
Ibn Sa'd Besinda 46; *al-Tabaqat al-kubra* 47
Ibn Taymiya 89–90, 95–96; as father of modern political Islam 95
Ibn Tulun, Ahmad (Tulunid sultan) 63–65, 66
Ibn Walkashi, Radwan 77
Ibrahim, Vivian: *The Copts of Egypt: The Challenges of Modernization and Identity* 2, 157
idolatry 190
Idris, Yusuf 100
al-Ikshid, Muhammad ibn Tughj 66–67, 69
Ikhshidi dynasty 4, 66–67, 68
IMF (International Monetary Fund) 186, 192, 201, 210
India 91, 111, 139, 141, 155; Amritsar Massacre 146
Industrial Revolution 111, 132
Internet 161, 199, 207, 215–16
Iohannis Ephesini (John of Ephesus) 25
Iraq 56, 60, 162; Arab conquest of 40
ISIS (the Islamic State of Iraq and al-Sham) 230
Islam: capitalism and socialism 184; festivities 114, 130, 152–53; Friday prayer/sermon 63, 78, 82, 84–85; history of 1, 2, 33, 161–62, 202, 206; prayer 39, 65, 89, 190; tolerance 65, 69–70, 229, 236; *see also the entries below related to* Islam; Muslims; political Islam; Shi'a Islam; Sunni Islam
Islam, conversion to 81, 93; Abbasid dynasty 62, 91, 93; 'alternative conversions' 97; changing demography in the South of Egypt 96–98; Copts 36, 40, 49, 53, 54, 61, 62, 74, 75, 88, 89, 91, 129, 190–91, 209–10; forced conversion 61, 77, 79, 97, 192; al-Hakim bi-Amr Illah and 75, 91, 93–94; Islamization of Egypt 93; Jews 54, 73, 74; *jizya* and 61, 62, 93; Mamluk dynasty 89, 91, 93; marriage and conversion 98–99; persecution and conversion 98; rich Coptic administrators and tax collectors 98; sham conversion 97; shift from Coptic to Arabic language 99–101; threats to Islam from

Mongols and Europeans 94–96; waves of conversion 62, 75, 89, 91, 93, 98
Islam in Egypt 3, 49; Arab ancestry, importance of 49; caliphs and governors 50–51; conditions imposed on non-Muslims 43–44; corruption 47, 51, 55, 57; Egyptian Islamic culture 100–101; *fiqh*/Islamic jurisprudence 41, 59, 170; Islamic art, architecture, and literature 50; treaty vs force 41, 49; *see also* Arab invasion
al-Islambouli, Khalid 198
Islamic banking/financing 185–86, 200, 210; FIBE/Faisal Islamic Bank of Egypt 185–86; Mit Ghamr Bank, Germany 185; Muslim Brotherhood and 185, 186, 192, 219–20, 221; political Islam and 185–86, 210; support from American and international financial institutions 186; *see also* Banque Misr; Harb, Muhammad Talaat
Islamic Conference: 1911 Conference: 147, 148–49; 1966 Conference 184; 1969 Conference 184; 1977 Conference 184, 194–95
Islamic investment companies (Sharikat Tawzif al-Amwal) 210–11
Islamic law (sharia) 146, 185, 186–87, 192, 202, 210; replacing secular law with 186, 194–95, 213
Islamic organization 194, 200
Islamic scholar 108–109; Azharite 108–109, 115, 120, 184, 198, 203, 234; Mamluks and 4, 89; Muhammad 'Ali/shaykhs relationship 123, 124; Ottomans/shaykhs relationship 108, 123; wealth 108; *see also* al-Azhar Mosque/University
Islamism 2, 101, 191, 200, 230; death penalty for renouncing Islam 191, 203; dress code 199, 212–13; educational system and 206, 211, 212; repressive effect on cultural life 211–12; violence during Mubarak period 202–204, 208; *see also* Islamization; jihad/jihadist; Muslim Brotherhood; political Islam
Islamization 4, 90, 199–200, 230; conversion to Islam 93; Islamic influence in the educational system 6, 199, 200, 206; media and 199–200, 207; political Islam and 187; *see also* Islam, conversion to; Islamism; political Islam
Isma'il Basha (khedive, Muhammad 'Ali dynasty) 129–31, 132, 141; abdication 131; the army 131; educational system 129–30, 131; expenditures and debts 131–32, 135; foreign intervention 131–32; modernization of Egypt 130–31; Suez Canal 130–31
Isma'ilis 68, 75
Israel 221, 238; 1977 Sadat's visit to 189, 193, 194, 195, 196; Israeli occupation of Sinai 188; Likud Party 189; *see also* 1967 Six-Day War; 1973 Arab-Israeli war

al-Jabarti, 'Abd al-Rahman 107, 108–109, 112, 115, 116, 118, 119–20
Jahin, Salah 100
Jamal al-Din, 'Abd al-'Aziz 49, 60, 75, 79, 142
al-Jamali, Badr (Armenian ruler) 76–77
Jawhar al-Siqilli 68
Jerusalem 9, 60, 65, 74, 79, 188, 194; Church of the Holy Sepulcher 69, 74; Persian invasion of 34; pilgrimage to 78, 107, 194; Salah al-Din and 80
Jews 61; conversion to Islam 54, 73, 74; dress code 73, 77, 79, 88, 106; extreme brutality suffered by 73; as infidels 208; Jews of Alexandria 28; *jizya* 42, 43, 77; Muslim Brotherhood, attacks by 165; People of the Book/*ahl al-kitab* 71; persecution of 68, 70, 74; Persian invasion and 34, 35; wealth 98; wearing a bell 74; *see also* Judaism
jihad/jihadist 6, 71, 90, 143, 178, 184, 186; jihadist ideology 95; jihadist violence 175; *mujahidin* 203;

Muslim Brotherhood and 201; *see also* Islamism; Muslim Brotherhood; political Islam
jizya (poll tax) 43, 44, 52–53, 67, 168; abolition of 5, 125, 128; Christians/ Copts 43, 69, 77, 83–84, 208; clergy/ monks 53, 54, 67; conversion to Islam and 61, 62, 93; Egypt's surrender treaty with Ibn al-'As and 39–40, 45; Jews 42, 43, 77; Muhammad 'Ali dynasty and 126; Muslims 52, 53–54, 80; non-Arab Muslims 57; Ottoman dynasty and 104, 105, 128; *see also* tax
John Chrysostom 28
John of Nikiou 18, 20, 35, 37, 38, 39, 40, 43
John the Writer 61
Johnson, Harry, Sir 236
Judaism 19, 70, 185; synagogue 28, 96; *see also* Jews
Justinian (Roman Emperor) 13, 33

al-Kabir, 'Ali Bey (Mamluk 'Ruler of Egypt') 106
Kafur 67
Kamel, Mustafa 144–45, 151; *al-Liwa'* 145
Karim al-Din (ruler of Alexandria) 87, 88
Katakhda, Ibrahim 106
al-Kawakibi, 'Abd al-Rahman (shaykh) 248
Kefaya ('Enough'), 213
al-Kharasani, Abu Muslim 57, 58
Khumarawayh (Tulunid sultan) 64, 65
al-Kindi al-Misri, Abi 'Umar Muhammad bin Yusuf 60
Kissinger, Henry 183
Kléber, Jean-Baptiste (French General) 116, 117, 120
Kora ibn Sheriek 54, 55
al-Kush, 208, 209
al-Kutla al-Wafdiya 159, 246–47

League of Nations 155
Legislative Assembly (1913) 151
el-Leithy, Tamer 94, 97–98
Lesseps, Ferdinand de 128–29, 130
Liberal Constitution Party (al-Ahrar al-Dusturiyun) 156, 157
Library of Alexandria (Royal Library) 11, 27, 42–43, 121; destruction of 27, 42–43; Serapion 27, 43
Louis IX (King of France) 81, 82
Lutfi al-Sayyid, Ahmad 100

Madi, Abu-l 'Ila 213
Maher Basha, Ahmed 163, 166, 241, 245
Mahfouz, Naguib 101, 202–203; *'Abath al-aqdar/Mockery of the Fates* 237; *The Cairo Trilogy* 166–69, 237; *Children of Gebelawi/Children of the Alley* 203; Nobel Prize for Literature 169
al-Mahgoub, Rif'at 202
Mahmud, Abd al-Halim (shaykh of al-Azhar) 194
Mahmud, Nur al-Din (King of Damascus) 78, 79
Majlis al-Sha'b (People's Assembly) 177
Majlis al-Shura 130
Makram, 'Umar 119, 124
Mamluk dynasty 4, 58, 83–92, 123; Abbasid puppet caliphs 84; conversion to Islam during 89, 91, 93; Coptic–Muslim relations 4, 72, 83–90, 96; decline of 91–92, 103; end of 124; French in Egypt and 112, 115, 116, 117; internal power struggle 83, 91; Islam and 81, 83, 89; legitimatized by Muslim religious leaders 4, 89; Mamluks as slave warriors 81, 83; Ottomans and 4, 103, 106, 108; revolt 91
al-Ma'mun (Abbasid caliph) 58, 59, 60, 72
Mansour, Adly (Judge) 226
al-Mansur, Abu Ja'far (Abbasid caliph) 58
al-Maqrizi, Taqi al-Din: *Kitab al-mawa'iz wa-l-i'tibar bi-dhikr al-khitat wa-l-athar*, 34, 35, 40, 43, 51–52, 53, 54–55, 56, 59–60, 65, 73–74, 85–89, 90, 100; the first Coptologist 89
Marcian (Roman Emperor) 30
marriage 179, 187; conversion and 98–9; intermarriage 44, 49, 99; polygamy 109, 229; *see also* divorce

Marwan II (Umayyad caliph) 58
Marwan ibn Muhammad (Umayyad caliph) 56
Mashhour, Mustafa 208
Maspero massacre 223
al-Masri, Iris Habib 13–14
al-Mas'udi, 'Ali ibn al-Husayn 42, 66
Mecca 42, 45, 57, 65, 67, 115; Ka'ba 57; pilgrimage to 96
media 1, 160, 165, 178, 192, 196; dress code 212; Islamic extremism in 207, 208; Islamic presence in 199–200, 207; Muslim Brotherhood and 190; *see also* Internet; newspaper; press
Medina 49, 57
Melchite Church (Chalcedonian) 57, 61, 69, 79, 90; Melchite patriarch 57, 60, 69
Melitius/Melitians 24–25
Menou, Abdallah de 114
Middle East 91, 94, 100, 103, 111, 175, 178, 186, 192, 230, 240; *see also* Crusades/Crusaders
Mikhail, Emad Shehata 223
the military *see* the army
Milner, Lord (British colonial secretary) 154
Milner Commission 154
al-Miskin, al-Abb Matta (Father Matthew the Poor, Yusuf Iskander) 24, 26, 74, 181, 182, 197
missionary 5, 132–34, 148; American missionary 133–34; Catholicism 108, 109–10, 132, 133; colonization 132, 133; Copts' conversion to Catholicism or Protestantism 109–10, 132, 133; missionary school 132–33; Protestantism 108, 109–10, 132, 133, 148
Mitri, Najib 249; Dar al-Ma'arif/The House of Knowledge 249
modernity/modernization 230, 242; al-Azhar University 120, 232, 236; conservatism vs modernity 120, 232; Isma'il Basha 130–1; Muhammad 'Ali 5, 119, 124–27
Mohammed al-Faisal (Prince of Saudi Arabia) 185
monastery 96; Abu Nafar's Monastery 96; al-Baghl Monastery, Muqattam Mountain 87, 90; building of 27, 29, 77; destruction of 68–69, 73–74, 76, 84–85; Kellia 17; Monastery of al-Baramus 179; Monastery of the Holy Family 180; mutiny at 180; Nitria 13, 17, 28; Pachomian monasteries 16–17; Persian invasion 34; Quseir Monastery 14, 73–74; St. Anthony's Monastery 33; St. Bishoi Monastery 31; St. Catherine's Monastery 33; St. Macarius Monastery 15, 18, 74, 182, 197; Wadi al-Natrun 17, 18, 59–60, 74, 75, 180; *see also* monasticism
monasticism 3, 15–18, 53, 97, 181; Abbasid dynasty and 59–60; Anthony, St. 16; Arab invasion and 18; influence of 18, 29, 53; iron bracelet in monks' wrist 54; *jizya* on monks 53, 54; manuscript/book collections 18; nuns 16, 17, 56, 85; origins of 15–16; Pachomian Rule 17; Pachomius 16–17; revival 18; Roman Catholic monasticism 17; Shenoute, St. 17; Theophilus of Alexandria 27–28; *see also* Christianity in Egypt; monastery
Mongols 4; Baghdad, conquest and sack by the Mongols 84, 91, 94; invasion of the Abbasid Empire 81; Islam and 81
Moroccans 70, 97, 115, 213
Morsi, Muhammad 7, 226; as president 224–25; removed as president 7, 226, 229
mosque: al-Aqsa Mosque 80; building of 83; church converted into a mosque 29, 74, 91, 96; converted into church 80; destruction of 4, 67; Ibn Tulun Mosque 64, 65, 82; *mihrab* 65, 115; political Islam 186, 190; *see also* al-Azhar Mosque/University
Mu'awiya ibn Abi Sufyan (fifth caliph) 47, 52
Mubarak, Gamal 204, 214, 217, 218, 219

Mubarak, Hosni 201; assassination attempt 203; as military man 201, 202; Sharm al-Sheikh, Red Sea 204; stepping down from power 7, 217–18; *see also* Mubarak period
Mubarak, Suzanne 212, 214
Mubarak period 7, 201–16, 224; 2005 election 204; 2010 election 204; 2011 revolution 217; the army and 7, 201, 205; changing political, social, and economic climate 207–16; Coptic–Muslim relations 7, 205–10, 215; Copts elected during 177, *252*; corruption 204, 210; decline 214; demonstrations and riots 204, 214, 217; emergency law/state of emergency 7, 204; false democracy 214; fossilized and autocratic government 204, 224; Islamist violence 202–204, 208; Muslim Brotherhood and 201–202, 203, 204–205, 208, 214; Nag Hammadi incident 215; opposition to 213–14; political Islam 7, 213; political repression 7, 202, 204; sectarian tension and violence 206–10, 215; Shenouda III 205–207, 215, 219; United States 204, 222; *see also* 2011 revolution; Mubarak, Hosni
Muhammad, the Prophet of Islam, 12, 33, 36, 42, 47, 67, 162, 184; descendants of the Prophet/*ahl al-bayt* 57; distribution of the booty 38, 41; festivity of the birth of 114; hadiths 161
Muhammad 'Ali 5, 92, 123–27, 242; agriculture and trade 125; the army 124–25; Azharite shaykhs 123, 124; Coptic–Muslim relations 5, 126–27; education and educational system 5, 127, 129–30, 131; Egyptian expansion 127; forced-labor/*sukhra* system 125; *jizya* 126; Mamluks and 124; modernization of Egypt 5, 119, 124–27; tax collection 126; Wali al-Nassara/"The Ruler of the Christians' 119, 126; *see also* Muhammad 'Ali dynasty
Muhammad 'Ali dynasty (after Muhammad 'Ali's death) 5, 127–32; Abbas Basha 128; Coptic–Muslim relations 5, 128, 129, 133–34, 143–44; Ibrahim Basha 127; *jizya*, abolition of 5, 125, 128; Suez Canal 5, 128–29; *see also* Muhammad 'Ali
Muhammad ibn Sulayman 65–66
al-Mu'izz li-Din Illah (Fatimid caliph) 68, 69
Mujahid, Muhammad 208, 227
Mukhtar, Mahmud 160
Musa, Abd al-Halim 202
Musa, Salama 100, 160, 234–39, 247, 249; books by 239; Fabian Society 236; *al-Hilal* magazine 236; *al-Majalla al-jadida/The New Magazine* 237; *al-Mustaqbal/The Future* 236; *New Statesman* 236; political Islam and 238; social reform 235; socialism 237, 238
al-Musawwar Magazine 221
Muslim Brotherhood 2, 7, 143, 213; 1952 revolution 173–74; 2011 election 224; 2011 revolution and aftermath 7, 219–20, 224–27, 229; 2012 election 224; anti-Coptic hostility 164, 208; anti-Jews hostility 165; assuming the authority of the caliphate 162; ban on/suppression of 164, 175, 178; democracy and 163; dissolution of 165; educational system and 190, 199, 205; emergence of 6, 160, 162; encampments at al-Nahda and Rab'a 226–27; financing/Islamic banking and 185, 186, 192, 219–20, 221; Hassan al-Banna as founder of 133, 163; influence in Europe and United States 186, 192, 205; jihad and 201; media and 190; Mubarak period 201–202, 203, 204–205, 208, 214; Nasser period 175, 178, 185; paramilitary wing of 163, 164; political system and 214; popularity of 163, 164, 201–202, 205, 214; Rida, Rashid 143; Sadat period 6, 184, 189, 190, Saudi Arabia 175; SCAF and 7,

219, 220, 221, 222, 224; secretive, well-organized system 205; strategy of chaos and instability 163, 175, 226–27; violence and terror 163–65, 175, 203; *see also* Morsi, Muhammad; political Islam
Muslims 6; the army 38; exclusion from highly profitable jobs 70; expulsion from Spain 94; *jizya* on Muslims 52, 53–54, 80; pilgrimage 96; *see also* Coptic–Muslim relations
Mustafa IV (Ottoman sultan) 123
al-Mustansir (Fatimid caliph) 76
al-Mustansir bi-Allah (Mamluk King) 84
al-Mutawakkil (Abbasid caliph) 58, 61
Mu'tazili theology/movement 58–59, 61

al-Nabulsi, Abu 'Amr 'Uthman: *Tajrid sayf al-himma li-istikhraj ma dhimmat al-dhimma/The Sword of Ambition* 94–95
Nag Hammadi incident 215
Nag Hammadi Library 17
al-Nagar, Ahmed 185
al-Naggar, Said 213
Naguib, Muhammad 173
al-nahda (Egyptian Enlightenment) 127, 159–60, 211, 231, 247, 248
al-Nahhas, Mustafa 159, 165, 166, 167, 244, 245–46
al-Naqqash, Raga' 119
al-Nasser, Gamal Abd 173–78; assassination attempt 174; death 178; Non-Aligned Movement and 175; resignation as president 177; *see also* 1952 revolution; Nasser period
Nasser period: 1967 Six-Day War 6, 177, 183–84; the army 6, 178; Aswan High Dam project 174–75; construction of new churches 176–77; Copts elected during 177, *251*; education 6, 175–76; industrialization 6, 173, 175; land reform 174, 176, 210; Muslim Brotherhood 175, 178, 185; as police state 175, 183; political Islam 183–84; socialism and social agenda 6, 173, 174, 175, 210; Soviet Union 175; Suez Canal, nationalization of 174, 175; United States 173, 174; weakening of democratic institutions 6, 178; *see also* al-Nasser, Gamal Abd
Nasserites 6, 184, 188
Nastoris, 'Issa ibn 70, 73
National Party (al-Hizb al-Watani) 137, 138, 145, 147, 151, 167; Copts in 145; 'Egypt for the Egyptians' 136
nationalism 167; Arab nationalism 247, 249; democratic nationalistic movement 6; Egyptian nationalist movement 143, 144, 146, 149, 153, 243; as substitute for religion 169, 195; *see also* Wafd Party
NBE (National Bank of Egypt) 241
NDP (National Democratic Party) 204, 209, 212
Neda, Youssef 186
Nelson, Horatio (Admiral) 111, 112
Nestorius (bishop of Constantinople), 28–29
New Civic Forum 213
newspaper 145, 151, 232; *Al-Ahram* 190, 203; *al-Liwa'* 145; *al-Manara al-misriya* 164, 238; *Misr* 238; *al-'Urwa al-Wuthqa/The Indissoluble Bond*, 143; *al-Watan* 179; *see also* media, press
Nicene Council 23, 24, 29; Nicene Creed 23, 24, 26, 28; *see also* church council
Nigm, Ahmad Fu'ad 100, 178
Nile Delta 17, 35, 39, 55, 56, 77, 81, 138, 145, 185, 214
Nile River 18, 36, 42, 66, 74; flood 39, 51, 63, 76, 81, 92
Nile Valley 15, 99
Nixon, Richard 198
North Africa 68, 76, 96, 97, 103, 149
Nubar Basha 130, 136
Nubians 35, 39, 40
al-Nuqrashi Basha, Mahmud Fahmi 163–64, 166, 245
Nur al-Din, al-Mansur (Mamluk sultan) 83–84

OAU (Organization of African Unity) 203
Obama, Barack 222

Okasha, Osama Anwar 221
Old Cairo 56, 86, 125, 153, 187; Bab Zuwayla 84, 88, 103; the Citadel 79; fortress of Babylon 37–38; *see also* Cairo
Origen 12–14, 15, 23, 27; allegorical interpretation of scripture 3, 12, 27; condemned by Demetrius I 9, 10, 13, 14; condemned by Theophilus of Alexandria 13, 14, 27–28; declared a heretic/excommunication 13, 14; as head of the School of Alexandria 10, 12; *Hexapla* 12; Origen's work condemnation 13; works by 12–13, 14, 16
Osman (third caliph) 45–46
Osman, Tarek 202
al-Osmani, Muhammad (Ottoman caliph) 161–62
O'Sullivan, Shaun 98
Ottoman dynasty 4, 103–10; after French withdrawal from Egypt 123; al-Azhar shaykhs/Ottomans relationship 108, 123; Coptic–Muslim relations 105–109; decline of 104–105, 106, 108, 109–10, 123; end of 145, 149, 152; French invasion of Egypt 105; *al-iltizam* taxation 104; *jizya* 104, 105, 128; Mamluks and 4, 103, 106, 108; Russian attacks against 105, 106; Sufism 109; territory of the empire 103; Turkish sultan 104; World War I 145, 149, 152; *see also* Turks

paganism 26, 27, 43
Pakistan 155, 212
Palestine: Arabs in 36, 40; Camp David Accords and 194; Crusaders in 4, 80; Persian invasion of 33–34
pan-Arabism 175
pan-Islamism 142, 149, 175; *al-'Urwa al-Wuthqa/The Indissoluble Bond*, 143
Paris Peace Conference, Versailles 152, 154
People of the Book (*ahl al-kitab*) 71
Persians 33–34; Abbasid dynasty and 57, 58, 59; *jizya* 57
Phocas (Roman Emperor) 33
police 131, 209; 2011 revolution 217, 220; police state in Nasser period 175, 183; violence suffered by 163, 198, 202, 227, 229; violence/brutality of 187, 215, 217
political Islam 119, 143, 160–64, 173, 230, 238; 2011 revolution 221; British occupation 143; building churches and 171; Copts and 164–65, 186–87; Ibn Taymiya and 95; Islamic banking/financing and 185–86, 210; Islamic government 163, 189, 193; Islamization and 187; legal system and 211; mobilization from abroad 192; mosques and 186, 190; Mubarak period 7, 213; Nasser period 183–84; political system and 213, 214; popularity 189; Qur'an and 162; rise of 2, 158, 160, 177, 186, 230, 238; Sadat period 6, 184, 186–90, 193, 196, 198, 199; Saudi Arabia 186; sophisticated operations 203; terrorism 186; violence and harassment by 186, 163–64, 199, 202–203, 208; *see also* Islamism; jihad/jihadist; Muslim Brotherhood
political system and Copts 5, 6, 129, 130, 169; 1995 election 209; constitutional reform 149; Copts as prime minister 144, 247; Liberal Constitution Party 156; Mubarak period 177, *252*; Nasser period 177, *251*; National Party 145; Parliament 156, 158, 177; Sadat period 177, 191, *252*; Wafd Party 151, 154, 155, 156, 159, 167, 169, 209; Zaghlul's administration 157; *see also* politics
politics 6, 157, 166; appointment system 177; al-Azhar University 6, 152; Coptic Church and 6, 22, 24, 177, 191–92; exclusion of non-Muslims from leadership positions 71; leftists 6, 173, 188; minorities in Parliament 156; multiparty system 177; Muslim Brotherhood 214; Nasser's one-party system 177; political assassination/

violence 155, 163–64, 202–203; political Islam and 213, 214; political parties 6, 214, 230; Shenouda III 191, 192, 194, 195, 206–207; women and 153; *see also* democracy; election; political system and Copts
poll tax *see jizya*
press 226; censorship 201, 238, 242–43; freedom of 147, 156, 183, 202; *see also* media; newspaper
Proterius, Chalcedonian Patriarch 30–31
Protestantism 107–108, 133; demographics 133; Syrian Protestant College 247; *see also* Christianity; missionary
Ptolemaic dynasty 99
Pulcheria 30

al-Qaeda 190, 220, 230
Qal'aji, Qadri 78
al-Qaradawi, Yusuf (shaykh) 186, 219
Qena 222–23
Qur'an 43, 77, 135, 161, 170, 215, 219, 245, 248; classical Arabic 100, 101; dealing with non-Muslims 70–71, 95; interfaith tolerance 95; interpretation of 12, 44, 59, 96, 163; memorization of 231–32, 235, 239; political Islam and 162
Quraysh tribe 42, 45
Qus 77, 96, 97, 100
Qutb, Sayyid 175, 193

Rabin, Yitzhak 198
racism 142, 168
al-Rashid, Harun (Abbasid caliph) 50, 58, 59; succession war 59–60
Reagan, Ronald 196
revolt 3, 5, 21, 51, 59, 62; Abbasid dynasty 59, 60, 62; Alexandria 19–20; Bashmuric Revolt 56, 59; 'first revolt against the French' 114–15; Hammam bin Yusuf's revolt 110; Mamluk dynasty 91; 'second revolt against the French' 116, 117; tax collection and 56–57, 59, 93, 104, 105; Umayyad dynasty 56–57; Zaghlul revolt 133; Zanj rebellion 60; *see also* 1919 revolution; 1952 revolution; 2011 revolution; Urabi revolt
Rida, Rashid 143
Rifki Basha, Osman 136
Riyad Basha 136–37, 143, 148
Rizq, Mu'allim 106
Roman Empire 18, 19, 31, 33, 73; Christianity as official religion of 18, 22, 23, 26; Egypt and 20, 36; persecution of Christians 3, 12, 15, 19–21, 24, 25
Rousseau, Philip: *Pachomius: The Making of Community in Fourth-Century Egypt* 17
Rufila, Ya'qub Nakhla 53, 60, 116
Russell, Gerard 230
Russia 123, 127, 131, 142; Bolshevik Revolution 160; *see also* Soviet Union

Sabbahi, Hamdeen 224
Sabry, Musa 191
Sabunji, Louis 136
Sadat, Anwar 6, 247; 1977 visit to Israel 189, 193, 194, 195, 196; 1979 press conference at Isma'ilia 195; assassination of 6, 184, 186, 198, 222; a controversial figure 183; funeral of 198; al-Miskin, al-Abb Matta and 182, 197; 'Mr. Yes Man' 183; Nobel Peace Prize 189; peace process 193–5; al-Ra'is al-Mu'min/'The Believer President' 187; Sadat/Shenouda III relationship 6, 182, 187–88, 189, 191, 194, 195–97; *see also* Sadat period
Sadat period 6, 183–200; 1973 Arab-Israeli war 6, 186, 188–89, 194, 195; construction of churches 187–88; Coptic–Muslim relations 190–92, 194, 196, 199; Copts and political system 177, 191, *252*; corruption 178, 192–93, 210; coup d'état attempt 189; demonstrations and riots 192–93, 196; financial developments 184; Islamization 199–200; jihadist groups 184; liberal economic policy 178, 210; Muslim Brotherhood 6, 184, 189, 190; 'open door

policy' 210; political Islam and 6, 184, 186–90, 193, 196, 198, 199; political repression 6, 197–98, 201; sectarian tension and violence 188, 190, 191, 194, 196, 199; Soviet Union 188; United States and 183, 195, 196; *see also* 1973 Arab-Israeli war; Sadat, Anwar
Sa'dist Party 245
al-Sadr, Mohamed Bakr 185
al-Saffah, Abu-l 'Abbas (Abbasid caliph) 58
Said, Khalid 215–16; 'We Are All Khaled Said'/Kolona Khaled Said 216
Said, Rushdi 212
Sa'id Basha (Muhammad 'Ali dynasty) 128, 135
Sa'id Basha, Muhammad 154
Salafism 208, 212, 219, 221, 223, 226
Salah al-Din (Ayyubid sultan) 78–79, 80
Salah al-Din, al-'Adil (Ayyubid sultan) 80
Salah al-Din, al-'Aziz (Ayyubid sultan) 80
Salem, Mamdouh 191
Salih, Subhi 219
al-Salih Ayyub, al-Kamil (Ayyubid sultan) 80, 81–82, 96
Samuel, Bishop (Saad Aziz) 181, 197
Saria, Saleh 189–90
Saudi Arabia 46, 124, 152, 163, 178, 184, 185, 220; female dress code 212; Muslim Brotherhood in 175; political Islam and 186; *see also* Wahhabism
Sayf al-Din Qutuz (Mamluk sultan) 84
SCAF (Supreme Council of the Armed Forces) 7, 217; 1971 Constitution, amendments to 219; 2011 temporary Constitution 224; Constitution Committee 219, 220; Maspero massacre 223; Muslim Brotherhood and 7, 219, 220, 221, 222, 224; Parliament dissolution 224, 225; use of force 222; *see also* 2011 revolution aftermath
School of Alexandria (Catechetical School of Alexandria) 3, 10, 11–15, 23; Athenagoras 11; curriculum 11, 12; Heracles 14; Pantaenus 11; *see also* Christianity in Egypt; Clement of Alexandria; Didymus the Blind; Origen
sectarianism 207; 2011 revolution aftermath and sectarian violence 221–23, 227, 229; British occupation 144, 145, 146, 147–48; French in Egypt and sectarian violence 112, 114, 115, 117, 118; Mubarak period 206–10, 215; Sadat period 188, 190, 191, 194, 196, 199; sectarian tension 1, 29, 165, 206–207; sectarian violence 97, 108, 171, 208, 229, 238; *see also* Coptic–Muslim relations
Sedki, Aziz 175
Selim I (Ottoman sultan) 103
Selim III (Ottoman sultan) 123
Severus of Ashmunayn (Sawiras Ibn al-Muqaffa'), 10, 34, 53, 55, 56, 65, 74; *The History of the Patriarchs/Tarikh al-batarika* 9, 19, 61
Shabab Muhammad (Muhammad's Youth) 189, 238
al-Shabrawi, 'Abdullah (shaykh) 107
Shafiq, Ahmad (General) 217–18, 224
Shajar al-Durr (sultana) 81–82, 83
Shamir, Yitzhak 198
Sharaf, Essam 218, 219
sharia *see* Islamic law
al-Sharif, 'Abd al-Latif 186
Sharkey, Heather J. 133–34
Sharon, Ariel 198
Shawir, Abu Shuja' 77–78
al-Shazly, Kamal 209
Shenouda III (Coptic patriarch, Pope) 177, 181–82, 190, 209; criticism 191, 205–207; death penalty for conversion into Christianity 191; exile/house arrest 197, 205; meeting with President Jimmy Carter 189; Mubarak period 205–207, 215, 219; Nazeer Gayed 181; opinion on Israel 189, 194; politics and 191, 192, 194, 195, 206–207; 'Pope of the Arabs' 194; Sadat/Shenouda III relationship 6, 182, 187–88, 191, 194, 195–97; Sadat's claim of a

Coptic state led by 195–96, 206; *see also* Coptic patriarch
Sherif Basha, Muhammad 137
Shi'a Islam 46, 67–68, 69, 185; as Egypt's official state religion 68; *see also* Isma'ilis
Shinin, Muhammad (shaykh) 108
Shukri, Ghali 212
Sidqi, Isma'il 233, 238, 240, 241
al-Sisi, 'Abd al-Fattah (General) 7, 226, 227, 229–30
Sitt al-Mulk 69, 76
social media 161, 217; *see also* Facebook; Internet
socialism 160, 184, 220, 235, 236, 237, 238; Nasser period: socialism and social agenda 6, 173, 174, 175, 210
Soviet Union 174–75, 188, 203; *see also* Russia
Spain 4, 94, 96, 162
Stack, Lee, Sir 158, 159
Sudan 68, 110, 127, 128, 147, 155, 158, 248
Suez Canal 139, 147, 185; construction of 5, 128–29, 130, 147; inauguration 130, 131; nationalization of 174, 175
Suez Canal Company 139
Sufism 96, 97, 109
Sulayman al-Qanuni (Ottoman sultan) 105
Suleiman, Omar 217
Sunni Islam 67, 68, 77, 78, 89, 142, 168, 169
Swanson, Mark 90; *The Coptic Papacy in Islamic Egypt 641–1517*: 61, 80–81
Syria 4, 33–34, 78, 79, 90; Arabs in 36, 40; Byzantines and 67, 69

al-Tabari, Muhammad ibn Jarir 39, 40
Tagher, Jacques: *Christians in Muslim Egypt* 2, 29, 64, 114, 115, 126
al-Tahtawi, Rifa'a (shaykh) 109, 127
al-Takfir wa-l-Hijra 193
Tamarod 225, 226
al-Tanuhi, Usama ibn Zayd 54
Tawfiq Basha (Muhammad 'Ali dynasty) 131, 135, 136, 139, 141, 145, 146, 151; Urabi revolt, 137, 138;
tax 50–1, 237; Abbasid dynasty 3, 51, 52, 59, 60, 61–62, 63, 67, 93; British occupation 141, 143; British school for tax collection 144; Byzantine tax system 46, 51, 53; Coptic–Muslim relations 3, 51, 52, 56; Copts as tax collectors 3, 44, 52, 69, 70, 83, 90, 95, 98, 105, 114, 118, 126, 144; corruption and extortion 105, 106, 107, 126; end of Copts as tax collectors 44, 52, 98, 114, 144; excessive tax collection 3, 45, 51, 61–62, 91, 104; exemption 52, 53; Fatimid dynasty 72; French adventure in Egypt 113, 114, 116; *al-iltizam* taxation 104; land tax/*kharaj* 40, 52; Muhammad 'Ali dynasty 126; revenue decline 44–45, 46, 50–52, 53, 54, 55, 62; revolt and 56–57, 59, 93, 104, 105; taxation amir 50, 55; Tulunid dynasty 63, 64
types of 52; Umayyad dynasty 3, 52, 53–56, 93; use of force 105; *see also jizya*
al-Tayyib, Ahmad (shaykh of al-Azhar) 226
terrorism 186, 189, 203
Theodoretus (Roman Emperor) 26, 27
Theodosius II (Roman Emperor) 28, 30
Tiberius II (Roman Emperor) 25–26
Tulunid dynasty 4, 63–66; Ibn Tulun as founder of 63–64; Mosque of Ibn Tulun 64, 65; al-Qata'i' 63–64, 65; tax collection 63, 64
Tuman Bey (Mamluk sultan) 103
Turan Shah (Ayyubid sultan) 81, 82
Turkey/Turks 63, 66, 76; Abbasid dynasty and 58; abolition of the caliphate 160, 162; French in Egypt and 115, 116, 117, 118, 119, 120; governorate of Egypt 63; *jizya* 57; *see also* Ottoman dynasty

'Umar ibn 'Abd al-'Aziz 53–54, 93
'Umar Ibn al-Khattab *see* Ibn al-Khattab, 'Umar

Umayyad dynasty 3, 50, 51, 52–57, 68; Arab immigration to Egypt 55; Coptic–Muslim relations 52, 53–57; Mu'awiya ibn Abi Sufyan as founder of 47, 52; revolt 56–57; spread of Islam 47, 57; tax collection 3, 52, 53–56, 93
Umm Kulthum 160
al-Umma al-Qibtiya (the Coptic Nation) 180
United States 142, 218; 1973 Arab-Israeli war 188–89, 194; 2011 revolution 221, 222; American missionary 133–34; Mubarak period and 204, 222; Nasser period and 173, 174; Sadat period and 183, 195, 196
university 208, 211; Egyptian University 232; Farouk University/Alexandria University 233; Fu'ad University 179; University of Ibrahim/Ain Shams University 234; *see also* al-Azhar Mosque/University; Cairo University
Urabi, Ahmed 135, 136–37; exile 5, 138, 139; *see also* Urabi revolt
Urabi revolt 5, 135–39, 143, 144; Battle of al-Tal al-Kabir 138; British colonization of Egypt 5, 135, 137–39; Cyril V, Pope 133; egalitarian principles 136; impact of 139; Tawfiq Basha 137, 138; unity between Coptic and Muslim leaders 135, 138; *see also* Urabi, Ahmed

Volkan, Vamik: *The Need to Have Enemies and Allies* 208

Wafd Party 156–60, 167, 169, 176, 234, 238, 241, 243, 245–46; 1923 election 156; 1925 election 159; 1926 election 159; 1950 election 158, 165; beginnings of 151–52; Copts in 151, 154, 155, 156, 159, 167, 169, 209; Egypt's independence 154; members' exile 155, 156, 159; nationalism 169; Paris Peace Conference, Versailles 152, 154; popularity 152, 157, 158, 159, 209; 'Religion for God, and the nation for all' 151; secular principles of 151, 153, 159, 170; *see also* al-Nahhas, Mustafa; Zaghlul, Sa'd
Wahba, Magdi 206
Wahba Basha, Youssef 154
Wahhabism 124, 163, 175, 184, 208
al-Wakil, Zaynab 245, 246
al-Wardani, Ibrahim 146, 147
wealth 45, 46, 47; Coptic Church 64; Copts 52, 90, 98, 104, 148, 210; equitable distribution of 244; Islamic scholar 108; Jews 98
Wilson, Charles Rivers, Sir 136
Wilson, Woodrow 154
Wingate, Reginald Francis, Sir (British high commissioner) 151
women 209–10; burka 212; dress code for 174, 186, 199, 212–13; education 130, 234, 242; Egyptian feminist movement 153; *hijab* 153, 187, 199, 212–13; *niqab* 199; petition against the British occupation of Egypt 153; unity of Copts and Muslims women 153; *see also* al-Yusuf, Rose
World Bank 174, 192, 201, 210, 213
World War I 145, 149, 152, 236
World War II 159, 170, 233, 240, 245, 246

Ya'qub, Mu'allim 4–5, 115, 116–19; allied with French occupiers 4, 117–18; as patriot and visionary 5, 118–19; as traitor 5, 118, 119; *see also* French adventure in Egypt
Yarbrough, Luke 94–5
Yazid bin 'Abd al-Malik 54
Yazid ibn Mu'awiya ibn Abi Sufyan 52
Yemen 11, 68, 76, 79, 105, 131
Yusuf, Ahmad 101
al-Yusuf, Rose 160, 242–43; *Rose al-Yusuf* 160, 242–43

Zaghlul, Sa'd 151, 154, 167, 242, 244; arrest and exile 153, 155, 156; death 159; Egypt's independence 154; Wafd Party 151–52, 154, 157, 159; Zaghlul movement as secular movement 153; Zaghlul revolt 133;

Zaghlul's administration 157, 158; *see also* 1919 revolution
al-Zahir (Fatimid caliph) 76
al-Zawahiri, Ayman 190
al-Zawiya al-Hamra 196
Zaydan, Jurji 100, 160, 236, 247–49; *The Arabic Language as a Living Being* 248; historical novels 249; *Tarikh al-tamaddun al-islami, 1902–1906*: 249
Ziedan, Youssef: *'Azazil* 29
al-Zubayr ibn al-'Awam 46
al-Zumar, Abbud 198